CUSTOMER-EFFECTIVE
WEB SITES

ISBN 0-13-087827-8

90000

9 780130 878274

FT.COM

There is a new world which we can look at but we cannot see. Yet within it, the forces of technology and imagination are overturning the way we work and the way we do business. ft.com is both gateway and guide to this world. We understand it because we are part of it. But we also understand the needs of businesses which are taking their first steps into it, and those still standing hesitantly on the threshold. Above all, we understand that, as with all business challenges, the key to success lies not with the technology itself, but with the people who must use it and manage it. People like you. See the world. Visit us at www.ft.com today.

CUSTOMER-EFFECTIVE WEB SITES

Jodie Dalgleish

Prentice Hall PTR
Upper Saddle River, NJ 07458
www.phptr.com

Library of Congress Cataloging-in-Publication Data

Dalgleish, Jodie.
    Customer-effective web sites/Jodie Dalgleish.
      p. cm.
    Includes bibliographical references.
    ISBN 0-13-087827-8
    1. Web sites—Design. 2. Internet industry. I. Title.

    TK5105.888. D35 2000
    005.7'2--dc21   00-029128

Editorial/Production Supervisor: *Kerry Reardon*
Project Coordinator: *Anne Trowbridge*
Acquisitions Editor: *Mike Meehan*
Editorial Assistant: *Linda Ramagnano*
Manufacturing Manager: *Alexis R. Heydt*
Manufacturing Buyer: *Maura Goldstaub*
Marketing Manager: *Bryan Gambrel*
Art Director: *Gail Cocker-Bogusz*
Cover Designer: *Anthony Gemmellaro*
Cover Design Director: *Jerry Votta*

© 2000 Prentice Hall PTR
Prentice-Hall, Inc.
Upper Saddle River, NJ 07458

Prentice Hall books are widely used by corporation and government agencies for training, marketing, and resale.
The publisher offers discounts on this book when ordered in bulk quantities.
For more information, contact

    Corporate Sales Department,
    Prentice Hall PTR
    One Lake Street
    Upper Saddle River, NJ 07458
    Phone: 800-382-3419; FAX: 201-236-7141
    E-mail (Internet): corpsales@prenhall.com

Printed in the United States of America

10 9 8 7 6 5 4 3 2 1

ISBN 0-13-087827-8

Prentice-Hall International (UK) Limited, *London*
Prentice-Hall of Australia Pty. Limited, *Sydney*
Prentice-Hall Canada Inc., *Toronto*
Prentice-Hall Hispanoamericana, S.A., *Mexico*
Prentice-Hall of India Private Limited, *New Delhi*
Prentice-Hall of Japan, Inc., *Tokyo*
Pearson Education Asia, Pte. Ltd
Editora Prentice-Hall do Brasil, Ltda., *Rio de Janeiro*

ABOUT THE AUTHOR

Jodie Dalgleish is a Director of Consulting with Gartner in California. She has worked with Web development and design teams across all facets of Web site development from conception through implementation and has been a leader in the practice of soliciting feedback from e-customers, in New Zealand and, now, in the US. She currently consults on a wide range of e-business issues.

*This book is dedicated to Cookie, who always dreamed of writing
a book, and to Callan, who has helped me realize a dream of my own.*

CONTENTS

PREFACE

Two potential book titles came to me while I was writing this book. One was *Internet Services for Real People* and the other was *The Internet Service Revolution*. Neither title was quite right, as pointed out by my editor, but each encapsulates my underlying motivation for writing this book.

In a nutshell, I want to see "real people" better served on the Internet. Real people need to do everyday things to run their hectic lives, and the Web can help them do that. I want to see the Internet come of age as a service medium because it has the potential, if harnessed correctly, to emancipate customers rather than frustrate and restrain them.

Over a period of two years I was actively involved in many forms of customer and internal testing of e-service concepts and Web sites, across a number of industries and in relation to many different e-service offerings and e-customers (for a comprehensive description of testing techniques see Chapter 3).

In doing this testing, a theme kept recurring: Give customers something useful because if you ignore what they're trying to do by visiting your Web site, your Web site will only be irrelevant to them and frustrate them. It was customers' frustration that first made me think about writing this book.

I feel that, if I encourage all parties involved in Internet development to ask their customers and themselves the right questions, for the right reasons, we will all be a lot better off. And this needs to be an integrated effort, within and between businesses and their development partners. I feel frustrated, however, because I observe many people with motivations fueled by the search for the "quick buck," rather than the search for lasting customer value.

For years, marketers have talked about the market-of-one phenomenon as the lynchpin for creating lasting customer value. We now have a medium that allows us to market to individuals more effectively than we ever have before. And yet, people carry over their old, constrained, and ineffectual, so-called customer-relationship strategies to the Web.

Despite this, I feel encouraged because things are starting to change. I salute those people who realize that the Web needs to be a part of peoples' everyday lives, and are creating useful Web sites that address real customer needs.

That's important because we're on the verge of what I call the "e-service revolution"—a revolution than can be created equally by service providers and their customers. E-service providers need to take the initiative to talk to customers and do things differently as a result. There's nothing new in talking to customers; we just have a better chance of getting results with the Web in the mix, and we have a lot more to lose, a lot more quickly, if we don't find out what we need to know and change the way we do things.

And so, in the interests of helping e-service providers, and their development partners, harness the opportunity to do right by their e-customers, and create lasting value, I have made the effort to describe the necessary Web site development process from beginning to end. In doing so, I have addressed what it takes to create not just "Web sites," but Web-based e-service systems or applications that are integrated with an e-service provider's business.

It takes discipline to create a good Web site. Part of that discipline is talking to customers and effectively translating their needs, attitudes, and behaviors into the requisite Web site experience. And I hope what I have written helps you translate customer needs into strategies and practices at every step in your development process.

That doesn't mean that this book will give you a list of shrink-wrapped instructions you can tick off as you go. If that's what you're expecting, you're reading the wrong book. However, if you're prepared to be challenged to think about things differently, and to take concepts and ideas and develop them further in the context of your own e-customers and what they're trying to do, this book is perfect for you. And I hope you'll get a lot out of reading it.

To get the most out of this book, bear in mind that the pictures are an integral part of the story. If you skip the pictures, you'll miss a lot of the new ideas and concepts that make this story different. If you take the time to inspect and understand the pictures, you'll be rewarded with new ideas and insights, because I've put some things together in new ways.

In fact, exploration is a key tenet of this book. I see us exploring, together, how the e-service revolution can be brought about. And I'm thankful to those who have come before, because I've borrowed from their ideas to explore how they can be aggregated and applied to the Web.

I wish you well in your endeavors to provide lasting value to real people and in creating the e-service revolution. And I believe that you are an important part of our collective learning process, and would like to hear from you as you have insights and create new ideas.

Jodie Dalgleish

LIST OF FIGURES

CUSTOMER-EFFECTIVE WEB SITES

CHAPTER 1

BEING CUSTOMER-EFFECTIVE

An evolution has occurred.
But there are still many more barriers to break through.

THINGS HAVE CHANGED

The evolution of electronic service has been swift and convincing. Businesses have adopted Web technologies and so have customers. Customers can now do anything from order a pizza to actively manage our investment portfolio—if they have the patience and the know-how.

While businesses have been taken with their rapid evolution in applying the Web, they've been, unwittingly, overtaken by customer expectations. Customers now expect more than is being delivered. A game of tag has occurred between businesses and their customers, and at the moment customers are "it."

Businesses and their suppliers have focused on taming the Web as a new medium, and that hasn't been an easy task. And it's far from over yet. In many ways, businesses have led customers into the new era of electronic servicing. They've tagged customers and said, "You're it. If you want to use it—here it is."

And customers have learned quickly. They've been getting themselves connected, working out how to find their way around cyberspace, and starting to "do stuff" on the Web. They've stuck with us as we've struggled to make a go of e-commerce. But now they want more. They want Web sites that are driven by their needs; the things they need to do as customers.

Of course, it's not as if we haven't done well. We've done amazingly well, if you think about the rate at which we've had to do it. We've learned how to design good Web sites (which is not as easy as it sounds). We've started to develop content that is more than online brochures. We've learned that information architecture and navigation are important, and we (sometimes) create structures and scenarios for our Web sites. We've even developed new off-the-shelf technologies making core functionality accessible to small and big business.

But we can't rest on our laurels. We need to let customers tag us and pass on the challenge. We need to be asking customers what we need to do now. Customers will quickly let us know whether we've developed electronic services that meet their needs.

On balance, it seems we've fallen short somewhere. We haven't had enough time or resources to get everything right the first time. We've not been able to completely understand customers' needs in an electronic environment and translate them into customer-effective Web site design, content, or functionality, all of the time.

Customers have been happy to learn with us, but now they have a grasp of the Web and they're ready for more. Unfortunately, this often leads to disappointment as customers go to Web sites and find it's a painful or frustrating experience.

Customers have tagged us. They have learned to do useful things, and they're waiting for us to tag them back with e-services that are better, smarter, and faster.

We need to break through the barriers that prevent us from developing e-services that are useful to customers and start developing more customer-effective Web sites. And that is the subject of this book.

GOOD VERSUS CUSTOMER-EFFECTIVE WEB SITES

Customer-effective Web sites allow customers to do things they need to do as customers, such as set-up, change, or discontinue products and services. Customers adopt customer-effective Web sites into their everyday lives because it makes their dealings with businesses easier, more efficient and more rewarding.

Customers don't understand connectivity, interface design, information architecture, navigation, or business process design, and in general, they don't want to. We may do a good job on all these fronts and still fail to be customer-effective.

Good Web site design is a means and not an end. The end has to be the end user—the customer. We need to approach Web site development from the perspective of what customers need to do online.

Consider the following scenarios:

A customer selects a product on a Web site and then tries to order it. The Web site moves the customer through a number of screens based on the information the customer provides. A designer has created some great screens, but they do not address the customer's need for information or reassurance throughout the order process. The customer goes through only a few screens and then bails out—another lost sale, and chances are that no one will ever know about it.

Now, say, the screens are well designed and give the customer everything necessary to complete the order—the customer successfully completes the order and it reaches the business providing the purchased product. But the business process presents requirements that weren't met in the online process—there are holdups in fulfilling the order, and a service representative has to phone the customer to get more information. The customer was expecting the product to arrive, not to answer any more questions. The result is a disgruntled customer who decides to use the phone the next time—so much for the time and effort that went into developing online ordering.

To be customer-effective in either scenario, we would have to provide both a Web site that makes it easy for customers to find, evaluate, and choose the exact product desired and an order process that is easy and comfortable to use. Underpinning this would be an organizational fulfillment process that is at one with the Web-based order process and that provides the product more conveniently than ordering it by any other means.

To provide a customer-effective order process, we need to understand the way customers seek, evaluate, and choose products; consider the way the Web site takes the customer through the process (which involves interface design, information architecture, navigation, and content); and understand how the order is received and dealt with by the service provider (business process design and its relationship to the Web site).

Being customer-effective is about finding out what customers need to do on your Web site to operate effectively as customers, and creating an end-to-end electronic service experience that makes that activity painless and rewarding.

WHY IS IT SO HARD TO CREATE CUSTOMER-EFFECTIVE WEB SITES?

We can be honest here: it isn't easy for businesses, and in turn their development partners, to be customer-effective.

There are a number of forces at play, and they all add up to making our job difficult. If we understand what stands in the way of creating customer-effective Web sites, maybe we'll be better at doing it.

So why is it so hard to create customer-effective Web sites?

IT REQUIRES NEW WAYS OF DOING BUSINESS

Over time, organizations have become more and more marketing-oriented. In other words, they've become more aware of what customers want to buy and are concerned with providing products and services that meet customer needs (in a way that is hopefully better than their competition).

Being marketing-oriented requires customer involvement. Somewhere along the line customers have to be factored into the business to find out what they want to buy and how to best develop and deliver it. Unfortunately, customer involvement is not as easy as it sounds, and businesses have had to work around the constraints of noninteractive media as best they can.

Without the Web and its integration with e-mail, dialogue with customers is very difficult. Businesses rely on traditional research techniques such as focus groups, interviews, and questionnaires to find out what customers think and want. Businesses also use traditional marketing techniques such as direct mail, competitions, and coupons to solicit feedback.

The Web has allowed us for the first time ever, to have a real chance to get close to our customers, in real time. Businesses have talked about the "market of one" phenomenon where they can tailor their offer to an individual, for ages, but there hasn't been a medium intimate or immediate enough to achieve it. Until now.

The problem is that businesses are not geared for the opportunity. Business structures inherently reflect the constraints they have always encountered. Business process has been developed for organizational efficiency and effectiveness and has been fine-tuned on the basis of customer feedback as it has been acquired, not driven by customers as part of the business.

Now businesses and their development partners have to deliberately think about letting customers get as close to the business as they want, and this is new. At the same time, we need to start engineering our business to make that closeness real.

And that's not all. We all have to deal with higher customer expectations and find new techniques for getting close to our customers because traditional business and Web development techniques aren't enough anymore.

The Web is an intimate medium, and as soon as customers use a Web site, they're getting closer to your business than they ever have before—because they're interacting with you in real time.

In his book *Customer Service on the Internet,* Jim Sterne gives us a model for thinking about increased customer expectations and access to a business. As customers get closer and closer to a business on the Web, their expectations of what they should have access to increases. Customers started off with access to information and then wanted access to problem resolution. As customers were given access to problem resolution they then wanted access to people. As customer were given access to people they then wanted access to business process. The more you integrate your e-customers into your business, the more they will want to be a part of your business (see Figure 1-1).

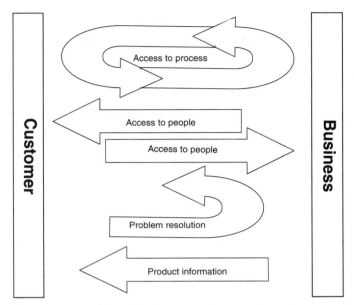

Figure 1-1 Each level of customer integration raises customer expectations of being given access to the next level.
Source: Customer Service on the Internet by Jim Sterne. Copyright © 1999. Reprinted by permission of John Wiley & Sons, Inc.

The Web, by its very nature, brings customers closer. The fact that businesses aren't really integrating customers into their business processes is obvious to customers. Businesses are caught in the upward spiral of increasing customer expectations, and customers now expect to get closer and closer to business processes as a result of being on the Web.

This book will help businesses determine how they can bring their customers closer, translate that into specific requirements for customer-effective Web sites, and integrate electronic servicing into their business processes.

E-SERVICE IS EXPERIENTIAL

The Web is an active medium. Web sites are places where customers can do things. Customers can click on objects to go to different places and enter information into tools and forms to receive immediate, or delayed, results and feedback. Customers partake in an experience when they interact with Web sites.

This means that we have to anticipate and understand peoples' random and often, unpredictable behavior and the context of those behaviors. And we are subject to all the complications that come along with humans trying to successfully use a computer interface.

THE COMPLEXITIES OF BEHAVIOR

Behavior is a complex issue because everybody behaves differently, and that behavior is often random. Customer behavior has always been difficult to pin down. Unfortunately, in e-space this is compounded even more because everything is driven by an action.

Behavior can be seen from different angles in e-space: as the path people take through cyberspace, the way people learn to use Web sites, and the context in which they use those Web sites.

People can take multiple paths through cyberspace, both within and between Web sites—they can jump around all over the place if they feel like it. It becomes a nightmare trying to anticipate every path to or within your Web site—the possible variations are endless. So how can we anticipate people's needs while they're on a Web site if we don't know the way they are going to behave?

We have to make some informed guesses about what people want to do on our Web sites and how they came to be there, and then we have to respond appropriately. This gets translated into an interface that allows customers to do what they want. Unfortunately, this is also fraught with issues.

INTERFACE ISSUES

When people are faced with a computer interface, they have to learn how to use it. There are "rules" that apply. Think back to when you were a novice Web user and were learning to find your way around. You had to learn the cues—the language and images that indicate what you may do and how it should be done.

People learn in different ways and draw on previous experiences when learning new things. This is compounded on the Web where people learn through doing. We are faced with a circular problem. We have to help customers learn to use our interface, and yet we don't necessarily know how they will behave and, therefore, how they will learn. Neither do we necessarily know the previous experiences and assumptions they draw on when using a new interface.

The temptation is to develop interfaces that we can use ourselves, that make sense to us. The problem is that, in almost all cases, we're not the actual user and, generally, we've forgotten what it was like to be a novice user.

To complicate matters even further, interfaces aren't easy things to design well anyway. The presentation and navigation of information is multidimensional, and yet an interface is two dimensional. The choices that people make when interacting with an interface are multivariate. In other words, people have to make multiple choices when interacting with a Web site. When we try to visually present multiple choices, we run into trouble—two dimensions just isn't enough.

In his book *Envisioning Information*, Edward Tufte points out that "nearly every escape from flatland [two dimensions] demands extensive compromise trading off one virtue against another…even our language…lacks immediate capacity to communicate a sense of dimensional complexity." We have no choice but to make trade offs when presenting multidimensional information in two dimensions.

And how do we know what we should be trading off if we don't know exactly how a customer is going to behave? Who is to say whether a certain path through complex information is more logical than another?[1]

People struggle every day to categorize information in a way that makes sense to themselves and others. We try to order our thoughts. When we do this on a Web site, we run into problems because people organize information in different ways. If we could understand what motivates people to behave a certain way on a Web site, we might have a better chance of presenting information in a way that makes sense to them.

And once we've categorized information and presented it in two dimensions, we have to provide visual cues that help customers find their way around. Visual cues are extremely powerful, especially in the Web environment, where they are associated with doing things. We can send customers off on a wild goose chase when they interpret a visual cue differently from the way we thought they would. In trying to provide visual guidance, we create a double-edged sword for ourselves. Unless we know all the ways a cue can be interpreted by our customers, how can we be sure they mean what we think they do? And does a cue change meaning depending on the context customers find themselves in?

A customer's use of a Web site is not a stand-alone experience; it is likely to be part of a range of Web sites visited in relation to a range of pursuits. Baecker et al. in their book, Readings in *Human-Computer Interactions* liken human-computer interaction to "the blind person's interface to a cane. Yet like blind users of canes, computer users want to be primarily focused on their work in the world, not on their canes." The cane covers lots of different surfaces on a number of different routes. Each place encountered is part of the journey. This is true of customers on the Web, who use a computer interface to access a whole range of Web sites in their efforts to explore and traverse their world.[2]

It seems that good interface design is both a science and an art.

This book will help us to better understand customers and will offer some ideas on how we can better create Web site experiences that allow customers to do what they need to do as customers.

WE HAVE MULTIPLE AUDIENCES

In the world of traditional marketing, we're used to defining our target audiences and selecting media to reach them. This doesn't really work on the Web, because we have far less control over who sees our Web sites—they can be browsed by anyone who visits a cybercafe or who has access to a PC, an Internet connection, and a browser.

[1] Envisioning Information by Edward R. Tufte. Copyright ©1990, Graphics Press.

[2] *Readings in Human-Computer Interaction Toward the Year 2000* by Rondi M. Baecker et al. Copyright ©1995, Morgan Kaufman Publishers, Inc.

There is a range of audiences that could come to your Web site, for very different reasons. They could be customers, prospects, researchers, the media, or even competitors. Can we possibly create rewarding experiences for all these different audiences—and would we want to? Probably not. However, we need to be aware that a Web site is not sacrosanct to one particular audience, and we will need to juggle or trade off different audience needs.

This book will give businesses insight into defining their audience and balancing different customers' needs.

IT REQUIRES INTEGRATION

Creating customer-effective Web sites is obviously a multifaceted endeavor. We need to understand the complexities of customer behavior and also need to know how to translate customer behavior into effective interface design and development on many levels. Many skills are needed within and across businesses and suppliers.

To illustrate, consider again the scenario in which a customer tries to order a product on a Web site.

To develop a process for progressing the customer through the order process, a business needs to take into account marketing and customer service requirements and relate this to existing service processes and systems. Then these requirements need to be communicated clearly to Web site developers and system architects who will, together, create the Web site and realize e-customers' end-to-end service experience. And then there's also the customer research and testing that must be factored into the development process.

A variety of disciplines are required to create customer-effective Web sites because we need to understand the way people behave and learn as well as how to translate this into effective interfaces and systems. Information technology has come together with other disciplines, such as psychology, sociology, and anthropology.

Not surprisingly then, a lot of different professionals have come into the Web site development arena in the past two years, from a variety of backgrounds and disciplines. This has resulted in the availability of rich and eclectic skills and ideas, but also fragmentation of the industry into multiple areas of specialization. We have behavioral analysts, cognitive architects, creative architects, information architects, system architects, content strategists, program managers, project managers, producers, consultants, and interactive strategists—all working toward creating the ultimate user experience.

The risk with multiple areas of specialization is that the overall thread will be lost—and that thread is what the customer needs to do on the Web. We have to make an effort to integrate because, in this environment, it won't happen as a matter of course.

This book describes the integrated activities businesses and Web site development companies need to undertake to develop customer-effective Web sites, within their own teams and across all teams required during the project.

Businesses need to have an integrated internal project team to ensure that all business requirements are covered. Similarly, external development teams need to be integrated to ensure that design and technical competencies are combined to produce customer-friendly and technically efficient Web sites. And then, the internal business and external development teams need to be integrated to bring together people with relevant skills and similar goals at the right times during the life of the project (the integrated project team is illustrated in Figure 5-1).

WHO IS INVOLVED?

Creating customer-effective Web sites is clearly a team effort within and across businesses, their suppliers (the "Web site development company"), and customers. Each party has a key role to play and responsibilities to accept.

The integrated team will need to comprise:

- Businesses
- Web site development companies
- Customers
- Strategists
- Researchers

1. BUSINESSES

A business is responsible for understanding its customers' service requirements and providing its suppliers with a good description of what customers need to achieve as a result of visiting its Web site. And the business should provide the overall strategy and direction for how it wishes to manage customers via the Web in the short and long term.

This gets the development process started. From there, the business is responsible for providing the information (or "content") that needs to be on the Web site along with guidelines on how this information could or should be structured. The business is also responsible for making sure its infrastructure supports the Web site strategy; business structure and processes need to be examined along with resources.

As the Web site development company delivers iterations of the concept and the Web site, the business is responsible for providing feedback and direction. That feedback and direction should be based on internal quality testing as well as customer testing.

And once the site is up and running, the business is responsible for keeping it running. This involves keeping all of the information current and ensuring that the site continues to provide a quality customer experience.

2. WEB SITE DEVELOPMENT COMPANIES

Web sites that give customers access to business process, such as an order process, require integration with businesses' existing systems. Someone needs to make sure that this integration is achieved and that the system acts efficiently and effectively as a whole, from the Web site interface to execution of customer activities within existing business systems. Integration may be a primary supplier function performed by a development team or by a specialist team of system integrators, or it may be undertaken by the business itself.

Overall, the development company is responsible for helping the business work out what it should be doing with its Web site. External organizations that deal with the Web every day are in a better position to understand the fundamentals of successful electronic servicing than businesses that may not have the same exposure.

Once the strategy is established, the development company is responsible for translating that into a Web site concept and product specification. The product specification will describe the system required to meet the business' requirements. The development company keeps refining the concept until it meets the business' requirements, and then the development company produces the Web site for real.

3. CUSTOMERS

Customers keep both the business and the Web site development company honest. They provide information and feedback that allow the business, in partnership with the development company, to provide a customer-effective experience.

The thing to remember is that customers won't tell you what you need to know unless you ask them. And you have to ask them the right things at the right times. Chapter 3 will give you a good many things to think about when planning and executing your customer testing.

4. STRATEGISTS

Sometimes strategists, such as consultants who specialize in Internet strategy, can give an even bigger view of what is going on in the world of electronic servicing. Strategists will probably always strategize, but their strategies will not be specific to your business or your customers unless you've directly employed them. If you're lucky, you may already have some people on your team who can offer this level of insight. If so, make sure you use them.

5. RESEARCHERS

Researchers whose primary function is to research customers' perceptions, attitudes, and behavior, are required to keep us in touch with customers, their big-picture needs as well as their specific needs. Failing to understand customers' needs results in lost opportunities for competitive advantage.

Traditional research companies may not yet be up with the play on researching e-services and customer responses to Web sites. If they just use traditional interviewing and focus group techniques, and don't take into account the electronic medium in their research, you may not be getting the full picture.

You may have people within your business or the Web site development team who can perform a research function, but remember, it's always useful to get an objective perspective on what you should, and have, developed.

PUTTING IT ALL TOGETHER

An integrated project team is one of the keys to success in creating customer-effective Web sites. Integration is required within the business, within the development company, and across both.

Figure 1-2 illustrates some of the responsibilities that go into the integrated development of customer-effective Web sites across businesses, Web site development companies, and customers.

At the beginning of the project, businesses and their development partners must form Internet business strategy and their component Web site strategy on the basis of customer service requirements (customer testing techniques are covered in Chapter 3 and a business' e-service requirement definition is covered in Chapter 4). Businesses must define their specific requirements for a Web site while their development partners begin to develop concepts and a specification for their Web site (a Web site development company's product, or Web site, specification is covered in Chapter 5).

Once the specification is agreed between Web site development companies and businesses, then businesses begin sourcing content and developing guidelines for the presentation of information on their Web site while their development partners begin Web site production and database design (the content challenge is covered in Chapter 5). While development partners are continuing production at the Web site, businesses complete the set-up and process design required to support the Web site and the e-customer's required service experience (business process improvement is covered in Chapter 5).

Web Site Development Company			
Business	**Front End**	**Back End**	**Customer**
Internet business strategy and Web site strategy			Service Requirements
Definition of requirements	Web site concept and product specification		
Content sourcing, collation, and generation and site guidelines (ongoing)	Web site production (ongoing	Database design	
Business setup and process design and redesign (ongoing)		Programming	
Definition of changes required	Debugging and fixes		
Testing (internal and customer)	Integration and testing		Feedback on Web site experience
Migration of Web site to a live environment			
Site maintenance and enhancement			Feedback on Web site experience

(bracket at right labeled: Iterative)

Figure 1-2 Responsibilities within an integrated development team

Once the Web site reaches a point where business requirements have been met, all parties, including the customer, go through a process of testing and redevelopment until the Web site delivers against customers' service requirements. And then the Web site is migrated from a production to a live environment and the ongoing task of keeping the Web site alive begins.

We will look at the integrated activities of organizations and development companies, and a recommended integrated project team structure, in detail in Chapter 5. Project milestones are also given in Figure 5-2.

Meanwhile, we will turn our attention to the customer, who is, after all, the starting point in all customer-effective Web site development.

CHAPTER 2

WHAT CUSTOMERS WANT

In a nutshell, customers want e-services that are better, faster, and smarter. And you may only get one chance to provide them.

As I've stood behind customers, in the moment before they experience a business' Web site for the first time, I've been poignantly aware of all the expectations they have poised in their fingertips as they anticipate swinging into action once the home page downloads.

I have found that, basically, customers expect a Web site to improve the service they receive from the business in question. To a customer, this means getting things done easier, faster, and smarter. As soon as customers download a Web site, they expect to experience something superior; they expect businesses to have applied this great, new technology to enhance their service experience and to help them, personally, get things done.

And what does it mean to get things done? Well, let's put ourselves in the customers' shoes for a moment and think about the things they need to do to find, set up, and maintain the services they need.

Consider things you have to do as part of everyday life: managing your finances, looking for a place to live, refinancing the mortgage, setting up cover for the new car or home, putting in a second phone line, setting up an electricity account, advising of a changed address, remembering birthdays and organizing gifts, ordering stuff you can't find in the shops, getting someone to come and fix something, and understanding how something works even when you've got the instructions spread all over the place.

Sound familiar? Now, consider customers in pursuit of superior customer service on the Web. What are the types of things they want to do while on a business' Web site?

They will want to seek out pertinent information and ask questions, evaluate alternatives, make choices, and make things happen as quickly as they can once they've made up their minds. And, once they've made a decision, they want to be kept in the loop, just to make sure they made the right decision or in case something better comes along. They'll keep an eye on what the business and their competitors are up to. Or else they'll be busy concentrating on other decisions and go back to the business only when something's broken or they need something else.

The Graphics, Visualization and Usability (GVU) Center of Georgia Technology Institute have made some inroads into finding out about why people use the Web and the experiences they have. The center runs an annual Web user survey, and the results are publicly available online (see Netography for the Web site address). It includes some pretty smart questions about such things as primary uses of the Web, problems using the Web, use of different types of information, important features of Web vendors, dissatisfying experiences, purchase decisions and preferences for the Web over other media, and pursuits. Questions like these help us to appreciate the dynamics underlying customer usage and create more customer-effective Web sites.

The GVU user survey gives us insight into the fact that customers use the Web to perform specific tasks related to the services and products businesses provide. In the tenth user survey the most popular pursuit was gathering information for personal needs, followed by work/business, education, and shopping. "Time wasting" was ranked almost lowest. In addition, people were visiting Web sites weekly to seek out product information.

The survey also shows that the Web is only part of a customer's service experience. Customers don't necessarily want to do everything, like purchase, on the Web. GVU found that people use the Web as the primary source in making a purchase decision about once every one to two months, whether they purchase on the Web or not. In addition, people browse product information without the explicit intent to buy once to several times each month and search with the explicit intent to buy several times each week or month The Web experience may or may not lead directly to purchase, but, irrespective, it is an important part of a customer's decision-making process.

So customers use the Web as a service medium and they go to Web sites to perform specific tasks. The Web may also be only one medium a customer relies on during their overall service experience.

FIVE "DOING-AREAS"

We can categorize what customers want to do on the Web under five "doing areas," as follows:

1. Evaluate competing businesses and products.

2. Select products and transact with e-service providers.

3. Get help.

4. Provide feedback.

5. Stay tuned in as e-customers.

These five areas are all important. Customers will operate in one area more than another at a given point in time, depending on where they are at with what they're trying to do. We can think of the five areas as a rough progression, from evaluating businesses and products to becoming customers to receiving after-sales support and information.

Now, let's look at each of these "doing areas" in more detail.

1. Evaluate Competing Businesses and Products

Customers have to decide between businesses and products. Web sites are a part of that decision-making process.

When deciding among businesses, customers will either actively or passively get information from a company's Web site. Customers want to make sure they like a company enough to do business with them. Customers are more likely to actively search for, and evaluate, information on a company when they are new to the market for a product. They're likely to look at parts of the site that give them an idea of what the company is up to. Customers who already have dealings with a business are less likely to actively seek out their general company information. However, they may actively seek out information on a particular incident or company activity if it affects their preference for that company.

Potential and existing customers will get a feel for a company just by being on its Web site. How customer-centric the site feels will give them an idea of the quality of the customer service they can expect. How well the company has used technology will give customers an idea of how switched on it is.

Of course, a company must be the type a customer is looking for, and must offer the type of products a customer wants. The search for, and evaluation of, product information is key for new and existing customers. Customers will evaluate different products offered by one company and by different companies. Sometimes that evaluation will result in a sale (either online or offline) and sometimes it won't, but it is all critical to the decision-making process. Customers may also evaluate product information available in other forms, like brochures, as part of their decision-making process.

The importance of being able to find useful product information has been reinforced in GVU's tenth user survey. The survey showed that the provision of quality information is the most important attribute of a vendor's site. In addition, the greatest cause for customers to leave a site is not being able to find the information they were looking for.

Customers' evaluation of product information is not about passively viewing product blurbs. Customers seek out product information and interact with Web sites, and a business, to find out what suits them best. Customers are quick to use any sort of useful interactivity to get a better view of what a product offers them, how much that will cost, and how easily they can get it. The more usefully interactive product information is, the more the customer will use it.

Mortgage calculators provide a good example of useful interactivity. Customers enter the amount of the desired loan, and the various features they require, to find out how much it will cost them, over a certain loan period. By changing the variables and running the process a few times, customers get a good idea of what they're in for.

Customers will provide information on themselves to get an intelligent response. This can take many forms, not just strictly mathematical as in the mortgage calculator example. They will enter information to get a personalized response. And they want as much help doing that as possible. They want to compare the various scenarios they've generated and the responses they've got, and they may do that right then and there on the Web site or come back a few times to try things out.

Customers will take time out to evaluate products. The more useful the information, the more likely they are to spend time evaluating them. If product information is not useful, chances are customers will abandon your Web site for someone else's. The tenth GVU user survey showed that Web users can spend up to half an hour looking for the information they want.

Sometimes, you can't tell customers everything they need to make a decision. In these cases they will ask you questions or request more information. Or customers may not be able to locate the information they need, and they'll come straight to you and ask for it.

At this point, customers are pretty single-minded, and they're unlikely to give you a whole lot of background information when asking questions. This can make it difficult to direct and respond to customer questions. You can lead customers to ask more meaningful questions, if you give them some simple selections to make when entering their comments. In fact, sometimes this makes inquiries easier for customers.

2. SELECT PRODUCTS AND TRANSACT WITH E-SERVICE PROVIDERS

Customers are faced with a lot of choices when they go to a Web site. They will make selections to personalize their experience and the services and products they receive. That selection will comprise the choices they make to get around your site and identification of the things that they want or that particularly interest them. This may involve choosing a particular product there and then or setting themselves up to receive information and services later.

And sometimes, that selection will lead to a transaction. This transaction may or may not be financial. When customers transact with you, they give you something in return for a service. Sometimes that is simply information, for example, when they register to receive particular information online.

Customers have to select the path they take through your site as much as the particular services and products they want. They are using your Web site to create a context that is relevant to them personally. Selection, then, is the process of personalization.

When making their selections, customers rely heavily on tools to seek out personally relevant information, such as site maps, search functions, indexes, and shortcuts. They also use tools that help them receive personally relevant information and services, such as entering personal information to create profiles and receive personalized content.

Personalization is an all or nothing proposition. Personalization should allow e-customers to modify the information and functionality they receive on Web sites, based on facts related to their own particular situation. E-customers will find Web sites irrelevant and intrusive if they do not receive something personally relevant and useful in return for the information they have provided. E-customers are more likely to provide personal information on Web sites that clearly offer valuable and useful information and functionality in return for the information they have provided.

3. GET HELP

Customers may seek help at different times, as part of their evaluation process or after they have made a selection and transacted. Customers will also seek out help on different levels: getting around the site, evaluating what is best for them, and getting the best out of something, and solving a particular problem.

Customers will interact with your site to:

- Work out how to use your site. Customers want to learn how to get around and optimize the use of your site as quickly and easily as possible.
- Find out how something works once they have it.
- Resolve a problem online.
- Find out where to go, or whom to talk to, if they have a problem that can't be easily resolved online.

And don't forget, a Web site is only part of a customer's experience. Customers may also seek help outside of your Web site. Tailored advice is still very important and, oftentimes, this only comes from talking to someone.

4. PROVIDE FEEDBACK

Customers will provide feedback. This may be voluntarily provided by e-customers (unprompted) or solicited (prompted).

Customers sometimes want to provide feedback on an experience they've had with you, either on your Web site, or in general. A Web site provides a medium where people can have a good moan without having to talk to someone in person.

Customers will complain and unprompted feedback is usually negative, unfortunately and fortunately. It's unfortunate because it can create a skewed view of how well you are doing and fortunate because it provides an outlet that customers may not otherwise have. It also gives you a chance to get things right where you may not have otherwise known something was wrong.

Feedback on your Web site may not be particularly helpful, because customers don't understand the way your Web site works as well as you do. "Your Web site stinks" might be all the feedback you get after a customer has spent half an hour unsuccessfully trying to do something useful. You may never find out what the customer was trying to do or exactly what went wrong. However, if you prompt feedback in places related to specific things you know customers are trying to do, and give them some guidance on what you want to know, you're more likely to get useful feedback.

Customers are more passive when it comes to prompted feedback. However, customers will give you information, provided they get something worthwhile in return. A customer who is very involved with your company or your product may want to have some involvement with the decisions your company makes. Those customers still need to see payback for time spent. This payback does not equate to a bribe either. Seeing the difference the feedback makes may be enough for a customer.

5. Stay Tuned In as E-Customers

The level of day-to-day involvement e-customers have with businesses as e-service providers will determine how much they want to "tune in" to their Web site. For example, a bank's customer is more likely to want to use a Web site for frequent transactions than a computer supplier's customer who may only purchase once a year.

Even if customers are not transacting with you on a frequent basis, they will still use your Web site to:

- Access and maintain any information they've given you or that you share as a result of your service relationship.
- Be sure they've gotten the best deal you can provide.
- Access special deals or offers.
- Get the most out of the product they've purchased.

And, again, let's not forget that a Web site is only part of a customer's service experience. Customers may have relationships with people within the service-providing organization, and these are also an integral part of day-to-day support.

SEVENTEEN CUSTOMER DIRECTIVES

When we get in the way of what customers want to do on the Web, they get frustrated. What they want to do will comprise getting around a site and making use of the content and functionality it offers.

There are some complaints, or requests, I've heard over and over again, in relation to a whole range of Web sites and industries. Customers don't know all the marketing and business reasons behind the way a business has done things, they just know what they want it to do, and they'll state it in simple terms they understand.

Here I will share with you what I have come to know as fundamental customer directives. There are 17 of them, and they're all given in customers' words. I have also provided examples to illustrate the types of roadblocks that drive customers mad. These examples are hypothetical but are closely related to real-life experiences that customers have had. I have called them "blunders," because that is how customers describe them. We know the reasons why these things happen, but customers don't.

That doesn't mean to say that customers will be equally frustrated by all these blunders. They will be most frustrated by what gets in the way of the things they want to do the most (and this will change depending on where the customer is at). Also, customers will take your Web site on balance. If you give them some very useful things, they may put up with some blunders and learn how to get around them (but that's not an excuse for making the blunder).

The following customer directives will give you some triggers for thinking about all of the factors that contribute to a frustrating customer experience, the thinking and planning that goes into a site, the content that ends up there, the visual interface and interactive functionality, and the performance of the system in general. All of these dynamics will be explored in depth in this book, and these customer directives will set a frame of reference for later. If businesses and Web site designers are aware of what frustrates customers they will be more likely to direct their energy into areas most likely to result in customer effectiveness.

And, remember, nothing can replace the value of doing customer testing tailored to your own customers and service offerings. The next chapter looks at ways you can do effective customer testing and the methods used to uncover these customer directives.

An overview of the seventeen customer directives is provided in Table 2-1.

Now let's explore each of these customer directives in more depth. We will look at examples of some blunders being made on Web sites to illustrate just how often businesses are unwittingly violating these simple customer directives. (The Web sites making the blunders, have not been identified, but the scenarios given are based on experiences customers are having on those, and similar, Web sites).

Table 2-1 Seventeen customer directives and their implications

Customer Directive	Implication
1. This better be worth the wait	Every piece of content , functionality and design should be complete and have a clear purpose.
2. Tell me what I get if I do this	Make the results of interactions, such as registration, very clear to e-customers. Never ask for information without stating what the e-customer will get in return, especially if some e-customers are excluded or a significant time investment is required.
3. I'll ID myself when I'm ready	Be sensitive about when e-customers want to be anonymous and when they don't. Make it clear when e-customers are well known to businesses but are anonymous on their Web sites.
4. Use what I give you	Every action should have a logical consequence.
5. Let me build my knowledge	Offer information and functionality that lets e-customers build on what they already know about a business.
6. Let me make a valid comparison	Make it easy for e-customers to compare products within and across Web-sites.
7. Don't expect me to make a decision without the facts	Don't prompt actions at inappropriate points in e-customers' decision-making processes.
8. Be careful second-guessing my needs	Don't make recommendations or offer personalized content unless you know enough about the e-customer to be relevant and useful.
9. Let me get to where I need to go	Let e-customers go straight to important parts of a Web site, such as those related to frequently required service requests.
10. Yes, I want it now, what?	If e-customers can express their desire for a product or service they should be able to go about getting it right then and there.
11. Signpost my journey	Provide a centralized, consistent and helpful navigation system that doesn't send e-customers off to disparate sub-sites. Always show e-customers where they are, where they've been and where they can go next.
12. Don't lock me out	Don't invite e-customers to engage in any interaction, such as authenticating themselves, when they may be excluded from the results of that interaction. Make it very clear when different e-customers have different privileges.

Table 2-1 Seventeen customer directives and their implications (cont.)

Customer Directive	Implication
13. Don't limit my choices	Whenever Web sites offer selection criteria to e-customers, there is a risk the criteria will be wrong or incomplete. E-customers should have as much control as possible over what content they receive in relation to certain criteria.
14. Give me digestable chunks	Use the interactivity of the Web to layer the delivery of information so that e-customers don't get overloaded with more information than they need at one time.
15. Call a spade a spade	Be honest about what Web site functions will do for e-customers. Avoid using fancy labels that overstate the usefulness or sophistication of Web site components.
16. Tell me the info you need	E-customers should not have to use trial and error to complete an online process such as ordering or sending an e-mail form. All mandatory fields should be clearly stated and error messages should be specific and relate to all errors generated in the previous interaction.
17. Don't ignore important relationships	If e-customers have important relationships with people in businesses, they will expect that to carry over to their Web sites. This is particularly relevant in the case of business-to-business relationships.

1. "THIS BETTER BE WORTH THE WAIT"

Everything we offer on the Web is subject to higher expectations because customers have to wait for it.

On the Internet we have to wait for things to download; that's a given. Slow download speed is still rated by customers as the biggest negative in their experience of the Web, but they live with it. Customers get mad when they wait for a page to download and then find there's very little on it. Sometimes it's just obvious that that part of the site is under construction. Customers feel that companies should make the effort to complete each page before offering it online.

Under construction

This doesn't necessarily mean that a business should refrain from presenting a page that is "under construction," but it does need to be handled appropriately. Customers will feel cheated if they spend time following a path only to find their ultimate destination under construction.

Dead ends

It is surprising the number of times a customer comes to a "dead end" on a Web site, a point where no new content is delivered. This is especially true of Web sites where a standard navigation (such as frames) has been used across all product content. A page should not be offered if there is no new content available on it.

Multiplicity

Another common frustration is taking one path to find information and then taking another, only to find yourself receiving exactly the same information. Customers expect different paths to reflect different customer needs, and they get annoyed when they find the same information having taken different paths. This is particularly problematic in relation to calculative or scenario-based functionality, where the customer sees quite different variables and considerations leading to exactly the same outcome. If the outcome is the same for all the different variables, why would a customer bother going through the process of generating scenarios always to end up at the same place?

Gratuitous content and functionality

Download time also makes customers more sensitive to time wasting. Customers will see anything that doesn't exist for a reason as gratuitous. This doesn't mean they don't want graphics or other interesting and creative devices on Web sites; they just want these things to be a worthwhile part of the journey, and, therefore, worth the wait.

Blunders

Navigation leading to nothing

Say a Web site offers "tips from other customers" as part of the standard navigation for evaluating products. However, only one in five products actually has customer tips associated. When the customer clicks on "customer tips," chances are, there won't be any. This will get annoying after a while. The level of annoyance would be even greater if it was something fundamental, like product prices, that was sporadically available.

Worthless downloads

Consider a company who has run a series of TV ads and has decided to profile those ads on their Web site. Customers can click on a picture of a screen shot from each of the TV ads and this starts a download. The download takes about five minutes. Customers who complete the download find it to be a reproduction of the TV ad, nothing more, nothing less. They wonder why they bothered taking the time to see something they've already seen on TV. After all, TV is a better medium for the ad anyway. They expect the Web site to give them more information, to complement the ads, not just reproduce them.

2. "TELL ME WHAT I GET IF I DO THIS"

Web sites can't show everything all on one level. It's just physically impossible. We have to put different information on different levels and give customers paths to navigate their way through it.

Customers need to make an informed decision of whether or not it is worth their while to head down a particular path or partake in a particular process. The more we can tell customers about the consequences of their actions, the better. And "telling" a customer what's going to happen, or is happening, will involve written and visual cues.

Blind action and hidden consequences

Unfortunately, we often don't make a certain path clear to customers and they don't know what they're committing to when taking a certain action. The result of an action isn't always clear. This means that customers will not try the action or will try it and be disappointed or confused.

This is particularly problematic when customers become eligible for something as a result of a transaction, but don't know exactly what that is until after the transaction. This might result in customer delight if they are eligible for more than they expect, but, chances are, they'll be disappointed.

Also, when customers are considering whether or not to purchase online, they want to know what the process is and need help every step of the way (including confirmation of a successful purchase at the end of the process). Customers often feel uncertain about what's happening to them if they don't understand the steps they're going through. This lack of understanding sometimes results in fear, and this will prevent some customers from purchasing online.

Hidden time requirements

Some processes take up a lot of customer time, but the customer doesn't know that up front. Customers don't mind investing a bit of time if the payback is good, but they get angry when things unexpectedly pop up along the way. Downloads are particularly problematic because of the time taken to complete them. Many customers also aren't comfortable with performing downloads; they feel they don't know enough about what's going on. Some customers will venture a download, but they need to know exactly what's involved up front and receive help along the way.

Blunders

Blind registration

A researcher comes to a Web site to find out about a particular piece of research they know has been completed by a research organization. They are not a client, as such, but are prepared to register and pay for the research if necessary.

On coming to the Web site the researcher finds that the information they want is not publicly available. The Web site does, however, offer registration. There are two types of registration, one for clients and one for a complimentary account. There is no explanation of what the registration processes will offer. Irrespective of this, the researcher is willing to register for a complimentary account, because they expect it to give them access to the piece of research they're looking for.

The researcher goes through four screens to complete the registration process. (It would have been five or six if someone else had chosen the same username or password as they did.) On completing the registration process, it finally becomes clear to the researcher what they are eligible for. It turns out that they can access the research they want, but they can't access the full transcript without client access.

The researcher now has to go back and find out what is required to qualify for client access. They are perturbed that they didn't know, up front, what they had to do to get the information they wanted. Let's hope the research, if they can actually get hold of it, is worth all this hassle.

The sequence the researcher goes through is shown in Figure 2-1.

3. "I'LL ID MYSELF WHEN I'M READY"

Sometimes customers want to be anonymous and sometimes they want you to know exactly who they are. Customers use their anonymity as a basis for getting impartial advice and information without any sales pressure. This tends to be early in the process when a customer is evaluating alternatives.

The importance of anonymity is reinforced in GVU's tenth user survey, where people agreed strongly with the statement that they valued their anonymity on the Internet and enjoyed online shopping because of the absence of sales pressure.

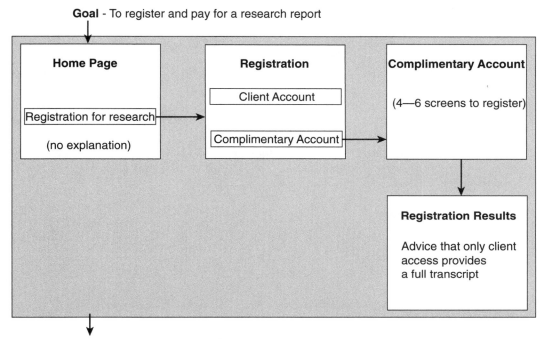

Figure 2-1   Blind registration.

However, if customers want to transact with you, and if they have a history with you, they may well want you to know who they are. This is likely to be later in the process when identification benefits the customer.

Problems arise when we misjudge when people want to be anonymous and when they want to be identified. Forcing customers to identify themselves too early in an inquiry process could prevent them from going through with it. Additionally, Web sites sometimes don't make it clear whether customers are anonymous or not. Customers can sometimes incorrectly surmise that they have been identified, and then get disappointed when they don't receive personalized information.

4. "USE WHAT I GIVE YOU"

If you ask customers for information, they expect you to use it in some way. This applies to information that returns a response then and there, as well as later on.

If customers are using functionality, such as a calculator, or a drop-down menu, to create outcomes from different scenarios or selections, they expect the information they enter to directly affect the outcome. Customers get frustrated when they enter information and it doesn't change the outcome.

Similarly, if customers give you information about themselves during their Web-site experience, and then you don't use it for anything useful to them, they wonder why you needed it in the first place.

In addition, customers expect Web sites to remember things so they don't have to tell you the same thing over and over. This is particularly true when customers transact—if they seek to do a number of transactions sequentially, and they give you personal information the first time, they expect you to remember it, to save them from rekeying it each time.

Blunders

Go-nowhere selection

A customer wants to find out the cost of a phone call to, say, part of the United States. They find a calculator that allows them to enter where they're calling, and when, to find out the cost of the call. The calculator returns the cost of the call, and also presents a drop-down list from which the customer can select the time at various places called. The customer would have to select the exact place they are calling from the drop-down list to find out the time there. The customer is confused as to why the tool couldn't tell them the time at the place they were calling at the same time as telling them the cost of the call—they had already provided information on where they were calling.

Insufficient memory

A customer wants to buy a mobile phone. They go through some scenarios on the Web site to work out what they need. The Web site recommends a particular type of mobile phone and the customer decides to get it. The customer clicks through to purchase the product but finds that the form needs some information identical to what they've already entered.

OK so maybe they can live with that. They then fill out the form to purchase the product. They then realize that they also need to sign up for the call plan that goes along with the mobile phone. Having ordered the mobile phone, they go on to sign up for the call plan they want. They get a form to sign up and discover that a lot of the information they just filled in on the previous mobile phone form hasn't been captured in this form either, and they have to rekey it.

By this time the customer is getting a little frustrated and is thinking, "This could have been easier." The customer submits the form to sign up for the call plan but they get an error message telling them that they haven't filled the form in correctly. They go back to fix the form but find that some of the information they filled in the last time has disappeared. Now the customer is really annoyed. If the error messages or the forms aren't very helpful as well, this customer could end up going back and forth a number of times to rekey, rekey, and rekey.

Chances are that this will be the last time they try and order something on that Web site.

The sequence the customer goes through is shown in Figure 2-2.

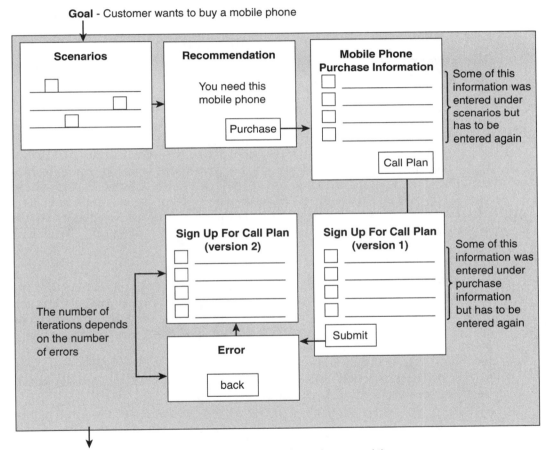

Figure 2-2 Insufficient memory.

5. "LET ME BUILD MY KNOWLEDGE"

Because Web sites are not the only medium that customers have to find out about companies and their products, they expect Web sites to "make sense" in relation to all of the dealings and exposure they have with a company.

Customers expect businesses to tell them more than what they already know, not repeat everything they've already been told without offering anything new. It also sticks out like a sore thumb when known parts of the business or product offerings are obviously excluded from the Web site.

If customers already know your company, they expect to be able to learn more.

Of course, this directive is largely to do with integration; integrated marketing and customer service. And this is something we will explore in more detail later in this book.

Blunders

Incomplete offering

Consider a telecommunications company that offers connectivity to the Internet through an ISP (Internet Service Provider). A customer goes to the company's Web site to find out about its ISP's rates relative to their current ISP. But, mysteriously the company's Web site makes no mention of its ISP. The customer is baffled and confused as to why such a relevant service would be missing from the Web site. They then find out, in "other links," that the ISP has a separate Web site, so they go there. But, they still can't understand why there are two Web sites. Both sites may represent two companies, but they're all part of the same service as far as the customer is concerned.

Insufficient interactivity

A customer who is evaluating different mortgage options goes to the Web site of a financial services provider. The customer has already gathered information from a few other Web sites and is hoping to be able to decide among them. However, when the customer gets to this particular Web site they find the available information to be nothing more than what they already have in the provider's brochures. The Web site does not provide the customer with information relevant to their particular situation. Chances are that this company will not win the sale as the customer moves on to check out the next Web site.

6. "LET ME MAKE A VALID COMPARISON"

Customers evaluate products and services against each other; those products may be offered by one company or across companies. Customers also want to compare the value of the different information offerings on your Web site.

Inconsistent product information

Customers get frustrated when product information is presented in such a way that it makes a valid comparison difficult. Lack of consistency in how product information is presented makes comparison difficult for customers, and that relates to consistency in visual presentation and access as well as it does to the nature of the content that's provided.

Ignoring relativity

Customers also struggle when Web sites ignore obvious relationships between products they are evaluating. Some products are obviously related, or maybe even packaged, by the service provider, and yet the customer finds that the Web site does not relate those products at all through content or even basic navigation.

Blunders

Difficult product comparisons

Consider a customer who wants to select a day-to-day checking account. On visiting a site they find information on a range of checking accounts. The customer starts off with a list of the accounts available and clicks through to evaluate the first one. Having evaluated the first one, the customer has to go back in order to click through to evaluate the second one, and so on for the seven checking accounts available—forward and back seven times.

But then the customer realizes that the last three accounts are actually complementary to the checking accounts; they detail the different ATM and card options. The customer then has to work out which of the previous four checking accounts these three options relate to. It would have been helpful to evaluate those options at the same time as evaluating the checking account, not to mention being able to get between products without having to go forward and back all the time.

Company structure versus product comparison

A customer of a global management consulting company receives good consultancy advice on a project and wants to find out what other areas the company could assist with. The customer goes to the consulting company's Web site and clicks through on "products and services" to get a list of broad service areas. However, none of those services can be clicked on for more information.

The customer then goes back to the home page and realizes that this is an international home page and that they will need to select a country-specific Web site in order to get information on services. Given that this customer is in the United States, they select the U.S. Web site. Now they click through on "products and services" and get a list as long as your arm; the list appears to detail every service and subservice available, plus a lot of other items that don't even look like products and services.

The customer starts to go through the list, clicking on the ones that look interesting. However, the customer finds that each click returns a new Web site—one for every service (each with its own home page). Each of these Web sites is completely different and each seems to be more of a brag book for a subsidiary company or department than a guide to products and services.

Needless to say, evaluating services on the Web site would be a labor of love. The customer decides it's probably quicker and easier just to call the head consultant on the project already completed to find out what other areas the company may be able help with.

The sequence the customer goes through is shown in Figure 2-3.

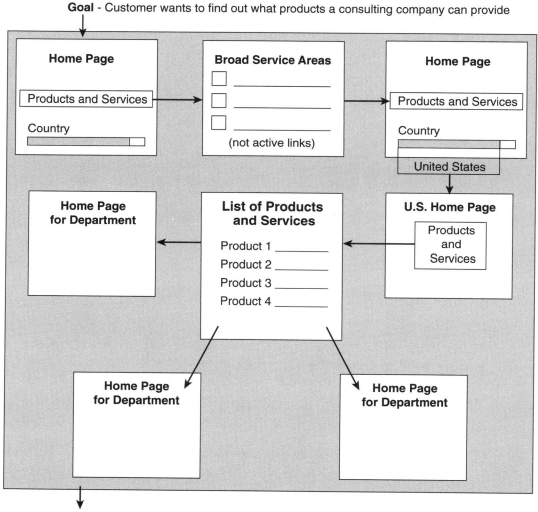

Goal - Customer wants to find out what products a consulting company can provide

Result - Customer phones consultant

Figure 2-3 Company structure versus product comparison.

7. "DON'T EXPECT ME TO MAKE A DECISION WITHOUT THE FACTS"

Customers are likely to feel like they're being subjected to a hard sell if they do not have sufficient information before being faced with a decision or an invitation to purchase. There will be some fundamental information that a customer wants before deciding whether to purchase. The nature of these fundamentals will depend on the service being offered.

Blunders

Inappropriate timing

Consider a customer who is evaluating products offered by an electronics company. The customer interacts with a tool that helps them identify some solutions to common desktop publishing problems. By identifying with some problem scenarios, the customer receives some recommendations; a list of software and hardware products with a brief description of each product. Next to each product name is a button inviting the customer to "buy now." The customer feels uncomfortable with the process at this point because they don't feel they know enough about any of the products to purchase anything at that point.

Missing facts

Continuing the above scenario, the customer chooses to ignore the inappropriate invitation to "buy now" and clicks through to the product page for one of the recommended products, a printer. From the product page the customer clicks through to a page that allows them to choose the printer model. Here they are again invited to "buy now," but unfortunately no prices are given for the different printers, probably because each printer must be packaged with software, thus making each combination a different price. The customer feels they can't possibly purchase a printer without knowing how much it is going to cost, and they bail out of the process at that point.

8. "BE CAREFUL SECOND-GUESSING MY NEEDS"

This area is fascinating. I have observed customers making brilliant and smart use of the Web, only to find them ambivalent toward it (or, when too much liberty is seen to be taken; disdainful). You would think that anything that helps customers personalize or customize what they get from a Web site would be a good thing. Wrong.

I've had to put my disappointment aside to realize that usefulness is just that. We are limited in our knowledge of our customers, one way or another. The better we know our customers, the more we can directly address their needs. But that's stating the obvious, right? Maybe. But sometimes we need to remind ourselves of the obvious because lots of Web sites just aren't getting this right.

Be very careful assuming you know what customers need—what they need to know or what they need to get. Remember that their use of a Web site is only part of their whole experience, and what you know from a customer's Web site behavior may not tell you enough to second-guess what makes them tick.

Personalization

Many Web sites invite customers to personalize content and functionality for their own uses. Creating a home page has become quite a common concept—and maybe that's part of the problem. People take an idea that may have worked on another site and apply it to their own, without realizing the fundamentals of what it takes to make it successful.

To work well, personalization is dependent on what's being personalized. Personalized irrelevance is never going to be relevant. Customers just can't be bothered with the process of personalization unless they get something that's useful to them. And, of course, the process has to be user-friendly as well. Customers do not want to go through a painful process to create something that may not end up being useful to them.

Recommendations

Many Web sites also make recommendations to customers. Customers may find these useful, be ambivalent, or find them a waste of time and space. Why? Because, to state the obvious again, the better we know our customers, the more we can directly address their needs. And sometimes we don't know them as well as we think we do.

So we can make recommendations on what we know we know, and find out what we don't know, before making recommendations. For example, we do know what a customer has done on our Web site (well, we should). If we base our recommendations on a good dose of Web site behavior, then we might have a better chance of being useful. Also, if we ask customers to select the things that they find important, or identify with, before we start making recommendations, we will also have a better chance of being useful.

In general, if customers' needs are not well understood, it is better to provide customers with adequate, quality information and leave it up to them to make their own decisions, rather than take the liberty of second-guessing their needs.

Decision support

Customers want to find out which product or service is best for them, and some Web sites will offer content and/or functionality to help them make the best choice. That's fine, but sometimes this help is couched as "customized solutions"—generating solutions on the basis of customer needs. This type of decision support is an all-or-nothing proposition to the customer who would say, "Either make a recommendation based on adequate knowledge or don't bother making a recommendation."

Hopefully, this directive will become less needed over time as we utilize the Web to better understand our customers. In the meantime, care needs to be taken not to make the worst of a good idea.

Blunders

Ill-informed solutions

A business customer wants to evaluate the types of advertising and promotion they should be engaging in. The customer goes to one of their favorite Web sites, which has a center just for small businesses. The Web site says that it can offer helpful advice and solutions to small businesses. The customer finds a section on advertising and promotion right away—it's obviously a hot topic for small businesses that have tight budgets and need focused results.

The customer is given three areas of selection: type of business you are in, what you are likely to spend, and how well you pitch yourself against your competitors. The customer makes a selection under each of these areas and clicks on "solution" to get some advice on the type of advertising and promotion that might work best for them. The results come back as a list of different types of marketing approaches, a long list it seems, and a lot of the approaches don't seem that suitable.

The customer decides that the tool doesn't know enough about their business, who their customers are, the products they sell, geographic considerations, things that have, or haven't, worked in the past, etc. The tool hasn't told the customer any more than what they already knew. Fortunately, it didn't take a lot of time to go through, but the customer is unlikely to go back to the Web site for advice.

Personalized irrelevance

"Why would I want to personalize that?" was a good question from a CEO trying out an extranet now on offer from their service provider. Apparently, the extranet is aimed at sharing privileged information with the industry's top decision makers.

Unfortunately, the site offers content areas that don't really seem to relate to what this customer wants to do, or know about, as CEO. However, the site assumes that personalization of the extensive database of articles will deliver most of the site's value. While this type of personalization is a good idea, this CEO can't be bothered trying to find some content that might be of interest, and anyway, they can only personalize by broad subject areas, none of which, on the face of it, are particularly relevant.

The CEO decides this particular site is of little value and not worth the effort.

9. "LET ME GET TO WHERE I NEED TO GO"

Some Web sites just don't allow customers to do the things they need to do as customers. The things they want to do are likely to fall into one of the five "doing areas" identified earlier.

Lack of utility

One of the most common areas of customer frustration is not being given access to people within a company. A Web site that only gives a generic e-mail or mail address or phone number, may not be seen to be particularly helpful.

Frustration also commonly arises when customers can't transfer their everyday transactions to the online medium. The level of that frustration will increase if those transactions are routine and frequently performed.

Customers also get frustrated when they can't access their personal information online, especially if they think it is required to perform routine, everyday transactions. Of course, access to personal information is a lot easier than it sounds. Customers generally don't understand the complexities of providing access to internally held information via the Web.

Customers expect to be able to get closer to the company they're doing business with, and noncapitulation is often taken by customers to be inferior customer service. These customer expectations were illustrated by Figure 1-1 in Chapter 1.

Information classification

Information has to be classified into areas that customers can access. That information can be cut many different ways, and the particular approach adopted may help or hinder customers.

There is a lot of debate over the most effective way to categorize information. I too have been involved in this debate and have observed customers' preferences with interest, keen to discover "one best way of doing it." However, I can't say there is "one best way." What I can say is that, when information classification gets in the way of customers doing the things they need to do, they get annoyed and frustrated.

Needless to say, few Web sites classify information on the basis of what customers want to do or tasks they want to perform. Often the necessary utility is buried deep in a site and the customer has to ferret it out. Some Web sites don't even provide obvious links to frequently required utility.

Obtrusive content

Customers get frustrated when they come to a Web site already knowing what they want and end up going through an interminable process of unnecessary persuasion. They want to go straight to the object of their desire, not churn through marketing blurb.

Frustration increases when customers are very familiar with a company's products; they may even know the name of the product they want (which is no small feat if brand names are given to different products). If a company has a high market profile, at a product level, customers need to make direct access to those products as quickly and easily as possible.

Blunders

Hidden utility

A customer finds out that their electricity supplier now has a Web site, and they have heard that it's supposed to offer good customer service. This customer is about to move to another home in a few weeks and wants to notify their supplier. Rather than sit in a long phone queue, the customer decides to advise their supplier online.

The customer goes to the Web site. The home page presents "Electricity for the Home" as an area for selection, and the customer clicks on that. Then the customer gets the "Home Page" for "Electricity for the Home." There is no obvious link to the type of activity the customer wants to perform, but there is a section called "Customer Service." The customer clicks on "Customer Service" and goes to a page that categorizes services under a few headings. The customer is not sure which one is exactly the closest to the activity they want to perform, but thinks "The Bill" is probably closest, since they will need the bill sent to the new address. The customer clicks on "The Bill" and gets a page that explains a typical bill. Just when the customer thinks that they haven't found what they're looking for, they remember to scroll down. And there it is, "Notify Change of Address." Clicking on this brings up a form that the customer fills in and sends.

It was there, just four layers down.

Helpfulness as hindrance

A customer goes to a car manufacturer's Web site. This customer knows exactly the make and model of the car they are interested in, they've seen it advertised everywhere recently. They go to the Web site and, on the home page, are met by a "guide" that offers to help the customer plug in some simple requirements to generate a list of models that meet those general requirements. The customer doesn't want to head down that route, because they already know what they want.

The customer notices that they can click through to a product search at this point, or they can click on a few other areas, but these are general categories and the customer is not sure which category this particular model would fall under. So the customer decides to risk the search function (their experience with search engines is checkered at best). After clicking on "Product Search" the customer receives a page that just lists the same product categories as were presented on the home page. At this point the customer scratches their head and asks themselves "How am I supposed to get to this product?"

Depending on how keen the customer is, they may go back to the home page and try to generate a recommendation for the model they want, so they can click through from there. Or, they may just go make a cup of coffee instead.

The sequence the customer goes through is shown in Figure 2-4.

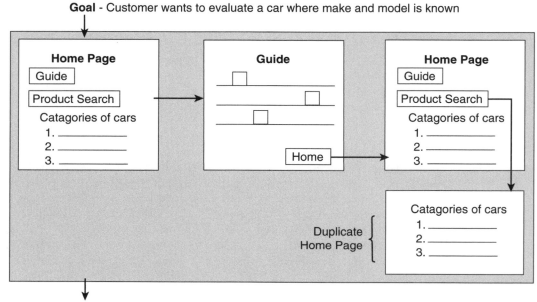

Goal - Customer wants to evaluate a car where make and model is known

Result - Customer fails to find the car they want to evaluate

Figure 2-4   Helpfulness as hindrance.

10. "YES, I WANT IT, NOW WHAT?"

Customers get frustrated when a Web site leads them down a path to a product and then they can't get it. Either the Web site does not give them the option to select or purchase, or they have to go through some convoluted process to end up doing something other than purchasing it.

This happens with frightening frequency in relation to special deals.

Blunders

Hype and no hustle

A customer goes to a software company's Web site for business customers to find out about its special deals. They click on "Special deals" off the home page and get a page with mini-ads for three hot specials. One of them looks interesting; this new software could help the customer manage business forecasting a whole lot better. The customer clicks on this special to find out more.

A promotional Web site comes back, with good explanatory information about what this software can do for businesses. It's only a beta version of the software, but it sounds great and it's affordable. The customer decides they want it and clicks on "Get It." This results in a page that details what you need to run the software, terms and conditions and how to install it, as well as a link to "Register Interest" in the final version of the product. But nowhere does it actually tell the customer how to get hold of the beta version of the software, only a contact for more information. Since there's nothing else, the customer clicks on "Contact for More Information" and receives an e-mail form that allows them to enter comments; the customer simply types, "So, how do I get it?" and sends the form.

11. "SIGNPOST MY JOURNEY"

Given that we have to create layers of information, and paths through them, we need to provide signposts that show customers where they're going. We need to help customers navigate.

When a Web designer designs a navigation system, they are designing a system of visual cues that helps customers find their way around a Web site. We can think of navigation as the framework that helps customers understand what they are doing on a Web site.

Some navigation systems are better than others. That said, there are some common areas where navigation systems frustrate customers. Within these systems we use navigation devices that provide the cues as to where we are, where we've been, and where we're going. Some of these are also better than others.

Customers get frustrated when you throw them too many curve balls. When they go to your Web site, they have to learn to use your navigation system and devices. Customers become angry when you don't allow them to learn your system, because you're inconsistent or it just "doesn't make sense" (and, remember, that *sense* is defined by the customer).

Information architecture and navigation are huge topics. We will look at them in more depth in Chapter 7 when considering customer-effective Web site design. Here, we will look at the common things that trip customers up.

Navigation systems

Inconsistency seems to be the thing that most often trips customers up. If a Web site introduces customers to a navigation system up front, they expect it to apply throughout the whole site, without exception. The main "anchors" for customers are navigation bars and frames—when these differ, for no apparent reason, customers start to flounder.

Consistency is also particularly important in relation to site hierarchies; often Web sites don't clearly show levels, or layers, of information, or they mix them up.

Customers very quickly lose their grasp of your navigation system if the hierarchy is messed up.

Many sites revert to different navigation systems within one site (particularly in cases where the site is structured around the company and not the customer). Unless customers can see the relationships between these different systems, up front, and have some common way of navigating between them, they're likely to get lost. A single, consistent system seems to work best—in fact, if it works, customers don't even really notice it's there; they just use it intuitively. (And note here that a system can be consistently made up of a number of approaches that all function as one system.)

Interestingly, customers seem to be comfortable with a reasonable amount of complexity in the navigation system, as long as it makes sense to them and they can learn it quickly. An overly simple navigation system doesn't necessarily win points if it "hides" the site from the customer (as is sometimes the case). Sometimes customers won't go digging into a "hidden" site, because they don't know its value, or they will start to dig, find some useful stuff, and get annoyed that they didn't know about it in the first place.

Another, very interesting, and disappointing, discovery is that many customers treat their browser as an inseparable part of your navigation system. For example, some customers blame a company's Web site that doesn't do what they want when they hit "back" on their browser; they don't get mad at the browser. This is particularly problematic in transactional processes where the customer uses the browser to go back and forth while entering and sending information—many Web sites aren't technically able to cope with this and the customer ends up getting error messages, losing information, or giving up.

Navigational devices

Within the navigation system there will be a number of navigation devices—elements of the Web site that allow customers to get around within the basic navigational structure.

One of the most common frustrations is not being able to work out where they are at a certain point in time or where they've been. From your home page, customers get a path (or paths) in mind. Customers will want to roughly follow that path and make sure they're roughly on track as they go.

There are some simple devices that help customers, and, when these are not used properly, they cause the most problems:

- *Inconsistent or non-existent highlighting to show where the customer is on the site.*

- *Changes in the color of links.* Sometimes the links don't change color when selected or the colors are inconsistent. This leaves the customer wondering what the different responses mean in relation to where they've been.

- *What is clickable?* Every clickable object should be obvious. I have observed many customers who run their mouse over a page to see what's clickable or "live" once a page has downloaded. If you don't consistently show customers what is clickable, they will get frustrated quickly. I have seen customers curse because they've tried, repeatedly, to click on something that they expect to take them somewhere, only to find that it's not "live". Passive images, such as "wallpaper" images, seem to be particularly problematic, because customers try to click on them.

- *Sending no feedback on where customers have been.* Some sites provide feedback on the layers and/or sections of the site customers pass through. In very deep sites, this seems to help customers to keep track of things. Many sites offer no feedback or only sporadic feedback. Customers get confused about the cues they are supposed to be using to find their way around.

- *Misleading or nonexistent labels.* We don't have room on a single screen to write full explanations of what each object is; we use labels. In truncating instructions to labels we create a real risk of confusing customers. Many labels just don't make sense to customers, particularly when the label is "company-speak" and not "customer-speak." Labels that are different from the "standard" labels customers are used to seeing on Web sites are also problematic.

- *Unknown search functions.* Often search exists at a number of levels on a site. Not surprisingly, customers expect the search to relate to the level of the site in which it is offered. Usually the search is general, vague, and not particularly well directed. To avoid customer frustration, a search function should appear in the appropriate context and customers should know what the search is being performed on.

- *Inconsistent and misleading use of iconography.* Sometimes sites combine words and labels to form their own icons, and these are often key to the navigation system. However, many attempts at iconography only go so far, and not far enough—they disappear leaving customers wondering what their signposts are.

- *Multiple windows.* Some Web sites use new windows to present new information. If customers can't understand why this new information has appeared in a new window, or don't even realize they are in a new window, they will get confused, and lost, very quickly. I've seen some customers panic when a new window opens and heard them ask themselves, "How did that happen?"

- *Misleading visual symbols.* Sometime sites use common visual symbols as a way of showing meaning. However, these symbols often mean something different to customers, who take them at face value. Also, common symbols may be loaded with meaning over and above what a customer would normally expect. For example, an arrow shows direction. Some web sites use arrows to indicate movement as well as direction (e.g., using arrows to indicate that customers can order a list of items by moving them). This additional meaning may be lost on customers.

- *Vague use of indexes.* Customers sometimes face indexes that they don't understand. This makes the indexed information inaccessible to the customer. For example, a product index that is simply shown at the top level as A B C D, etc., means nothing to a customer. I've observed customers totally stumped by this sort of thing; they have no idea how you would categorize your products, and, chances are, they certainly don't know all your product names.

Blunders

Conflicting navigational systems

A customer goes to a company's home page, which introduces a main navigation bar across the top of the screen. This navigation bar categorizes the site by product groups. The home page also provides a list of links to all parts of the site (under the navigation bar).

The customer clicks on one of the product categories in the main navigation bar. This takes them to a page that lists all the links available within that "section of the site." However, the customer later discovers that these are, in fact, "pseudo" sections and not actually core to the navigation of the site, because when they click on one of the links from the home page they get a different Web site with a different navigation bar. And there are no links between the two navigation systems. The customer sits for a few moments going forward and back trying to work out the relationship between the home page and the next level of pages, trying to decide which system they want to use (i.e., they are about to make a trade off).

It seems the top-level system (the main navigation bar on the Web site and the pages on each product category) has just been wallpapered over the underlying navigational system (the list of links on the home page and the Web sites they correspond to). This has introduced conflicting navigation systems and confused the customer, who has been forced to either lose the perspective of one system in favor of the other, or learn both.

The sequence the customer goes through is shown in Figure 2-5.

Absence of a navigational system

A customer goes to a company's Web site. The home page is roughly in two halves. The top half includes three images that the customer can click on, "Articles," "Introduction to the Firm," and "Special Feature." The bottom half looks more like a list of links to different sections of the Web site: "Contacts," "Services," "Search," "Clients," etc.

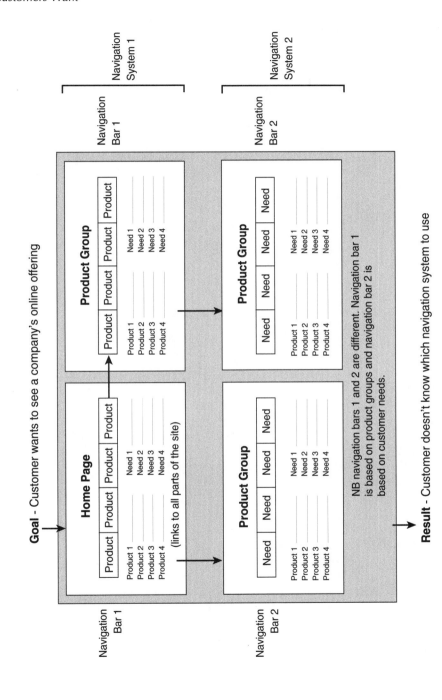

Figure 2-5   Conflcting navigation systems.

The customer discovers that clicking on the top half and the bottom half generates a stand-alone section relative to the area selected. To get to a new section of the Web site the customer has to go back to the home page and make a selection from there.

This is extremely time-consuming, and cumbersome, and the customer asks themselves "Why couldn't they just put links to all the sections on all the pages to save me going backward and forward all the time?" Good question.

Too many Homes

A customer goes to the Web site of an international company to find out about the services offered by some of its local offices. The home page downloads and it relates to the international company. From here the customer selects the first local office they are interested in.

Selecting the local office brings up a local office home page with its own "home" icon. There's also a link to the international home page at the top of the left-hand frame set.

The customer looks around for a while and then decides to go back to the international home page they received on entering the site, so they can select another local office. The customer absent mindedly clicks on "Home," forgetting that this relates to the local site and not the International site. Remembering that the international site is linked to at the top of the frame set, the customer clicks on that to get the international home page. Phew.

From here, the customer selects the next local office and they receive yet another home page. This time the customer discovers that the "home" icon does actually take you back to the international home page and not the local office home page. The customer slips up a couple of times while looking around this local site and hits "Home" to go back to the local office home page, only to end up at the international home page.

The customer decides, rightly or wrongly, that this company has no international coordination of local Web sites.

The sequence the customer goes through is shown in Figure 2-6.

12. "DON'T LOCK ME OUT"

Some Web sites offer different access to different users. In other words, some customers can get at some information while others can't. The users who can get at this privileged information will have to identify, or authenticate, themselves to gain access.

Customers don't always react positively to this, wondering what lies behind those magic doors and why they can't get at it too. This negative reaction is greatest when the Web site doesn't explain what the different privileges are or doesn't give customers equal access to the parts that should be available to everyone.

Goal - Customer wants to peruse services offered locally

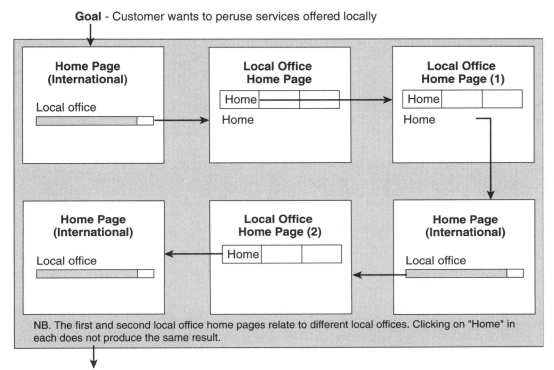

NB. The first and second local office home pages relate to different local offices. Clicking on "Home" in each does not produce the same result.

Result - Customer decides there is no international coordination of local Web sites

Figure 2-6 Too many homes.

Blunders

Badly placed and poorly explained authentication

A customer of a consultancy company goes to its Web site to find out what research it has done lately. The home page does not offer any obvious links to research, but there is a navigation bar that offers "Client" as an option. The customer clicks on "Client," given that they are a client, to receive a screen asking for a login id and password. Well, the customer doesn't have a login id or password. There is no explanation as to who has access here or how they go about getting it. The customer then notices a search option in the navigation bar.

Selecting search brings up the same screen as before, just a request for a login id and password. The customer thinks, "Hang on a minute, why can't I search the site to find out about your research, why are you locking me out?" The customer surmises that the search probably relates only to the "locked" information and not to the site in general.

The customer decides to try another route. They go back to the home page and select "Products and Services." This brings up information including mention of an article on one of the consultancy company's recent research studies. The customer thinks, "Aha, I can find out what this research is here." They select the link to the article and get the same screen again, just a request for a login id and password. The customer thinks, "I just want to read the damn article!"

By now the customer has decided that they're not going to get the information they want. They grab the phone and call their consultant demanding to know why they aren't allowed to see the consulting company's research. It turns out that all the customer had to do was register, but didn't know that. It's some time before the customer goes back to attempt to find, or complete, the registration process.

The sequence the customer goes through is shown in Figure 2-7.

13. "DON'T LIMIT MY CHOICES"

Poor navigation will, of course, restrict the choices customers have because they won't be able to make the appropriate selections to get to where they need to go.

The broader issue of navigation aside, we will look at some specific instances where customers are directly offered choices and where those tend to be problematic.

Classifying customers

Different customers have different needs, and many Web sites classify customers to help direct them to different information. This might work if you know who these different customers are along with their needs. Too often, customer classifications are made from a company's perspective and are not meaningful to customers.

Beware of putting your customers in boxes, unless you really know they'd put themselves in a box, without a moment's hesitation. Your marketing segmentation approach may make sense to you and mean absolutely nothing to your customers.

Incorrect classification will anger your customers because it gets in the way of them doing what they want to do on your Web site.

Drop-down lists

Drop-down lists can be double-edged swords. They offer finite parameters to customer selections, and that can be very helpful and useful to customers. However, these lists often fall short because they just don't include the options customers are looking for, or they don't allow customers to send the right messages about who they are, their problems, their needs, or what they need to do.

Lists that require mutually exclusive selections stump customers. What do customers do when more than one, or maybe even all, of the possible selections apply

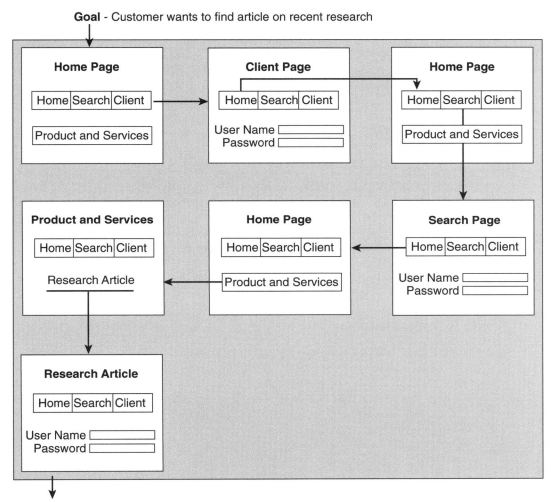

Goal - Customer wants to find article on recent research

Result - Customer research company to find out why they don't have access to research articles

Figure 2-7 Badly placed and proorly explained authentication.

to them? They are forced to limit their response to one selection, and it just isn't enough. I've observed customers who sit and look at lists like this, scratch their heads and say, "What do I do now?" Some customers will make a single selection and make do while others will just decide not to interact on the basis of limited choices. If customers bail out, it can have significant consequences, especially if they're in the middle of buying your product.

Search

"Search" is one of the areas most likely to frustrate customers. This is probably because it is potentially one of the most useful tools customers have to get where they want to go. Get it wrong, and it's a double whammy.

Search functions can limit customers' choices when the functions present search criteria unrelated to what the customer is looking for, and by "anchoring" searches to criteria other than those the customer is interested in at a particular time (anchors are discussed further in Chapter 7).

Customer service

Customers also get very frustrated when they are presented with limited online services. They get annoyed when they want to make a particular transaction, and can't, or are forced to limit their interaction.

This problem is particularly prevalent when customers are completing forms to receive certain services. Some forms ask the customer to check certain boxes and obviously limit the nature of the service available.

Blunders

Insufficient choices

Consider a customer who is thinking about getting a mobile phone. They go to a Web site and select the section on mobile phones. The site offers a link that provides "guidance" to customers wanting to evaluate mobility products. Clicking on this link brings up a series of drop-down lists. The customer is able to select one of the scenarios in each list to generate advice in relation to each selection. A drop-down list presents the following options:

I would use a mobile phone:

- To have one just in case, but not make many calls
- But don't want monthly contracts, monthly bills, or fees

The customer thinks to themselves, "Hang on. I'll probably make lots of calls and I don't mind having monthly contracts. What do I select, since neither of these apply?"

The customer proceeds down the other lists and finds that none of them apply. The customer has to go straight to the product list so they can work out what they need for themselves.

Restrictive search criteria

A professional goes to a Web site that offers job-finding services. The professional wants to see the types of roles on offer, to see whether there is a fit with their skills and experience.

The professional clicks on "Search Available Jobs" to receive a search function. However, the search function they are presented with only allows them to search against location. Actually, location is the least relevant criteria for this professional because they are happy to be located anywhere, provided they're in a good job.

To avoid wading through jobs classified by location, the professional goes onto another company's Web site. This one allows them to search against lots of different criteria: type of role, salary range, skills, etc. However, every time the search engine produces results, they are all "pinned" to, or "anchored" on, location. To view jobs by role, the professional has to also click through location (and sometimes there are up to three or four levels of locations to click through). Well, this isn't perfect but it's better than the last site. Depending on how good the roles look, the professional might wade through locations as well, or, then again, they might not...

Limited customer service

Continuing the above scenario, the professional finds a link on the Web site inviting them to "Provide Feedback on the Site". They decide they'll do just that and click on this link to receive a form they can complete and send. However, this form only allows them to check boxes in relation to "bugs encountered" on the Web site. Can frustrations with a search engine be classified as a bug? Probably not. The form doesn't allow them to enter any comments either, and the professional is forced to give up.

14. "GIVE ME DIGESTABLE CHUNKS"

Many customers seem to hate scrolling, and scrolling, and scrolling, to get at a company's information. Customers get angry, in fact, when they feel like they're drowning in your information. They expect to receive information in chunks they can digest, and quite often, they'll even suggest what those chunks might be. For example, in the case of product pages, customers prefer to see links to product information within the page so they can go straight to the part of the page they are most interested in without having to scroll through all of the other information available.

15. "CALL A SPADE A SPADE"

Customers often feel that a site overpromises and underdelivers. In some ways this is almost unavoidable given that we can't always do everything customers want online. However, we would manage customer expectations, and stave off disappointment, much better if we called a spade "a spade"; i.e., called things exactly what they are.

"Too clever" is what many customers would call fancy, and often misleading, labeling on a Web site. "Just tell me what it is," they would say, "straight up."

In addition, there are a lot of labels that have taken on a certain meaning in the Web world. Many sites use these terms and deliver something that is a far cry from what has come to be expected, and incur customer criticism as a result. Some examples of customer criticism follow:

- Home—"Don't call it home unless it is."
- Site map—"Is it a map or just a basic list of links that doesn't help direct me"
- Search—"Is it actually a way of searching relevant information or just a rudimentary index."
- Contact—"So, give me the contacts then!"
- Buy now—"This doesn't mean register interest, or see if you qualify, or anything else, it means buy now!"
- Help—"Don't give me vague information on irrelevant stuff; I need to know how to solve my problem."
- Feedback—"I don't think you actually want it."
- Special deals—"Doesn't look like much of a deal for a customer who's especially come to your Web site to find it."

16. "TELL ME THE INFO YOU NEED"

Customers get very frustrated when they're transacting with you and you don't tell them the information you need them to provide, or the format that you need it provided in. They can waste a lot of time going backward and forward, "correcting things," to get a transaction accepted.

Blunders

Success through trial and error only

A customer decides to purchase a weekend holiday package at a hotel they've been wanting to stay at for ages. They call up the package information and click on "Buy Now." They receive a form which they can complete and send. The form asks for lots of different information, but some of it doesn't seem to apply particularly well to them, so they leave those particular fields blank. They complete the form and click "send."

An error message comes back saying, "You have not filled in all of the necessary fields, try again." "Which fields?" the customer asks themselves. They engage in a process of trial and error to find out which fields have to be filled in.

The customer then gets to the point where all the fields are filled in and the form is still generating an error message. This time the error reads, "You have not entered information correctly, please try again." "Which information, and what format should it be in?" the customer now asks themselves. They go back and look at the fields most likely to be required in a different format, such as date and phone number. Trial and error reveals that the phone number shouldn't have had any spaces in it, and the form is finally accepted. Success at last!

The customer decides that, next time, it's probably easier just to call the toll-free number and organize it over the phone.

17. "DON'T IGNORE IMPORTANT RELATIONSHIPS"

Web sites are only one part of customers' relationships with a business. Some customers have very important personal relationships with the people inside. Customers often expect these relationships to carry over to the Web, particularly in a business-to-business environment, where customers will expect to have access to someone like their account manager.

Web sites that ignore important relationships to provide a less adequate level of service will frustrate customers. Of course, sometimes anonymity is a good thing, but as discussed before, if it means losing out on the benefits of good service, customers will identify themselves and their personal relationships.

CUSTOMERS AND ORGANIZATIONS

Now, having thought about what customers want to do on the Web, and the directives they might give us in providing what they want, we are faced with a very fundamental issue—customers and businesses don't necessarily want the same things. Businesses often want to create or change customer behavior. Businesses want to influence the services customers use in different situations and the way they use them. This may not always line up with what the customer is trying to do. While businesses can use Web sites as a means to influence e-customers, that influence should be in harmony with what e-customers are trying to do. When businesses try to explicitly mould a customer's Web site experience, contrary to a customer's natural expectations, it is seen as obtrusive and the customer becomes frustrated.

Conflict between business and e-customer goals becomes very apparent in cases where bricks-and-mortar companies begin to migrate some of their services online. Sometimes bricks-and-mortar companies will introduce new service processes and relationships on their Web site, and they can be contrary to what the customer normally experiences offline, and potentially expects online. This won't be a problem for bricks-and-mortar companies or their customers, as long as customers needs are recognized and the company works with customers to change service processes over time in a way that makes sense. If bricks-and-mortar companies are seen to immediately offer a lesser quality of service (through the absence of physical contacts and services, for example), then there will be a direct conflict between what companies and customers are trying to achieve.

It is unlikely that we will be able to provide all of the content and functionality required to service every need customers have. Some of those needs just can't be met (well, not now anyway), and sometimes the business chooses not to meet them for their own reasons. For starters, it may not be technologically possible to provide customers with the experience they want.

Creating customer-effective Web sites can be a win-win proposition—it's just a balancing act. A company has to deliberately consider the customer needs they cannot meet and work out how that is going to be handled.

A business that does not consider the balancing of organizational and customer needs may be seen to be ignoring its customers and offering inferior customer service. And a company's apparent silence on the matter will make it "guilty as charged."

In addition, if a business gets its first attempt at electronic service so wrong that customers have a bad experience, it may not be given a second chance to get it right.

Ways that businesses can establish their requirements with customers' needs in mind, understand the balancing act required, and manage and implement Web sites that effectively meet customer needs are explored further in Chapters 4 and 5.

Meanwhile, we will look at customer testing and some ways to go about getting quality information from our customers.

CHAPTER 3

CUSTOMER-EFFECTIVE TESTING

Testing is the single-most important thing you will do.
Unfortunately, it could also be the most ignored.

WHY BOTHER TESTING?

When we create customer-effective Web sites, we are concerned with developing Web sites that make it easy for customers to do what they need to. What customers want to do is the context for development and must also be the context for testing.

To find out what customers want to do, and how they actually need to go about doing it, we must find out about customer behavior. We need to understand the big picture as well as the specifics of what customers will want to do on a Web site. And that requires some smart planning and execution across the business and the Web site development company.

Customer needs drive the development process and are our touchstone for success throughout that process. We need to talk to customers, up front, before development and pull them back in at critical points in the development process prior to launching a Web site to the public. The testing gets more and more specific as we go. A lot of companies run into problems when they try to test generalities when they need specifics, and vice versa. General customer feedback is appropriate early in the development process, but later on when development has progressed to specific designs and functionality, specific customer feedback will be required. The level of the testing, its timing, and the techniques used all affect our ability to get the right information when we need it.

If we don't know what we need to know about customers, we will not develop customer-effective Web sites. We may develop good Web sites, but if customers can't, or don't, adopt them into their service relationships, then we've failed.

So we test our ideas with customers in an attempt to offer them the best e-services we can. And this implies an iterative process where we have to potentially redevelop concepts or parts of a Web site and then retest them.

Iterative processes often send businesses and Web site developers into a spin. It's not surprising when we are all working with tight deadlines. We simply don't have the time to redo, redo, redo. Do we?

As with all things, it's a matter of striking a balance. It is possible to work against tight deadlines and still benefit from customer testing. That said, if you have no intention of revising what you're doing as a result of customer feedback, it's probably not worth asking customers what they think in the first place.

Of course, we don't have to deliver a perfect e-solution from day one. Customers will learn with us and help us along the way, as long as we give them something useful in the first iteration of our Web site. And therein lies the problem. Too many companies continually save revisions to "the next release" and launch a Web site that offers little or no value to their customers. Customers don't think in releases; they think about what they need to know and do, now, not later. If you provide customers with useful content and functionality in the first iteration of your Web site, and then continue to deliver additional useful content and functionality in the first iteration of your Web site and then continue to deliver additional useful content and functionality when it is needed by e-customers, you can keep them on board.

A business needs to take e-customers' priorities into account when deciding what content and functionality will be released and when. If e-customers are all asking for a specific service function, such as view and pay their bill online, because it is the most important thing they want to be able to do on a business' Web site, then this should be the first thing to be developed by the business.

Sometimes e-customers want things businesses can't deliver straight away, and this needs to be understood and managed by the business. Sometimes e-customers want things that can be delivered straight away, but they would have been overlooked had e-customers not been consulted. Testing, therefore, is necessary to really understand e-customer priorities and how businesses can create for e-customers from day one.

If we set the right direction at the start, then we avoid having to reinvent during the development process. Reinvention, late in the development process, is a waste of everybody's time and resources. More often than not, companies will roll out an inadequate Web site, rather than redo what has already required a lot of time and money. And that's a risky move, if you know you're not on the right track with your customers. We may lose our customers by providing our competitors with the opportunity to offer them something better.

Customer testing should lead to invention, not reinvention. It's just a matter of good management and timing.

And, of course, customer testing can also be a way of fixing obvious problems we miss. Many of the mistakes we make relate to the way information and functionality is presented on Web sites and can be easily fixed. Being aware of the 17 customer directives in Chapter 2 will give businesses and Web site developers many potential mistakes to avoid.

PRACTICAL EXAMPLES

In his Web site on usability, useit.com, (see Netography) Jakob Nielsen gives us an example of how we can improve things simply be asking customers for feedback. He relates an "icon intuitiveness" test that was conducted as part of developing an intranet for Sun Microsystem's employees. Figure 3-1 lists the icons that were tested, and the ways in which they were interpreted.

Intended Meaning: Benefits
Different Test Users' Interpretations: Health field, money, health care is expensive, Clinton's health plan, hospital, benefits

Intended Meaning: What's new (bulletin board)
Different Test Users' Interpretations: Bulletin board, laundry

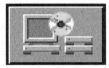

Intended Meaning: Product catalog
Different Test Users' Interpretations: System oriented, disk, computer, CD-ROM

Intended Meaning: Specialized tools (toolbox)
Different Test Users' Interpretations: Briefcase, personal info, toolbox

Intended Meaning: Public relations (TV with commercial
Different Test Users' Interpretations: TV, video

Intended Meaning: World Wide Web
Different Test Users' Interpretations: Networking on a world scale, map, location, dimensions of the planet, networking around the world, geography, global

Figure 3-1 Icons tested for intuitiveness.

The icons for the toolbox and the World Wide Web were the most problematic. The toolbox was seen as a briefcase and the WWW icon was interpreted too closely to the icon representing the geography of the company. All of the other icons did well enough, when taken on balance and in context.

In total, twenty versions of the toolbox icon were designed; seven tool metaphor icons, nine shopping metaphor icons (including a shopping cart and a grocery shelf), and four chest icons. The original and four revisions were tested with users as seen in Figure 3-2.

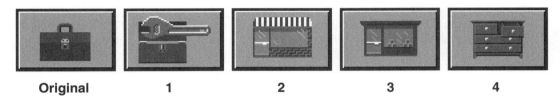

Original   **1**   **2**   **3**   **4**

Figure 3-2 Revisions made to Sun's toolbox icon.

The first revision was too strong and users thought that everything that could be deemed a tool on the site should be found in this section. Unfortunately, some of the site "tools" belonged in other sections. In order to use a weaker metaphor for special-purpose applications, a storefront icon was adopted in the second revision.

However, the second revision was too easily interpreted by this audience as a circuit board. From there, several alternative storefront and shopping icons, such as revision 3, were used. These interfered with the "product catalog" icon. The idea of an application store was then dropped.

The last icon, the application chest, was finally settled on.

Another practical example of the difference testing can make is given by Jeffrey Veen of Wired Digital in his article on Webmonkey; "Test your designs on people". He says:

> When our designers redesigned the Wired News Web site, they included a navigation panel down the left side of the screen. It pointed to the various sections behind the frontdoor: an area to check stock prices, the week's top 10 stories, and a collection of articles from trade magazines. However, when our testing subjects saw the navigation bar and its respective links—Stocks, Week's Top 10, From the Trades—they instinctively grouped the sections together. When asked what they thought the links pointed to, users all agreed the "Week's Top 10" was about the best-performing, publicly traded companies, and "From the Trades" must be about large buys and sells from the exchange floor. They mentally grouped everything around stocks.

A simple test—a half-dozen subjects using the Web site for a half-hour each—uncovered a potentially confusing design. Armed with this data, our designers modified the link placement and made the site less obtrusive and easier to use.

The modified design can be seen in Figure 3-3.

Figure 3-3 Wired screen resulting from customer feedback.

TYPES OF TESTING

To establish your own testing strategy, you need an overall view of all the testing that may be required as part of a major development project. Then you can decide what testing approaches and techniques are most relevant to you.

Here I will provide an overview of all the types of testing required, across a number of disciplines. We will touch on testing that must be completed externally with customers as well as internally by businesses and Web site development companies. Our focus in this chapter is customer testing; however, we will also touch on internal testing critical to the delivery of a customer-effective Web site to provide a complete overview of all the testing you are likely to encounter.

CUSTOMER TESTING

This section examines the different types of testing that directly involve external customers, including:

1. Exploratory research
2. Concept testing (of e-service and Web site concepts)
3. Prototyping (of Web site components and slices of system functionality)
4. Usability testing
5. Beta testing

1. EXPLORATORY RESEARCH

Exploratory research is carried out by businesses to find out their competitive position in the market and the general service needs of their customers. This knowledge is needed to understand how e-services fit within a customer's overall service experience, and needs, and how the Web might be used to meet those needs and create competitive advantage.

This type of research is the most general "testing" required. It sets the scene. It may involve pulling together general research already done by the business and user surveys done by research companies. A word of caution, however. Businesses may find that current research does not adequately factor in the Web as a service medium, and it may be difficult to create linkages between their own customer data and that given by general user surveys. Also bear in mind that current user surveys tend to provide quantitative, rather than qualitative, data on Web usage. Quantitative data may not be enough to give businesses an idea of their customers' attitudes and behaviors.

If businesses end up having to do exploratory research from scratch, they should remember it is just that—exploratory. Businesses want to get a broad view of the opportunities open to them. They want to know what makes their customers tick in e-space and what customers want them to provide there. Businesses should be gathering information on customers' propensities to use certain e-services alongside other service channels and their basic requirements in doing so.

Businesses and their research companies should not be afraid to test the boundaries of customer usage and adoption to find out how customers may, or may not, respond to new e-service and Web site concepts. But also remember that it can be difficult for customers to envision themselves using new technology and techniques, particularly where they would need to modify or develop new ways of doing things, and you may not be able to rely on their view of their intended behavior. However, customers will be able to tell you about the things they want to do as customers, and from there it's up to you to apply technology for their benefit.

Also, businesses should avoid engaging research companies that come back and tell them things people hate about the Web in general because, given the amount of writing and discussion that has been had about the weaknesses of the Web and the way people feel about them, this is stating the obvious. Businesses should engage research companies that can look at customers' unique reactions toward a business' particular e-service offering. Understanding what people hate, and like, about the Web is only a background to the testing businesses and research companies need to do.

Remember that the information businesses gather will provide a useful steer for both them and the development company throughout the life of the project and beyond.

2. CONCEPT TESTING

Concept testing can occur at different times within the life of a project. It is required early on to help a business define its e-service offering and later on when design concepts have been developed by the Web site designer.

E-service concept testing

A business will have an idea (possibly based on exploratory research) of what customers want and it will consider its business goals and capabilities alongside customers' to develop a concept for its e-service offering. This concept will support the business' e-service strategy. At this stage, the business can go to customers to test the viability, and appeal, of its proposed e-service offering.

It's a matter of bouncing ideas off customers to see if you're heading in the right direction with your e-service offering. At this stage you're not concerned with putting visual concepts in front of customers; it's too early for that. You are concerned with creating "doing scenarios" that customers can relate to—they put themselves in the position of doing certain things and tell you what they think about being able to do it and how much they like doing it that way. And they'll tell you what you're missing.

Concept testing also gives you the opportunity to prioritize what you will deliver to customers. Of all the things the customer wants to be able to do on the Web site, what is most important? Understanding this will help you decide where to direct your energies and what to develop first.

Web site concept testing

When coming up with a proposed solution, the Web site designer will start with a concept for your Web site. For example, the Web site might be based on a particular "metaphor" that helps customers relate their knowledge of another object or experience to what they can, and need to, do on your Web site. The shopping cart metaphor is an example of a common metaphor for a Web site where customers go about shopping online.

Metaphors can be double-edged swords, and it is a good idea to test them on customers before basing a whole system around them. The risks, and opportunities they present are discussed further in Chapter 6. You will quickly find out whether or not a metaphor conjures up the right associations with customers.

There are other fundamental ideas that your Web site will be based on: the system by which customers get around (the navigation system) and the navigation devices (such as icons) used to help them on their way, the type of content provided, and the tools provided to support particular e-customer activities. These may be tested at a high level, but chances are they will also be subject to a prototyping process where customers get to interact with physical examples of different ideas.

3. PROTOTYPING

Let me preface this section by saying that *prototyping* is one of the most confusing terms commonly used; everyone seems to have a slightly different interpretation of what it means.

From what I have observed and read, there seem to be two basic approaches:

1. *Prototyping components.* Concepts such as navigation, content, and tools are prototyped as stand-alone components or objects.
2. *Prototyping slices of the "system."* This is where a formative part of the Web site is tested along a particular thread. Concepts such as navigation, content, and utility will form part of that thread.

Both of these approaches can be employed at a high level when development is only rudimentary or later when development is more advanced.

Prototyping components

This approach may be useful to the Web site designer as they seek to "sanity check" their ideas early on in development. Navigation is something that can be presented in a fairly abstract way and tested as a "stand-alone" system, for example. (Of course, navigation is not truly stand-alone and should also be tested in the context of the entire Web site system. However, a stand-alone test will provide feedback on whether the navigation system makes sense to customers and fits with the mental model they use when doing things.)

As an example, imagine you are testing the highest level of the basic navigation system used on the Amazon.com, reputedly one of the Web's most successful online stores. We want to present the "essence" of Amazon's navigation system, or its most simple way of working, to see if it makes sense to customers and can be used by them.

The navigation system would be abstracted and would be presented without other Web site components such as graphics or content. Using either simple interactive screens, or paper-based mock-ups, the test facilitator would walk through the flow of the navigation system with customers.

In testing the highest level of Amazon's navigation system, the customer would move between the home page and each of the next-level pages. Of course, your test could be broader than this and include more layers and dimensions of the navigation system.

Figure 3-4 shows the representation of the Amazon home page followed by the "Books" page at the next level in the navigation system (received as a result of clicking on "Books" on the top navigation bar on the home page).

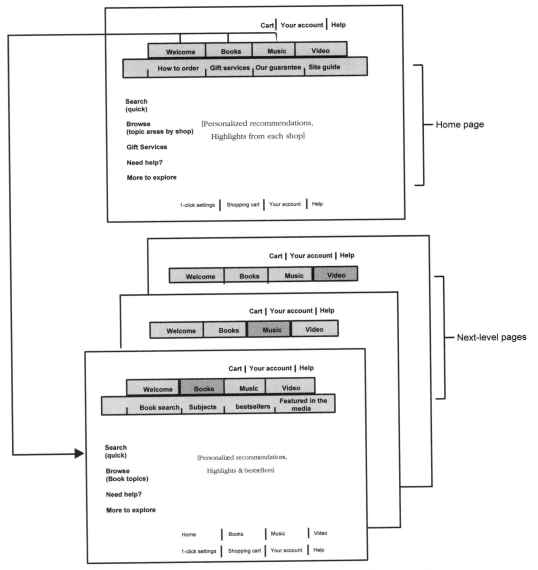

Figure 3-4 Testing the highest level of Amazon's basic navigation system.

The test facilitator would be interested in finding out things like:

- How well the navigation system reflects what the customer expects to find on the Amazon site, and why.
- What customers expect to receive as a result of each interaction with the navigation system, and how this compares with what they do receive and their relative level of satisfaction.
- How well customers are oriented as they move around the navigation system: i.e., if they are aware of where they are, where they've been, and where they're going next.
- How comfortable customers are in using the navigation system: i.e., if they avoid making common errors or misjudgments and if they use the system intuitively without explanation.

Prototyping slices of the system

This approach may be useful to businesses that need to ensure the Web site system will deliver the required experience to their customers. By testing customers' reactions to a critical slice of the system, they get an idea of customers' reactions to the whole system. In my experience, this approach works best when slices are interactive because customers can experience something naturally (as they would in real life), making their feedback that much more meaningful.

As an example, imagine you are testing the basic search functionality on the Amazon site. Given that customers go to Amazon to browse for, and purchase, books, CDs etc., the search function is critical to customers who may know exactly, or roughly, what they are looking for.

This critical "slice" could include the search entry screens, customer entry of search criteria, and the search results generated from those criteria. You would be interested in finding out things like:

- How customers use the search functionality, how they expect it to behave, and their relative level of satisfaction.
- How well the search function allows customers to search against their search criteria (such as keywords they naturally expect to produce search results).
- The general usefulness of search results and how well they meet customer expectations.

You could give Amazon customers a list of items for which they can search without giving away the "rules" that you want them to intuitively work out for themselves. In addition, providing a list of search items will allow you to develop the test slice against a manageable dataset. Too often "Search" does not get tested until development is complete (if at all) because it is seen to be dependent on a complete database.

Figure 3-5 shows how Amazon's search function, as a critical slice of the Web site system, might be represented.

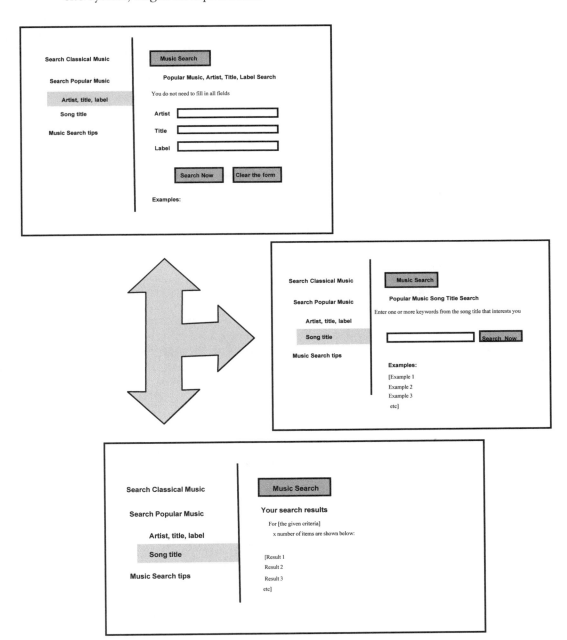

Figure 3-5 Testing Amazon's basic search system.

Fundamentals

Regardless of your approach to prototyping, the underlying premise is customer participation. This is the point in the project where you can put something reasonably tangible in front of customers and find out how well it fits with what they need to do as customers. To do this, we need to show enough of the system for customers to relate it to their intended actions. And this can be tricky in the early stages of development. However, some people are happy to prototype earlier on and have developed techniques that work in that context. Some of these techniques, such as paper-based prototyping and "walkthroughs," are covered later under "Testing Techniques."

Prototyping is also fundamentally different from usability testing. However, the two often get confused or combined. Given the rapid development of many Web sites, prototyping and usability testing often get rolled into one. Prototyping is about the fit with customer intentions and actions; usability is about whether the Web site is usable. While some usability testing includes exploration into customer behavior and expectations, it is important to realize, however, that usability doesn't necessarily equate to prototyping.

Whatever you want to call your testing, make sure you do test your Web site's customer behavior and its usability.

4. USABILITY TESTING

Having just discussed the difference between prototyping and usability testing, we will define usability testing as the task of measuring users' performance against set tasks to ensure that the tasks can be done with ease and efficiency.

Usability can come late in the development project when fine-tuning of the visual interface is required and earlier in the development process as part of the Web site designer's "sanity checking".

When testing usability late in development, the structure and organization of the Web site should be determined already. Such usability testing should not have to deal with last-minute structural problems. At this late stage in development you can't fix structural problems with band-aids, and designers should not be faced with this task. Structure can be fixed only with restructure. For this reason, concept testing or prototyping should ideally occur before final usability testing.

Ten usability "heuristics"

The previous icon intuitiveness test is an example of usability testing. In his Web site useit.com (see Netography) Jakob Nielsen gives ten heuristics that can be used as benchmarks in usability testing. These heuristics have become pretty well-known, so, rather than just regurgitate them, I have put my spin on them, as follows:

1. Visibly provide feedback on what the system is doing when it's doing it, or shortly thereafter.

2. The system should adopt real-world language and concepts to be natural and logical to the customer.

3. Give users the freedom to do and undo tasks.

4. The system should consistently follow its own standards.

5. Make the system error-proof.

6. Lead the customer with dialogue and don't expect customers to retain information on behalf of the system.

7. Cater for the experienced and novice user by providing shortcuts for frequently performed actions.

8. Provide only the information required by the user; "fluff" just gets in the way.

9. Help users recognize, diagnose, and recover from, errors.

10. Provide customer-centric help online.

Nielsen based these heuristics on a large volume of usability problems. In heuristic evaluation, you would rate the Web site's success against each of the above heuristics.

5. Beta Testing

While testing occurs during development, beta testing is required in the live environment once development is complete and before the Web site goes public. This is the only time customers have to experience the fully functional Web site before its launch and a business' last chance to ensure that, overall, customers have a rewarding and quality experience.

Beta testing is the final, customer-driven, quality assurance for the Web site. Inevitably, this testing will retest the concept, interactive site components and usability. It also tests the interface with a business' internal systems (if any) and site performance in a live environment. It is important to keep testing focused on specifics so that changes can be meaningfully defined in terms of system modifications and process improvements. Additionally, customer reactions will help businesses sanity check their ideas on positioning and promoting their Web sites.

By the time businesses do beta testing they should know they've got things roughly right. After all, they don't want to redo things at the last minute. Chances are businesses will also need to prioritize changes and decide what must be changed before the site goes public, and what can occur later as part of ongoing development modifications and improvements.

INTERNAL TESTING

Businesses develop Web sites to meet business and customer objectives. Testing should ensure that these objectives can be met (and the reconciliation of the business' and customers' needs should have been taken into account in concept definition and testing). Internal testing is the process by which a business can judge development against business objectives. This can run parallel to customer testing, or a company may prefer to fully test internally before testing with customers (however, this can lead to protracted testing timeframes).

In addition, businesses and Web site developers should always avoid putting a substandard product in front of customers; this aggravates them and gets in the way of meaningful testing. Irrespective of whether or not internal testing is carried out before external customer testing, some sort of quality testing is always required before Web sites, and their components, are seen by customers.

We will examine different types of testing that businesses will complete internally before going public with any online offering (either a completely new Web site or any changes to an existing Web site):

1. Acceptance testing
2. Quality testing
    1. Interactivity testing
    2. Integration testing
    3. Compatibility testing
    4. Security auditing
    5. Performance testing

ACCEPTANCE TESTING

There must be formal process whereby the business signs off the Web site before it is accessible to the public. This sign off is formal acceptance of the product delivered by the Web site developers. Of course, the business sign off will be hugely influenced by feedback from customers, but there also needs to be an internal process of testing and feedback.

To keep this process manageable, it is best to define acceptance testing in terms of meeting agreed Web site objectives. Criteria that realize these objectives need to be clearly established and benchmarked against by business stakeholders who are able to focus on evaluation against their area of responsibility and not become would-be Web designers. Of course, this is easier said than done. Guidelines and scripting can help focus internal testers, and this technique is covered later under "Testing techniques."

QUALITY TESTING

At the same time, business sign off will be contingent on internal quality testing. The business must be sure that the Web site system functions the way it should, as a customer interface and in relation to internal systems and processes. To achieve this surety, the system must be subjected to:

1. Interactivity testing

2. Integration testing

3. Compatibility testing

4. Security auditing

5. Performance testing

1. Interactivity testing

Interactivity is the means by which customers get around a Web site and receive the information they are looking for. To ensure a quality customer experience, all interactive objects, such as external and internal links and navigation devices must, on interaction, return the expected response. The system should also return expected responses, such as appropriate error messages, when the customer does the "wrong" thing.

Also, some interactivity, such as calculators or decision support tools, provide customers with intelligent responses. It is a good idea to identify these intelligent components and test them as stand-alone pieces of functionality. The tester should be provided with the rules regarding inputs and associated outcomes. Testers must ensure that every input and action generates the right output. This can become difficult if the logic behind the functionality has not been clearly defined, and this situation should be avoided. Any process of input-process-output must be defined according to some rules, and these can be captured in test scripts.

Too often, businesses try to define rules at the same time as testing functionality. This usually results in confusion over what is being tested and results in a poor-quality product. If a business does not know outcomes relative to customer inputs, how are customers supposed to make any sense of the results they receive? If interaction promises an intelligent response, customers will expect it. It is better not to promise this type of intelligent interactivity than to provide something that is only half thought through.

2. Integration testing

Some Web sites interface with a business's internal systems and processes. An online order process, for example, interfaces with internal systems receiving the order and the systems and processes used to process the order and provide the product.

The interface between a Web site and internal systems must deliver customers with a seamless, end-to-end service experience, whether it be ordering, making an inquiry, requesting information, or activating a service.

The flow of each process should be known and documented, and tests should be carried out to trace customer actions and requests through these processes to their logical conclusion. (The mapping of such processes is discussed in Chapter 5 under "Process Improvement"). If a business already tests parts of these processes, then only those parts affected by the Web site interface may need to be tested.

3. Compatibility testing

Different development languages can be treated in different ways by different browsers. Early on in the development process, the business and the Web site development company should agree on which browsers must support the Web site. Testing should determine that the Web site runs as expected on each appropriate browser, and browser version.

Different operating systems and different machines will also render Web pages differently. Again, the necessary user configuration should have been agreed on early in the development process, and testing should ensure that the Web site runs as expected on each appropriate configuration.

4. Security auditing

Security auditing refers to the testing of the Web site and Web server configuration to eliminate any security or access loopholes.

5. Performance testing

Performance testing involves making the Web site and its server as efficient as possible, in terms of download speed and the efficient running and responsiveness of machines and servers.

TESTING TECHNIQUES

Different techniques can be used when carrying out various forms of testing. I have presented an overview of different techniques you might find useful, including:

1. Interviews
2. Focus groups
3. Demos
4. Questionnaires
5. Online surveys
6. Usability inspection
7. Modeling techniques

You should take care when selecting testing techniques. You need to be sure that a technique will yield results appropriate to the nature and goals of each test you wish to complete. Guidelines on matching different techniques to different stages within the life of your project is covered later in this chapter under "Ten Success Factors." For now we will explore each of the techniques in turn.

1. Interviews

One-on-one interviews are commonly used to solicit customer feedback throughout all stages of development and in relation to prototyping and usability testing in particular. Interviews are useful when you need a reasonable level of detail about a customer's interaction with the Web site. However, they are problematic because they often encourage a higher level of intervention than a customer would ever experience in a real-life environment. Leading a customer too much during the interview process removes the real-life dynamic of customers' intended actions and unpredictable behavior and can create a false test environment yielding misleading results.

Close-range observation is the most useful characteristic of interviewing. This can be useful when evaluating a customer's use of a proposed Web site or an existing Web site you wish to improve or redevelop. However, useful observation requires a skilled observer.

In their book *Contextual Design*, Beyer and Holtzblatt provide some guidance for would-be observers. They talk about various relationship models that interviewers and interviewees fall into and recommend the master-apprentice model as the most effective.

The master-apprentice model forms a basis for the interviewer (the apprentice) to learn about what the interviewee (the master) is doing and trying to do. To avoid gleaning information too abstract to provide the level of detail required for design, the interviewer is required to reflect on and clarify the actions of the interviewee throughout the interview. The interviewer can also find out about the motivators and past experiences behind certain actions, and this creates a richer understanding of the context a system will be used in.

Beyer and Holtzblatt describe four parts of a contextual interview, as follows:

1. *The conventional interview.* The start of the interview is based on the conventions of getting to know the interviewee and establishing rapport.

2. *The transition.* This is where the interviewer sets up the master-apprentice model.

3. *The contextual interview proper.* This is where the interviewee teaches the interviewer about what they are doing.

4. *The wrap-up.* This is where the interviewer reflects their understanding back to the interviewee for clarification.

Beyer and Holtzblatt also offer some good advice to interviewers: "Take the attitude that nothing any person does is done for no reason; if you think it's for no reason, you don't yet understand the point of view from which it makes sense."[1]

---

[1] *Contextual Design: Defining Customer-Centered Systems* by Hugh Beyer and Karen Holtzblatt. Copyright ©1998, Morgan Kaufmann Publishers, Inc.

Customers must perceive an interviewer to be objective and open to their feedback. An interviewer also needs to be knowledgeable and informed enough to observe customer actions and mentally translate these into specific system changes and improvements (on the spot and later on). This isn't an easy balance to strike. For example, a system developer may be too close to the system to be objective and may be seen as an expert by the customer (getting in the way of the master-apprentice model). At the same time, a developer may be in the best position to extract meaningful results from the testing.

When deciding who should interview customers, the merits and characteristics of each would-be interviewer should be taken on balance, having considered the nature and goals of each interview.

2. Focus groups

Focus groups are also commonly used to solicit customer feedback throughout all stages of development. They are used in relation to concept and beta testing, in particular. Focus groups are useful when you need more general information about customers' needs, attitudes, and behaviors. However, they are problematic because they often result in too much abstraction and can be biased by "groupthink," where the views of one or two strong individuals influence a whole group.

If you can counterbalance the cons of groupthink, and exploit the pros of group excitement and idea generation, focus groups give you an efficient and cost-effective way of generating customer feedback. It is just too time-consuming, and costly, to conduct many interviews where a focus group could suffice. (Bear in mind, however, that in specific tests such as usability testing, a large number of interviews are not required to uncover obvious usability problems.)

In my experience, focus groups that comprise an interplay between exercise and discussion provide the most meaningful customer feedback.

Exercise-creation can be difficult early on in the Web site development process because you don't have anything "physical" customers can interact with. You can, however, create good exercises by showing simple visual abstracts and by sharing simple stories of what customers can, or might like to, do. Avoid presenting visuals that customers perceive as designs because then they'll focus on the look and not on the idea. Showing other Web sites and discussing and whiteboarding common customer experiences can also be good bases for exercise and discussion.

In addition, I have found the development of group decision support software to enhance the productivity and effectiveness of focus groups. There are also exciting opportunities for remote, asynchronous participation through the networking of group decision support software. This is discussed in more detail later in this chapter under "Another Contextual Test Methodology?"

3. Demos

Demos can be useful when you need flash-in-the-pan feedback from a group of users. However, demos often get confused with prototyping. Demos do not allow customer participation and are, therefore, not prototyping. You should have modest expectations of the feedback you get from demos. Without being able to interact with the system in real life, customers do not have enough of a feel for how useful the system will be.

Demos may be most useful for gaining high-level acceptance from stakeholders within the business (i.e., as part of internal testing) but are not ideal for soliciting customer feedback.

4. Questionnaires

In general, questionnaires are more useful for generating quantitative, rather than qualitative, information. Sometimes quantitative information is required to complement qualitative testing, particularly during exploratory research when businesses need customer demographics and statistics on general customer usage, or later when the propensity to adopt a particular product needs to de quantified.

Some practitioners use short questionnaires after a tester has had a "real-life" experience of a Web site to gather rankings against certain criteria. This may be a useful approach, but without the ability to also conduct qualitative investigation you are limiting the feedback you receive by using your own criteria.

Additionally, some user survey providers use questionnaires as follow-ups to online surveys.

5. Online surveys

As mentioned previously, under "Concept Testing," the results of numerous online Web user surveys are available, and these should be adopted with caution. Some are useful to provide necessary orientation, background, and direction, but information relative to your own audiences, and service offering, needs to be unique. Some user survey providers also offer customized online testing. They use predefined sample audiences to generate online survey results relative to your particular area of interest.

Online research is not a thoroughly tested methodology; however, there is a reasonable body of work and experience to draw on. GVU (Graphics, Visualization and Usability Center) of the Georgia Institute of Technology has been a pioneer in the area of online research. By the time it conducted its fifth user survey, it had collected responses from 55,000 Web users since January 1994. GVU shares a number of its learnings and experiences on their Web site (see Netography) as follows:

- The greatest challenges to online surveys are, firstly, the constraints introduced by self-selection, which can introduce bias in the sample, and, secondly, limited sampling, which can inhibit the generalization of results.

    1. Self-selection. When people decide to participate in a survey, they select themselves. There is very little researchers can do to persuade people to

participate if they don't want to. This may exclude some types of people from the survey and bias results toward those who do participate.

2. Limited sampling. Sampling is not random, because participants have to see an invitation to participate and respond deliberately. Nonrandom results can't be taken as representative of all Web users. However, GVU has minimized the limitations of their sampling by promoting the survey through diverse media to attract as broad an audience of Web users as possible.

- With each survey, GVU has advanced survey technology in line with new Web capabilities. On its Web site (see Netography), GVU reports its major advances to have been:

  - Adaptive questioning

    As they complete a survey, respondents will dynamically receive an adapted set of questions based on answers they have submitted. This decreases the number and complexity of questions each respondent is asked and removes common errors that result from human encoding of collected data.

    Adaptive questioning also ensures better survey completion. Questions the respondent did not answer the first time around would be returned with the dynamically generated follow-up questions.

    Java has been trialed as a means to facilitate more dynamism. The Java applet allows the connection between the respondent's action (clicking) and the system's action (adding the question) to be more explicit.

    The fact that the Java applet runs within the browser means that new sets of questions can be dynamically generated on the basis of a user's response to a particular question, right then and there within the browser. The Java applet is a program that can run itself within the browser, independent of the Web server. Each mouse click has the potential to trigger new questions which can be asked immediately.

  - Longitudinal tracking

    User-selected IDs were used to relate a respondent's answers across different sections in a survey. After entering an ID, respondents were given a URL (Web address), which contained their ID, to add to their bookmarks (stored Web addresses) and which they could use to participate in future GVU surveys.

    When respondents identified themselves as having previously participated in a survey, either by using the URL they had stored, or by remembering their ID, their identity was loosely checked and a partially completed survey was returned giving respondents the ability to review previously supplied information and modify it if necessary.

As well as being a component of concept testing, online surveys can be a part of ongoing learning and evaluation, after a Web site has been made available to the public. There are ways and means of gaining customer feedback on a Web site, and this may not equate to the formal "online survey." In fact, one of the best, and most underutilized, forms of feedback is e-mail.

Whatever form online testing takes, you must make sure that its placement and nature fit with customer goals and activity; do not get in the way of customer activity with online surveys or perpetual requests for feedback. The most useful point at which to gain feedback is when it is relevant to customer usage. If you want feedback on your order process, for example, offer an optional, short e-mail form at the completion of your order process.

6. Usability Inspection

Jakob Nielsen gives usability inspection as the generic name for a set of methods that are all based on having evaluators inspect a user interface to find usability problems in the design. These usability inspection methods can be used early, and later on, in the development process.

Useit.com (see Netography) gives an overview of usability inspection methods, which are abbreviated as follows:

Involves individual inspection (probably by a usability specialist or expert developer/s):

- **Heuristic evaluation** is the most informal method and involves having usability specialists (not customers and probably developers) judge whether the ten usability "heuristics" (summarized previously) are upheld.
- **Heuristic estimation** is a variant on heuristic evaluation. Inspectors are asked to estimate the relative usability of two (or more) designs, in quantitative terms (typically expected user performance).
- **Cognitive walkthrough** is a more detailed procedure that simulates a user's problem-solving process, step by step, to ensure that users can act correctly to meet their goals.
- **Feature inspection** lists sequences of features used to accomplish typical tasks, checks for long sequences, cumbersome steps, steps that would not be natural for users to try, and steps that require an unrealistic level of knowledge and experience.
- **Standards inspection** is where an interface standard expert inspects the interface for compliance.

Involves group inspection (probably by specialists and users):

- **Pluralistic walkthrough** involves group meetings where users, developers, and human factors people step through a scenario, discussing each dialogue element.

- **Formal usability inspection** combines elements of both heuristic evaluation and a simplified form of cognitive walkthrough in a six-step procedure with strictly defined roles.

- **Consistency inspection** is where designers, who represent multiple other projects, inspect an interface to see whether it does things in the same way as their own designs.

Useit.com (see Netography) also describes the process of allocating severity ratings to usability problems. Severity ratings combine a number of factors in a single rating and are used to allocate resources and provide a rough estimation of additional usability efforts required. The severity of a usability problem is given as a combination of three factors, as follows:

1. The frequency with which the problem occurs. Is it common or rare?
2. The impact of the problem if it occurs. Will it be easy or difficult for users to overcome?
3. The persistence of the problem. Is it a one-time problem that users can overcome once they know about it, or will users repeatedly be bothered by the problem?

Underlying these three factors is the market impact of a problem. Some problems can have a devastating effect on the popularity of a product, even if they are "objectively" quite easy to overcome.

7. Modeling techniques

There are a number of testing techniques that help us model customer behavior and perceptions. These techniques help turn something abstract (customer actions and thoughts) into something conceptually "concrete" (narrative and pictures).

Card sorting

This technique allows you to find out about people's mental models; the way they think about things. By asking them to allocate cards to different ideas, you can better understand the way a customer thinks about a particular concept. This general technique is particularly useful when developing the information architecture of Web sites.

By asking customers to sort cards into piles that make sense to them, we get an idea of how customers clump together the information and activities they would find on a Web site. (Of course, the cards assume what information and utility should be available to the customer, and therefore card sorting is not a way of measuring customers' satisfaction with the information and utility offered.)

In the previous example of how employee feedback enhanced the development of Sun Microsystem's intranet, we considered what Nielsen called an "icon intuitiveness" test. Prior to completing this test, a card-sorting exercise was carried out to help design the information structure of the intranet site. On useit.com (see Netography), Nielsen describes the process as follows:

> ... the SunWeb development group had brainstormed about possible information services to be provided over the system, resulting in a list of 51 types of information. We wrote the name of each of these services on a 3-by-4 inch notecard. In a few cases we also wrote a one-line explanation on the card.

> Before each user entered the lab, the cards were scattered around the desk in random order. The users were asked to sit down at a table and sort the cards into piles according to similarity. Users were encouraged not to produce too small or too large piles but they were not requested to place any specific number of cards in each pile. After a user had sorted the cards into piles of similar cards, the user was asked to group the piles into larger groups that seemed to belong together and to invent a name for each group. These names were written on Post-it notes and placed on the table next to the groups. The users typically completed the entire process in about 30 minutes, though some took about 40 minutes.

The results gave Nielsen's team categories of information to work with. Without trying to be overly scientific about it, "eyeballing" of the data yielded a rich understanding of ways information could be presented to make sense to users.

Intuitiveness tests

Many elements on a Web site require an intuitive response from customers, such as the use of particular metaphors or navigational devices such as icons. By simply showing customers these elements and asking for their intuitive response, we can get an idea of what will, or will not, conjure up the right meaning with customers.

On useit.com (see Netography) Nielsen describes the process used in the previous "icon intuitiveness" example as follows:

> Based on the results from the card-sorting study, we defined fifteen first-level groupings of the information in SunWeb and designed icons for each of them for use on the Home page. The icons would be presented with labels to enhance users' ability to understand. Even so, we wanted to make the icons themselves as understandable as possible, and in order to achieve this goal we conducted an icon intuitiveness study where four users were shown the icons without labels and asked to tell us what they thought each icon was supposed to represent.

Paper-based prototyping

Early prototypes are often paper-based and are used as a guide for the design of actual screens and their interactivity. Of course, interactivity is ideal for getting meaningful feedback on a customer's experience, but in the absence of it, paper-based mockups can provide a useful guide.

This technique is quite popular among designers and developers who want feedback on core elements of system design before committing to bits and bytes. Testers are invited to walk through a paper-based scenario while describing what they would expect to do, and find, along the way. Sometimes rough sketches are used to reinforce that the test is high level in nature, and sometimes more defined screen shots are used.

To continue the Sun Microsystem example, having conducted the "icon intuitiveness" test and refined icon design, Nielsen's team completed a walkthrough of a paper-based prototype. Nielsen describes the process as follows:

> ... we printed out a magnified color screendump of our design for the SunWeb Home page. We wanted to test a paper version instead of a screen version to avoid the problem of users clicking on buttons that, at that time, had no effect. The test users were asked to point to each button and think aloud what information they thought would be accessed through that button. At the end of the page walkthrough, the users were asked to comment on the aesthetics of the icons and to list the icons they liked the most and disliked the most.

Workflow modeling

We can conceptualize models that describe the "work" customers want, and need, to perform on a Web site on the basis of information gleaned from interviews or focus groups. However, these "work models" can be explicitly solicited and tested, not just interpreted. Testing work models helps us ensure that our interface facilitates tasks and activities that are optimally useful to customers. (The definition and use of these work models is a key part of business process improvement, which will be discussed further in Chapter 5.)

We can ask customers to help us create our initial workflow models. Getting customers to simply draw out the flow of certain activities gives us an idea of the order in which customers do things and what they need to complete at each step in the process.

I used this technique with a small group of customers involved in booking travel on behalf of their business organizations. There were many dynamics within their travel booking processes and a lot of organizational procedures involved. By asking these customers to draw their process, and describe it to a group, we were able to generate discussion of the types of booking processes encountered. From this, we then developed a list of mandatories for a potential online travel booking service. These mandatories, and the flow diagrams, could then be translated directly into initial designs.

We can also check workflow models with customers later in development. Previously, under "Prototyping" we discussed using interactive, critical slices of the Web site system as prototypes. Some of these slices can relate to workflow models explicitly, such as online ordering. By asking the customer to perform a particular task, such as placing an order, we can determine how well our workflow model fits by assessing how easily customers complete the online process and how likely they are to use it.

Guidelines and scripting

When testing within a business, we need to provide testers with as much guidance as possible. Internal testers who are not clear on what they are testing, and who have a particular barrow to push, will get in the way of meaningful testing, and, ultimately, the formal sign off of the Web site Guidelines provide parameters for testing and scripts provide the process.

Guidelines need to describe the testers' area of responsibility, the criteria against which they are testing, and the process by which a "fault" or discrepancy should be reported and how it will be resolved.

Scripts take testers through the testing process, step by step. Scripts should describe the action they need to perform and the response they should receive on completion of each action.

For example, a sample script for interactivity testing of a Web site's "check my personal details" is shown in Table 3-1.

Table 3-1 Example of an Internal Test Script

Check My Personal Details				
Test No.	**Test Item**	**Test Action**	**Expected Response**	**Pass/Fail**
4.1	Process	1. Click on "Check My Details" from the Navigation Bar. 2. Change your details and click on the "Send" button.	1. Are you presented with a screen populated with your existing information? 2. Are you presented with a thank you message confirming the changes have been made?	
4.2	Receipt	1. Upon completion of 4.1.2 the email is received.	1.The e-mail is received in the inbox of jodie@xorganization.com.	

The script walks the tester through the testing of the Web site's performance against very clear criteria related to inputs (test actions) and outputs (expected responses).

ANOTHER CONTEXTUAL TEST METHODOLOGY?

The phenomenon of electronic collaboration and the development of groupware have presented some opportunities to conduct richer customer testing; testing that tells us more about the real-life context a customer operates in.

Group decision support software, such as GroupSystems by Ventana, has been developed to support the decision making of groups. By harnessing the ability of electronic systems to gather a large amount of potentially asynchronous data, group software provides an environment in which groups can gather and process information quickly and effectively.

Ventana's GroupSystems has been designed principally to improve the effectiveness of electronic meetings. However, it presents some fundamental attributes that lend themselves to effective, and contextual, customer testing. (You can explore Ventana.com to find out more about the GroupSystems software and how it is being used.)

I have found GroupSystems, and associated facilitation centers, to be useful in conducting high-level, and more detailed, customer testing. The software and setup is excellent for brainstorming and idea generation, and provides an environment where customers can naturally interact with Web sites and provide comments. The testing and setup would be characterized as follows:

- You would have a group of about seven to twelve customers sitting behind desks in a horseshoe, all with their own laptop or PC in front of them.

- Each laptop or PC is running GroupSystems, and customers can contribute comments anonymously using the software.

- The software allows customers to complete "exercises" such as commenting on specific topics, brainstorming, categorizing information, and voting.

- Every interaction the customer has with the software is centrally captured and can be projected on a screen visible to all participants.

- An accredited facilitator controls the central projection of customer responses and the use of the software. This facilitator may also run the testing session, or work alongside another facilitator dedicated to running the testing, rather than the equipment.

- By guiding the group through a series of exercises, in conjunction with traditional focus group techniques, the facilitator is able to get the required feedback on the object of the testing.

- All the customer interactions the system captures are held in a useful report that can be disseminated by e-mail or printed out. No customer comments are lost.

A typical testing room, such as the Santa Rita group room at Ventana headquarters in Tucson, Arizona, may look like this:

Figure 3-6 A typical Ventana-style testing room.

This, and other, testing rooms can be found on the Ventana.com Web site along with other useful resources such as the University of Arizona's learnings after having built six generations of decision support software, conducted over 150 research studies and facilitated over 4,000 e-sessions over twelve years.

While using group decision-support software offers some exciting new opportunities, it is not perfect (as is the case with any testing methodology). I have found there to be a number of pros and cons in this kind of testing, as follows:

Pros

- Rapid, effective and efficient collection and storage of data for analysis.
- The environment allows very quick generation of a lot of ideas and encourages spontaneity in customer feedback.
- Anonymity allows customers to contribute comments without being directly influenced by the group (however, I'm not suggesting that "groupthink" is eliminated, because it isn't).

- Customers can interact with a Web site naturally, without mediation (provided a browser is available on their laptop/PC as well as the GroupSystems software). This better reproduces true customer behavior and removes the disadvantages of leading customers through an interview process.

- Data can be synthesized there and then, allowing analysis and reflection to occur within the testing session. This generates more meaningful results and reduces the overall time spent in analysis and reflection.

- The facilitator can use the electronically generated data to direct other non-electronic activities.

Cons

- The facilitator, and the group, can suffer from information overload and this can get in the way of meaningfully using the data generated.

- The technology can be seen as the end and not the means to an end. The facilitator has to work hard to generate discussion.

- Sometimes anonymity can get in the way of further exploration. This can often be overcome by the facilitator, but the depth will never be the same as that gained in a one-on-one interview.

I have generally got the best from this approach by using it alongside one-on-one interviews and, within the testing session, by alternating electronic exercises with group discussion.

It takes a little practice to facilitate these sessions effectively and, if you wish to explore this approach, you should probably talk to someone from the facilitation center nearest to you about available centers and facilitators. (Contacts can be found on Ventana.com.)

Ventana is also exploring the application of "distributed systems" to group decision making. The prospect of being able to achieve group collaboration electronically, over distributed locations, also offers some potentially exciting opportunities for customer testing across geographically spread (and maybe even global) markets. The Web itself renders time and space largely irrelevant, so it will be an interesting prospect to be able to effectively conduct testing in this same context.

PUTTING IT ALL TOGETHER

Now that we have considered different types of testing and testing techniques, we are faced with the challenge of putting together our own testing strategy.

Many books and articles have been written on the software development cycle, and testing is a part of that cycle. Some commentators claim that software development approaches cannot be applied to Web development. I disagree. I think the process is similar while the inputs, outputs, and timeframes are different.

My version of the software development cycle, as it applies to Web site development, is given in Figure 3-7.

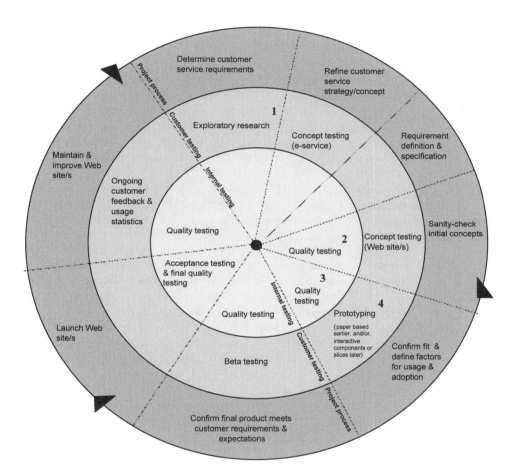

Figure 3-7 E-service development cycle along three coincident streams of activity.

The model shows three coincident streams of activity: project process, internal testing and external customer testing.:

Notes

1. Exploratory research may not need to be as in-depth on the second, or subsequent, times around the cycle. However, you should try to stay abreast of competitive activity and technological development because these will quickly, and radically, change the environment your customers operate in.

2. Quality testing, prior to testing Web site concepts, could include simple usability checking by the development company.

3. Quality testing, prior to prototyping, needs to be more thorough, since the product is more developed, and possibly interactive. Testing may include usability checking, interactivity testing and some integration, compatibility, and performance testing (to make sure the customer can complete test processes reliably).

4. You may choose to prototype earlier in the development cycle, before the product is interactive (e.g., with paper-based mockups) or later when the test product is interactive. You may not necessarily do both. For optimal results, early prototyping may be useful to test core concepts such as the navigation system and, later, prototyping may be useful to test the usefulness and attractiveness of core processes (of which navigation will be a part).

The internal testing, customer testing, and project process activities build on one another, as we move from one stage in the cycle to the next. Activities also build on one another, within each stage, as we move from the inside to the outside of the circle. So, for example, the project process activity of sanity checking of initial concepts is based on the criteria defined during requirement definition (building on the previous stage in the cycle), and you would start with some initial quality testing before exposing customers to the elements being tested (moving from the inside to the outside of this stage in the cycle).

You may not necessarily end up following this cycle exactly. You may decide to do some tests and not others. For example, you may skip e-service concept testing and go straight to Web site concept testing, or even prototyping. If testing is skipped at a given stage in the cycle, it introduces more risk of being further away from meeting customer requirements when you do test.

The pros and cons of skipping testing at various stages must be taken on balance given the level of familiarity you have with your customers and providing them with e-services. If you do skip testing at some point, make sure you don't test fundamental concepts too late. The Web site is just the manifestation of your e-service strategy; if your strategy isn't right, your Web site won't be either.

The danger is that you may develop a great Web site that is of little use to your customers. It is tempting to assume we know our customers' needs and the way they behave, translate that into a Web site concept, and then test it late in development or on completion. At this stage, we are past the point of no return, and we may be faced with having to launch a substandard service or fundamentally start all over again. It is surprising the number of times Web sites go public when they are known to be out of touch with customer needs.

Each testing activity doesn't have to be a project in itself. In fact, if you follow the above cycle, each testing activity is optimally efficient because testing can be simply focused on supporting one particular project activity. Problems arise when you try to support too many project activities and execute a complex testing brief.

Typically, you end up getting general information about not very much. Also bear in mind that the testing techniques we have discussed don't require large test audiences or arduous processes. Asking small groups of customers simple and straightforward questions at the right times will save you the pain of redevelopment or customer disdain later on.

TEN SUCCESS FACTORS

To help you put together an optimal test strategy, and test plans, we will consider some of the secrets of successful testing; testing that will ensure a customer-effective Web site results.

The ten success factors for an optimal test strategy and plan are as follows:

1. Strike a balance between methodologies, design and redesign, competing business and e-customer desires and make a balanced interpretation of e-customer requirements
2. Match research techniques to desired outcomes
3. Time testing to produce the right results when you need them
4. Optimize expertise and resource for objectivity and optimal test results
5. Ask the right people, more than once to benchmark changes in needs over time
6. Create the right context for testing
7. Ask the right questions
8. Employ a good feedback process
9. Use the results you get
10. Plan your tests

Now, let's explore each of these success factors in turn.

1. STRIKE A BALANCE

Balance is required in a number of areas: to select methodologies and techniques and to get the right information without having to test forever, or compromise the design process.

Methodologies and techniques

You should be familiar with the different types of testing, testing techniques, and the pros and cons of each. No test is perfect. However, you can cover your bases by combining methodologies and techniques to achieve a balanced approach overall. For example, consider the following methodologies and techniques that complement each other:

- *Quantitative and qualitative research.* Quantitative research will provide quantification of market demand and demographics, while qualitative research will give you a better understanding of people's attitudes and perceptions.
- *Interviews and focus groups.* Interviews will give you more detailed insight into the needs of individuals while focus groups allow you to generate ideas and explore concepts with groups.
- *Online surveys against other sampling and selection methods.* Online surveys are expedient and can be skewed toward certain types of Web users; other tests such as questionnaires allow more rigorous sampling and selection of respondents and can verify, and flesh out, online results.

Information quality, not quantity

You should avoid unhelpful information overload, whenever, and however, you test. Hone in on the essence of what you need to know at a given point of time and be very clear about what you are testing. Decide on what is manageable and what will make a tangible difference to where you are at.

Start with the answers you need and map these back to a few simple questions. Lots of peripheral information just gets in the way and does not provide value for the money. It is better to get a two-page summary of what you need to do, than 50 pages of dialogue that you will only struggle to do anything useful with.

Design versus redesign

You will need to balance the need to revise concepts and development with getting the work done. In this medium, you could revise forever and still not feel like you're getting close enough; things move that quickly.

At some stage you will have to put a stake in the ground and make something available to the public. That's not an excuse to get the basics wrong, but is recognition of the fact that the Web is dynamic and immediate and you can improve things as you go (as long as you do it in a way that delivers value to customers and encourages them to stay with you).

Reconciling different desires

In deciding what is good enough, you will have to balance customer needs and goals with business goals, because customers and business seldom want exactly the same things. You will have to make trade offs.

You will be given many directives as a result of customer testing and many directives as a result of internal testing; and they won't always line up. This is why it is critical to find out what customers want the most and what the business wants the most.

It only takes a minute to ask customers to rank things for you. For example, if customers have identified a workflow they have to perform online, ask them what absolutely has to be done online and what doesn't, and if customers identify a list of functionality they want on your site, ask them what is most, and least, important to them. Then judgment has to be used to decide who gets what they want and when; and that decision needs to be an informed one.

Reality versus fantasy

There's a phenomenon I have seen time and time again when testing in e-space. I call it the "expectation-plus" phenomenon. As soon as customers and business people start thinking about cyberspace, they seem to conjure up images of the "wizardry" of computers and the Internet. Sometimes you wonder if they really do think it all happens by "magic." You have to create a meaningful frame of reference that grounds customers in tangible and practical terms and avoid getting carried away by hype. Staying focused on what customers do and need to do, is always grounding and something customers can act as authorities on, without a moment's hesitation.

As well as counterbalancing the "expectation-plus" phenomenon, you will also have to balance customer expectations against what your company can deliver; without limiting possibilities or inhibiting insight into what customers really need and want from you. It's a difficult balance to strike.

I find it best to allow customers to "blue-sky" things (i.e., generate their wish list) and not limit their thoughts and ideas. Later on, as you start to zero in on priorities, you can add a dose of reality. And generally, customers will say, "Well, they obviously can't do all of this right now; not all at once." Customers will help you prioritize realistically. However, it does take guidance and your testing facilitators should have a feel for technological boundaries; otherwise you can spend a lot of time chasing rainbows and find no pot of gold.

Balanced interpretation

Interpreting test results and translating them into recommendations take as much careful thought as designing and executing the testing. You have to take everything on balance when making recommendations. You need to consider the dynamics that have led to the results; things like the obvious effects of groupthink and customer frustration with technology may need to be recognized and accounted for. (especially if you have experienced problems during testing).

You can't please everyone all of the time, and test results should not be taken literally as recommendations. The key is to get to the essence of what customers need to be able to do to act successfully as customers. Sometimes, you have to realize that customer requirements may have been given in another guise; for example, when I got feedback on a proposed home page. All the customers gave a different view: "Shouldn't it look like this instead?," "What about some animation?," "What about some more color?" etc. What they were trying to say was that the home page was boring and unexciting, but they didn't have the requisite knowledge of e-space to volunteer a smart solution, so they just offered the best solution they could come up with at the time. To go back to the company and say, "You need some animation on your home page" would have been treating a symptom (actually, probably creating another one) rather than solving a problem.

2. MATCH TECHNIQUE TO OUTCOME

We have an awesome grab-bag of techniques we can use in our testing, as we saw previously in this chapter under "Testing Techniques." We must bear in mind, however, that some techniques are more appropriate than others, depending on what we're trying to find out and when. Each technique will provide a different spin on the information we need.

Figure 3-8 provides some ideas of techniques most likely to be used as components of the test plan at different stages in a project:

3. TIME THINGS RIGHT

Matching techniques to outcomes helps you to get detailed feedback on the area of most interest at the right time. For example, interviewing helps provide detail on exactly what customers do, usability tests provide detail on what they can use, and focus groups can provide detail on usage boundaries.

If you're redesigning an existing Web site, you have an initial reference point for discussion, but avoid getting minutiae on the existing site too early in the process.

Of course, you can also get detailed feedback too late to be able to do anything useful with it. It is critical not to leave the testing of strategic and conceptual fundamentals until late in the development process. I have observed cases where concept testing was inherent in prototyping; late in the development process. By this time, flaws in the basic e-service offering and concepts, such as the navigation system, will be costly to fix, not to mention downright inconvenient.

To avoid rework as much as possible, testing should be timed with development. The testing plan should follow the development plan and the Web site designer should advise possible test components in line with their deliverables and timeframe. If the Web site designer is clear on the testing a company wishes to complete, the designer can ensure the company adopts an appropriate development process. Agreeing on critical Web site components and planning their delivery can help a business and their Web site development company plan, and execute, their respective testing and development tasks.

4. OPTIMIZE EXPERTISE AND RESOURCE

As we have seen, some testing is general and some more specific. The more specific the testing gets, the more likely that expert testers (such as usability experts and expert Web site developers) and facilitators will be required to conduct the test-

	Forming Strategy	Developing Concepts	Doing Development	Ensuring Quality Prior to Launch	Ensuring Quality Ongoing
Interviews	Some as counterbalance to Focus groups and to get some in-depth feedback on unmet customer service requirements (see Modeling).	In-depth exploration of usage against a suite of e-service concepts.	Key part of gaining detailed feedback on fit with customer requirements during prototyping.	Could conduct a few with previous test participants.	Some to benchmark changes in customer uses or requirements (see Modeling).
Focus Groups	Idea generation and scene setting across audiences.	Sanity checking and ranking of usefulness and attractiveness.	Contextual testing of Web site components (e.g., using group decision support software).	Final checking through Beta testing.	Some to generate ideas when rejuvenation is required.
Demos	Web sites might act as triggers for Focus Groups/Interviews. Not a stand alone activity, however.		May be part of a business' internal buy-in process.	May be part of internal sign-off process.	
Questionnaire	May be used to quantify audience characteristics and usage characteristics.				
Online Survey	May be used to zero in on attitudes of a particular audience important to strategy formulation.				Online feedback in relation to specific activities and customer problems.
Usability inspection	Too early for this.	Too early for this.	Sanity checking by the development company and formal tests with customers.	Last troubleshoot for usability problems, or "showstoppers."	Benchmark testing with a small group of users and/or feedback from the site regarding general usage problems.
Modeling	Workflow modeling, probably as part of interviewing. Too early to model concepts, however.	Card sorting against basic site structures.	Intuitiveness tests and paper-based prototyping.		To stay abreast of changing customer e-service requirements.

Key:

■ Core component ▨ Partial component ▧ Subsidiary component ☐ Probably not a component

Figure 3-8 Techniques relative to project stages.

ing. However, all testing demands an understanding of the e-service environment and the operation of e-customers within it.

It is difficult to keep a balance between objectivity and familiarity. A partnering of professional researchers and facilitators with Web site development experts can help strike that balance, and this may involve cooperation between the business that must deliver the Web site and the development company they have employed to create it. This cooperation may go something like this:

- *Exploratory research.* The company will take the lead and may even complete this phase before appointing a company to develop their Web site. However, if a working relationship already exists, an outward-looking development company may be able to offer a business some valuable background orientation.

- *Quality testing prior to concept testing.* Both the business and the Web site development company will complete quality checking independently.

- *Concept testing.*
  - *E-service concepts.* The company will take the lead, since it is largely refining its own e-service strategy.
  - *Web site concepts.* The Web site designer will take the lead, since it is testing its initial concepts.

- *Quality testing prior to prototyping.* Both the business and their Web site development company will complete quality checking independently. The development company may introduce usability or development experts into its quality testing.

- *Prototyping.* The business and Web site development company may act in concert to strike a good balance between strategic objectivity and product familiarity.

- *Quality testing prior to beta testing.* Both the business and Web site development company will complete quality checking independently.

- *Beta testing.* The business and Web site development company may again act in concert, but there will be less dependence on experts to interpret feedback into system changes at this point.

- *Acceptance testing.* This is the responsibility of the business.

- *Final quality testing.* Both the business and Web site development company will complete quality checking independently. However, the development company may play a role in helping the business complete integration and performance testing, given the likely migration of the system from the development company to the business' production environment.

5. Ask the Right People, More Than Once

It is likely that you will need to recognize a number of different Web site audiences, although only one or two may be your focus (refer back to "We Have Multiple Audiences" in Chapter 1). Your testing, at least early on, should try to keep a broad perspective on audience; this will give you a better idea of what not to do, as much what to do to avoid alienating customers from different audiences. Later on, you may want to narrow in on specific Web site uses by audience. Beta testing may also include participants from subsidiary audiences to ensure they are not alienated by the focus on key audiences.

It is also important to cover a cross-section of technological abilities when testing. You should not confine yourself to novice users or experienced users because your customers could be either or anywhere in-between. However, beware the dynamics of putting different experience levels together in focus groups. It can become exceedingly difficult to manage exercises, and the pace at which they are executed, when experience levels are too diverse.

And once you've worked out whom you should be talking to, talk to them more than once. This will help you benchmark and track attitudinal and behavioral changes as customers learn about e-space and use your Web site.

6. CREATE THE RIGHT CONTEXT

Our inquiry should be contextual; it should help us create e-services that fit with the way customers need to work as customers. We are more interested in customers telling us stories about what they do, and why, than we are in generating loads of statistically significant data. We need to create test environments where customers can think in metaphor and scenario.

In addition, the customers' use of the Web site must be as natural as possible; we shouldn't interfere too much with the way they would normally interact with Web sites. If we want to be sure our interface is intuitive, we must allow customers to interact with it without our direction or interference. The more researchers direct e-customers to parts of a Web site, the more unnatural the e-customer's usage will be. When a customer sees a Web site for the first time, they can interact with it any old way they want. This random and undirected usage is part of an e-customer's experience and will affect their impressions of a Web site.

Early in this chapter we looked at a contextual test methodology that utilizes group decision support software within focus groups. This approach seems to create an environment where e-customers can interact with a Web site naturally and where researchers are able to collect and explore test responses.

7. ASK THE RIGHT QUESTIONS

We must identify the fundamental questions, requiring answers, at each stage in the life of our projects. We must match our questions, and not just our techniques, with outcomes. And we should build on what we know and avoid restating the obvious. Results like "the navigation needs to be consistent" and "the site should be useful" are givens—we need to understand the specific applications of these principles as well as the principles themselves. With the relevant principles in mind, we can ask more pertinent questions that help us get to the crux of what we need to do.

Simple, direct questions work best. And those questions should break ideas down into bite-sized chunks. Asking customers, "what do you want?" or "what do you think of this idea…?" will just lead to blank looks. If you keep things grounded in exercises and tangible examples, customers will be able to respond to more useful thought triggers and provide you with better feedback.

While providing customers with tangible exercises and examples, avoid "selling" your concepts to your audience. There is a real temptation to do this in a demo or prototype environment, where you may have to present information to customers.

8. EMPLOY A GOOD FEEDBACK PROCESS

There is no point doing great testing if it will be ignored due to an inadequate feedback process. A sound feedback and evaluation process, and the related activities of specific individuals, should be nailed down before testing starts.

The process shown in Figure 3-9 can work well, as long as decision makers are clearly identified and can act quickly.

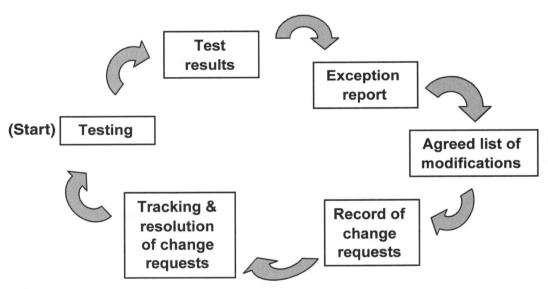

Figure 3-9 A process for making changes on the basis of test results.

An exception report translates test results into a precis of recommended modifications that are agreed on (or not) and then itemized in a final list of modifications. The parties responsible for the changes must advise progress against the specified changes and then these can be retested as required.

9. USE WHAT YOU GET

A good feedback process will help you make sure things happen as a result of your testing, and this takes time. You must factor in time to interpret and act on your test results. Good planning early on in the project will allow you to run tests and make changes in parallel, so you don't get unduly held up by the change process. However, you can't always redevelop and develop simultaneously because Web sites reuse common components in many different parts of the site. Sometimes you will have to put the brakes on and make the necessary changes before you do anything else.

And you must make sure that you don't lose the value of your testing in the interpretation of results. Someone has to be dedicated to quickly translating results into usable directives for being customer-effective. In addition, somewhere along the line, someone is going to have to act as final arbitrator on behalf of the business, the Web site development company and customers. Final arbitration should be a part of the process and not come as an unwelcome surprise to designers flat out making what they understand to be final modifications. (See the discussion on the "customer advocate" in Chapter 5 under "Setting up the Project.")

10. PLAN YOUR TESTS

In every test you do, you should be crystal clear about exactly what is being tested, and how. Writing a test plan will help you crystallize exactly what has to happen. You will need to ask yourself:

- What is the test subject and its scope? For example, if you're testing an order process, where does it begin and end?

- What are you testing for? Be as specific as possible. If you are going to test one aspect of the test subject, make that limitation clear. You must understand what you are testing; if you're testing specific functionality, you must know exactly how it's supposed to work.

- What are the test criteria? How will you know whether something has passed or failed? Wherever possible, you should describe necessary outcomes, relative to inputs through scenarios, scripts and test cases.

- What is the test process? Map out the process, allocate specific people to specific tasks, and tell them how long they have to complete them, and why.

DECIDING WHAT IS RIGHT FOR YOU

How you choose to combine the various types of testing with the various stages of your project will be key to your success. There is no standard approach that can be adopted in every case, but some of the ideas and guidelines we have covered will help you on your way. However, the closer you can get to the development cycle shown in Figure 3-7, the better.

When deciding your testing approach, you will need to consider the following:

Timing

Take a good hard look at your schedule. When will it be imperative to get customer feedback before and during development? Think about the decisions being made and the information needed to make them with a customer perspective in mind. If there isn't enough time to do the testing you need to do, then consider the risk of not doing it and whether you can live with that. Of course, being customer-effective requires you to talk to your customers. How much attention you want to pay to your customers is, ultimately, up to you.

Fit with your project

Testing will need to fit with your project methodology. There may be strong principles guiding what happens, when and by whom, and you should establish what these principles are at the beginning of the project and consider how they affect testing. For example, if there is a clear approval process, this should be adopted in your testing feedback and change control process.

Level of rigor required

Different organizational cultures demand different levels of rigor; some cultures are founded on a more scientific view of the world, and a more thorough and substantial testing approach may be required to reach consensus and get things done. Other cultures are founded on a more empirical view of the world, and testing may be more inductive or intuitive. It can be a good idea to run the proposed testing approach past key stakeholders at the beginning of the project to see how comfortable people are with what, and how, testing will be done.

How results will be applied

It is worthwhile doing testing only if the results are applied. Consider the types of outputs from each type of testing and whether they would, or could, be used within the infrastructure of your project. It should be clear where there is not a good match; bearing in mind, however, that a mismatch between outputs and their use may mean your project team and tasks may not yet be fully defined.

Expertise and resource available

Also, with each type of testing you will need to consider who is available to complete the testing, across all parties involved. Talk with suppliers to develop a cooperative approach to testing. Testing is a resource-hungry task and the more hands on deck, the better.

Redesign versus first-time development.

First-time development will probably demand a broader scope and more detailed results than subsequent development. How much you can shorthand your test approach, subsequent times around, will depend on how close you have got to your customers and how familiar you are with them.

As time passes companies will be able to optimize their Web sites to get to know their customers better, and, provided this customer knowledge is captured and applied, the need for discrete test exercises will reduce.

However, companies will always need to keep an eye on the big picture and think about what other e-service opportunities and audiences exist. Additionally, some Web sites are just not up to having more and more bits "tacked on over time." In these cases, it may be advisable to test with a blank sheet of paper rather than try to leverage previous testing and feedback, particularly if the focus, and development, of the Web site has shifted between different tasks and different audiences over time.

CHAPTER 4

E-SERVICE REQUIREMENT DEFINITION

> *How well you describe what you need to develop relates directly to your ability to win and retain e-customers. Your suppliers can't make up for lack of thought and clarity within your business.*

Having considered what customers want from e-service providers, we will now consider how an e-service provider goes about establishing and defining their e-services and the associated infrastructure.

The requirement definition process occurs internally within the e-service providing organization and then these requirements are communicated to the development company. To give e-service providers a head start, we will look at some best-practice fundamentals, and the key decisions that organizations have to make, before looking at how they can successfully complete the requirement definition process.

ELEVEN BEST-PRACTICE FUNDAMENTALS

E-business hasn't been around long enough for us to empirically establish best practice. However, in a short time, there have been enough examples of what has worked, and what has not, to intuitively establish some best-practice fundamentals. Based on my research, reading and experience, these best-practice fundamentals are as follows:

1. Innovate.
2. Be an e-citizen.

3. Create value early.
4. Deliver on a clear value proposition.
5. Integrate.
6. Balance the physical and virtual.
7. Know whom you're dealing with.
8. Create a useful experience.
9. Operate in real time.
10. Match business capabilities.
11. Use technology as an enabler.

We will explore each of these fundamentals in turn.

1. INNOVATE

The e-business phenomenon has redefined the way people do, and will do, business, in the following ways:

1. Some industries have fundamentally changed the services they offer, how they are offered, by whom and to whom. Decreased margins, wholesale buying and selling, and increased market coverage have changed the fundamental business decisions that organizations make. Online pioneers, such as Amazon, with its discounting and range of titles, are transforming the way business is being done online and offline.

2. The boundaries between industries have become blurred and the traditional demarcation between types of business may no longer be valid. Intra- and interindustry cooperation and consolidation have occurred in e-space, particulalry through the advent of portals that give access to a range of products and services.

3. New industries and markets have arisen as a result of new e-business opportunities, such as offering new types of information and processes, in new ways, for financial gain.

4. Disintermediation has occurred where companies have been removed from the supply chain (such as in the case of removing agents and brokers from the sales process), along with increased mediation where companies have been added to the supply chain (such as adding online brokerage services on behalf of new buying groups).

These changes are a threat to traditional industry but are also an opportunity to innovate. By thinking outside traditional boundaries we can tap into new markets and find new and better ways of doing business. We can also engage in what I call "information innovation" as we provide customers with access to information that they couldn't get anywhere else but on the Web, and we can do it in new and exciting ways.

In addition, we can optimize the interactivity and immediacy of the Web, and associated Internet technologies, to innovate. For example, we can now provide online demos and simulations, customizable content, and tailored solutions. We can also bring the customer further into our business than we ever have before. For example, we can allow customers to interact with their own data and directly affect business processes and outcomes as a result.

And we can be the first to innovate in a particular way. Innovative application of Internet technologies differentiates us from our competitors and may put us in a leadership position. Leadership, even if it is not sustained over the long term, can establish a window where customers are won, which then provides the opportunity for those customers to also be retained (through various means) over the longer term.

2. BE AN E-CITIZEN

When you create "real estate" in cyberspace, you become part of much greater whole. You cannot act in isolation on the Web; you are a citizen in an e-community; and that community has its own set of protocols and cyberculture. Your e-customers will move to and fro in cyberspace, and your Web site may be only one of their destinations. You should not act as if you exist on the Web in isolation. Participation in the e-community is implicit in being on the Web.

Now, participation in the e-community can be made explicit. Communities can be created within and across e-customer groups and within and across industries. Oftentimes, businesses make weak attempts at creating communities—just because the Web facilitates the interactions of many people doesn't mean that those people necessarily want to interact, or interact in the way businesses think they do. When considering the community aspects of your Web site, you should consider all the parties that make up your customers' e-service experience, and why, and consider how those should be brought together on the Web.

Once you become a member of an e-community, you are better able to tap into, and reach, the e-customers who move around in that community. And how you do that will be captured in your Web marketing plan.

3. CREATE VALUE EARLY

As we know, value drives a business as much as cost and revenue do. Value is often elusive because it is hard to quantify and qualify. However, what people perceive as valuable is a major determinant in whether they choose to do business with us.

In e-space, there are many ways to create value through the services we provide to e-customers and the communications we have with them. The first most obvious value opportunity is to become customer-effective and utilize the Web for the benefit of your customers. In addition, a good hard look at how your industry is serving e-customers will give you plenty of ideas of how you can enhance e-service in general. You can create value just by doing better than other e-service providers.

Once you've got the basics right, the potential is limitless. However, you do have to get the most critical basics right (at least). Customers may give you only one shot at serving them online. If you deliver a bad experience, chances are they won't stick around until you do. You need to ensure there is value for customers right from day one.

The mentality of making software releases, where people put up with bugs until they get them fixed, has been, dangerously, carried over to Web development. The Web is a dynamic and agile environment and people won't put up with a staid "release it and fix it later" mentality. You don't have to be perfect, but you do need to offer enough value to keep e-customers interested.

4. DELIVER ON A CLEAR VALUE PROPOSITION

Clearly communicating a value proposition is important to position organizations and manage customer expectations offline, and even more important when a business is online. Customers will go to your Web site for a reason and, for every visit, you have to make that reason very clear, before the customer gets to your site and while they're there.

And because the Web is an experiential medium, where customers create value through their actions, you must be clear about the value you deliver throughout your site as well, as follows:

- Make it very clear to your e-customer what your Web site will, or will not, do for them.

- Make it very clear to your e-customer how your Web site offering fits with your whole service offering (comprising online and offline services).

- Provide a reason for every customer interaction, and deliver against it (recall customer directive number 2, "Tell me what I get if I do this").

5. INTEGRATE

E-business strategy should be an integrated part of overall business and marketing strategy. The strategy process used to formulate e-business strategy should be in harmony with other strategy processes. Overall, business and marketing strategy will feed e-business strategy and vice versa. Of course, if e-business is your business, then business and e-business strategy are one and the same thing anyway.

Customers know when the e-services they receive are not integrated with the rest of your business. Customers know when they get inconsistent or conflicting marketing messages and communication, when they can't complete an online process because something "didn't get through" or got lost in business processing, and when someone tries to sell them something they have already bought, or inquired about, on the Web, for example.

And, of course, there's integration of the customer into the company, as per Figure 1-1 in Chapter 1. Customers expect organizations to provide convincing access to:

- *Product and service information.* Your customers will expect to have direct and easy access to quality product and service information.

- *Problem resolution.* Customers will expect to be able to "solve problems" via your Web site, and you need to give them real ways to do this.

- *People.* Contacts should be provided in relation to particular activities and areas of expertise. This goes beyond offering an e-mail address such as info@....

- *Process.* Transactional functionality inherently achieves this, but you should also find ways to involve customers in developing or improving business processes, even if it's simply involving them in the development of your Web site.

6. BALANCE THE PHYSICAL AND VIRTUAL

Many customer service experiences combine physical (offline) and virtual (online) communication to deliver an overall service experience. If this is the case, care must be taken not to force customers to be physical when they don't want to be, or virtual when they don't want to be.

Customer empowerment puts the choice of being physical or virtual in the hands of the customer. Of course, this shift in the balance of power is not particulalry attractive to companies seeking to save on the costs of physical assets by migrating customers to online platforms. However, even if a company replaces physical services with virtual services, it must still provide the customer with access to personal support. There should always be a human behind the "system," someone you can talk to when all else fails.

An optimal service provider will always strike a balance between maximum efficiency and maximum personal service, and will balance the physical and virtual to achieve that overall balance. This physical-virtual balance is particularly important in facilitating customer adoption of new online services.

The more high-tech a system in general, the more high-touch the counterbalance required to encourage its adoption. This is especially important when a company is principally responsible for the adoption of online services. Sometimes, a company is able to deal with customers who have already adopted the Web, or adopted certain online services, but this is not always the case. Companies that are breaking new ground in online servicing have to educate, and woo, e-customers.

7. KNOW WHO YOU'RE DEALING WITH

The premise of this entire book is that you must understand and respond meaningfully to e-customers. Before you do that, you need to know who your e-customers are—the ones you seek and the ones you don't. You will need to determine which e-customers you will focus on, and how you will deal with visitors who you do not target as customers (bearing in mind that a range of audiences may come to your Web site).

Having decided who your key audiences are, you must find out how they do, and will, behave, how they need to "work" as customers, and what their "work" context is. You will also need to find out how expert e-customers are (their level of familiarity and understanding in your field), how technologically proficient they are, and what software and hardware they are likely to be able to support.

Different e-customers may need to be treated in different ways, depending on their characteristics and needs. In addition, you may want to selectively sustain relationships wth e-customers over time. You have to get to know your e-customers to find out the best way to create dialogue and exchanges that keep relationships alive, without alienating other ancillary audiences.

8. CREATE A USEFUL EXPERIENCE

Relevance

E-customers will have a useful experience as long as the content and functionality they encounter on a Web site is relevant to them and supports what they're trying to do. The interactivity of the Web should allow us to better tailor information and utility to individuals who create their own experience of our Web sites.

However, to do this, we need to understand whether "one size fits all" or whether our e-services need to be customized by our e-customers. It is easy to overlook the opportunities for personalized actions and responses in real time and fall into the trap of offering averaged products and services that don't really meet the needs of selective individuals. Despite its ability to provde tailored experiences to individuals, the Web has become a breeding ground for "mass impersonalization" rather than "mass customization."

Additionally, companies that tailor their products and services to the Web tend to be more successful. Sometimes companies try to rehang existing services and processes on the Web; they think they can simply "offer that service on the Web." However, being useful on the Web comes with a whole new set of rules and e-customer expectations. Your services may not transfer to the Web; you may have to re-create them, or offer something completely different or new, to be useful to your e-customers.

Convenience

A Web site must make existing processes more convenient. If it doesn't, you will not be meeting customers' basic service expectations. In addition, every interaction on your Web site should be easy.

Utility

You must facilitate the "work" customers need to do as customers, and this means providing the necessary utility on your Web site. Customers must be able to get things done on your Web site.

Useful information

Content must usefully create a context for what customers need to do as customers. Gone are the days of providing content for its own sake (i.e., the traditional publishing model). Content must exist for a reason, such as:

- Facilitating and supporting e-customers' decision-making process.
- Helping the e-customer get around and use the Web site.
- Helping the e-customer transact with you.
- Helping the e-customer stay in touch with you.
- Creating a dialogue with the e-customer as they move around your Web site.

This doesn't mean that content has to be boring and instructional. "Useful" is defined by e-customers in relation to what they're trying to do. What an e-customer is trying to do will depend on who they are, what their relationship is with you, and what you're offering. A customer may be trying to participate in a discussion forum, for example, and you will need to provide a context to make that experience meaningful and easy. Content facilitates all interactions, whether those are e-commerce related or not.

In addition, the way content is organized and presented is a key determinant of how useful it will be. Many Web sites bury important and useful content as a result of bad information design.

9. OPERATE IN REAL TIME

If any information or functionality is time-critical to your customers, you will add value by making it real time. The Web gives businesses and customers the ability to act in a synchronous fashion (i.e., to be getting things done, together, at the same time). However, we still tend to operate according to the traditonal modes where "I ask and you get back to me," as opposed to "I ask and we make it happen now."

As customers become more and more a part of our business, the more likely it is that we will be operating with them in real time. Customers and businesses can work together in a synchrounous environment based on two-way workflow.

10. MATCH BUSINESS CAPABILITIES

Of course, if the company is not capable of offering value to e-customers, then it should think twice about being in e-business. Sometimes companies have to reinvent all, or parts, of their business, or create new businesses, capable of delivering customer-effective e-services.

What e-services you offer, and how, will depend on what you can improve on, or do anew from scratch, and what you can support through the interface and at the back end. Don't think you're going to do real-time, online ordering from day one, for example, if you have no capability for connectivity with internal systems or a secure and reliable environment for handling external transactions.

You have to be the expert on how all the pieces fit together to deliver e-services to your customers. A development company can't build you an interface if it doesn't know what the customer is interfacing with, and how. And that interface won't offer the customer any value if the infrastructure that supports it is inadequate.

It is always best to bite off only as much as you can chew at one time, while making sure that you are providing enough value to your e-customers.

11. USE TECHNOLOGY AS AN ENABLER

Customers see technoloy as an enabler; it is a means to an end and not the end in itself. Technology enables e-customers to have direct and convenient access to the business and a better quality of service. "Whizz-bangery," in itself, does not add value. You must look for ways to leverage technology in a way that adds value to e-customers, such as the provision of real time processing and greater integration with the business.

The choice between technologies has to be largely driven by what will enable the requisite customer experience. Unfortunately, personal agendas seem to be a key driver within businesses where zealots push one technology over another without really understanding the effects their preferred technologies will ultimately have on the customer experience.

KEY DECISIONS YOU WILL HAVE TO MAKE

Sometimes, making the right decisions starts with asking the right questions. Here we will list many questions you will need to answer to be able to define your requirements. I have envisioned that businesses could refer to these questions within the meetings and workshops they will have to determine their e-business strategy and Web site requirements. Those questions fall under the following headings:

1. Strategy.
2. Marketing.
3. Customer service.
4. Web site characteristics.

You may not have the answer to every question, but you should at least be thinking about them.

Problems arise when an issue gets addressed too late in the development process, a decision is made to change tack, and previous development becomes redundant. This is a waste of time and effort for everyone involved. Addressing all of these questions up front internally, and with your suppliers in the early stages of the product specification process, will help you establish a clear direction, and stick to it. (Product specification is covered in Chapter 5.)

If you want to avoid all the hype that goes along with e-business, and want to get straight to what you actually need to do, ask yourself these questions.

1. STRATEGY

When defining your e-business strategy you will need to address the following issues:

1. What is my new industry?
2. What is my new economy?
3. What is my new business?
4. What is my new e-community?
5. Who is my e-customer?

6. Is my e-customer integrated?

7. What e-services do I offer?

8. Are we ready for this?

We will explore each of these issues in turn.

1. The new industry

The Web creates new connections between companies that participate within industries. These connections can create new ways for different companies to work together more efficiently. This phenomenon is giving rise to new industry structures such as those seen in business-to-consumer and business-to-business Net markets. These Net markets are creating new buyers and sellers and bringing them together within a whole new business model. Once industry relationships fundamentally change, so do the rules of business in that industry. In fact, sometimes the industry is dismantled and new industries emerge. And so, businesses today need to ask themselves the following questions:

- What is our new industry structure?
- What are the risks and opportunities for e-businesses in this new industry?
- How will maximum value be achieved throughout the value chain? Where does that place our business within that value chain?
- Has disintermediation occurred where companies have been removed from the supply chain (e.g. direct selling)? Or is mediation just as, or more, important (where companies, such as intermediaries for buying groups, have been added to the supply chain).

2. The new economy

As industry structures change the economics of an industry also change because different industry participants are faced with delivering against a different value proposition, and they will be remunerated in line with the value they create. When Amazon.com came online they started to change the economy for book-selling, for example. Amazon.com's low margin business forced bricks-and-mortar booksellers to re-engineer their business to be able to compete in this economy of lower margins and lower prices to consumers. Whether businesses are bricks-and-mortar, 100% Web-based, or a combination of both, they need to ask themselves the following questions:

- What is our new e-economy? What value do we provide within this economy and how can we be remunerated for it?
- What drives profit in this new economy?

- How does diversity and scale affect the profitability equation?
- How is real value delivered to our e-customers?
- What is the up-front cost versus the longer-term payoff? How will potentially deferred payback be factored into short-tem organizational cost and revenue objectives?

3. The New business

When industries change and businesses' financial models change, that challenges a business' very reason for being. Every business must decide what their core business is and too often they get caught up by not noticing that their reason for being has changed. Businesses don't adapt to their environment and they become extinct. This has been happening even without the Web in the mix. Now, the chance of becoming extinct is even greater as industry structures, financial models and business purpose change more fundamentally and more quickly than they have before. To be sure of the business they're in businesses need to ask themselves the following questions:

- Am I still operating in the same market or even the same business?
- In what ways can my business become a superior service provider through dedication to e-servicing?
- How can my business go beyond traditional boundaries in:
  - The products and services offered via our Web site. What's now adding value?
  - The information we offer e-customers and the dialogue we have with them. What new exchanges are most meaningful?
  - How those products and services are delivered. What's easier, quicker, and more cost effective?
  - The process that supports those products and services. What's now working smarter and harder for the e-customer?

4. The New community

- Is my business leading or following?
  - Are we motivating technology adoption within the industry? Among customers?
  - Are we driving a change in customer behavior?
  - Who else should be in our e-community and what should they contribute?
  - What internal and external parties (customers, suppliers, other contributors) participate in my e-community?

Businesses need to consider how Web-based technologies can be applied across their interactions with many different audiences and decide on the connections that should, or could, exist. It is particularly important to consider how connections between an Intranet (serving an internal audience), the Internet (serving external customers), and extranets (serving external parties that have privileged access to Web-based information and functionality) enhance the functioning of the entire community.

Personally, I believe too much differentiation is made between intra-, inter- and extra-nets. The benefits of shared information and functionality—with different access for different audiences—seem to be overlooked because of segregation between projects and development processes within businesses.

Businesses need to keep a holistic view of the e-community they participate in and their role within it by asking themselves the following questions:

- How does cyberculture alter and enhance our business culture?
- How do we create connections with other e-citizens (see "Marketing" below).

5. The e-customer

When a business' core business changes so does their customer base. The Web allows businesses to attract customers they may not have previously had any connection with. Businesses can also create new products made possible by the Web. These new products generate new e-customers.

All businesses with a Web-based service offering need to be very clear about which e-customers relate to online products and which customers relate to offline products. Businesses also need to be mindful of situations where a customer is both an online and offline customer so they can deal with those customers holistically. Businesses need to ask themselves the following questions:

- Who is our e-customer?
- Are we seeking new customers (new markets and/or increased market penetration)?
- What is our e-customer's "work" context? How has, and will, our e-customer's behavior change?
- How has access to information changed the balance of power in our e-customers' favor? How expert will our e-customer become?
- How technologically proficient is our e-customer?
- What technological infrastructure is our e-customer subject to (i.e., hardware and software capabilities?)

6. The Level of customer integration

Businesses must decide how integrated their e-customers will be. In other words, businesses need to decide how much they will let e-customers have a direct impact on, and involvement with, business processes as a result of using their Web site.

It throws an interesting light on this question to relate intranet strategy to Internet strategy. In her book *The 21st-Century Intranet,* Jennifer Stone Gonzalez provides four models that depict the way companies choose to approach their intranets:[1]

1. The publication model: "I publish, you read."
2. The asymmetrical interaction model: "I ask, you respond—you ask I respond."
3. The symmetrical interaction model: "We all have a chance to talk and listen."
4. The synchronous virtual environment model: "This is the way we work together."

There are two dimensions to the above models: symmetry and synchronicity. As we move from the first to the fourth model the interaction between server and client becomes more synchronous as people "work" together in real time and information flows become more reciprocal.

While it is going a little too far to draw a direct analogy between the relationship between internal intranet clients (or employees) and companies and external e-customers, it does challenge us to think about customers as an integrated part of our business.

Figure 4-1 illustrates the potential scope of customer integration. Where do you think your company, sits, or will sit, on the above continuum, and why?

Of course, external customers will never be involved in "work," to the same extent as internal employees, but customers do "work," or complete activities, that allow them to get what they need, and want, as customers. Who knows how far customer integration will go in the future? How far you go in integrating e-customers is a key part of your strategy.

7. E-services

Different businesses offer different levels of service on the Web. This is particularly true for bricks-and-mortar businesses that are migrating only some services to the Web, while keeping other service offerings offline. It is critical for businesses to be entirely clear on what their online value proposition is, and why.

Businesses that choose not to offer some services online may be missing out on opportunities for improved customer service and competitive advantage. However, if not all of a business' customer base is online, it will make sense to offer

---

[1] *The 21st Century Intranet* by Stone-Gonzalez, ©1998. Reprinted by permission of Prentice-Hall, Inc., Upper Saddle River, NJ.

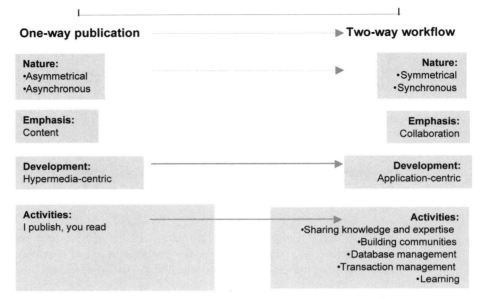

Figure 4-1 Applying Intranet strategy to the customer integration decision.

services offline. Businesses need to understand the necessary balance between online and offline services and must ask themselves the following questions:

- How broad is our e-service offering? Are we focused on one or a few key services?
- Are we enhancing existing services or creating new ones?
- Are we leveraging full-service capability to create integrated online solutions?
- Are we focused on e-commerce transactions or providing a broader e-service experience?

8. Business readiness

Businesses need to have the right orientation and infrastructure to provide e-services and must ask themselves the following questions:

- What is our commitment to innovation?
- How quickly can we innovate; how agile can we become?
- What e-processes can we support?
- Do we have an information technology strategy in place? Does it address the application of Internet technologies across the business? Do policies exist on the way Internet technologies will be applied?

- Are we prepared to develop applications using Internet technologies, or will we buy a pre-established off-the-shelf product (i.e., what is our stance on the make-or-buy question)?

- What technological infrastructure can we establish and maintain to facilitate meaningful connectivity with e-customers? What can we do from day one, and what will we do later? Will we implement staged implementation (to take into account increasing levels of connectivity with internal systems allowing increasing customer integration and synchronicity over time)?

Businesses also need to be honest about the level of resources they have to complete the necessary Web site development, business process design and ongoing Web site maintenance and support and must ask themselves the following questions:

- Will customer research, development, and consulting be outsourced or provided internally? Will cross-organizational teams be formed?

- If we can't maintain Web site hosting internally, will this be outsourced? How will this affect our ability to achieve connectivity with internal systems?

- What level of security can we offer e-customers and internal stakeholders?

- What capabilities do we have to publish Web site content and engage in content management?

- What resources and activities exist to keep our e-services and Web site interface current and functional?

- What support resource is available on a daily basis to provide assistance, answer inquiries, and service transactions?

2. MARKETING

As part of establishing e-business strategy, businesses need to develop a Web marketing plan. I could write a whole book just on Web marketing and the different approaches you could employ—but that would be a different book from this one and, needless to say, good books on the topic exist already (see Bibliography). Here we will talk about the decisions businesses need to make at the requirement definition stage—because they affect the way their site is structured, designed, and supported.

When defining your Web marketing strategy you will need to address the following issues:

1. How do we create competitive advantage?
2. What is our brand and how is it positioned?
3. How do we practice marketing?

4. How is marketing integrated?

5. How do we define our audiences?

6. How do we use our Web site as a communications medium?

We will consider the questions requiring discussion in relation to each of these issues in turn.

1. Competitive advantage

The Web has introduced new industries, economies, products, e-services and e-customers and this creates opportunities for competitive advantage. Businesses need to deliberately consider how the Web creates new opportunities for competitive advantage and must ask themselves the following questions:

- How can we be more customer-effective than our competitors?
- How can we offer better e-services than our competitors?
- How can we create more value in cyberspace than our competitors can, or do?
- How can we communicate better on the Web than our competitors?
- How can our Web site be superior in its information design, visual presentation, content and functionality?
- How can we build and maintain real-time relationships with select customers?
- What is the nature and degree of dialogue with e-customers? Are we engaged in one-way or two-way information flow and transactions?
- Do we need to learn more about e-customers, what and how?

2. Branding and positioning

Businesses now have to manage e-brands as well as physical brands and they need to understand the effect that those brands have on each other. E-service brands can affect the value of physical brands and vice versa. For example, a bricks-and-mortar business might significantly enhance their brand by also establishing that brand as an e-brand. However, some bricks-and-mortar brands may not be elastic enough to transfer to the Web. In other words, the bricks-and-mortar brand values make the e-brand unattractive. In these cases, bricks-and-mortar businesses establish new e-brands that can be perceived as independent from their bricks-and-mortar brands. To decide on their relative brand strategies and manage different brands businesses need to ask themselves the following questions:

- What is my e-brand? Am I enhancing existing brands and/or creating new brands?
- What is the value proposition surrounding our brand/s?

- What visual brand standards will transfer to the Web site and why?

3. Marketing practice

The interactivity of the Web and the ability for e-customers to share information and capture that information against a personal profile provides marketers with new opportunities to get to know e-customers. The Web is the medium that allows marketers to deliver on the market-of-one proposition. On the Web, delivering on a market-of-one proposition involves personalization of information and functionality that results in a customized e-service experience.

In addition, the Web is a service and communications channel that demands more singlemindedness and simplicity than physical channels, because those services and communications have to be delivered intuitively through a user interface. This is a good opportunity for businesses to rationalize and simplify their marketing approach. Marketers must ask themselves the following questions:

- How does customer intelligence change the way we market?
- Can we avoid unnecessary brand and sub-brand proliferation to achieve an integrated and seamless online presence?
- Can we avoid unnecessary product and feature proliferation to make e-customer decision making and selection as clean and convenient as possible?
- What behavior do we want to encourage and what rewards/responses will we provide in relation to particular customer activities/behaviors?

4. Integrated marketing

It has always been important for businesses to engage in integrated marketing where all media channels and their respective marketing messages combine to optimal affect. The Web is another medium that must be integrated into the marketing effort. Marketing strategies and plans should include the Web as much as any other medium. Marketers must ask themselves the following questions:

- How will our marketing approach and activities be integrated with the experience that customers have on our Web site?
  - In what way will marketing messages be tied into (linked) to our Web site?
  - How will existing market relationships be embodied on our Web site? What new relationships can be created?
  - How will content and functionality reflect or support marketing activities?
  - In what ways will our positioning statement be tangibly demonstrated on our Web site?
  - How do we launch new products on the Web, and how is this an integrated part of any product launch plan?

- How do we modify new products or the way we market them—how does this dynamism and process need to be translated into Web site content and design?
- How often do we launch and modify new products, and how will new products be added to our Web site on an ongoing basis?
- How do we plan and manage campaigns, and how will the Web be factored into our planning as a campaign tool?
  - What campaign content will need to be provided on our Web site—how frequent will our campaigns be and how explicitly do we want to link Web site campaign content and promotion in other media?
  - Will we set up separate (but linked) "mini" Web sites for specific campaigns or populate campaign content to a common Web site? (Bear in mind that you can provide different URLs to give customers access to a common Web site and track the effectiveness of different marketing collateral such as direct mail letters or broadcast advertising. You do not have to create a separate Web site to track entry against campaign-specific URLs. Mini sites can be useful in supporting shorter-term banner advertising or sponsorship, but they do make it more difficult for the customer to keep a holistic view of your service offering.)
- How, will integrated marketing activities affect the expected number of visitors to our site; for example, if we include our Web site URL on TV ads, will this cause surges in visitor traffic and when? How do we anticipate and plan for these surges?

5. Audience definition

Marketers need to define e-customers as much as they have always had to define any customer in order to market to them. Marketers must ask themselves the following questions:

- Are we focused on attracting new or existing customers, or do we need to maintain both pursuits in parallel?
- How do we deal with different audiences acquired as a result of unprompted site visits?
- Do we want our audiences to self-select themselves on our Web site?
- Are our audiences local or international?
- Do we need to cater to different levels of e-customers (e.g., novice and savvy users)?
- Do we need to limit the use of some technologies based on the likely PC, connection, and browser version used by our audiences?
- How will visitors find their way to our Web site, where are they likely to be coming from, what are they likely to be prompted by? Knowing this, how can

we make it easier for e-customers to find our Web site (see "Communication" below)?

- How will we use the Web to get to know our e-customers better?

6. Communication

Marketers must know how to optimize the Web as a communications medium, both as part of their marketing mix and in relation to communications required in relation to e-customers in particular.

Marketers should develop Webmarketing plans that detail the online marketing techniques they will use to promote their Web site offering and generate visitors to a business' Web site (see Netography for links to online resources on Webmarketing techniques). In doing so, Marketers should ask themselves the following questions:

- How do I best utilize the Web as a communications medium? Where does the Web fit in our marketing mix?

- How does the Web enhance communication with our e-customers (bearing in mind that the Web is intimate and immediate and allows information "push," where information is sent out to a selected audience as well as information "pull," where audiences select themselves by coming to our Web site)?

- Do we need to educate customers to adopt new online business processes? What do we need to do to encourage customer learning and comfort with new technology and processes?

- To what degree do I need to "sell" to e-customers—how familiar are they with our company and our product and service offering?

- How explicitly will we involve customers online—will they generate their own content for their own viewing or the viewing and comment of others?

- What feedback do we want from customers? Will this be prompted or unprompted? Will we explicitly allow customers to submit complaints, and how will these be resolved?

- How much contribution will e-customers make to Web site development and how explicit will this be? Will we tell e-customers about the changes we've made on the basis of their feedback?

- Who will be involved in generating content on our Web site (in addition to our company), customers, suppliers, related vendors, lobby groups, other contributors?

For example, if you and your customers deal extensively with another third party, your Web site could provide the platform for that third party to directly publish content of use to your customers—this will save you having to create and manage content on behalf of a third party. (Bear in mind, however, that you will need to put controls in place to manage the quality of content populated to your site.)

- What are the benefits and constraints of facilitating cross-customer communication (through community-type components) on our Web site; e.g., do customers wish to remain anonymous, are they hesitant to share precious knowledge that gives them an advantage, or can they all benefit from sharing and pooling their knowledge?
- What Web marketing techniques will we use to increase the number of visitors to our Web site, for example:
  - Register with search engines and Web directories.
    - How will Web site construction and design facilitate easy search by search engines. It is important for the development company to know how meta tags, descriptions, and keywords should be used when building your site. Also the placement of introductory content on each Web page will be important if it is used by search engines that don't reference meta tags (a special tag that provides information about a Web page without affecting the way it is displayed).
  - UseNet newsgroups.
    - Will tnewsgroup participation be a public relations function (since it deals with monitoring what online communities are saying about your organization and contributing to the emergence of opinion and direction in your industry)?
  - "Cool" sites (sites that identify other sites as "cool" or worthy of particular awards).
    - Which cool sites do we want to register with (to try and get nominated as a "cool" site)?
  - Web advertising and sponsorship.
    - Who will establish our Web advertising and sponsorship portfolio—will it be a combination of internal and external resource (possibly utilizing existing relationships with communications/advertising suppliers)?
    - What opportunities exist to leverage existing relationships to provide coverage (links or content) on complementary Web sites? How can all parties get the most value out of this exchange (i.e., over and above traditional practices such as trading links or banner placement)? What content can you "own" on one another's Web sites to optimize value to all parties involved?
  - Online media management.
    - How explicitly will we offer the media content and direction on our Web site? Who will the Web site direct the media to?

- Links.
  - To what extent will we link customers to other people's Web sites? What is the context for this? How do we ensure that this adds value to the customer and not lose Web site visitors to other sites? Who will maintain the quality of those links (i.e., ensure the link to the Web site, and back, is always active)?
  - Many businesses avoid offering links to other Web sites for fear of losing customers to other sites—this is an anticommunity stance and is based on a lack of understanding of the importance of operating within an e-community for the benefit of all e-citizens. Having said that, you have to be smart about the links you provide and where.
- How will we use e-mail as a promotional medium?
  - Will we provide marketing content in automated or manual e-mail responses, such as:
    - Responses to general, or product-specific, inquiries—will we follow up with prompts back to related products and services or special deals on our Web site?
    - Confirmation of a product or service order—how will we affirm our role as a value-added online service provider. Will we provide links to related product deals and after-sales support information and functionality on our Web site?
- What other push content do we want to provide to e-customers (e.g., consider approaches such as that adopted by Amazon with their "Eyes" and "Amazon.com delivers" services)?

Amazon describes its Eyes service as follows:

> Tell it [Eyes] what authors and subjects interest you, and it will track every newly released book matching your interests, author by author and subject by subject. Sign up with Eyes and we'll send you e-mail when the books you want to know about are published.

Amazon describes its "Amazon.com delivers" service as follows:
> Tell us what you like, and our editors will e-mail you recommendations, reviews, articles, and interviews—all tailored to your tastes. Plus, from time to time, your favorite authors, artists or actors will drop you a line.

3. CUSTOMER SERVICE

When defining your customer service requirements you will need to address the following issues:

1. What is our e-service offering?
2. How do we deliver integrated customer service?
3. What stance will we take in relation to service fundamentals such as:
   - What we remember about e-customers.
   - How we identify customers.
   - What service processes we support, and how.

We will consider the questions requiring discussion in relation to each of these issues in turn.

1. E -service offering

- What will our business provide better, smarter, and faster than it does now?
- How can we make existing processes more convenient? What are the main problems our customers currently experience and how can these be addressed? What customer service needs can't be met offline—can these now be served by integrating the Web into our service offering?
- Will the total customer experience be provided online? What other service channels exist and how will these fit with our online service offering (e.g., at what point is a product actually delivered to the customer—who else is involved in this process and should their activities be factored into our interface)?
- What key customer activities will we support online? Which translate from existing service processes and which are new to our company? Which existing processes need to be migrated to an online environment for cost-effectiveness and efficiency?
- What key pieces of utility (useful functionality that allows the customer to get something done) should, and could, we offer? What principal actions can they perform on a regular, and less frequent, basis? What level of utility will customers expect at a minimum?
- What level of customer support will we provide (after-sales service and help using the Web site and services)?

2. Customer integration

- What information needs to be provided to facilitate an e-customer's decision-making processes, i.e., the facts and tools required to enable customers to take a certain action on our Web site?
- What access will customers have to information we hold on them? Will the Web site solicit e-customer information and where will this be held (within the Web site database or within other company databases)?

- Who can we give our e-customers access to (i.e., real people)? Through what combination of media? What e-mail addresses will be given? How will e-mails be routed to the appropriate recipients and how will they be expected to respond? In what timeframe? How will we know whether they've responded? Will we keep a record of customer responses and at what level—a customer level, category level, department level or against some other criteria? Will we analyze customer responses so we can improve our service?

- How can we empower customers to resolve their own problems online (e.g., by giving them access to internal databases, involving them in the creation and use of knowledge bases and discussion forums, and by providing frequently asked questions (FAQs) and linking these meaningfully to the things we know customers will be trying to do, and, most probably, having difficulty with)?

- What different transactions will customers be able to make? Which of these are financial? Who within the business is responsible for processing them? Within what timeframe? How will we know when the transaction is processed? How will we know whether what we have provided has met e-customer expectations? Will we keep a record of customer transactions and at what level will they be held?

- When is the customer integrated into other business processes? When is the customer able to change or affect business processes and at what point? Will we invite the customer to participate in some businesses process, e.g., in the product development process?

It can be useful to simply draw the process-flow of the main interactions customers need to have with us. An example of one particular Web site's process flow is shown in Figure 4-2

As can be seen if Figure 4-2, this company is at an early stage of customer integration. It will not have connectivity with internal systems and cannot respond in real time. This means that it has had to identify which service interactions will be fielded initially by phone (via its existing call center) and which can be dealt with by e-mail. (Note that this basic drawing can be overlaid with other factors, such as the identification of likely usage by audience (in this case "prospective customers"), to build up Web site concepts over time.

3. Service fundamentals

Memory

- How much does the e-customer expect us to know about them? How can we manage these expectations if we do not have access to that level of knowledge?

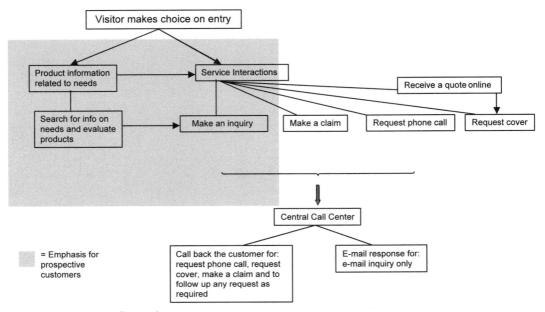

Figure 4-2 Process-flow of e-customers' main service interactions.

- How much of what e-customers tell us do we want to remember and why?
- What personal details do we expect e-customers to have to rekey within each visit or each time they visit?
- Should we know the service activities of particular individuals? Should customers be able to access a history of their own service activities?
- What minimum personal information do we require? Will we solicit free-form comments and what will we do with them?
- What anchors are required for the e-customer to follow up a service request, e.g., a query or order number?
- How does our company feel about the use of cookies (text files stored on the customer's browser and used to identify the customer each time they visit our site)?

Customer identification

- Do different customers have different privileges—can they access information or functionality that others can't, why? How will e-customers, with no privileges, respond to this and what considerations should be factored into Web site design, e.g., how should privileged audiences be dealt with as opposed to those who are not? Do privileged and nonprivileged audiences share information and functionality, or will they have an independent experience?

- Do I need to authenticate customers? What method of authentication is most meaningful to our customers, (e.g., do we use authentication in other media already—through an IVR (Interactive Voice Response) interface to our phone system)? Do we want to provide a common authentication method across media? Does authentication already provide some customers with access to internal systems? If so, what method of authentication will be compatible with these internal systems? (Some different methods include PIN numbers, account number, name and password.)

Service process

- How can we provide easy and quick access to frequently required service requests and activities? Should this quick access be on entry to the site, throughout the site, or only in certain areas of the site?

- How can we make our service processes transparent to e-customers? How many stages of the process can we make visible on our Web site? What aspects of our service process does the e-customer need to interact with and/or change?

- Are we serving customers in real time? What information and functionality are time-critical, i.e., the customer must have current information to act as a customer, e.g., flight cancellation information)? Which interactions make things happen right there and then? Which interactions have delayed results? What will customers expect and how should we manage these expectations?

- What facts does a customer need to make choices and selections (e.g., is price required to transact)? What details does the customer need to provide to complete the transaction, at each stage in the process? How can these be provided? What is the necessary flow of the transaction process (e.g., placing an order)?

- It can be useful to simply draw a picture of the necessary flow of a particular service process. The more direction you give the Web site designer, the better. They will translate your directions into screen and information design. Exactly how the process will work online will, to some extent, depend on the level of connectivity you have with internal systems (i.e., what information you know and what information you need to get from the e-customer) and what technologies you are using to develop the Web site (some technologies give you less ability to engineer processes than others, such as those that come "out of a box"). Such an exercise is the beginning of your business process improvement endeavor, and this is explained, along with the drawing of an e-customer's order process in Chapter 5 under "Process Improvements".

- What common customer problems and complaints can we anticipate and how can we address them online (e.g., with FAQs?).

- How can e-mail be crafted to help customers make common inquiries?
  - By designing e-mail forms around common activities and inquiries, you make things easier for e-customers. In addition, the way you design those forms will make things easy, or difficult, for your company to deal with—the clearer you are about the exact nature of the inquiry, the more efficiently you will be able to deal with it.

On their "Contact Us" screen, Bank of America offers access to e-mail forms along with FAQs (see Figure 4-3). If customers cannot find what they're looking for within the FAQs, they can use an e-mail form to send a specific inquiry. (Note, you have to be careful how you design this, however; while you want to be helpful, you don't want to get in the way of an e-customer making an inquiry.)

The Bank of America "Contact Us" screen is shown in Figure 4-3.

You may want to use e-mail forms in relation to specific service requests, such as:

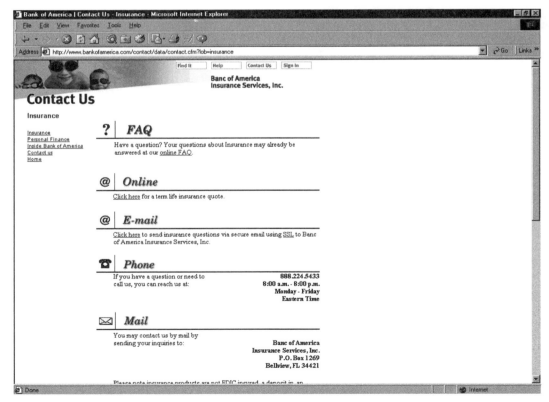

Figure 4-3 Bank of America's "Contact Us" screen combines e-mail and FAQs.

- Product inquiry.
- Campaign inquiry (relative to integrated marketing campaigns).
- Requests for more information (you may make other marketing or business collateral available on your Web site).
- Policy questions.
- Activating a specific service request (e.g., order, register, update personal details, view account history, track or follow up on delivery, discontinue a product or service).
- Making a change to a product or service.
- Reporting a problem with a problem or service (e.g., a fault).
- Feedback (on the Web site and placed in the context of service interactions to get feedback on specific service processes).
- Paying or querying an invoice.
- Calling (requesting to be contacted by phone).
- Applying for a job with your company.

- Will e-mail be automatically routed within the company? If so, what criteria will this routing be made against (e.g., according to type of request, recipient, geography and/or degree of urgency)?
- What service level will we communicate to e-customers before and after they have completed a service request? What will the e-customer be told about what will happen next? What information should be provided to the e-customer to allow them to follow-up their request?
- What response do e-customers get when they submit a service request; e.g., do they get an automated e-mail response—if so, what will it tell them? Will an automated response include information that might help customers while they wait for a resolution (e.g., sending FAQs or links back as part of automated responses)? What messages do customers need to feel comfortable that we have received their order correctly and will deliver what we have promised?

- If we are engaged in financial transactions, what payment mechanisms can we, or do we want to, support (e.g., credit cards and/or billing against existing accounts)?
- What data needs to be validated at the point of entry; i.e., do we want to dynamically gauge the quality of the information provided as it is provided by e-customers? What data validation rules will apply? What will be mandatory fields (i.e., what fields will e-customers absolutely have to fill in for us to do our job)? How will we make it obvious to e-customers what are mandatory fields and what our data rules are, so they can enter information right the first time and avoid the frustration of having to go backward and forward to get data accepted?

- What service processes do we require feedback on? Who will receive this feedback and what will happen to it? Will it contribute to service improvements, how? What are the most appropriate places to solicit customer feedback?

    - Consider placing requests for feedback right in the context where the service process is being used, such as in the case of Amazon where it invites customers to send feedback after setting up its Eyes service: "If you don't think this free service is both cool and useful, please send mail to feedback@amazon.com and tell us why."

4. WEB SITE CHARACTERISTICS

There are many decisions you will make about the nature of your Web site, in conjunction with your Web site development company. The ones I have covered here seem to be the decisions that need attention early on as part of requirement definition.

To get a better background understanding of how your Web site development company goes about developing your Web site, see Chapter 6. For now, we will consider the areas you may want to provide some direction on early in the process, as follows:

1. Will we offer some Web site components and not others?
2. What does our Web site's information design need to achieve?
3. What does our Web site's navigational system need to achieve?
4. What, and how much, interactivity will we provide to e-customers?
5. What kind of content will we provide to e-customers?
6. What reports do we need on e-customer interactions?

1. Web site components

- Will we expect e-customers to make software downloads to be able to optimally use the site? Will we present documents in downloadable format such as PDF format?

- What level of graphics and/or animation is acceptable? What standards will apply to ensure quick page downloads in the context of our user environment?

- Will we open windows within windows ("child windows") to differentiate between different sources of content?

- What explicit "community" components will we use (e.g., discussion forums, chat groups, billboards, and/or threaded discussions)? Will these be mediated or unmediated? If they are unmediated, how will we ensure a participant's quality experience?

- What will be searchable on the site? At what levels does search operate and what is the scope in relation to each search function? What search criteria are most meaningful in each case? (See the discussion of search design in Chapter 7 under "Navigation" and "Anchors.")

2. Information design

- What is the scope of information housed on our Web site? How will that scope change over time? What contexts need to be created now for expanded use later on (i.e., what future proofing needs to occur now)?

- In what ways can information be bundled, or classified, to make sense to e-customers? What information needs to be provided around transactions and service processes to facilitate ease of use? What are the key selections e-customers will make when dealing with our company (i.e., who they are [self-selection] or what they do [activity selection] or what they need to know [knowledge selection]?

- What comparisons do customers need to make between our products and services, and those of our competitors, and how can our information design facilitate comparison?

- Do we need to create strong relationships between information on certain products and services (e.g., as a result of packaging or solutions provision)? How will these be made explicit within our information design?

- How will, or should, different user privileges affect information design? Who should be made aware when, and why, privileges exist, and how do we manage the expectations of nonprivileged customers or prospects?

- How will the structure of the company be reflected in the Web site, if at all?

- Will the site be central or de-central (i.e., one site with content areas or several related sites that can operate quite independently)?

- What metaphors do our e-customers already understand, from existing applications or service experiences within the industry or across related industries?

3. Navigation system

- How familiar is our audience with different navigation systems and what are we able to maintain? What degree of complexity is acceptable?

- Do we require the navigation system to singularly apply across the Web site, or are we happy for different navigation systems to operate in different areas of the site?

- How changeable will different areas of content be—which ones will be the most volatile and how can we build a navigation framework that will allow us to make the necessary changes over time (i.e., what future proofing is required now)?

- What is time-critical information or utility and how visible, and accessible, does this need to be (i.e., does it need to be part of the navigation system, or a shortcut within the navigation system)?

4. Level and nature of interactivity

- Will we offer decision support to e-customers? If we make recommendations to e-customers, what criteria will these be based on, and how will we access, or solicit, the necessary e-customer information to be able to make meaningful recommendations?

- Will we allow e-customers to build personal profiles? Will these profiles capture all, or part, of an e-customer's activities within a visit and over time (i.e,. can e-customers save and retrieve their profile or is a profile active only during one continuous visit)? Will e-customers be able to change the information contained in their profile?

- What level of help will be provided to e-customers—in relation to use of the Web site, completing transactions, and resolving other service problems? Where are customers likely to encounter problems? Will we utilize existing support staff or channel inquiries somewhere else (in-house or external)?

5. Nature of content

- How familiar are e-customers with our products and services? Do we need to cover product and service information available in other media—which aspects are necessary and which are redundant? What new, value-added information could be provided to build on what e-customers already know?

- How much should similar information be standardized? (And how does this translate into how content is generated, stored, and presented via the navigation system?)

- What layering of information is required? How much scrolling is necessary, and how can we chunk information and present it efficiently and effectively?

6. Reporting requirements

- What standard Web site usage statistics do we require to assess the volume and nature of visitors?

- What tailored reporting is required to relate any stored customer data with usage data to create additional understanding of e-customers and their Web site usage? Who will hold the necessary data, and who will perform the collation, analysis, and generation of reports?

THE REQUIREMENT DEFINITION PROCESS

Having covered best-practice fundamentals in e-servicing and questions that businesses need to ask themselves, we will now consider a process that busienesses can use to develop a statement of their requirements.

The proposed requirement definition process comprises six stages that progress the business from its big-picture requirements through to specifics. This statement of requirements will form the basis for initial concept testing with external customers and the brief for the development company/s.

The process-flow diagram in Figure 4-4 illustrates the six stages of the requirement definition process.

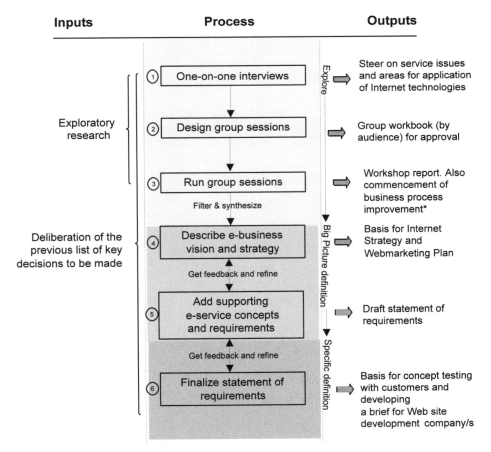

*Identification of business process occurs along with discussion of improvement. This becomes very specific, by process, during development (see Chapter 6)

Figure 4-4 The six-stage requirement definition process.

As much as we want to use narrative, metaphor, and scenario to enrich our understanding of e-customers, we also want it to enrich the business's vision for, and understanding of, the ways in which it will serve e-customers.

The main forum for this internal story creation, is the "group session." The group session provides a creative context for companies to explore their e-business strategy from a number of different vantage points all grounded in what e-customers need and want. A representative cross-section of the company should be involved in the group sessions, from strategy makers through to people who deal with customers ear to ear, or face to face.

Preparing for, facilitating, and translating the results from the group sessions is demanding because it requires a good understanding of the relevant e-environment and e-customers. Whether you use external consultants to facilitate the group sessions, and the requirement definition process, is up to you. The key is to ensure that the people driving the process don't miss opportunities for your company to create competitive advantage, by either missing the big picture or detail relative to the business you are in.

Of course, at the time of requirement definition, compaines don't have perfect information about what customers want, and need, from them. While exploratory research gives companies a lead on e-service opportunities and constraints, companies have to go through the requirement definition process before they can put some definite ideas in front of e-customers for feedback.

During requirement definition, companies have to put some stakes in the ground about what e-customers want, and need, from them. Then, once their ideas are better formed, companies will be able to assess, and revise, their requirements on the basis of e-service concept testing. This revision will be made before the Web site designer is briefed, to ensure that the requisite Web site is customer-effective. Oftentimes, the revised statement of requirements becomes the brief provided to the Web site designer. (An example of a brief's content is given later in this chapter.)

In addition to kicking off the briefing process, requirement definition also kicks off business process improvement and the formulation of an Internet strategy and Web marketing plan. Business process improvement gets kicked off because requirement definition requires the business to identify processes and consider how they could be improved. Then, more rigorous examination of each process would occur later in the development phase of the project. (Business process improvement is covered in Chapter 5.)

To help you formulate and plan your own requirement definition process, we will look at each of the six stages in more detail.

1. Conduct one-on-one interviews

The design of the group sessions is key to their success. You may have only three hours in which to guide group members through a process by which they can describe what they think needs to be done for e-customers, and you'll get only one shot at it. A three-hour investment is a lot these days, and you'll need to do a top-notch job.

By conducting some one-on-one interviews before designing the group sessions, you can get a feel for some of the current service dynamics and issues and discuss some initial thoughts on the application of Internet technologies. The responses you get will give you a good sense of the areas you must address in the group sessions and relevant case studies and customer scenarios to explore.

You should interview a representative sample of company participants—but don't go overboard; you want a flavor of what's going on in the company and not the recipe. A good facilitator will be able to adapt the group session to take into account new information and perspectives as they come out.

Interviewing people from different areas in the company will also help you decide on the best makeup of the group sessions. You'll need to put participants into groups of up to twelve, and finding commonalties within groups makes for more effective facilitation and more interactive group sessions. Interviews will also give you a picture of the different levels of understanding within the company, so you can design around them.

2. Design group sessions

Through hands-on experience, I have found the following basic agenda to work very well:

1. Introduction to the Internet and e-servicing.
2. Introduction of a model for thinking about application of the Internet.
3. Exploration of some case studies and sites illustrating different approaches.
4. Group application of the model to participant's own business situation.
5. Groups presentations.
6. Central discussion of ideas, issues, and next steps to wrap up.

Overall the process flow is:

1. Educate.
2. Create a meaningful frame of reference.
3. Apply.

As companies become more familiar with the Internet and e-servicing, the need to educate participants on the characteristics of e-servicing, and the fundamentals of best practice, will reduce. However, it is useful to establish some agreed-on ways of thinking about e-servicing before you get started. Then looking at a range of different Web sites, and discussing them as a group, will create a very rich context for thinking about the company's own approach.

You will have time to look at only bytes of other Web sites, so you need to do a lot of preparation to decide which parts of those Web sites will create the most meaningful context for discussion. Generally, I find that focusing on two or three competitive sites and a completely off-the-wall (seemingly), nonrelated, site works best. Putting participants face to face with the world as e-customers experience it can be a sobering experience for them, and they will quickly react to what they are seeing by demanding a higher standard of performance from themselves.

3. Run group sessions

I use models as triggers to help companies think about what they need to develop to serve e-customers better, smarter, and faster online. The models are useful frameworks for thinking about things. Some professionals are happy to use very free techniques, such as inviting participants to create free-form pictures, mind maps, or whatever else channels their creativity. Free techniques are good for visioning and less useful for gathering the detail needed for requirement definition.

Of course, you could run two lots of group sessions, rather than one. The first lot of group sessions could be dedicated to visioning (and utilize more free techniques) while the second lot of groups can be dedicated to fleshing out the vision. I find that, for the purposes of alignment and buy-in, it is best to keep everyone involved as much as possible, and running one lot of group sessions helps achieve that. In addition, the logistics of running two lots of group sessions involving the same people can be prohibitive, and I find that one session can be designed to give birth to vision and concepts; as well as explore them (because the two pursuits are intertwined anyway).

I have found two models to provide meaningful triggers, and the two models and their respective uses are discussed below.

Model 1

The first model shown in Figure 4-5 works well within companies that have identifiable "exchanges" with customers; in the form of information exchanges and sales and service processes, for example.

Model 1 simply gives us a way to illustrate how we relate to different groups of customers; to think about the nature of the different exchanges we have with them and how the Internet can be applied. And because the Internet is an active medium, we can also associate specific outcomes to each application of the Internet. This helps remind us of the behaviors and responses we are creating.

Model 1 can be used to consider the application of Internet technologies across a range of audiences such as internal audiences or other suppliers and vendors. In this way, companies can think generically about the application of Internet technologies, and these may be translated into related intranet and extranet requirements. Sometimes there is an intuitive fit between Inter-, Intra- and Extranet requirements, and this fit can be explored efficiently and holistically in one group session.

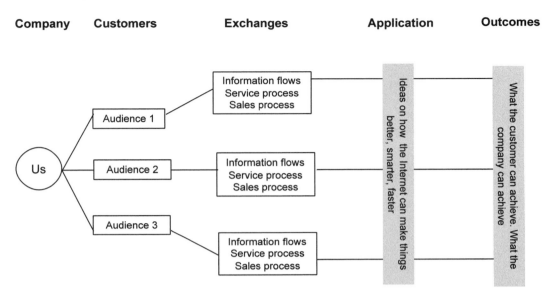

Figure 4-5 A workshop model for exploring the application of the Internet to audience-specific exchanges.

I have found Model 1 to be successful because it helps participants break things down simply into people, actions, and applications. The process of identifying audiences tends to be intuitive; people identify groups of people according to the nature of the exchanges they have with them. Audience identification is not meant to be a rigorous customer segmentation exercise and is not treated as such.

Also, in thinking about how the Internet is applied, participants are not expected to suddenly become Internet gurus or Web designers. Rather, participants think in general terms about how Internet characteristics help facilitate better customer exchanges (and those characteristics, and examples of how they have been applied, are discussed earlier in the same group session).

And because we start by identifying customers, and the nature of the exchanges they have with the company, a customer-centric focus is inherently adopted and carried through the application of Model 1.

In applying Model 1, participants complete five activities, as follows:

1. Identify key audience groups.

2. Identify the key exchanges that currently exist between the company and customers, and the nature of those exchanges.

3. What are the outcomes of those exchanges for customers and the company?

4. Identify any ways the Internet could improve those exchanges and outcomes.

5. Are there other exchanges that would also add value to the customer? Identify whether there are desired outcomes not currently met through existing, or known, exchanges, or exchanges that could create new outcomes for customers.

Model 2

The second model, shown in Figure 4-6, works well within companies that have quite different areas of emphasis for different customer groups; and that need to understand and explore the differences in those emphases.

Model 2 shows the relative stages within the marketing and sales cycle and follows this with a curve, along which various customer groups can be placed. The placement of Audiences 1–3 below is hypothetical and would translate to Audience 1 principally requiring after-sales support, Audience 2 principally requiring sales, and Audience 3 requiring presales support. Different audiences could require quite different areas of emphasis because of their different nature and the different service offering the company offers within different service contexts. Establishing different areas of emphasis up front can help avoid a one-size-fits-all mentality creeping in later on.

Of course, the two models can be used together or with different groups within the same company. Model 2 is easily understood by marketing and sales-oriented people while Model 1 is easily understood by customer service personnel (mind you, neither model is particularly demanding and should be understood by all company participants).

In applying Model 2, participants complete five activities, as follows:

1. Identify key target audiences (groups that are similar or do similar things).

2. Consider marketing and sales activities with each audience.

3. Identify the role of the Internet in helping facilitate these marketing and sales activities. Where do they sit on the curve? What is the relative value proposition?

4. Given where customers sit on the curve, what "experience" (interactivity and content) is required to "encourage" e-customers to complete marketing and sales activities?

5. What do the customer and company achieve from partaking in the Web site experience?

While questions are provided to help participants apply the models, each group (within a group session) tends to adopt its own approach. The questions are provided only to answer the first question every group asks itself before embarking on a joint activity—"So, what are we doing?"

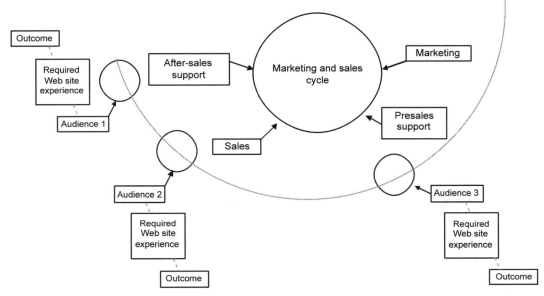

Figure 4-6 A model for placing different audiences within the marketing and sales cycles.

Groups will present back using flip charts and notes. It's always worth encouraging groups to write as much down as possible, so you have a record for later. Sometimes a recording of the session also helps establish, at least, an audio memory of the occasion. I find an audio record useful when issues come up and I haven't fully understood them, or had time to explore them. By going back and replaying the comment, I can explore the issue and catch something, potentially, vital.

A workshop report would be generated as a result of the group sessions. This report should capture the core activities of the groups, their outputs, and the issues discussed. The workshop report can include an emergent vision statement, or this can be synthesized and distributed separately. The benefit of combining the vision statement with more specific requirements identified in the workshop report is that it creates more tangibility and results in increased impetus and buy-in within the company.

4. Describe E-business Vision and Strategy

You will get a lot of output from your group sessions, a lot of great ideas and a surprising amount of detail about possible initiatives and areas the company needs to address. At this stage, the idea is to gather the central thoughts of all that output and formulate a central vision. Doing this first gives you a platform from which you can achieve organizational alignment and filter and synthesize all the detail you have to to produce a list of requirements for the company's approval.

Oftentimes, the statement of e-business strategy and vision will be part of the executive summary of the workshop report. This allows participants and other organizational stakeholders to see quickly how the strategy and vision were arrived at.

5. Add supporting e-service concepts and requirements

The person involved in translating the workshop output into an initial statement of requirements bears a great responsibility. He or she must find common themes in a diverse, and possibly eclectic, array of group-generated information. And he or she must add value to the information that has been generated by finding additional meaning as a result of collation and additional deliberation. Rather than just regurgitating participant inputs, you will be looking for common e-service concepts and their supporting requirements.

Sometimes it can help to go back to the people who were interviewed in the one-on-one interviews and "sanity check" some of the themes and concepts that come out of all the group-generated information.

6. Finalize statement of requirements

After another round (or two) of feedback from participants and stakeholders, you should have arrived at the final statement of requirements. Well, as final as it will get at this stage prior to concept testing with customers. Requirements may then be revised as a result of customer feedback before briefing the Web site's development company/s.

And a final tip relating to the presentation of the company's requirements: you will facilitate quicker signoff from company stakeholders by centering everything on scenarios of what e-customers want, and need, to do.

THE BRIEF

Your statement of requirements will form the basis of the brief you give to your development company/s. As discussed earlier, when you revise your requirements on the basis of customer feedback, your revision may well become the brief itself (i.e., your requirement definition and brief can be the same document).

The brief should communicate the vision and e-service concepts that have come out of your requirement definition process and should also address many of the pertinent decisions covered under "key decisions you have to make." Figure 4-7 outlines the contents of a sample brief you may wish to adapt to suit your purposes.

Introduction or background

Context for the project

E-business environment being recognized and addressed.

Competitive environment being recognized and addressed.

E-customer opportunities and constraints.

Task (of this supplier as differentiated from other suppliers)

Vision

} These may differ across stages of project implementation

Objectives

Audiences
Characteristics, behavior, technological proficiency, hardware and software constraints.

E-service concepts

What customers will be able to do (scenarios).

Requisite content (types of content and known content areas). ⇒ Will feed into the company's content process

Requisite functionality
Use of e–mail
Search functionality
Help functionality (online and offline)
Interactive components such as calculators or decision support
Service processes and transactions made ⇒ Will feed into the company's business process
Community components (such as billboards, threaded discussions and chat) improvement initiatives
Push content
User identification and authentication
Customer profiling
Reporting and analysis

Infrastructural context
Technical architecture of current system, and policies and constraints for systems development, along with business process implications.

Branding and presentation requirements

Product and service coverage
List of products and services the Web site covers, probably as an appendix.

Budget parameters

} These will need to be confirmed with the Web site development company/s as part of product specification

Project timeline

Figure 4-7 An example of brief content.

There are a number of areas, such as business process improvement and content identification and generation, that start in the requirement definition stage and are continued in the development stage. There are also a lot of other processes and activities that the company needs to complete during development. And these activities are the subject of the next chapter.

CHAPTER 5

E-SERVICE DEVELOPMENT AND IMPLEMENTATION

> *Now you're working with your suppliers*
> *to make your vision a reality.*
> *How well you set up your infrastructure, and work with your suppliers,*
> *will determine how customer-effective you end up being.*

Some companies are in such a hurry to enter the e-business fray that they just don't do what is necessary. Typically, these companies end up dumping too much responsibility on their suppliers, who end up, inevitably, not rising to the occasion.

No one knows your business, or your customers, as well as you do—it's your job to engineer your project, your processes, and your content for customer-effectiveness. And you must provide your Web site development company with as much concrete information as it needs to deliver the requisite experience to your e-customers. Contrary to what seems a common belief, Web site designers can't use "their intuition" to design your customer-effective Web site—they need a lot of help and direction from you.

In this chapter we will look at how to set up your project, handle the often-elusive process of product specification, deal with the content challenge, practically address business process improvement, and work with your supplier for customer-effective results.

SETTING UP THE PROJECT

In Chapter 1 we established that creating customer-effective Web sites is a multi-faceted endeavor requiring the integration of many skills within and across companies and their suppliers. An integrated project team and project methodology are required to bring all the disciplines and skills together.

Books have been written on project management (see Bibliography) and I'm not here to reinvent the wheel. My focus is on guiding you on the types of people required to do get everything done and the necessary relationships and tools to ensure things get done well.

THE INTEGRATED PROJECT TEAM

The integrated project team relies on partnership between a company and its suppliers. That partnership translates to matching roles and responsibilities within and across the company and its suppliers. And the roles on the company and supplier sides match requisite project activities to skills.

It is important to strike a balance between minimizing necessary communication flows to ensure everyone knows what is going on and not having so many chiefs that it takes forever to make a decision. To address this, and recognize the important composite activities that must be discreetly recognized and managed, I have described the project team as made up of three core groups:

1. Management team.

   This team is responsible for directing the project. They are responsible for major decisions throughout the life of the project, such as:
   - Setting e-business strategy and defining strategic e-service concepts.
   - Managing project resourcing.
   - Approving items at each milestone.
   - Providing direction within their own organization to ensure integrated activity and quality deliverables.

2. Requirement owners.

   This team is responsible for the day-to-day, week-to-week, running of the project. Together, requirement owners are responsible for defining the company's requirements and seeing them met. They are hands-on with the design, development, and implementation of e-servicing and are involved with:
   - Being the day-to-day points of contact for development related to their business area.
   - Contributing to the development of e-service concepts.
   - Defining and clarifying requirements related to their area.
   - Actively participating in the requirement definition process.
   - Reviewing all relevant project documentation and raising issues as required.
   - Determining the most appropriate service and technical infrastructure and ensuring its implementation.

Sometimes it will be most effective for requirement owners to deal with central contacts within supplier companies (such as the project manager and producer) and sometimes dialogue will be required with developers themselves.

3. Activity owners.

    I have identified this separately, even though it crosses over requirement ownership, because it is important to explicitly recognize these processes—to ensure they receive the adequate level of focus and resource required.

    Of course, people can be activity owners as well as requirement owners, but this may not necessarily be the case. Some activities will require specialized and dedicated resource, in the areas of testing, content management and process design, for example. Activity owners contribute to requirement definition because they understand a level of detail that others don't, but they may not be held directly responsible for the definition and implementation of those requirements.

The matching of personnel in the three core groups can be seen in Figure 5-1.

As seen in Figure 5-1, the strategic visionary and customer advocate are also required to act as "glue" between the company and suppliers. Strategic visioning and customer advocacy are ways of behaving more than roles, however, someone within the integrated project team needs to keep the strategic vision or "big picture" alive, and the customer advocate needs to keep the customer at the forefront of development.

Sometimes a key person involved in testing acts as customer advocate, and he or she works closely with the strategic visionary to help reconcile customer and business needs and goals. Sometimes the strategic visionary is from within the management team, and sometimes not. The strategic visionary has to be objective enough to not get bogged down in detail but familiar enough with project issues and decisions to be able to lead in the right direction.

INTEGRATED PROJECT TOOLS

Project Charter

Once you have selected the Web site development company/s you want to work with, you may want to establish a charter for the project. The charter details the project team members, their roles and responsibilities and contact details, the project process or methodology, and the milestones of the project. The charter would probably be put together jointly by the company and supplier's project managers, in consultation with other team members.

A charter can be particularly useful when there are a number of parties involved in the project, and clarity is required to know who is doing what, what the most appropriate channels of communication are, and what the agreed-on development process is (different development companies sometimes adopt differ-

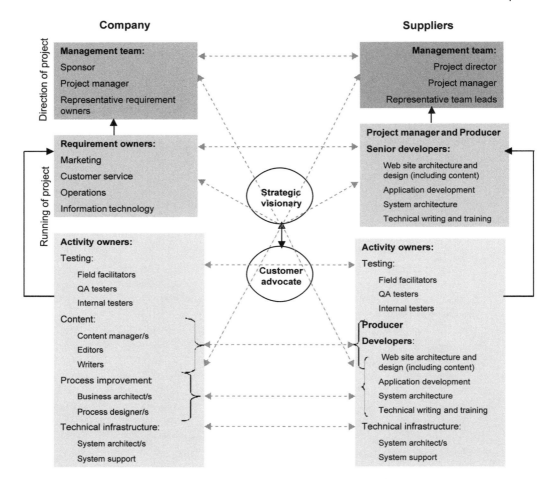

Figure 5-1 The integrated project team.

ent processes, and businesses also have process requirements that need to be reconciled). If this clarity is not required, then don't bother with the charter; there is no need to create unnecessary bureaucracy.

The charter is not a project plan or a service level agreement; it is, however, a practical guide to the project for all parties involved. The following areas can be covered within the document:

- *Project purpose.* A statement of why the project exists and how its success will be measured. This statement may come directly from the project sponsor.

- *Project fundamentals.* You may want to note down some of the guiding tenets of the project if they are of particular significance to working together effectively. Otherwise, avoid stating the obvious unless you feel it needs to be stated.

- *Roles and Responsibilities.* You may like to use Figure 5-1 as a guide, just to make sure you cover all the bases. The more parties involved in the project, the more detail is required on the delineation of responsibilities.

- *Milestones.* Project milestones are shown in Figure 5-2. (Note these milestones build on, and augment, Figure 1-2 which depicts the broad responsibilities of an integrated development team):

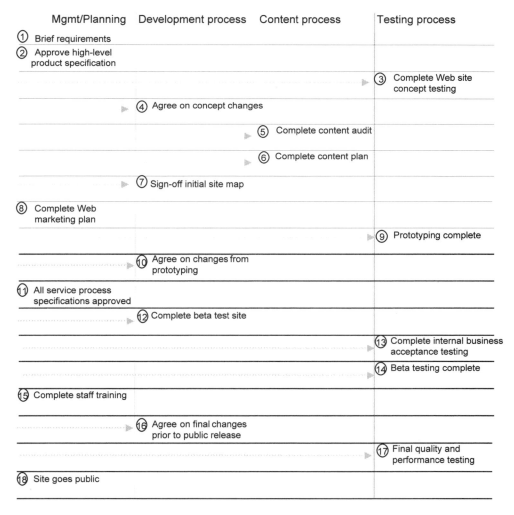

Figure 5-2 Integrated project milestones.

- *Project considerations.* You may like to identify any red flags, such as intra- or interproject dependencies that could impact on the process and timings.

Project Web site

The charter could be available online as part of a project Web site (or extranet accessible to the integrated project team and other affiliated stakeholders).

The project Web site adds a whole other dimension to the charter because it allows you to dynamically keep track of what's happening throughout the life of the project. The charter is a good starter for the project, but the project Web site allows you to support integrated activity on an ongoing basis.

The project Web site could even help facilitate group decision making, allowing sign offs or exceptions to be centrally captured and addressed online.

A possible project Web site concept is shown in Figure 5-3.

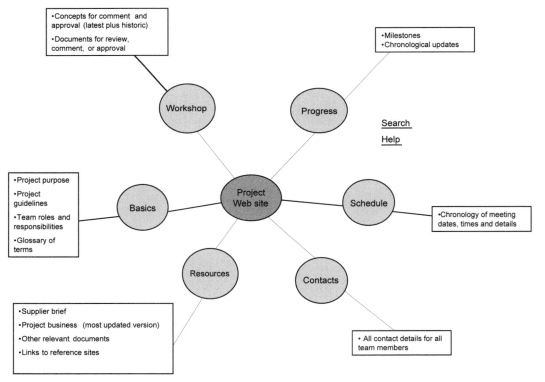

Figure 5-3 Concept for a project Web site.

Despite their obvious usefulness, and the best intentions, project Web sites often don't eventuate, because everyone is too anxious to get on with the "real" project development. Also, some of the functionality that could be used in developing the project Web site may be developed as part of the project proper, making development of the project Web site premature in the development process. However, it is worth putting something together as best you can at the beginning of the project and adding to it as more sophisticated functionality is developed.

The project Web site can be housed and maintained by the business or Web site development company. Chances are, however, that the development company already has such sites operable for other clients and may be able to adapt the concept to your project. Secretsites.com gives an example of a template project site, such as a development company could adapt to each project.

PRODUCT SPECIFICATION

The "product specification" is something we have inherited from the traditional software development process. It is the document by which the product, as it will be designed and developed, is described in detail, and agreed on, before work commences. It has acted as a contractual agreement as much as a guide for development.

However, even in the world of traditional software development, the "product specification" has become problematic. The assumption that software can be document-driven has been the subject of debate since about 1970, when the "waterfall model" was first introduced. The waterfall model stipulates that software development is stepwise; development occurs in successive stages. One stage flows into the next like a waterfall. However, a primary source of difficulty with the model has been its emphasis on full documentation of development prior to design and development.

The document-driven approach has been found to work in only a few cases where systems are small and unsophisticated and not the product of programming in higher-generation languages. In most cases, however, the attempt to complete full documentation early has led to the specification of poorly understood user interfaces and decision support functions, followed by the design and development of large quantities of unusable code.

If this has been the experience in traditional software development, it is even more so in the case of Web-based development. Web development uses rapid and iterative design techniques and technologies, and this can be difficult to plan for. In addition, the integration of Web technologies into business tends to be more far-reaching in its effect, and not all process changes and requirements can be anticipated from day one.

In a knee-jerk reaction to the waterfall model and its emphasis on upfront and detailed specification, evolutionary models, that allowed development to evolve without upfront and detailed specification, were explored. However, these were found to be too loose, leading to a lack of coordination and direction in the design and development process.

Perhaps we need an approach that gives us the best of both worlds, a way of documenting what will be built and creating enough flexibility for requirements and development to evolve during the development process.

PRODUCT SPECIFICATION PROCESS

Here I will describe an approach I have seen to be fairly workable in large-scale projects.

The approach requires the development company to establish a product specification in response to the company's brief. That specification deals with what is known and expected at the time it is written. Then, during the development process addenda are added to the product specification. These addenda are succinct descriptions of more fully defined process components, as they become known. These process components are likely to reflect the progress made with business process improvement and the particular processes that become necessary to activate the Web site in a live production environment.

A product specification process is shown in Figure 5-4.

The initial product specification defines the scope of operability the company expects the Web site development company to deliver (so this acknowledges the work completed in the addenda, without trying to define it beyond the level of knowledge held at the time).

Pinning down deliverables can be a very challenging problem, sometimes leaving development companies in the position where they do far more work than they ever, perhaps, expected, or get remunerated for (although the inverse can also occur!). Deliverables get blurred because of the dynamic and evolutionary characteristics of Web development.

The traditional idea of delivering a "release" of software does not transfer to Web development because the job is just never done. How do we know when the development company's job is done? It is difficult for development companies to draw that line in the sand and say "we've done our job," and companies need to be sensitive to that. All I can suggest is a process of review or "reflection" at agreed-on project milestones where both parties fairly assess what has been delivered against the scope of operability agreed in the initial specification.

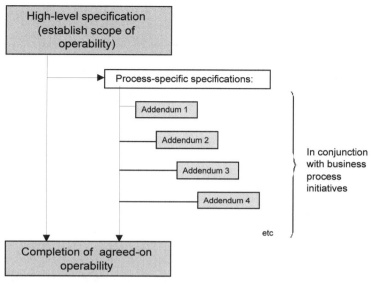

Figure 5-4 A proposed product specification process.

THE SPECIFICATION DOCUMENT

The specification will deconstruct the company's brief into discrete components that they must use to design, build and support the Web site system. The development company takes your ideas and turns them into the nuts and bolts of a Web application.

Figure 5-5 presents the content you may expect to see in a specification.

Of course, this figure is closely aligned to Figure 4-7 depicting the content of a company's brief. The brief and the specification may be an RFP (Request for Proposal) request and response; however, I have not made that assumption, because I believe that the market will start to move away from this very costly and time-consuming way of awarding business.

THE CONTENT CHALLENGE

Most commentators, writing from experience, testify to the fact that the biggest roadblock in developing Web sites on time is not technological or infrastructural as you might expect, but absence of necessary content. And how many Web sites,

---

Introduction or background
Our understanding of your strategy and objectives.

Task
Definition of the scope of deliverables in terms of expected system operability. This may be detailed against staged development should this be a requirement of the project.

Required e-customer experience
Holistic description of the experience that the intended system will create for different e-customers. This anticipates the combined affects of design, development, and the supporting technical infrastructure.

Functional components
Holistic description of the experience that the intended system will create for different e-customers.

    For example, specification of:
        Use of e-mail
        Search functionality
        Help functionality (online and offline)
        Interactive components such as calculators or decision support
        Service processes and transactions made
        Community components (such as billboards, threaded discussions, and chat)
        Push content
        User identification and authentication
        Customer profiling
        Reporting and analysis

Content management
Description of the content management capabilities of the system and the related content management processes.

Technical architecture
Recommended technical architecture and technologies used for design, building and ongoing support.

 Budget

 Project timeline

Figure 5-5 An example of specification content.

sadly, go live to the public with great design and functionality and vapid content? Why does this happen?

UNDERSTANDING THE CONTENT CHALLENGE

If we better understand the content challenge perhaps we will be able to manage it better.

Businesses often get overwhelmed by the amount of content they need to generate. This is largely because they underestimate the volume of content that needs to be generated—they assume the necessary content already exists, in some form within the company or on an existing Web site. All they will need to do is put it online, right? Wrong. Generally, the content that already exists will need to be significantly remodeled to fit your Web site, or written from scratch.

First, this is because Web sites create experiences—content is contextual. The content you already have may sit in a context totally different from what it needs. Second, the content you already have offline might be as welcome in the online medium as a runaway wild pig in your (recently vacuumed) living room. And third, you may now want to have more real and intimate dialogue with your e-customers because you know them better and you're changing the way you market. You now want to use a completely different tone of voice, one that is more intimate and impersonal.

Oftentimes, it is late in a project before a company catches on to the scope of the content generation required.

In addition to getting to the content problem too late, we are also subject to a problematic development process. The reality is that we can get in a rather annoying chicken-and-egg situation during development. There is a "fluid" relationship between information design and content. Information design depends on content, and content depends on information design. The process of information design and content generation is iterative.

When designing a Web site, you need to develop a big-picture view of how information will be categorized and how it all interrelates (the process of information design). However, that information design is affected by its components, all of the pieces of content classified. Now, the information contained on your Web site (content) can be shaped to fit the overall information design. And the information design can be shaped to fit the content. In reality, they work iteratively to create an optimal whole, as simply illustrated in Figure 5-6.

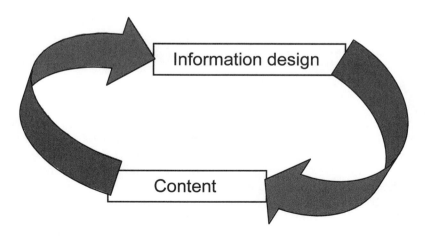

Figure 5-6 The iterative nature of information design and content generation.

The fluid relationship between information design and content can be problematic because your development company will want to start information design as soon as possible, because the way the site is structured (as illustrated by a site map, for example) is a key determinant of what visitors will experience and, therefore, encapsulates the development company's initial Web site concept.

To start information design, your Web site designer has to have a good feel for the content that will be on your Web site. Problem is, without a picture of how the site might be structured around a central concept, you will find it difficult to provide meaningful detail on content. In fact, you will probably want to establish a "style guide" for content so you can create content in such a way that it fits the Web site. And that style guide will rely on the information design of the Web site.

And so, you sit there asking for an explanation of how the site will be structured, and for a suggested style guide even, while the designer sits there asking for content details. And on and on it could go, ad infinitum, if we let it.

A PROPOSED APPROACH

You can address these problems by scoping the content challenge early and by feeding the development process with content detail, piece by piece, as you can manage it. Figure 5-7 describes a possible approach to managing content throughout the development process.

The initial brief captures the basic scope and nature of content you believe to be required on your Web site, along with the ways you intend to go about creating and managing content. In the context of what e-customers need to do, this gives the Web site designer an initial lead on the experiences the Web site needs to create, and therefore allows them to establish some initial concepts for your Web site.

On the basis of these high-level concepts, and in parallel as much as possible, you need to start to get a handle on the scope of the content challenge ahead of you. From experience, this is a necessary and sobering experience for companies that are better able to deal with a challenge that has been quantified than one that hasn't.

THE CONTENT AUDIT AND CONTENT PLAN

The process of the content audit involves identifying each content area and the core information contained in each and completing a "gap analysis" to identify what content you don't already have within the company, outside of the company or on other Web sites. Then, knowing the scope of content you will have to reshape, or create from scratch, you can establish an action plan.

To help you identify the core information required against each area of content, you may like to establish some simple standards for different areas of content. (These standards relate to the nature of information and not the style in which it is presented—it is too early in the process for that.)

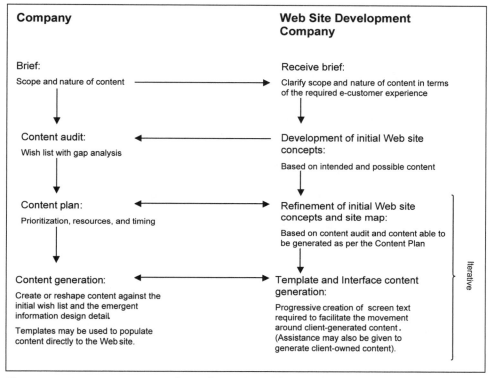

Figure 5-7 Content activities throughout the Web site development process.

For example, one client who wanted to facilitate the comparison of its products, in support of the customer's decision-making process, decided that each of its product pages would contain the following "chunks" of information:

- Introduction—a short statement that positions the product.
- Benefits—a bullet-pointed list of the key benefits of the product.
- Features— a list of the main product features.
- Options—an explanation of the different product variations available.
- Helpful hints/FAQs—a bullet-pointed list of common questions e-customers have about getting hold of, and using, the product.
- Pricing—a clear statement of the price along with information on any related discounts and rebates available.
- Purchase—the online order process (the definition of this online process will probably come later but you should identify any information that needs to specifically be given in relation to purchase, such as details on product availability).

Using this as a guide, a hypothetical client's content audit (in relation to content available on their existing Web site) is shown in Table 5-1.

Table 5-1 Content audit on product information

Product Name	Introduction	Benefits	Options	Helpful Hints	Pricing	Purchase
Home-replacement Insurance	An OK intro is given on current Web site at …	None on current Web site or in current marketing collateral	Need to reshape existing Web site content to properly detail the different options	None currently exist; however, hints on valuation could be helpful	Need to establish a clear statement on price. Some discount info exists on the Web site at …	Need to inform e-customers of terms of purchase—these exist in Policy Documents but would have to be summarized and reshaped
Home contents insurance	As above	Current Web site lists features that are actually benefits, at (given Web address)	As above. Existing Web site text is too expansive and the options need to be clearly summarized	None currently exist; however, hints on how to calculate your sum insured could be helpful	As above	As above

Key

☐ New content required   ☐ Content needs reshaping

It is best to start the audit with areas of content you know are most necessary and least dependent on the Web site context, such as the core product information in Table 5-1.

A content audit is a big job and it should be carried out by (at least one) dedicated resource such as a content manager (see Figure 5-1), who would be responsible for also managing the content plan and content generation against content schedules later in the development process.

Having gotten an idea of the scope of the task ahead, you can create the content plan. You will need to look at who owns existing content (online and offline) and start to allocate specific tasks to individuals.

In the above example, ownership of the product information sat within the auspices of the marketing department, and resource was allocated, over a given time period, in line with product management responsibilities. Product policy details, however, were owned by the underwriting department, which would provide the necessary detail and direction to another resource responsible for generating the Web site text.

You will also need to prioritize content delivery. The content most key to the required e-customer experience must be completed first. If there are areas of content that are just not going to fall within the timeframe for the project, then this needs to be clearly established and reflected in the Web site design and build. You may need to earmark some content as coming after the site has been launched to the public.

A content plan can be a stand-alone document. It will also form an important part of the overall project plan—because it is such a key dependency for progressing with, and completing, development. Knowing when different content areas will be complete will affect what you can test through interactive prototypes, and when, for example.

CONTENT GENERATION

Who should generate content?

There are different types of content and, therefore, different parties involved in the generation of content. Those parties will traverse both the business and the Web site development company. However, the bulk of the content will be in-depth and will be the responsibility of the business. I call this "substantive content." It is important to make the distinction between substantive and interface content because it helps us clearly allocate ownership and tasks in relation to each.

The development company will, in all probability, take the lead in creating content that facilitates the e-customer's experience on your Web site. I call this "interface content" because it is content that is seen at the interface with your e-customers. Interface content is closely tied in with information and visual design, which is why it usually ends up being the initiative of the development company.

The differentiation and respective roles are illustrated in Figure 5-8.

Interface content often "falls through the cracks" during the development process because it is not identified as a content requirement, and both the business and the Web site development company assume the other party is providing it—when, in actual fact, neither does. Then it ends up being done at the last minute and is not of sufficient quality to provide the e-customer with a meaningful interface. Thinking back to the seventeen customer directives, many of these relate to poor interface content—the e-customer just doesn't receive enough of the right information about what can be done and what is going on.

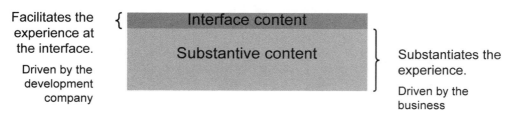

Figure 5-8 Differentiating between interface and substantive content.

Interface content forms some of the most important content on your site and should be carefully considered and, certainly, not forgotten. An order process, for example, requires interface content at each stage in the online process to guide e-customers through the process and manage their expectations. During an order process, interface content will need to provide an intuitive experience and reflect the business' service standards and protocols. The business and Web site development company will need to jointly determine the content required to facilitate these types of processes.

Generally speaking, development companies have experienced Web writers available. Businesses, however, tend to have a lot less experience with Web writing. Those companies that are inexperienced in Web writing will need to decide whether to train personnel within the company, employ a specialist resource, or outsource Web writing to a professional. Each approach comes with its own pros and cons.

If your company is committed to developing internal expertise in preparation for the demands of managing and maintaining your Web site after public launch, then it could be worth investing in existing and new personnel. Even if you do Web writing in-house, you may want to use a professional resource to edit and review what you have written—just to make sure it is appropriate for the online medium.

Tips for Web writing

Writing for the Web is fundamentally different from writing for other media. It is physically, and culturally, different. If we just pick up our current communications, reformat them a little, and put them online, we will get it wrong and turn our e-customers off.

As we know, Web sites are experiential and contextual; that is, people create an experience for themselves by interacting with Web sites, and the sites exist in a context affected by where visitors have been, come from, and what they are trying to do.

Web writing has to create a lot more context than any other form of writing. With a book or magazine in their hands, readers can tell a lot about the nature and quality of what they're reading. The Web, however, offers no such clues. The writer has to make the nature of the content, what it's doing there, and what use it is to the reader, crystal clear.

And the writer must not get in the way of what readers are trying to do or, conversely, presume too much about what readers are trying to do. The writer has to provide the tools, some good and relevant pointers, and then trust readers to build what they need for themselves.

You can provide your e-customers with a richer experience through your use of hypertext (links). Not by incessantly telling your readers to "click here" when they are only halfway through a paragraph, but by providing links that fit the context and add value to the visitor's experience.

Links change the look and feel of Web writing—they make the Web page imminently more scannable. You need to read your links as a pattern having their own syntax and rhythm, as well as a part of their surrounding text. And when including links in your writing, always keep to your subject, treating links as an inherent part of the text and not as alternate destinations.

On useit.com, Jakob Nielsen provides three main guidelines for Web writing as follows:

- Be **succinct**: Write no more than 50 percent of the text you would have used in a hardcopy publication.
- Write for **scannability**: Don't require users to read long continuous blocks of text.
- Use **hypertext to split up** long information into multiple pages.

Nielsen also advocates using "the inverted pyramid" in Web writing because, as known from several user studies, *users don't scroll* (however, this has begun to change and visitors seem a little more likely to scroll). The inverted pyramid puts general headline information at the top of an article and gives detail later in the article. Readers will often read only the top part of an article. Nielsen says that "very interested readers *will* scroll, and these few motivated souls will reach the foundation of the pyramid and get the full story in all its gory detail."

The inverted pyramid concept has been used by newspaper journalists for years, because they too know that people scan articles and may only read the first part of an article before moving on to the next. The journalist has to give readers all the important information up front so that, even if readers go away without reading the whole article, they take the most important facts with them.

Nielsen has found that, over time, readers have become more inclined to scroll. However, it is still important not to assume that all readers will scroll down to receive the detail they need.

As well as following a consistent framework, such as the inverted pyramid, content should be consistent enough to facilitate comparisons. Readers will compare like products, services, and ideas on your Web site and other Web sites, and you can make that easy, or difficult, for them. And write for searchability, with good, relevant, and consistent keywords that help e-customers find their way around the information they want to find.

Remember also that once e-customers get to a piece of content, a URL (uniform resource locator) will also be visible. URLs, as bookmarks, or references become their own shorthand for content, and you should try to make them as clear, relevant, and meaningful as possible.

In all of your Web writing, you are going to have to work hard to establish credibility with your readers. You need to establish yourself with visitors, so they know what you've got to say is worth listening to. E-customers have had to put up with a whole lot of poor content on the Web, and they won't hang around if they feel your writing is in the same vein.

The tone of voice you use will be a key factor in how your writing is received. If your Web writing sounds like a marketing brochure, or the one-sided musings of a corporate tycoon, you won't create a very favorable impression. Visitors expect more informality and intimacy in cyberspace—you have the opportunity to get to know them better and you should not talk to them in the aloof tones of yesteryear.

Your tone of voice also has to recognize the sophistication of your e-customers; and some are becoming pretty sophisticated. You have to recognize that some e-customers may have become expert e-customers; they may even know more about your products than you do.

And lastly, remember that you are part of an e-community. You don't necessarily have to create all your Web site content yourself—Web sites themselves can create content through the participation of e-customers and other parties affecting your e-service offering.

Content schedule

The content schedule is the detailed spreadsheet against which businesses monitor their progress in generating, and supplying, every piece of content required. It is also an important resource for the Web site development company, who will use the detail to finalize the site map and the inventory of every Web page (or page templates) it must create.

Both the business and the Web site development company need to realize that even at this stage, things can still evolve iteratively, and they should cooperatively review the status of the schedule frequently. The content manager will be key in facilitating this coordination and communicating changes, and chasing up the resources, as required.

The exact format of your content spreadsheet, or database, will depend on the structure most relevant to your project. For example, if you are serving content dynamically (creating Web pages "on-the-fly") the numbering system you use for each piece of content will reflect where that content is populated to on the Web site, and where it is stored, in the database.

Table 5-2 is an example of a spreadsheet format you may be able to adapt to your own situation.

Note that the schedule can be used to clearly prioritize content and distinguish between content that will be available when the site goes live to the public, and what will come later.

In my experience, interactive content, such as the home contents calculator in Table 5-2, is the most popular with customers who prefer to do something more useful than to scroll through static text. At the same time, you will have core products that you will want to cover on your Web site. Hopefully you'll have time to cover both. The golden rule, however, is to give customers what is most useful to them.

	No./id	Content Type	Content Owner	Source	Due Date	Received	File Name	Related Content	Search Keywords	Related E-Customer Activity	Template
Priority One—must be there for public launch											
1. Domestic products											
Home replacement insurance	1.1	Text with links	JD (market manager)	Current Web site at (URL)	7/11	Yes	Homereplacement (1.1).doc	All other domestic products (1.2 –1.5 incl)	Home, house, replacement, insurance, cover, valuation, fire earthquake, etc	Product evaluation	Domestic product page
Home contents insurance	1.2	Text with links	JD (market manager)	Current Web site at (URL)	7/11	No			Home, house, contents, insurance, cover, sum insured, theft, damage, etc	Product evaluation	Domestic product page
Home contents calculator	1.2.1	Text for table	JD (Market manager)	None		No			Home, house, contents, insurance, cover, sum insured, value, valuation, calculate, etc	Calculate sum insured for home contents	Calculator
		Rules for interactive table components	PB, (analyst)	None		No					

Table 5-2 A content schedule format you may find useful.

The schedule also identifies different content components, such as text, links, graphics, audio and video clips, and interactive decision-support-type applications (such as the calculators), and the associated customer activity. You will notice that the e-customer activity related to the home contents calculator is "calculate sum insured for home contents" while the broader e-customer activity of home contents insurance is "Product evaluation." The calculator (an interactive table) could be part of the content relating to home contents insurance but could also be a destination in itself (by way of a shortcut, for example).

Identifying related customer activities, or goals, helps determine the appropriate treatment of content components along with the their priority and who owns them. It will help the Web site development company develop the navigation system and templates for the different types of Web pages. It is also a good reminder of the fact that you are building the Web site to facilitate the actions of e-customers.

Content templates

Templates are designed by the Web site designer to carry a corporate design consistently through the Web site. Templates are common in projects where content is dynamically populated to a Web site "on the fly." Templates take into account the nature of the content components that make up the page, and the way they should be presented within the overall structure of the Web site. A large Web site could have as many sixty or seventy templates to cover the different types of content and activities found on the Web site. Obviously, it is best to avoid a proliferation of templates; however, you need to ensure there are enough templates to allow e-customers to adequately differentiate between the different activities available to them.

If templates are available, and approved, at the time content is ready to be delivered to the Web site, then the templates could be used by the business to directly populate content to the Web site database. This will remove double-handling later on. You should bear in mind, however, that, because of the iterative relationship between content generation and information design, templates take time to develop and will, probably, be released in succession (as more detailed content information becomes available).

Content management systems

While some Web sites allow dynamic population of content "on the fly" through the use of templates, other Web sites are static and each page has to be built and stored, ready to be served in response to an e-customer's request.

It is better to generate content dynamically than to create and store static pages. Dynamic content population will be faster, more efficient, and easier to maintain. When making updates, you just have to change one or two affected components, rather than, potentially, hundreds of static pages.

Content management systems that make dynamic content population possible, are one of the first indicators that object-oriented design principles (where objects form the basis of design as opposed to specific functions) are successfully being applied to

Web development. In fact, at the moment, there is a lot of work going into the development of Web object management (WOM) systems in general. WOM principles (that lead to the definition and use of objects that make up Web sites) cannot be applied only to content but can also be applied to facilitate application development, configuration management (that ensures that Web site concepts can be repeated in the future), and interoperability with related systems (inside and outside of the company).

This is an exciting area, and one you should be following with interest, because it could save you a lot of money and time later on, when these systems become more prevalent. You should keep an eye out for companies developing Web site applications based on object-oriented principles (links to some of these companies are given in the Netography under "content creation and object management"). It is my view that the application of object-orientated principles and technologies to Web development will enhance their application in traditional software development as well—both areas will feed off each other and contribute to improve, customer-centric, applications development.

But, to address the content issue at hand, WOM principles allow businesses to implement more sophisticated content management processes that ensure the quality of the Web site is maintained over time. These content management processes allow companies to implement processes where:

- Standards and styles can be applied through the use of templates.
- Any number of content components can be combined through the use of a template.
- Content components can come from different sources. This is particularly important where content ownership is spread across the company; you are likely to have people from different areas contributing content relative to their particular area of expertise. Once all of the components have been added by the various owners the template rolls them up into a Web page ready for publishing.
- All content additions can be controlled by a central resource, such as the content manager (while maintaining the ability for decentralized content generation).
- A staging environment allows changes to be made (as a result of editing, for example) and approvals can be given prior to content being available to the live system. Content can also be embargoed so that it is not "live" until a certain date, and similarly, can be deactivated on a certain date (in relation to campaign timings, for example).
- Decentralized and asynchronous approvals are supported. No content becomes available to the live system until all the requisite approvals have been given.
- Different versions of content can be managed (particularly given there is likely to be an iterative process of writing, editing, and approving, before each new piece of content is made available to the live system).

- Audit trails and reporting are provided. This is particularly important to achieve an overall view of content that has progressed through the system. Reports would probably be delivered to the content manager, who would ensure that content has correctly appeared in the live environment as anticipated.

- Different participants are offered different rights or privileges (this is important if different people in the company only have jurisdiction over some content areas or some administrative tasks). Of course, the content manager would maintain access to the entire system, as would the Webmaster.

- An easy-to-use front end allows stakeholders to add and change content and templates and administer the content system itself. This front end will be used in different ways by Web writers, editors, people giving approvals, the content manager, and the Webmaster.

PROCESS IMPROVEMENT

Your approach to e-business may be determined via a business process reengineering (BPR) exercise—you may be applying Internet technologies in an attempt to increase customer satisfaction through improved business processes. Your analysis of processes relating to your customer's Web site experience will be part of a much greater whole.

It is not feasible, or desirable, for me to explore such broad BPR activities in this chapter. Here I must focus on the processes critical to delivering a quality customer experience on your Web site. However, having said that, I will draw on recognized BPR ideas and methodologies.

First, we need to define some terms. BPR is concerned with designing processes, that optimally meet (hopefully customer-driven) business objectives. BPR is founded on the belief that it is better not to be constrained by existing processes; one must start with a blank sheet of paper. The upshot is that you may end up "obliterating" your current processes and have to redo things from scratch. BPR, therefore, is a high-risk approach to process improvement.

Business process improvement (BPI) is founded on the belief that it is good to start with existing processes. Once existing processes are modeled, they are analyzed and improved. Of course, that improvement could be relatively minor or particularly major. In theory, you should be able to completely replace the process with a new one, as in BPR, but the reality is that your knowledge of existing processes may hinder your ability to "think outside the box."

Both approaches require business process design, which you will implement to reengineer processes and to create completely new ones. Existing processes aren't always available as a reference point (if you want to use them as such). You will need to design and implement processes that have never existed before. Web site content management processes, for example, will be new to the company.

I don't think it really matters what label you use, as long as you are committed to putting processes in place that help create a quality e-service experience. I refer to this pursuit, generically as "process improvement."

AN APPROACH TO PROCESS IMPROVEMENT

On that note, we will explore a basic approach to process improvement that facilitates the identification of customer goals and the business' ability to support them.

This approach is built on the premise that customer goals should be matched to business goals and that this happens via the Web site interface. E-customers complete certain actions to achieve certain outcomes, or goals. Businesses also complete certain actions to achieve certain outcomes, or goals. The process of exchange between the e-customer and the company happens via the Web site interface. We can represent this e-customer-business exchange in Figure 5-9.

Figure 5-9 Matching e-customer and business processes via the Web site interface.

All of the component processes can be mapped; we can map e-customer processes, interface processes, and business processes, although the mapping techniques we use may differ. Business processes are likely to involve more sophisticated mapping techniques, as well as different levels of modeling to embrace the macro-to-micro- business environment.

We seek to understand customer processes and create an interface that facilitates them. The interface acts as the front end for business processes that fit seamlessly and effectively into the customer's e-service experience.

This highlights the importance of developing a quality interface and business processes. It also reinforces the importance of contextual design: designing an interface (and enabling it) so that customers can do what they need to do, in their context, as customers. (We will discuss the contextual design of interfaces further in the next chapter.)

To enable e-customer processes, business may end up improving existing processes, replacing existing processes, or creating new processes. To start off, companies will need to map e-customer processes, and, with the assistance of expert developers and process designers, relate this to interface and process design.

The nature of e-customer processes will depend on the type of e-services you are providing and to whom. In addition, some e-customer processes will require more deep penetration into business processes than others (depending on how much you have integrated the e-customer into your business). Some e-customer processes you will probably have to consider are as follows:

- Make a service request (and there will be different types of service requests, each requiring attention).
- Order a product or service.
- Provide input to online requests for information (i.e., not service requests but requests from the company for information such as participation in surveys or other Web-based forms that integrate e-customers with business processes, such as product development ideas).
- Register for a service.
- Update personal information held by the company.
- Request and receive e-mails or other push content.
- Evaluate certain types of products.
- Provide feedback (on the Web site and on a particular experience with your company).
- Get help (on using the Web site or a product or service).
- Contact someone who can help with a problem.
- Participate in an online forum.

More than one business process may support one e-customer process. In addition, some processes will be interrelated and will need to be considered in relation to one another, while others (such as the content publishing and management process) underpin a number of other processes. As with any process improvement exercise, you will describe and analyze processes at different levels and will need to relate and group processes to understand interdependencies and to avoid duplication of effort.

AN EXAMPLE

Let's consider an example of the approach as it applies to an e-customer successfully completing an order process. We can:

1. Map the e-customer, interface, and supporting business processes.
2. Analyze how well the processes match one another.
3. Make improvements to the processes on the basis of our analysis.

1. Mapping

E-customer process

We start off by mapping the e-customer process. Figure 5-10 shows an e-customer's order process.

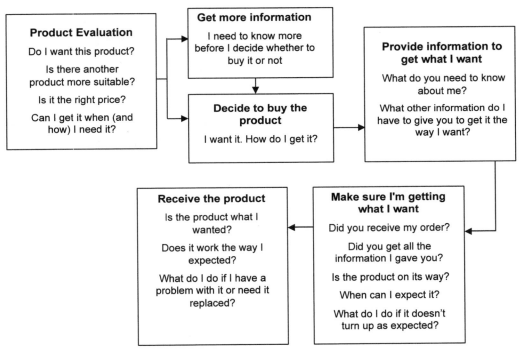

Figure 5-10 An example of an e-customer's order process

Interface process

Figure 5-11 shows the related interface process.

Business processes

The mapping of business processes presents us with more of a challenge; there are a number of related processes and a number of levels on which those processes exist.

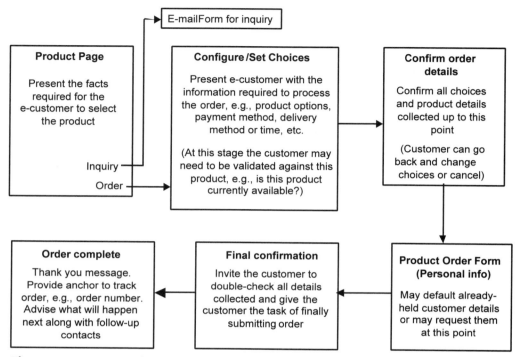

Figure 5-11 An example of an interface order process.

I have identified a number of business processes that support an e-customer's order process, such as:

- The receipt and routing of the order request (by which the company delivers the request to an appropriate person within the company).

- The product provisioning process (by which a company activates the product).

- The product fulfillment process.

- The complaints process (by which e-customers can register their dissatisfaction and get the product replaced).

- The product specification process (by which a company determines what it offers in relation to a product and what is required to provide it).

- The product pricing process (by which a company establishes and updates current prices of products).

- The campaign management process (by which companies determine which products are subject to campaign conditions and the management of those conditions).

And, of course, underlying all of this is the content management process, which ensures that the right information about the product, its price, its availability, its provision, and the relevant follow-up processes, gets served on the Web site. In addition, the content management process will, in turn, be affected by other business processes that provide content inputs, such as product pricing and specification processes and the campaign management process.

In addition, we can map or "model" these processes at different levels of specificity, depending on how much we want to get into the nuts and bolts of the processes involved. It is not feasible to go into all of the models you might create at this point. Figure 5-12 presents a model of the high-level relationship among processes.

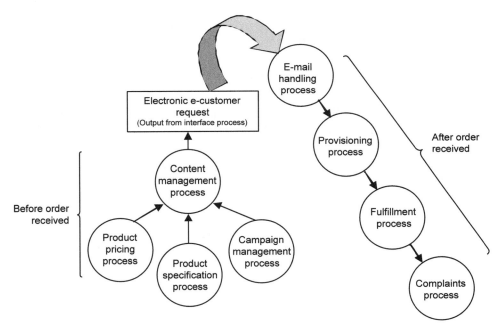

Figure 5-12 An example of supporting business processes.

2. Analysis

Matching the e-customer and interface processes

Applying the approach, we can match the e-customer and interface processes. In doing so, we address issues such as:

- Whether steps in the interface process logically match those of the customer process, i.e. does the interface intuitively facilitate the steps required in the e-customer process? We can match the previous e-customer and interface processes as follows:

- "Product evaluation" matches a "Product page."
- "Get more information" matches an "E-mail form for inquiry."
- "Decide to buy the product" matches "Order."
- "Provide information to get what I want" matches "Configure/set choices."
- "Make sure I'm getting what I want" matches "Confirm order details" through to "order complete."
- "Receive the product" also matches "order complete" which gives the e-customer information on what to do if they have a problem.

  The steps match pretty well because there is a step in the interface process for every step in the e-customer process. The e-customer should feel comfortable with the order sequence. Many online order processes don't follow a natural e-customer order process; steps are poorly defined or illogical.

- Whether the interface process offers the customer the necessary guidance throughout the order process.

  - The product page would have to provide the necessary content to enable the e-customer's evaluation of product alternatives. The product page would provide information on the fit of this product with others (what this product offers in relation to others), clear pricing information, and details on how and when, and to whom, the product is provided. (Refer back to the previous customer directives in number. 6, "Let me make a valid comparison" and number 7, "Don't expect me to make a decision without the facts.")

  - The "order" action has to be clear and easily accessible at the point the customer decides to buy. (Refer back to the previous customer directive number 10, "Yes, I want it, now what?").

  - The requests for information in "Configure/set choices" and "Product order form" should be clear and deliberate. (Refer back to the previous customer directive number 16, "Tell me the info you need".)

  - The customer understands, from "Order complete" exactly what will happen, along with when and how it will happen, in response to their order.

    We would be able to more fully assess how well the interface process guides the e-customer if we had actual screens to peruse. However, the process, as it is presented here, should enable the necessary guidance to be provided (going by the intended nature of each screen in the process. You would, of course, want to double-check this once those screens were developed.)

- What product information should be provided in product pages themselves and what is provided during the order process?

Some product information is more pertinent when e-customers are ordering than when they are evaluating a product. The goal is not to let unnecessary information get in the way of an e-customer deciding to buy while providing enough information to facilitate the customer's decision to buy.

Matching business processes

As part of your process improvement endeavor, you could focus on the most immediate business processes such as the e-mail receipt and routing process and then rely on the other existing processes to complete the customer's e-service experience. However, you could also take the opportunity to consider how the use of technology could automate the end-to-end process from the receipt of the order to its delivery. How much you want to bite off is up to you, but bear in mind that e-customers have higher expectations of timelines when they order over the Web. Therefore, you may need to look at streamlining a range of existing processes.

For the purposes of this example, we will relate the e-customer and interface processes to the e-mail handling process. In doing so, we need to consider issues such as:

- What is the minimum information an e-customer must provide to activate the related business processes?
- What are the rules relative to each product and who is responsible for defining them. How are the product rules integrated into the content process? Rules will be things like:
  - What particular service levels are associated with particular products?
  - What payment mechanisms are we able to use (e.g., credit card payment)?
  - Is the date the product is required likely to differ from the date it would be delivered?
  - How does a customer know whether a service has been activated (especially when it is not a physical product)?
  - At what stage is the availability of the product verified with the e-customer; is this done automatically online and a contingency of the customer request being accepted or does it happen in the service channel after the order has been received?
- Is each piece of customer-provided information used in the subsequent business processes. (Refer back to the previous customer directive number 4, "Use what I give you.")
- At what point is the output of the interface process (an electronic file) brought into related service processes? Efficiencies may be created by bringing the interface output in later, i.e., automating the processing of the output so that it fits into business processes at a later point.

- In what format should the customer request be provided to facilitate routing and integration with workflow and customer management systems once the request has been received by the company?

- What product options can be identified and fulfilled as part of the order process and what options require human intervention (e.g., more sophisticated products may not be able to be fully configured as a result of the online order process)?

- How do different customer choices affect pricing policy? Can activating these choices dynamically change the price online?

- Can related requests to affiliated suppliers be automated (i.e., if the company needs to involve another supplier in fulfilling the e-customer's order, can the acceptance of the e-customer order automatically trigger a request from the company to the supplier)?

Of course, there are other business processes you will also have to consider. Some of them will be as follows:

- *Product development process.* New products will have to be added to the Web site on an ongoing basis, and you will need to make sure that the process generates all of the inputs required to service that product on the Web site, such as template generation and/or application, content dimensions, service dimensions, transactional dimensions, the provision of rules related to decision-support-type functionality, and reporting requirements. You want to ensure that like products can always be effectively evaluated and compared by e-customers.

- *Product promotion process.* You will want to use your Web site as a promotional medium along with other promotional media. You will need to determine how promotional content is integrated into the Web site as much as new product information. Campaign conditions, such as price changes, will need to be tied in with product dimensions. You will also need to consider the embargo process, where you will manage the timing of the release and deletion of a campaign. Also, bear in mind that promotional content may be treated differently from other content, such as product information. Promotional content may be highlighted in relation to "what's new," or "what's hot," for example.

- *Customer management processes.* Your Web site may allow e-customers to store, retrieve and change personal information on the Web site database, or on internal databases (if you have connectivity between your Web site and internal databases). You will need to consider how this integrates with the processes you use for storing and maintaining customer data.

- *Service improvement process.* You may have a process in place whereby customer satisfaction is benchmarked according to certain indicators, such as the level of customer complaints. The Web site may provide information relevant to these indicators (deliberately, or not). You will need to determine how these indicators relate to an interface process and how they are integrated with offline indicators.

- *Strategy and planning process.* You will need to consider how the Web site fits into your evaluation of business strengths, weaknesses, opportunities, and threats to define what will make your company get ahead of its competitors. Your customer-effective Web site is likely to become a key weapon in the war against your competitors.

3. Process improvements

The types of general improvements you can expect to make as a result of applying this approach are as follows:

- *Shifting content from the call center to your Web site.* Web site visits are likely to directly substitute inquiries received by your call centers. How many customer inquiries can you defer by providing service support online (e.g., through FAQs and knowledge bases.
- *Removing steps that add no value to your e-customer.*
- *Removing control points that are no longer required as a result of integrating quality customer information deeper into business process.*
- *Web-based technologies that are integrated to achieve shared access to central databases, expert systems, decision-support tools, and automated audit and tracking processes.*
- *Decreased number of parties involved in a process through simplification of processes.* Indeed, there is the opportunity to greatly simplify many business processes as a result of the integration of Web-based technologies. Many businesses have become far more complex than they need to be to effectively facilitate e-customer actions.
- *The grouping of tasks around areas of specialization.* This can be particularly important in the company's management of its online presence—a centralized management function may be required to give that presence the necessary level of commitment and focus.
- *Expert service staff to deal with "cases" from end to end rather than being part of an "assembly line" of component tasks.*

TROUBLESHOOTING

You can avoid the pain others have endured! My aim here is not to restate what I have already stated, but to provide a little additional insight by highlighting some of the things businesses, sometimes unwittingly, get wrong.

Set up and development

"No-brainer" modifications

We discussed the set up of the integrated project team at the beginning of the chapter. The team should be structured in a way that minimizes the number of people who have to be involved in each decision. A classic blunder that you can avoid is taking, what I call, "no-brainer" modifications through a committee.

No-brainer modifications are the things that obviously have to be changed as a result of customer, or internal, testing—they're the little things that we can change so simply, as seen in the practical example given in Chapter 3 where the Wired team simply changed the order in which links were presented down the left-hand side of their News page to remove confusion over which links referred to stocks and which didn't. Surely, these no-brainer modifications don't have to be subjected to the same rigor as modifications that need discussion and clarification? I say, "just do it" and leave the other changes open to discussion.

Losing sight of e-customers

Sometimes a disconnection occurs between customer advocacy and project strategy. Strategy needs to be clearly expressed in terms of what the company will do for e-customers and it is up to the strategic visionary and customer advocate to make sure this happens. Customer requirements need to be translated into a language the company understands and that captures what customers need to be able to do.

Vision is, so often, expressed entirely from the company's perspective, and this is the beginning of a slippery slope for companies seeking to be customer-effective.

Specialists

It is important to appoint specialists early on in the project, people who can help manage and execute the content process, business process design, and the various facets of internal testing, for example. Identifying resource early on will make sure necessary tasks get under way sooner, rather than later. It is just too risky to wait and see what resource is required; chances are you will just meet a bottleneck later when it becomes apparent that critical tasks need to be completed.

Share methodology

You must agree on a development methodology with the Web site development company. Development processes (by which the development company goes about developing your product) shouldn't evolve; they should be planned. If you share a clear methodology, you will be able to make sure your respective activities are in synch and fit together logically. When activities get out of synch, things start to fall through the cracks and the product ends up suffering. Customer-effectiveness requires a great deal of coordination.

Change management

Earlier in this chapter we discussed the product specification process and the importance of defining the scope of the Web site development company's deliverables. You may like to integrate a change management process such as that outlined in Chapter 3, and seen in Figure 3-18. The change management process will be required to manage exceptions that fall outside the scope of the work that has been agreed on.

In addition, you must relate the prioritization of modifications (such as those resulting from customer testing) to the change control process. The Web site designer will drown if you give them a huge list of modifications without clear priorities.

Reinvention versus testing

Testing is not the process by which you go about reviewing and approving Web site concepts. Your project methodology should factor in approvals where they are needed. If not, you will encounter a whole group of internal testers reporting redesign requirements as if they were bugs. The Web site designer then has to try to discern what real fixes are required and work out how to politely deal with left-field design requests.

You need to give testers clear guidance to get usable results, and if they need to be involved in design decisions, that should have happened already.

Content

As we discussed earlier in this chapter, content is a challenging area. Here are the things that people often get wrong:

- Not clearly establishing the capabilities of the content management system. Sometimes a company's content management processes gets designed around a system that can't adequately support them.

- Not cooperating during the development process to manage the design and use of templates alongside the process of content generation. Sometimes people end up trying to use templates before they are finalized, or end up having to generate content and then "backfill" a template, only to find that the content doesn't fit the template.

- Prioritizing content from the company's perspective and not based on what is most useful to e-customers.

- Not recognizing decentralized content ownership and not providing resource (dedicated as required) for sourcing, writing, and editing. Some content owners, are not budding Web writers and will not feel comfortable creating or editing content. Cooperation is required across the company to complete the whole content task.

- Companies not identifying and specifying content that should be created by other parties (such as interface content or other third party content).

- Trying to add search criteria after content has been populated to the site.

- Expecting the development company to complete information design without any information on intended content.

- Assuming existing marketing material can just be reorganized to fit a Web page. You'll be able to use bits and pieces, but, generally, you'll either be reshaping what you have, or starting from scratch.

- Not establishing clear styles for Web writing. What framework will be used generically and within particular content areas? Inconsistency in style and approach results when styles are not established.

- Not including hypertext in Web writing. The resultant content is link-less and one-dimensional—which is great for a brochure, but not for a Web site.

- Providing content that hasn't been legally approved.

- Interface content being written as distinct from e-customer processes and without thought for supporting business processes. Too often, interface content is a facilitator of visual design and not the e-customer experience.

- The Web site designer is often not close enough to the company's content schedule and is unable to take a disciplined approach to modifying and updating Web site concepts and the related site map.

- Providing content without use of a numbering system to identify particular content components, their associated templates, and their ultimate destination once populated to the Web site.

- Not reviewing content after it has been populated to the Web site. Things don't always end up where they should. The site must receive a thorough review (including every page and every link) before it is deemed suitable for public consumption.

- Testing prototypes with no content in them.

Business process improvement

- Starting business process endeavors too late so they are not integrated with development. The Web site ends up poorly facilitating e-customer processes and poorly fitting business processes.

- Not establishing the rules related to certain products and their purchase. Sometimes, important product information ends up getting crammed into the product order process at the last minute, or left out altogether.

- Not integrating the campaign and product marketing process with Web site strategy and concepts forcing product and market managers to "do their own thing" (creating their own Web sites) on the Web. This leads to proliferation in customer interfaces and the risk of uncoordinated customer communications leading to e-customer confusion and frustration.

- Transferring product and brand proliferation, and undue product and process complexity, to the Web. Why not simplify!

- Not focusing on the business processes that will most directly affect the e-customer's online service experience.

- Not addressing the component processes where interface processes and business processes come together (at a micro-level).

- Not defining the required interface process outputs in enough detail so they can be fitted to business processes (and valuable e-customer requests and data end up getting lost!).

- Not creating an audit trail of e-customer requests through to their resolution, making performance measurement impossible.

Webmarketing

- Not identifying how current marketing activities and relationships relate to information design. A campaign, or sponsorship initiative, comes along and you can't find anywhere to include, or highlight it, in on your Web site.

- Not checking in with customers before praising your Web site characteristics and promoting its capabilities. You will heighten customer frustration if you send customers to your Web site, and it doesn't help them do what they want.

In the next chapter we will look more closely at characteristics of customer-effective Web sites and how Web site development companies, supported by businesses, can create more customer-effective Web sites.

CHAPTER 6

A CUSTOMER-EFFECTIVE DESIGN APPROACH AND PROCESS

> *E-customer actions are the context for customer-effective design.*
>
> *If we all start with what we know e-customers need, and want, to do, and learn how to make that happen effectively online, we can't go wrong. It's that simple.*

The structure of this book inherently reflects a customer-effective approach to developing e-services. First, you start by talking with your e-customer; second, you describe what e-services need to deliver to the e-customer, and third; you go about doing the actual design and development of those services. You don't start with design; you start with the customer.

Keeping a focus on your e-customers, from the first time you talk with them, through to the completion and delivery of your finished product, is a challenge. Oftentimes, businesses start out with the best of intentions and end up delivering something that is a far cry from what e-customers need and expect.

There are many reasons why disconnection occurs between e-customers and businesses. One reason is a lack of customer-effective design. While big strides have been taken toward use of the Web as a service medium, there is still a long way to go before Web design produces an interface that enables customer-effective e-services.

This chapter explores how to use e-customer actions as a basis for customer-effective design. It is exploratory, rather than directive; i.e. it will give you ideas, rather than instructions. This chapter will, hopefully, give you a new way to look at, and approach, Web design by seeing it as a means to seamlessly facilitate customer processes.

A CUSTOMER-EFFECTIVE DESIGN APPROACH

Customer-effective design is inherently contextual; it is based on an understanding of, and response to, an e-customer's context. The e-customer's context is the story behind why they are on your Web site, how they came to be there, what they're trying to do there and why, and what they're likely to do as a result of being there.

We have touched on the importance of understanding an e-customer's context throughout this book. We have seen e-customer actions as the root of requirement definition, product specification, testing, and process improvement. We will now turn our full focus on the idea of "contextual design," as it relates to the design of customer-effective Web sites.

APPLYING CONTEXTUAL DESIGN

Contextual design is a concept that has grown out of developing software systems for businesses; systems that allow businesses to work better. In their book *Contextual Design* Beyer and Holtzblatt describe a methodology for finding out how employees work and designing and developing a system that facilitates, and improves, the process of work.[1]

While e-customers are external to a company, they still seek to do "work" as e-customers. An online service channel, or Web sites that offer online services, are an important part of e-customers' work; the things they need to get done to choose, use, maintain and disengage from products and services.

We can learn a lot by applying some of the basic ideas of contextual design to the design of customer-effective Web sites. For a start, we can better orient the design process to what e-customers need to do when visiting our Web sites.

Many good books (such as David Siegel's, *Secrets of Successful Web Sites* and *Creating Killer Web Sites* have been written on Web design, and many of them are based on the fundamental belief that good design starts with understanding your e-customer. I do not want to duplicate discussion of good Web design; I want to explore how the application of contextual design ideas can result in more customer-effective Web design.

Too often, Web site design revolves around categorizing information (and not necessarily the information required by the customer to perform certain tasks) and finding a way to meaningfully present that information, intuitively, in an interface. Designers and developers have come a long way in developing systems that create good interactive experiences for customers. Problems arise, however, because those systems are often developed without explicit recognition of customer processes; they do not effectively allow customers to do what they need to do.

[1] *Contextual Design: Defining Customer-Centered Systems* by Hugh Beyer and Karen Holtzblatt. Copyright ©1998, Morgan Kaufmann Publishers, Inc.

Beyer and Holtzblatt introduce the idea of designing the process flow of a system around the work that (internal) customers need to do, not unlike the approach to business process improvement I introduced in Chapter 5. The system is designed around functions, within areas of focus, that allow users to do their work.

Designing the system around customers' work meets the design challenge of keeping the system coherent because the system enables work that is, in itself, coherent. Users can employ the system to seamlessly perform activities.

Beyer and Hotlzblatt provide an explanation of the coherence systems can provide when enabling customers to do their work, as follows:

> Coherence isn't just about consistency of the user interface—a coherent system keeps the user's work orderly and natural.

> When a presentation tool won't let users change slide notes and slide contents at the same time, making them jump back and forth between views, it breaks up the work. When a word processor provides three successive dialogue boxes to choose a bullet, it turns a minor function into a whole task, complicating the work.

> When an e-mail system lets users search the address book by providing a simple text entry field that filters the address book names but uses a separate query window to search the "sent mail" folder, it provides inconsistent structures for doing similar work.

> When the system model is coherent, it keeps the user's work coherent; when it fragments, it's the user's work that is disrupted.

Just as employees' work gets disrupted by systems that don't properly support their work, so the work of e-customers get disrupted by Web sites that don't naturally facilitate the processes they need, or want, to complete as e-customers.

To provide the type of coherence that Beyer and Holtzblatt refer to, Web sites (their information and interface design) need to be designed around a lot more than organizing and relating information. Web sites must be designed around the e-customer activities they are there to support.

Web sites can be designed around e-customer activities by identifying e-customer tasks and processes; we might call these "customer scenarios" or "themes" relating to what e-customers need, and want, to do. These themes are like a conversation or a dialogue about what the customer is doing, common threads related to activities or tasks. We can then establish structures around those "scenarios" or "themes" to create the kind of coherent system to which Beyer and Holtzblatt refer.

These scenarios exist on a macro and a micro level. At the beginning of the design process, designers and developers can establish a direction for the system by identifying the core customer tasks the Web site must support. Then as design becomes more refined, customer scenarios can be fleshed out by adding the component tasks associated with themes of activity.

In the book *Scenario-Based Design*, edited by John M. Carroll, the essay on narrowing the specification-implementation gap talks in detail about scenario as a basis for design. The importance of scenarios, from a macro to a micro level, is touched on as follows:

> Our approach encourages designers to first address the core tasks of the problem domain, to focus attention on what the system will support, and then to turn to how it will do this, and develop a user interface for these tasks.[2]

By starting with what e-customers need to do, we get a better sense of how our Web sites, as coherent systems that facilitate e-customer activities, need to be designed. Web sites can be conceptualized around what e-customers need to do and offer the requisite functionality through an interface that seamlessly leads e-customers through the completion of the activities they choose to complete.

AN EXAMPLE

So what is involved in starting with e-customer activities as a basis for the design of Web sites? What sort of discussion does this approach generate among designers?

To help us better understand a contextual design approach, we will use Amazon.com as a framework for discussion to illustrate a way of thinking about customer-effective Web site design. We'll identify some potential e-customer themes that could apply to Amazon.com and the design considerations that arise when exploring Amazon.com in relation to those themes.

Amazon.com has become part of the folklore of how real, ordinary people have gone about adopting the Internet into their everyday lives. It has set a shining example in so many ways, and in relation to its dedication to customer service, in particular. Therefore, Amazon.com provides a credible and well-known frame of reference for discussing contextual design.

Amazon is constantly improving its site, and even while writing this example, the site has changed. And it's likely that it has changed many times since then. That doesn't matter. This example will provide some useful triggers for thinking about customer-effective design, and the Amazon.com site, as it is captured in a moment of time, is simply the framework within which we have our discussion.

---

[2] *Scenario-Based Design*, John M. Carroll and Mary Beth Rosson, eds. Copyright ©1995. Reprinted by permission of John Wiley & Sons, Inc.

1. POTENTIAL E-CUSTOMER THEMES

While carrying out many one-on-one interviews and focus groups, Amazon.com has come up as a basis for discussion in relation to what people do on the Internet, and what they find easy, and what they don't. This, plus the fact that I've been an e-customer of Amazon for as long as I can remember, has formed the basis of some potential e-customer themes. These themes are common activities, or processes, that e-customers want to complete when they visit Amazon.com, as listed in Figure 6-1.

E-customer themes

① Find a book I know I want

② Buy a book I want

③ Browse books I might be interested in

④ Get recommendations on books that might interest me

⑤ Keep a note of books that interest me

⑥ Follow up on a book I want, but that is unavailable

⑦ Send someone a gift

⑧ Keep track of a gift I sent

⑨ Redeem a gift voucher

⑩ Update my personal information.

Figure 6-1 Specific e-customer themes we can use to consider the contextual design process.

Of course, I'm not saying these themes are definitive, but they do form a useful basis for discussion. We will explore each theme in turn and see what considerations would arise from applying a contextual design approach.

In addition to the specific types of activities e-customers may wish to complete on Amazon.com, there are other generic activities all e-customers wish to perform in relation to Web sites in general.

Referring back to our discussion of "Five Doing Areas" in Chapter 2, we can summarize these generic e-customer themes in Figure 6-2.

E-customer themes (generic)

①   Get help

②   Provide feedback

③   Find out what is on your Web site

Figure 6-2 Generic e-customer themes.

2. CONTEXTUAL DESIGN CONSIDERATIONS

As mentioned earlier in this book, e-customers take things on balance, before deciding how much use a Web site is to them. Therefore, looking at each theme in turn is a little artificial, since we would take them all on balance. However, looking at each theme in turn does provide a more meaningful discussion of contextual design principles. We'll take it as read that contextual designers would take all design considerations on balance.

Note also that Amazon.com has become much more than a bookstore. Although I have used a book as the subject within the e-customer themes, the item could well be something other than a book.

1. Find a book I know I want

The search function is the key facilitator for customers finding the book they know they want. Say customers know the title of the book and the author, they can go straight to "Book Search," enter the title and author, and find the book. (We saw an abstraction of Amazon's basic search "system" in Figure 3-5.)

Now, let's consider how easy it is for e-customers to find the book they know they want. On receiving the Amazon welcome page, they can either carry out a quick search, right there and then, or they can go to the appropriate store (in this case "Books") and do a full search.

The quick search is right there on entry to the Amazon.com site and allows one-dimensional searching against any of the sites stores (in this case "Books") as shown in Figure 6-3.

In most cases this quick search would suffice; however, e-customers may find that sometimes they're more likely to find exactly what they're looking for by using the full search, particularly when looking for more complex items such as classical music, where they may know the composer's work but not who has performed it.

If the quick search can return what they're looking for, it's only one click away. However, if they use the full search function, they have to go to the book store, select "Book Search" and then enter the details of what they want—at least three clicks away.

Figure 6-3 The quick search function available on Amazon.com's welcome page.

Would it be useful to be able to do a full search straight from the welcome page? And what effect would this have on information design? It may not be practical to offer full search at the highest level, and the distance of a couple of clicks may be inconsequential to e-customers anyway?

Now, finding books is also subject to their being available—and this is something that Amazon.com needs to help customers understand and manage. The book they know they want, which they have found through the search function, may, or may not, be available.

The world of publishing is prone to fits and starts—books get published in lots, and quite often, demand exceeds supply. That leaves the poor book readers pulling out their hair. There aren't any more copies of a particular book, and, quite possibly, the publisher may not be communicating whether it even intends to publish more copies.

On Amazon.com, e-customers may find out-of-print, and unavailable, books.

Amazon.com invites e-customers to order out-of-print books, and this can be done using the usual order process. From there, Amazon.com gets in touch with its network to find a second-hand copy of the book an e-customer desires. Once Amazon.com has located the second-hand copy, it e-mails the e-customer with the price and embeds a Web address they can click onto to directly confirm their order of that particular second-hand copy.

By the time Amazon.com goes away to purchase the second-hand copy, it could have, unfortunately, been sold already. This is disappointing for the would-be book buyer, but Amazon will keep trying until it has purchased a second hand copy. It's a service that saves e-customers a lot of time and effort scouting around second-hand bookstores or specialty Web sites (such as they exist).

As a contextual designer you would need to consider whether e-customers might like to be able to keep an eye on progress of a second-hand order. Or if they only need an update each time Amazon.com locates a second-hand copy.

Now, if the book is unavailable, as opposed to out of print, Amazon.com may not have information from the publisher and can only recommend that e-customers "Occasionally Check this Page to See if It's Been Reprinted".

When faced with availability glitches, an e-customer, relatively familiar with Amazon.com may search zShops (zShops "offer hundreds of thousands of new, used, and hard-to-find products from specialty retailers, small businesses, and individuals.") and Auctions, just in case those stores are carrying the book that is unavailable or out of print.

E-customers can also use Amazon.com's "zShop alerts" service where Amazon keep a vigilant eye out for items they have identified in a zShop search. The zShop alert service is shown in Figure 6-4.

Figure 6-4 Amazon.com's zShops alert provides an avenue for finding unavailable books.

As a contextual designer you would need to consider how the zShops alert service fits with the customer's goal of finding a book that happens to be unavailable and think about if, and how, it should be presented in that context.

In addition, you would need to consider what other actions you can create for e-customers; so they can be actively involved in finding the book they know they want.

For example, you could consider introducing functionality that automatically searches the Auctions and zShops stores for the unavailable book e-customers are trying to find. Maybe you could consider automating a sitewide search for the unavailable book and flick the e-customer straight to the store it is found in (if it is found).

You could also consider e-mailing e-customers when the book is republished. You could even facilitate e-mails from e-customers to publishers telling the publisher to "Please Reprint this Book!". And, taking this even further, extranet functionality could allow publishers to provide more information on likely reprint dates or give publishers the ability to take over the burden of advising e-customers of a book's availability.

As a contextual designer you have the opportunity to look at how industry problems and issues can be turned into an opportunity for offering customer-effective e-services on your Web site. How can the Web be used to reengineer industry dynamics that create customer problems? (Refer back to our discussion of key decisions you will have to make and "The New Industry" in Chapter 4.)

2. Buy a book I want

Of course, search is central to e-customers finding the book they want to buy, before they buy it, and the search function has been discussed above.

Having then found the book they want, e-customers go about ordering it.

Amazon.com offers a longer version of ordering as well as a shortcut, "1-click," order process. Amazon.com's longer order process is as follows:

1. Order from a product page (i.e., "Proceed to Checkout"—having been given all the facts needed to buy).

2. E-customers sign in by identifying themselves as a new user or returning e-customer.

3. Enter a shipping address.

4. Confirm selected items (this is the first time e-customers get feedback on what they selected from the previous product page).

5. Select a shipping method.

6. Provide payment details (select credit card, or pay be check).

7. Choose a billing address (defaults address previously provided under shipping address, Step 3, with the ability to "Use This Address").

8. "Confirm Your Order—the Last Step!" Here e-customers get to confirm all of the information they've provided along with final confirmation of the items they have selected.

9. Order confirmation screen.

There is a lot of debate over where the entry of personal information should come in an online order process. There is a trade off between creating efficiency by identifying, and defaulting information related to, known e-customers and letting e-customers get through an order process without having to identify themselves. (We will explore this further in our discussion of shopping metaphors in Chapter 7.)

Amazon.com puts the request for personal information early in the order process, before confirmation of order details (i.e., e-customers are required to provide personal information before getting feedback on what they have ordered.) Some people feel that early request for personal information, or "Registration," is invasive and unnecessary and that it should come at the end of the process (i.e., the provision of personal information should not act as a barrier to purchase).

There are also different views on the optimal length (i.e., number of screens) of the order process. There is a trade off between taking the e-customer through the order process step by step and consolidating the number of screens required to complete the process.

By contrast, one-click ordering is very short—select "Buy Now with 1-Click" from a Product page and instantly receive a confirmation message! With 1-click ordering Amazon.com provides an interface, and after-sales process, that effectively facilitates e-customer ordering.

To further explore the design considerations that come along with an order process, let's use the steps of my previously recommended order process (see Figure 5-11) as headings and explore the Amazon.com order process in relation to the following headings:

1. Order straight from the product page (having been given all the facts needed to buy).

2. Configure/set choices to specify the detail required to purchase the product.

3. Confirm order details.

4. Gather personal information required (or default already-held information).

5. Advise the order is complete, how the e-customer can follow up, and what will happen next.

1. Order straight from the product page

E-customers can buy with one click straight from the page on the book that they want, or they can add it to their shopping cart and then activate 1-click ordering from there. Whichever route they choose they are never left wondering how they go about getting what they want. The invitation to buy sits right up front on the product page and is shown in Figure 6-5.

2. Configure/set choices

In the case of the Amazon.com order process, products don't need to be configured—a book is a book is a book. On other Web sites, less tangible products do, however, require configuration (or selection of product options) before they can be purchased.

Figure 6-5 Amazon.com's prompt to buy.

3. Confirm order details

Once e-customers have selected "Buy Now With 1-Click," to buy the book *"Scenario-Based Design,"* for example, they receive a confirmation screen as shown in Figure 6-6.

Figure 6-6 Amazon's 1-click order confirmation.

Details on the 1-click order are retrieved by selecting "Review or Change Your 1-Click Orders," which returns comprehensive details shown in Figure 6-7.

This detailed confirmation screen clearly states what has been ordered, the order number, the price, the fact that any other relevant orders will be grouped with this one, and the delivery timeframe.

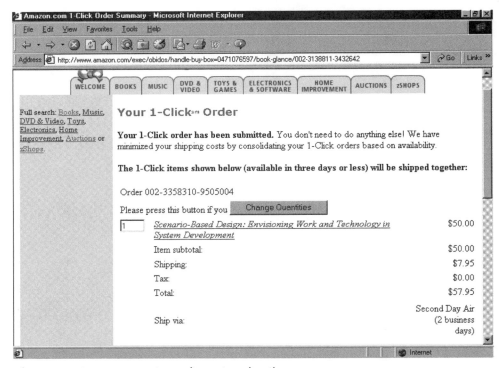

Figure 6-7 Amazon.com's confirmation details.

At this point e-customers may decide to cancel their order, in which case they would need to change the quantities on the confirmation screen to zero, or go into "Your Account," "View Your Order History," select their most recent, unshipped, order, and cancel it.

Amazon's confirmation e-mail also provides useful information on how to cancel unshipped orders, as follows:

> Please note that you can view the status of your account, examine your orders, cancel unshipped orders, change your e-mail address or password, or update your subscriptions to our Personal Notification Services at any time through the "Your Account" link on the navigation bar.

http://www.amazon.com/your-account

As a contextual designer you will need to consider what is required to provide the e-customer with an appropriate level of comfort throughout, and after, the order process, and visibility of, and access to, product cancellation is an important part of this. E-mail content is a good way to confirm cancellation details after an order has been received.

Amazon.com helps reassure new e-customers by providing feedback on order details during the order process. E-customers are also frequently advised that they can delete the order by changing the requested quantity to zero. At the end of the process, e-customers are presented with a screen entitled "Review and Submit Your Order—the last step!" This last screen clearly gives e-customers the task of reviewing all data accumulated during the order before confirming their order with the "Place Your Order" button.

Making this "Review and Submit" exercise so deliberate and clear reassures e-customers that they are getting what they want, the way they want, and gives them a definite last chance to cancel the order if they need to.

As a contextual designer you need to craft an order process that proves the trustworthiness of the order process to new e-customers. You need to consider how you can make an order process singular and consistent; any little quirks can throw a new e-customer off balance.

4. Gather personal information required (or default already-held information).

In the case of 1-click ordering, the personal information that has been captured, or set up, by e-customers, in their 1-click settings is defaulted to the order process. E-customers don't have to tell Amazon.com anything about themselves, and only need to confirm their 1-click order.

Of course, the first time around, if e-customers haven't yet set up 1-click ordering, they are required to register during the order process, and as previously discussed, this comes at the beginning of the order process.

5. Advise the order is complete, how the e-customer can follow up, and what will happen next.

In the case of 1-click ordering, Amazon.com provides, confirmation that the order has been received and is being processed along with confirmation of the order, as seen above in Figures 6-6 and 6-7.

In the case of the longer order process, Amazon.com provides confirmation that the order has been completed successfully at the end of the process, having already confirmed order details.

In addition, Amazon.com's use of e-mail extends the order process from the interface process. This allows Amazon.com to go the extra mile in providing e-customers with information about their order and assurance that everything is happening according to plan.

A confirmation e-mail is automatically generated as soon as Amazon.com has received an order via the Web site. This confirmation e-mail gives e-customers:

1. Instructions on how to get in touch with Amazon.com if they have a query (by e-mail and phone).

2. Confirmation of their personal details associated with the order.

3. Details of the ordered item: title, component prices, the total price and availability.

4. Instructions on how to view the status of their account, to review or cancel their order, or make changes to their personal details. A Web address is also provided so that e-customers can click straight through to that part of the Web site and make any necessary changes.

And then, once the e-customer's order has been shipped they receive another e-mail comprising:

1. Advice that their items have been shipped and their order completed.

2. A summary of the items shipped.

3. Confirmation of the shipping address.

4. A tracking number and a Web address that they can click on to go straight to tracking on Amazon.com's "Help" page.

5. Instructions on how to get in touch if you have a query (by e-mail, phone, and fax).

Many online order processes generate automated e-mail responses that confirm the basic details of an order. Amazon goes one step further than most by providing information on when ordered items have been shipped, and are, therefore, likely to arrive. Keeping e-customers in the loop, after the online order has been placed, is a good way to build trust and also to reduce the "noise" created by people ringing up to find out where their order is.

As a contextual designer you will need to consider how far you can extend online processes, such as the order process, through the use of e-mail.

3. Browse books I might be interested in

Amazon.com facilitates browsing and makes recommendations, as independent pursuits, but also uses recommendations as a key lever in facilitating browsing. However, should one pursuit suffer at the hand of the other, there would be a problem independently facilitating these e-customer themes and, therefore, meeting the basic requirements of a contextual design approach.

Amazon recognizes the importance of browsing on its Web site and it provides e-customers with plenty of useful levers to browse items that might interest them, and it does that throughout its site. Amazon.com successfully uses interesting "hooks" relevant to its products and online experience. As a contextual designer you will need to consider the appropriate emphasis given to browsing, and what levers are most relevant and useful to your e-customers.

Amazon.com's basic navigation system facilitates and encourages browsing. On coming to Amazon.com, e-customers are met by text greeting them by name (through the use of a cookie), advises them "We have recommendations for you," and provides links to "Recommendations home" and the recommendations pages within each store. Amazon.com also provides a "Quick picks" menu on the welcome page that summarizes an e-customer's top few personal recommendations.

The invitation to check out personal recommendations is then carried through to each store's welcome page at the next level of drilldown, allowing customers to browse items of interest at a store level. In addition, the lower navigation bar at the top of the page explicitly invites browsing within each store "Browse Subjects" in books, "Browse Styles" in music, "Browse Genres" in video, "Browse Categories" in electronics and software, and so on.

To further encourage browsing, Amazon.com's store-specific navigation bar is structured around content areas people are interested in browsing. The book store navigation bar allows e-customers to browse bestsellers, award winners, and books in the media as shown in Figure 6-8.

Figure 6-8 Amazon.com facilitates browsing in its bookstore.

Similarly, the content on each store's welcome page consistently provides a short-cut menu to browsing in that store, highlights, and something akin to a "What's Hot" for that particular store, such as "Amazon.com 100 Hot Books, Updated Hourly" in the book store.

Other content—such as Amazon.com's "Essentials," "Celebrity Picks", "Our Current Favorites," "Get started in... [a particular music style]", and "Mood Matcher" (in music)—provides useful levers for browsing.

Amazon.com's music and DVD/video essentials are shown in Figure 6-9.

This type of content (from the Amazon.com welcome page down) allows e-customers to start (and continue) their browsing without having to work through the navigation system (i.e., they can move around laterally, rather than up and down).

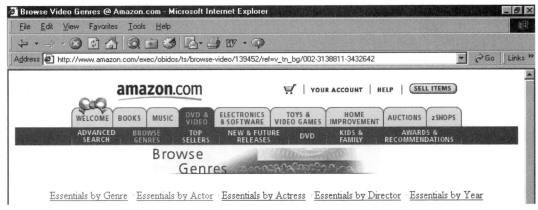

Figure 6-9 Browsing "Essentials" on Amazon.com.

As a contextual designer, you will need to consider what browsing triggers are explicit in the navigation, and what are simply provided as content. Triggers, or hooks, provided as content place more onus on the e-customer. Of course, the e-customer wants to do things other than browse, and there is a balance to be struck when choosing between the use of navigation and content.

Amazon.com provides a high-level and centralized part of the site for recommendations. These are linked to and from hypertext on the welcome page, as shown in Figure 6-10.

As a contextual designer you will need to consider the relative roles of content and the navigation system in directing e-customers to areas of interest. There are always trade offs because you can't give the same visibility to everything. How important parts of the site, such as "Recommendations Home," are found by e-cus-

Figure 6-10 Access to recommendations home is provided through hypertext.

tomers is a key decision when designing a site's navigation and templates for the presentation of content.

As a contextual designer you will also need to consider an e-customer's need for external browsing, as well as internal browsing. Will you provide external as well as internal links, and if so, what sorts of links and in what context?

There is always a delicate balance to strike when providing external links. You want to add value to e-customers' experiences, but you don't want them to take off into the Web and never come back to your site. Amazon.com is pretty modest in its provision of external links. A search across "All Products," for example, will result in a link to results generated from searching for the keyword on the Web.

As a contextual designer you would need to consider the degree of external orientation, and external links, required to meet e-customers' needs. If we decided that "Use Amazon as a key part of my research project," was an important e-customer theme, then more external orientation may be required. However, it is not a direct facilitator of the theme to browse and get recommendations on books, and therefore not a priority in relation to those themes.

4. Get recommendations on books that might interest me

Amazon.com's recommendations can be passively supplied online, as per its "Essentials" seen in Figure 6-9, and by e-mail, as with its "Amazon.com Delivers" service, or they can be actively personalized by Amazon.com and e-customers online and by e-mail.

Amazon.com learns from all of its e-customers' purchase behavior to make recommendations to e-customers. On the item product page, Amazon.com advises e-customers that "Customers Who Bought This Title Also Bought [recommended titles]" And on the order page Amazon.com advises e-customers that "Customers

Who Bought The Items In Your Shopping Cart Also Bought [recommended titles]."
Amazon.com also encourages e-customers to generate content that helps other e-customers, in the form of e-customer reviews.

As a contextual designer you would need to consider how interrelated e-customer activities should be, and how e-customers can help and support one another. Should e-customers be able to generate, and/or discuss, site content, for example? The interrelation of e-customer activities can be implicit, as seen in Amazon.com's purchase-generated recommendations, and explicit, as seen in Amazon.com's customer reviews.

As a contextual designer, you would need to decide how explicitly e-customer activities can, and should, be interrelated.

E-customer-generated reviews provide content that the site would not have otherwise had and that e-customers need to assist them in their purchase decisions. Of course, those reviews need to be useful, and Amazon.com encourages usefulness by allowing e-customers to rate reviews. These usefulness ratings are then represented as badges with a number of stripes corresponding to the usefulness of the review provided. Amazon.com also invites reviewers to set up member pages, giving reviewers a persona around their reviews and allowing potential buyers to check out other reviews posted by the same reviewer.

Once you have decided whether e-customers can generate content, you also have to decide whether that content will be subject to mediation. Amazon.com examines reviews before they are posted to the site and states that "Comments That Are Not Specific to the Item's Content May Not Be Posted on Our Site". Amazon.com also gives e-customers an e-mail mechanism to complain about comments provided by reviewers, should the e-customer find the comments offensive.

As a contextual designer, you may find other ways that e-customers could help and support one another. For example, could reviewers and potential buyers discuss a particular review online? And could potential sellers discuss sale items with potential buyers in relation to auctions or any other similar transactions facilitated?

As a contextual designer you will need to consider how explicit the community aspects of the site should be as well as who should be part of that community (i.e., are only e-customers involved or are other suppliers, such as publishers, involved as well)?

If bulletin boards and threaded discussions are used around certain topics, for example, you should consider how these can be related to other parts of the site. Could reviews themselves be discussed, and those discussions be linked to reviews, to help e-customers make a purchase? In what other ways could member pages also be leveraged to help provide e-customers with recommendations?

As well as leveraging e-customer content, Amazon.com also explicitly provides personalized recommendations. These "Instant Recommendations" are personalized on the basis of an e-customer's purchase history and/or that of all other Amazon.com e-customers.

Instant recommendations are also based on refinements that e-customers make to their "Instant Recommendations." An e-customer's personal recommendations update every time they make a purchase, or refine their recommendations. E-customers refine their recommendations by rating past purchases. The invitation to rate past purchases is shown in Figure 6-11.

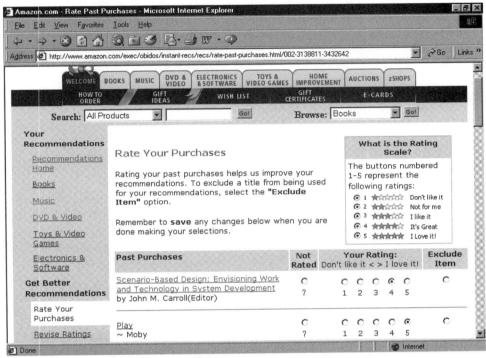

Figure 6-11 E-customers rate purchased items to refine their personal recommendations.

As a contextual designer you would need to decide how central personalized recommendations are to an e-customer's online experience and, therefore, how they should be accessed and how they should be presented in the context of other Web site content.

As a contextual designer you would need to consider how well, and how intuitively, the rating mechanism function reflects the different actions customers want to take in refining their recommendations (i.e,. how well does each piece of functionality relate to each intended action?). There may be other actions e-customers want to take to refine their recommendations. You would need to consider what these might be and what functions and structures would support them. For example, would e-customers want to arbitrarily add an item they really like so that recommendations for related items could be generated?

And you would need to consider how to recognize the fact that e-customers may already own some items recommended by the Web site, and find a way for the e-customer to factor this in.

On Amazon.com, e-customers are invited to "Advise" Amazon that they own a title by rating it. Amazon.com provides the following explanation:

How can I tell you that I already own a title you recommended?

Go to any recommendation product page and click on the "Rate These Items" link. This will take you to a page where you can rate titles that you own. This will both remove that title from your recommendations list and help generate new recommendations for you.

This combines the actions of rating a recommended product and advising that it is already owned. This may, or may not, be intuitive to e-customers.

A key consideration of offering recommendations on any Web site is the extent to which the site remembers e-customer information and activities. Amazon.com's recommendations are based on remembering purchases and the refinements (ratings) that e-customers attach to them.

Amazon.com does well by basing its recommendations on what it knows about an e-customer (rather than what it doesn't know) and by visibly using the information e-customers give to refine Amazon's recommendations. If e-customers make another purchase or rate an item they've purchased, their recommendations automatically update. This is important if we recall our previous customer directives: number. 8, "Be careful second guessing my needs," and number 4, "Use what I give you."

Now, this raises another interesting design consideration—how far does the site's memory extend? Is it applied to generate online personal recommendations only? Could e-customers benefit more directly from collective e-customer ratings by being able to view how items were rated, perhaps on average, by other e-customers? And could the site's memory also be applied to e-mail recommendations?

Amazon.com offers a subscription service called "Amazon.com Delivers." This service allows e-customers to select topics related to each store and receive e-mail from site editors on "hot," and interesting, items related to those topics. These e-mails contain generic (and not personalized) recommendations (i.e., Amazon.com does not apply what e-customers have when e-mailing recommendations—apart from the topics they know about e-customers checked against the Amazon.com delivers service). Does that matter? Maybe, and maybe not. It depends on the expectations of e-customers and what they find most useful.

Amazon.com also offers a service called "Eyes," which allows e-customers to nominate authors or topics that interest them, so that when a new book is published, they are informed by e-mail. This provides yet another trigger for e-customers to go and browse a new item, and it is a good way to bring them back online, if they haven't visited the site for a while.

Accessing recommendations

The "Amazon.com delivers" and "Eyes" services are mentioned in relevant contexts; "Amazon.com Delivers" information is generated along with recommendations, and "Eyes" information is generated along with some search results. This contextual placement of information is good because it puts the content where it is directly related to what e-customers are trying to do and, therefore, where it is most meaningful to the e-customer.

The "Amazon.com Delivers" information is shown in Figure 6-12.

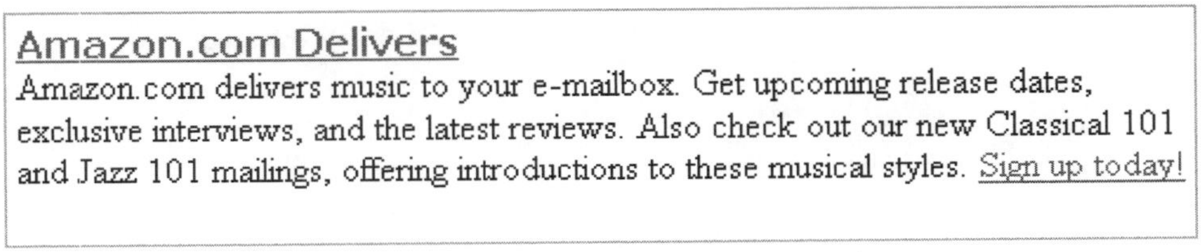

Amazon.com Delivers
Amazon.com delivers music to your e-mailbox. Get upcoming release dates, exclusive interviews, and the latest reviews. Also check out our new Classical 101 and Jazz 101 mailings, offering introductions to these musical styles. Sign up today!

Figure 6-12 Contextual "Amazon.com Delivers" information.

"Eyes" information is generated as a result of a search. The excerpt in Figure 6-13 was generated as a result of searching against the topic of "Web design."

Clicking on "Sign Up" takes e-customers straight to the "Eyes" registration screen, which explains the "Eyes" service and defaults the topic of "Web design." Then all they have to do is select "Sign Up" and they're done.

As a contextual designer you will need to consider how relevant content gets generated in response to e-customer actions, such as the contextual provision of "Amazon.com Delivers" and "Eyes" information. This consideration will be tied in with content planning and page template design. (See the discussion of content management in Chapter 5).

Eyes works while you play.
Eyes sends you e-mail every time a new book is released in which the subject words include "Web design".

Sign up for Eyes!

Figure 6-13 Contextual "Eyes" information.

Now, on entry to a Web site, e-customers try to work out exactly what your Web site allows them to do. Therefore, the welcome page is important in making e-services visible. On Amazon.com's welcome page, services such as "Eyes" and "Amazon.com Delivers" are grouped under a generic description of "Special Features" as shown in Figure 6-14.

Explanation of the "Amazon.com Delivers" and "Eyes" services are actually contained under "your account", which is seen at the top right hand corner of every page. Then, that explanation is found after responding to the invitation to "view or change your subscriptions".

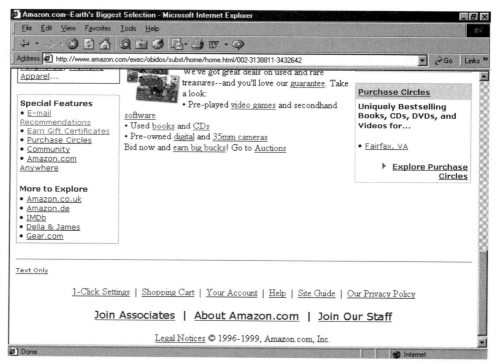

Figure 6-14 Mention of Amazon.com's special features on the welcome page.

There are always trade offs when designing a Web site; you can't give the same visibility to everything. How actual services, such as "Amazon.com Delivers" and "Eyes," get profiled and are, therefore, found and used, is a key decision when designing a site's navigation and templates for the presentation of content.

To create complete visibility of e-services, some sites have navigation systems explicitly structured around services and e-customer activities. Different approaches to the design of navigation systems will be explored further under "Navigation" in Chapter 7.

5. Keep a note of books that interest me

E-customers are encouraged to browse and will, no doubt, find all sorts of goodies that interest them, but they may not necessarily buy them right there and then. In fact, some items of interest to e-customers may not ever be bought—they may be triggers for finding other items that will be browsed and bought later, for example.

So how do e-customers keep a note of their favorite items? This relates to how the site's memory is used on behalf of e-customers and how that is presented. And when deciding on the appropriate level of memory the site should exhibit, you should also consider why e-customers want to remember an item and how that relates to other activities (or e-customer themes), such as purchase.

Amazon.com allows e-customers to remember items without having to buy them, and this is explicitly linked to the purchase process. E-customers select an item for purchase and can then select "Save for Later" next to that item in their shopping cart. When e-customers want to buy the item, they select "Move to Cart," as shown in Figure 6-15.

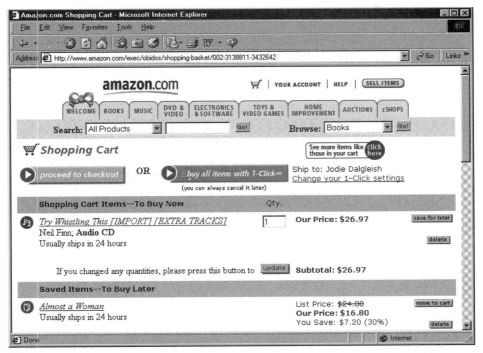

Figure 6-15 Amazon.com centralizes the memory of interesting items in the shopping cart.

Amazon.com also offers a "Wish List" service. This service is centered on keeping a note of things e-customers would like so that other friends and family members can buy them; making gift-buying easier at times of gift-giving and helping the e-customer receive a gift they like.

As a contextual designer you would need to consider what functions adequately facilitate this e-customer theme in light of what e-customers are trying to achieve as a result of remembering an item. You would probably need to associate specific e-customer scenarios with this theme and consider the goals related to each, and then decide how each is facilitated in relation to the others. Scenario goals could be:

- "I want the item, but I'll have to buy it later."
- "I want someone else to buy me the item."
- "I want to explore this item more next time I have a chance."
- "I want to explore items related to this one, when I have a chance."
- "I want to show these items to someone else who will be interested in them."

Having identified these component scenarios, you may decide to break this theme up into more specific themes, or keep the theme at this high level with its associated scenarios. In fact, as a contextual designer, you would associate more detailed customer scenarios with every e-customer theme considered here. You would then also consider how the themes, overall, should be categorized. We will discuss the categorization of scenarios and themes further under "A customer-effective design process" later in this chapter.

6. Follow up on a book I want

This theme is likely to be tied in with e-customers finding, and buying, the book they want. In particular, it is likely to be closely related to issues of availability.

On Amazon.com, e-customers can make second-hand orders, as we know. E-customers are made aware of the status of their order when they receive an e-mail from Amazon.com inviting them to authorize a second-hand copy they have located. E-customers can also check that their out of print order is still current under "Your Account" where it can be viewed as an open order; and the e-customer can change any of the details relating to that order, such as delivery address.

If the book is unavailable, and e-customers have had some way of notifying Amazon.com of their interest, then they would probably want to keep up with the status of the book's availability on an ongoing basis, until it becomes available. This would be a reversal of the "Check Back Regularly" invitation Amazon.com makes to e-customers.

And then, if a book has even been published, e-customers can use Eyes to be notified, by e-mail, when the new book comes out in print.

As a contextual designer you would need to consider how important this "follow-up" activity is and how much of an identifiable pursuit it needs to be on the Web site. You would need to consider whether the e-customer needs more continuous advice on the status of different orders. You would want to find out what, if any, e-mail inquiries a business gets about the status of orders, and the availability of products, and consider how site functionality can be used to displace the need for e-mail correspondence (i.e., let e-customers solve their problem online).

Should e-customers have access to a central area where they manage their interest in certain products with different availability characteristics? What affect would this have an relationships between themes that might share this type of functionality?

7. Send someone a gift

Amazon.com makes gift-giving easy. This aspect of its site provides a seamless experience around the noble pursuit of gift-giving. By providing a central area dedicated to gift-giving, Amazon.com is able to tie together all of the goodies on its Web site for the benefit of the giver and receiver.

Not only does Amazon.com give gift-giving higher-level visibility through its navigation system, by presenting "Gift Ideas" and "Gift Certificates" in its bottom navigation bar, but it also provides a menu of services that drills down to a thorough explanation of each of its "Gift Services," as shown in Figure 6-16.

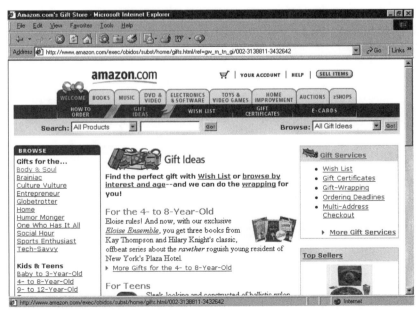

Figure 6-16 Amazon.com makes its gift services easily accessible.

Gift-giving is treated as a primary e-customer activity on Amazon.com.

Amazon.com gift-giving is the only activity presented within the navigation system. By being on the bottom navigation bar, gift-giving is visible only from the welcome page because the bottom navigation bar changes out to the store an e-customer chooses on entry.

As a contextual designer you would need to consider the visibility of gift-giving vis-à-vis other e-customer activities. You would also need to consider other activities e-customers need to perform on Amazon.com and consider the relative level of exposure required.

In addition, where gift-giving is concerned, you would need to consider the dynamics of both gift-giving and gift-receiving to offer useful and relevant services related to this e-customer theme. Gift-giving involves a giver and receiver, with different characteristics and completely different goals. You would need to associate scenarios to this theme that take into account the rich context of gift-giving, and then consider the giver's goals relative to the receiver's goals and the best way to facilitate both.

For example, what if the giver and receiver live on opposite sides of the world—how does this limit the gifts that can be purchased and sent and how should we advise e-customers of these limitations? When is it better to send a physical gift, a paper gift voucher, or an electronic gift voucher, considering aspects such as recipient location, cost, and reliability of delivery? What reassurance can we offer gift givers that their recipients, who may not be on the Internet or may be novice Internet users, will be able to successfully complete the process of finding what they want and redeem a gift voucher? Should senders be able to attach personalized tips and a list of items that they thought the recipient might like to their gift order?

8. Keep track of a gift I sent

We know that gifts are normally tied in with special dates, such as birthdays, and, therefore, e-customers are likely to want to know whether gifts make it on time and when they've been received.

As a contextual designer you would need to decide what gift givers need to receive by way of automated e-mail, or what information and/or functionality they should be able to access online, to keep track of gifts they have sent.

If there is no notification of when a gift certificate has been redeemed and received (i.e., receipt of an e-mail or mailed dispatch of a physical gift certificate), gift givers have a period of "silence" when they don't know whether their recipient has actually got anything from them, or not.

9. Redeem a gift voucher

As a contextual designer you would need to consider who will be redeeming a gift voucher. We know, for sure, that it's someone other than the e-customer who generated the gift voucher. And we also know that gift recipients are likely to be coming to Amazon.com expressly to redeem their gift certificates. We need to consider the different processes required at both ends of gift-giving; giving, and receiving.

I recently sent Amazon.com gift vouchers to my two brothers in New Zealand. The elder of my younger brothers had no access to the Internet at home or work, and would have probably never looked up a Web site before, let alone used one to generate an order! How does the process of redeeming gift vouchers need to welcome and guide the fortunate recipients of gift vouchers. And how does Amazon.com make the most of the opportunity to convert the gift recipient to an e-customer?

Amazon.com gives immediate visibility to "Gift Certificates" on the Amazon.com welcome page. Clicking on this item in the bottom navigation bar will take voucher recipients straight to instructions on how to redeem their gift voucher as shown in Figure 6-17.

Figure 6-17 "Gift Certificates" is visible on Amazon.com's welcome page.

Gift voucher redemption is done via the order process. So long as voucher recipients can make their way through the order process, they'll do OK.

In addition, you will need to decide what identifier the gift will be tracked against so that e-customers can follow-up on whether a gift voucher has been redeemed. This will be largely dependent on what is most congruent with the business' service processes. Amazon.com uses a voucher code (number) to identify vouchers for redemption.

10. Update my personal information

Having identified this as a separate theme, we gain an interesting perspective on Amazon.com's use of "Your Account." "Your Account" is a central place where e-customers go to proactively change or activate most Amazon.com services, including subscription services, as shown in Figure 6-18.

By considering distinct themes related to e-customer activity, as a contextual designer, you start to think about how intuitively things can be grouped, or not. For example, would you group the maintenance of services, such as subscription services, with the action of updating personal information? You would need to consider whether "Your Account" is intuitively obvious as the center for updating personal, and other, information.

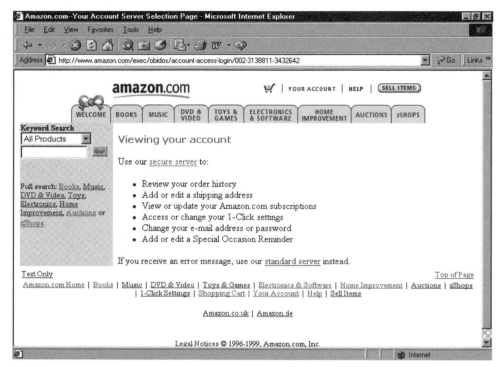

Figure 6-18 Amazon.com centralizes e-customer maintenance through "Your Account."

You could explore some alternatives with e-customers—such as renaming "Your Account" (e.g., to "Your Profile"?) and splitting out the function of updating personal information and activating and performing actions on groups of Amazon.com services into separate areas with distinct identities. This might also tie in with your testing of navigation system concepts (refer back to Web site concept testing in Chapter 3). You will soon find out what works best.

Generic e-customer themes

Now that we have considered specific activities e-customers may wish to complete on Amazon.com, let us, within the framework of this Amazon.com example, consider the generic activities that e-customers wish to complete.

We will refer back to the "Five Doing Areas" discussed in Chapter 2 to associate e-customer scenarios with these generic themes, and we will discuss related design considerations.

1. Get help (generic)

Related e-customer scenarios are as follows:

- Get help using this Web site.
- Resolve a problem online.
- Find out where to go, or who to talk to, if I have a problem I can't resolve online.

Get help using this Web site.

As a contextual designer, one of your decisions will be the nature and scope of help offered to e-customers. Many sites interpret the general function of "help" differently. When deciding the help you will offer, relevance and detail will be of prime importance. Many sites do lip service to helping e-customers use their sites—not so with Amazon.com. Amazon's Help centralizes a lot of information to help e-customers use their site.

Because "help" has become such a flaky concept on Web sites, it often isn't intuitively obvious to e-customers what will be offered. And so, unfortunately, even though help might be truly helpful, e-customers may not expect, or naturally seek, some of the services and content you provide under the label of "help."

Therefore, as a contextual designer you will also need to consider how your navigation system, and the dialogue provided as e-customers move about your site, clearly directs e-customers to help when they need it.

It is particularly important to relate "help" topics to e-customer usage. In other words, "help" should relate to e-customer themes. As a contextual designer, you will need to consider how "help" can be structured and presented to support e-customer activities, at the time the activity is being completed.

It would also be a good idea to provide information expressly for new users, should they need an extra helping hand. You will also need to consider how important it is for new users to see this help and how they are directed to it.

On Amazon.com we see advice for new e-customers given under "For first-time visitors" in the "Help" section, as shown in Figure 6-19.

As we can see from Figure 6-19, first-time visitors are helped under the heading of "Find What You Want" and are then offered a "Site Guide" by which they can acquaint themselves with finding what they want on Amazon.com. The site guide provides a useful list of links to areas in each store of the Web site, a complete directory of worthwhile places to browse on Amazon.com.

As a contextual designer, you will need to consider the balance between help for new, and more seasoned, visitors, and whether a distinction needs to be made between the help offered to both.

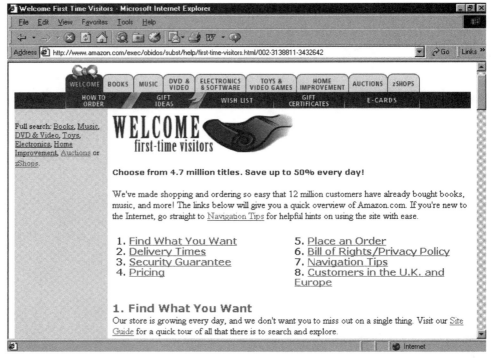

Figure 6-19 Amazon.com's "guide" for first-time visitors.

Resolve a problem online

E-customers may come to a Web site with a particular problem in mind. For example, say an Amazon.com e-customer orders a book and then gets that book as a birthday present; the e-customer promptly wants to get online and cancel the order. Now, the e-customer can do a few things—grab an e-mail address off Amazon.com and send an e-mail saying "Can I cancel my order?"; go to the order confirmation e-mail, if it still exists, to see if it tells them how to cancel the order (incidentally, it does); or try to find out how to cancel an order by perusing Web site content such as FAQs.

When businesses are analyzing and specifying their requirements, I recommend that they identify the top ten customer problems and then work out the best ways to give e-customers speedy resolution, online first, and then offline if necessary. (Refer to "Customer Service" and "Customer Integration" in Chapter 4 to see the types of e-service considerations facing businesses.)

As a contextual designer, you should specifically consider the use, and placement, of FAQs as a means to empower customers to resolve their own problems, which in turn removes unnecessary offline contact between the e-customer and the business.

FAQs are employed differently by different Web sites. FAQs can be centralized and de-centralized and can be presented in different ways and employ different functionality. On Amazon.com, an FAQ area is provided under "For First Time Visitors." This FAQ area covers some of the issues that are likely to concern first-time visitors (and possibly others as well). Amazon.com also offers quick-reference questions on the store home pages of "Auctions" and "zShops," as shown in Figure 6-20.

Top 5 Questions

1. How do I search?
2. How do I bid?
3. How do I sell?
4. Are there fees?
5. Why is it safe?

(a)

Top 5 Questions

1. What are zShops?
2. How do I buy?
3. How do I sell?
4. Are there fees?
5. Why is it safe?

(b)

Figure 6-20 Amazon.com provides quick-reference FAQs in (a) Auctions and (b) zShops.

Another aspect of helping e-customers use your Web site is the provision of useful responses when they generate an error. As a contextual designer, you will need to consider each specific error and how it will be handled. Generic error screens should be customized as much as possible to provide e-customers with guidance on what to do to solve their problem.

This is particularly important when e-customers are completing and sending e-mail forms, such as those used in an order process. You should carefully identify the data entry and validation rules and craft every message that e-customers receive when they enter information that doesn't conform to those rules. Simply telling customers they haven't completed all of the required fields, or have completed fields incorrectly, is not enough to guide e-customers. (Refer back to customer directive number 16; "Tell me the info you need" in Chapter 2.)

Find out where to go, or who to talk to, if I have a problem I can't resolve online.

A Web site always needs a quick-to-find summary of contacts. Sometimes this is presented alongside FAQs such as in the Bank of America example given in Figure 4-3.

Amazon.com offers a summarized list of contacts in "Contact Us." This is accessed by selecting "Send us E-mail" under "Other Important Info" in the "Help" section. The "Contact Us" screen is shown in Figure 6-21.

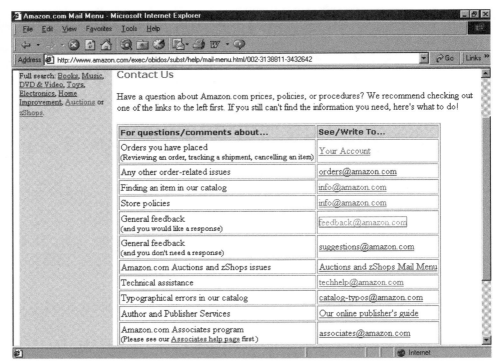

Figure 6-21 Amazon.com's "Contact Us" summarizes who to contact, and for what.

Amazon.com also provides help as content within the context of certain e-customer activities, such as completing an order, as follows:

> If you have any difficulties with this order, send e-mail to orders@amazon.com or phone (800) 201-7575. From outside the U.S. or Canada, phone +1 (206) 266-2992. You may want to bookmark this page before you phone us so you can come back quickly to this step.

When providing contact information, you will need to consider the respective roles of physical and virtual contacts. Amazon.com always offers access to a "real person" as well as e-mail access. (Refer back to "Eleven Best-Practice Fundamentals;" "Balance the Physical and Virtual" in Chapter 4)

As with other features, you will need to decide on the visibility of contact information. If a lot of e-customers come to your site to find contact information and talk with you, you'd best make it obvious. Some sites put "Contact Us" up front in the navigation and others put it up front as a content link.

2. Provide feedback (generic)

Related e-customer scenarios are as follows:

- Make a suggestion.
- Complain.

Make a suggestion

As with "Contact Us," you will need to decide how important it is for e-customers to provide feedback, and how up front it should be. Amazon.com provide requests for feedback in the context of particular e-customer activities, catching e-customers when they have a fresh recollection of what they've just experienced on the Web site and what they think of it. In this way, Amazon.com is more likely to get useful feedback from e-customers; and they do use it to improve their Web site.

We can see a request for feedback on the Eyes service within the context of an e-customer going about setting up the Eyes service, as shown in Figure 6-22.

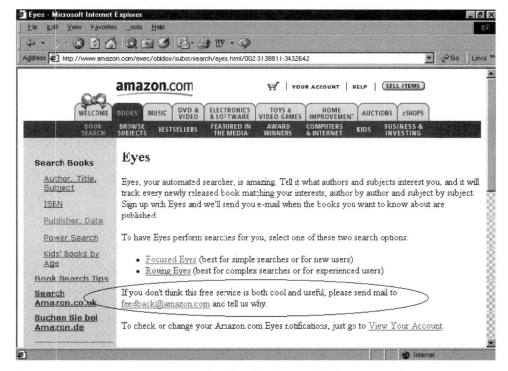

Figure 6-22 Amazon.com invites feedback when and where it is relevant to the e-customer

Complaints

It seems undesirable to ask an e-customer to complain. After all, we don't want complaints do we? Well, chances are, that e-customers will want to complain at some point. If you don't provide an outlet for e-customer complaints, e-customers will probably end up using some other e-mail form to suit their purpose. You will need to consider how "complaints" can be couched so that e-customers can easily let off steam if they need to, without creating negative overtones.

In addition, as contextual designers, you will need to consider the types of e-mail forms dedicated to different types of e-customer feedback. The nature of the e-mail forms required will reflect the common service requests that e-customers need to make online and will need to support your client's business process improvement efforts. Different types of service requests were discussed in Chapter 5 under "Customer Service;" "Service Fundamentals;" and "Service Process."

You will need to work with your client to develop interface processes that become the nexus between business processes and the processes that e-customers need to complete online. The matching of e-customer—interface—and business processes was discussed in Chapter 5 under "Process Improvement."

Amazon.com does not use e-mail forms to solicit e-customer feedback. Rather it uses a generic mail request generated by the e-customer's browser. This approach may work if there is a dedicated bunch of e-customer service personnel on the other end of e-mails ready to deal with any kind of request quickly and effectively. Most businesses, however, require some e-mails to be sorted and routed to be able to deal with them efficiently. In addition, putting some structure around e-mail forms can help e-customers who may need guidance on what the business is looking for.

E-mail forms can also capture meaningful e-customer information. Recall, however, customer directive number 4 "Use what I give you" and ensure that there is a reason behind, and a use for, every request for information.

Also bear in mind that while e-mail forms can provide a source of data about e-customers, you wouldn't want to start giving e-customers twenty questions when they're trying to complete and send a particular service request. One or two relevant questions might, however, be acceptable, and could provide some vital insight into e-customer requirements and motivation.

3. Find out what is on this Web site

Related e-customer scenarios are as follows:

- Get an overview of what is on this Web site.
- Look for something I believe should be on this site.
- Find out where I am in relation to other areas on the Web site.

Get an overview of what is on this Web site

The way the navigation system is designed and presented provides the key visual cues for e-customers who must quickly and intuitively work out where to go to do what they want to on your Web site.

As a contextual designer you will need to consider how to provide e-customers with obvious paths to the utility your Web site offers them. (The design of navigation systems to appropriately highlight site utility is discussed further in Chapter 7.)

A site map can help e-customers quickly get a view of the scope of your Web site and what it entails. A good site map provides e-customers with direction (that is, after all, the metaphor provided by using the label of "map"). Unfortunately, many site maps are rudimentary lists of links. Other sites bite the bullet and provide, what they call, a "site index" because they know what they're providing is not a "map."

As a contextual designer you will need to consider what form and function the site directory, or map, should take. If you can find form and function that works better than the current site map phenomenon, that is well and good. Whatever you design, make sure it helps the e-customer quickly find out what's on your site and how to get at it. And remember customer directive number 15, "Call a spade a spade."

Look for something I believe should be on this site

Site-level search is an important tool that provides e-customers with potential shortcuts to what they're looking for. It is interesting to note that there is no site-level search on Amazon.com. I guess that Amazon.com expects most e-customers to search against an item, such as a book, in which case the quick search and store-level search should suffice.

However, say an e-customer wants to search against a service or an issue. Much of the information in the "service" areas of the site, such as "Your Account," "Help" and "How To Order" are not searchable. Other product areas such as "Gift Ideas," "Wish List," "Gift Certificates," and "E-Cards" also remain invisible to store-level searches that search against product categories and not activities.

Many of the goodies that could be hard to find on the Amazon site might have been found using a site-level search—goodies like the "Site Guide," "Contact Us" and "Subscription Services" such as "Amazon.com Delivers" and "Eyes." An e-customer looking for e-mail recommendations, for example, might enter "e-mail recommendations," or just "e-mail," or just "Recommendations," to quickly find out about special services Amazon.com offers.

As a contextual designer you need to consider the key service and product dimensions that need to be searchable through a site-level search as well as the keywords used. Keywords should always be in e-customer-speak, not business-speak, and will, most likely, relate to e-customer themes.

Find out where I am in relation to other areas on the Web site

Navigation systems should be designed to provide e-customers with clues on where they are, and where they've been. You will need to decide what aspects of your navigation system will provide this feedback to e-customers. Amazon.com uses a change in color of links, and other navigational elements, as the key device for showing e-customers where they are, and where they've been.

As a contextual designer you will need to consider how overtly e-customers are given cues on where they are and where they've been. Some sites are very overt in providing orientation to e-customers and provide an online dynamic record of where the e-customer has been, particularly in cases where the e-customer is "guided" through a particular process online.

Site maps that are context-sensitive can provide e-customers with feedback on where they are and where they've been. However, this type of functionality seems to be the exception rather than the rule (as is the provision of a site "map" over a site "index.")

Site dialogue, or narrative, is also very important in providing customers with a handle on where they are, and where they've been. Amazon.com makes an effort to provide e-customers with dialogue that orients them throughout the order process, for example. (The use of dialogue in customer-effective design, and the dialog required to complete an order process, is discussed further in Chapter 7.)

ELEVEN DESIGN TIPS

From the Amazon.com example, a number of tips on customer-effective design emerge, as follows:

1. Tell e-customers about the Web site components and processes that relate to the things they are trying to do (and if they don't relate, what purpose do they serve?). Make these services visible and easily accessible.

2. Then tell e-customers what the service process is and design your site in such a way that a service process can be completed seamlessly across all related areas of the site. Make sure e-customers do not have to jump to different parts of your Web site to complete activities that are obviously part of the same process.

3. If your product is subject to availability issues, think about allowing e-customers to actively manage the situation. Think about:

   a. Allowing e-customers to track the availability of what is unavailable.

    b. Notifying e-customers when the item becomes available.

    c. Allowing e-customers to collect, save, and retrieve the items they want (e.g., as favorites).

    d. Considering how interdependencies (such as the activities of publishers in the case of Amazon.com) can be factored into the system (such as through integration of Internet, Extranet, and Intranet technologies) and how e-customers can interact to influence those interdependencies (such as giving publishers feedback in the case of Amazon.com).

4. Decide on the appropriate emphasis for browsing and deliberately identify and create levers to encourage e-customers to browse. Don't forget the important role of enmeshing links (content links that enmesh relevant areas of content in ways that e-customers may not find as a result of using the navigation system).

5. Use automated, and personal, e-mail responses to extend the e-customer service experience outside the Web interface. But make sure the e-mail fits into the required e-customer process; otherwise you'll have e-customers responding to automated e-mails in order to tell you the things they need to, to get things done. This becomes a fruitless and frustrating trap for e-customers who can get caught in a loop of automated responses, none of which take them in the direction of resolving their problem.

6. Whenever you ask e-customers to "Check Back Later," think "what functionality, such as favorites, can we offer customers to flip this around," so the business does the checking on behalf of the e-customer.

7. Realize that e-customers may want to collect items and not purchase them. Also consider how collected items, such as favorites, get quickly flicked over to purchase should the e-customer be ready to buy.

8. When e-customer themes start to share common functionality, think about centralizing those tasks around that functionality (while keeping component tasks identifiable to the e-customer). Functionality along the lines of a personal profile or personal manager may work here. (But make sure it makes sense to centralize tasks in this way—prototyping with real customers is a way to find out if it works.)

9. On e-mail forms—always indicate which fields are mandatory and which aren't, along with examples of fields or other instructions on field format if necessary. Error messages should always state the problem with a particular field and be cumulative (i.e., not dealing with only the first error encountered, and the others on subsequent, recursive, attempts).

10. Ask for feedback when e-customers complete key e-service processes (e.g., after taking an online tour, check on how you did vis-à-vis expectations).

11. As a rule don't give explanatory, and/or directive content unless it's meaningful in allowing a customer to do something. In general, less is more.

A CUSTOMER-EFFECTIVE DESIGN PROCESS

I have drawn on writings about contextual design and scenario-based design (see the Bibliography) and applied my own intuitive understanding of processes that I have used, and seen work, to compile a recommended customer-effective Web site design process.

The customer-effective design process is contextual and based on e-customer scenarios; it starts with e-customers and carries them as the most important element throughout the design process. Other writers have written about, and reported on, the effectiveness of creating scenarios around what system users need to do as a basis for design.

In their book *Scenario-based Design: Envisioning Work and Technology in System Development,* Mary Beth Rosson and John M. Carroll, describe scenarios as a basis for reasoning to:

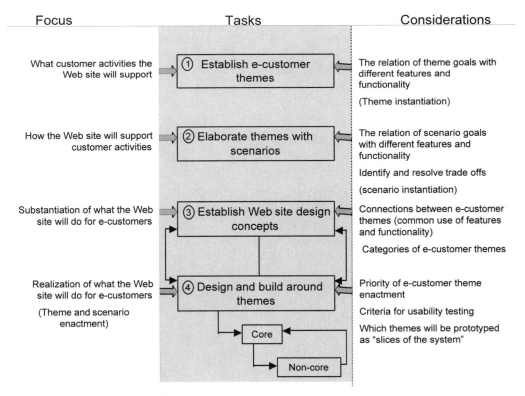

Figure 6-23 The customer-effective design process

... offer task designers a rich view of the goals, actions, and experiences of users interacting with the system. As such, they [scenarios] focus design efforts at the right level, on the tasks the system is intended to support. By developing a detailed account of a user's experience in a task, designers become more attuned to how the knowledge and goals the user brings to the situation interact with the services offered or implied by the system.

The definition of "scenario" is currently hard to pin down. But, in the case of Web site design, customer themes such as those covered in the Amazon.com example, along with more detailed scenarios, seem to work pretty well.

And what can we expect from applying a customer-effective design process? Well, if you consider design in relation to e-customer activities, and an e-customer's context, as in the Amazon.com example, you will be creating a Web site with:

- The utility required for e-customers to get things done.
- Interface processes that help e-customers do things easily.
- Dialogue that helps customers easily learn to do the things they need to do.
- A structure that makes sense to e-customers.

Figure 6-23 outlines the four stages of the customer-effective design process along with associated areas of focus and considerations.

Now let us explore each stage of the customer-effective design process in turn.

1. ESTABLISH E-CUSTOMER THEMES

By establishing e-customer themes, you are "putting a stake in the ground" regarding exactly what your Web site will do for customers. As in the previous Amazon.com example, some themes will be specific to your Web site and some will be general themes that should be found on any Web site.

You would have received a specification from the business outlining what it believes the Web site should do for e-customers, hopefully based on that company's own exploratory research and understanding of e-customer goals and opportunities. It is important for the Web site designer to "push the envelope" as much as possible to make sure the Web site is going to be useful to e-customers.

E-customer themes must be based on things e-customers need, and want, to do on your Web site. And there's a push-pull dynamic that goes on here. While talking to e-customers gives us an insight into what e-customers require, we also have the opportunity to meet customer needs in new ways, or even to meet needs e-customers don't even realize they have yet. There's a balance to be had between taking directions from e-customers and leading the way (and this relationship between e-customers and e-service providers was touched on in Chapter 1 under "Things Have Changed").

Once we have established a possible set of e-customer themes, we can then start to relate each theme to requisite Web site features and functionality and get an idea, at a high level, of the "personality" and purpose of the Web site.

2. ELABORATE THEMES WITH SCENARIOS

As you are exploring what the Web site will do in relation to different e-customer themes, you will need to start breaking those themes down into component tasks or usage scenarios, such as we did previously when considering our fifth Amazon.com theme, "Keep a note of books that interest me".

Going to this next level of specificity will help you instantiate scenarios (i.e., start wrapping something more tangible around abstract descriptions of e-customer themes). You will more closely identify Web site features and functionality with tasks, and start to prioritize those in relation to the tasks that are most critical to e-customers (within and across themes) and the purpose of the Web site as a whole.

This is the stage where you will be faced with trade offs. You won't be able to do everything for e-customers, or even within this medium, and you will need to make some tough decisions. Some of the trade offs we noted in the previous Amazon.com example are as follows:

- *Theme 1.* "Find a book I know I want"—trade offs that come with adopting one particular navigation system over another. (In fact, this trade off recurs in relation to most themes.)
- *Theme 2.* "Buy a book I want"—trade off between auto-populating e-customer details and asking for e-customer authentication early in the order process.
- *Theme 3.* "Buy a book I want"—trade off between taking the e-customer through the order process step by step and consolidating the number of screens required.

3. ESTABLISH WEB SITE DESIGN CONCEPTS

By now you will be getting a pretty good feel for the nature of your Web site, and you will need to start looking for connections between e-customer themes in order to establish concepts you can present to your client and subject to usability testing and prototyping.

Connections will exist between e-customer themes, such as the connection between browsing and generating recommendations in the previous Amazon.com example. Recommendations are a facilitator of browsing, and vice versa.

Themes may also use the same Web site features and pieces of functionality. A basic search function, for example, might support tasks in more than one e-customer theme. As you start to see how features and functionality relate to tasks, categories of e-customer themes will emerge, and these will affect the structure of your Web site, as well as help crystallize component concepts such as:

1. Web site purpose and function (perhaps as expressed through a conceptual metaphor) and the relationship of that to core content and functionality.

2. Core utility the system offers e-customers and what will be mandatory to realize the site's purpose.

3. Web site structure and how the navigation system houses the core content and functionality in a way that facilitates core e-customer processes.

You will be able to substantiate what the Web site will do for e-customers by describing the component concepts that combine to create an e-customer's online experience.

4. DESIGN AND BUILD AROUND THEMES

Now you will be able to start to design and create an interface that facilitates e-customer themes. This interface is the physical manifestation of how the system supports e-customer activities.

There will be an iterative, or circular, relationship between stages 3 and 4 As things become physical you will be constantly re-evaluating and refining your Web site's component concepts. This will be particularly noticeable in relation to content generation and information design (recall our discussion of the "Content Challenge" in Chapter 5).

You will build the most essential components first, bearing in mind that priorities are likely to change as you go as a result of customer testing and conceptual changes. In addition, building "core" and "noncore" components may not necessarily be a linear process, because features and functionality can be shared by core and noncore e-customer themes. If this happens, you may need to explain to your client that you're not diverting energy from essential Web site components; you are maximizing the efficiency of development.

Adopting this contextual design process gives rise to what we previously described as "slices of the system" in Chapter 3. These slices, or interactive themes, are threads of the system that embody e-customer and interface processes. Themes can form the basis of prototyping. Rosson and Carroll describe the creation of prototypes as a result of a scenario-based design process, as follows:

> ...designers begin implementing scenarios early in the design process, almost immediately developing an executable prototype of the task scenarios.

In addition, given that themes and scenarios are based on activities e-customers perform, they will inherently need to uphold certain usability characteristics and these will partly form the basis of usability testing (also refer back to "Ten Usability Heuristics" in Chapter 3.)

Having considered the basis of customer-effective design, and a process we can use to achieve it, we will now move on to consider specific design practices and how they can be improved to create customer-effective Web sites.

CUSTOMER-EFFECTIVE DESIGN PRACTICES

It takes a lot of careful thought, creativity, and discipline to create the online experience that e-customers require.

As with Chapter 6, this chapter is exploratory, rather than directive (i.e., it will give you ideas rather than instructions).

This chapter will look at some existing Web site practices, and what could be done to be more customer-effective, and explore the idea of e-customer themes and the potential practice of theming.

We will explore:

- Creating utility on customer-effective Web sites.
- The use of metaphor in interface design, what works, and how the real power of metaphor can be exploited.
- Providing dialogue to help e-customers learn to use an interface and do what they need to do.
- Types of navigation systems and approaches to designing more customer-effective navigation systems.
- The potential practice of theming where e-customer themes (introduced in Chapter 6) are embodied by utility, dialogue, metaphor, navigation, and content.

CREATE UTILITY

Here I am going to dedicate discussion to a concept that is central to customer-effectiveness—utility. Utility is Web site functionality that allows e-customers to do the things they need to.

If the Web is ever going to truly evolve as a service medium, designers and developers must look to create utility online. We need to harness the interactivity of the Web to provide e-customers with usefully interactive experiences.

It is the role of the Web site designer to "push the envelope" when it comes to utility. The designer is more conversant with the ways in which Web-based technologies can be applied to benefit e-customers. In addition, there is room for a lot of innovation in providing utility. Utility can reinvent existing customer processes or create entirely new ones. Designers have a unique perspective on how to help businesses and e-customers reinvent, and invent, the way things are done.

How do you go about creating utility? Well, there isn't any simple formula or shrink-wrapped application software you can plug in to get it. You have to take the Web-based technologies available to you and put them together in such a way that you benefit e-customers.

You start by talking to e-customers about what they need to do on your Web site. You then create scenarios of what e-customers will do on your Web site and wrap an interface experience around that (we will discuss this later in this chapter under "Theming"). Creating that interface experience requires you to marry concepts with Web-based technologies.

You need to be both smart and creative to come up with utilitarian concepts. And of course, over time, as Web site development companies become more and more adept at building utilitarian components, maybe they will start to be pre-built and bought off the shelf. But even then, these tools may, or may not, deliver the particular experience required by your e-customers and custom development will be required.

SOME EXAMPLES

Utility can apply at a Web site, or Web site component level. In other words, Web sites can be utilitarian (i.e., wholly dedicated to the provision of utility, or provide utilitarian components).

Whether you dedicate yourself wholly to the pursuit of utility and provide a utilitarian Web site will depend on what you need to create to meet your e-customers' needs. These utilitarian Web sites tend to be dedicated to providing a single-minded online service. And many of them are harnessing the ability of the Web to act as a facilitator, to create new online services and new ways of doing business.

I'm not advocating that all Web sites have to be utilitarian, but they do need to be useful to your e-customers. In fact, you can get it wrong with your e-customers if you try to create a utilitarian Web site that emphasizes utility over and above everything else. While utility is important, it doesn't have to be the sole focus of your Web site.

It's a matter of push versus pull, and getting the balance right. What actions should e-customers take initiative on (pull), and what actions should the Web site take initiative on (push)? For example, if e-customers wish to follow up on the status of an order, should they have to go in and seek it out (pull) or should the Web site generate the advice or send it out as e-mail (push)?

We will look at some different examples of utilitarian Web sites, and utilitarian components, and then we will discuss the critical success factors of creating utility.

The Web sites in the following examples might not win any design awards, and they may not necessarily be bastions of customer-effectiveness in their entirety but they offer components that are useful to the people they've been created for.

And you may notice that these examples are about a lot more than just online purchases, although that is obviously an important utility component on many Web sites. Of course, the Web can be applied for a lot more than financial transactions. It can be applied to support e-customers, in whatever it is they need to do.

CISCO.COM

Jim Sterne's book *Customer Service on the Internet,* provides a case study on Cisco Systems and its commitment to online customer service, including the history of how it got to where it is.

Cisco has always impressed me as being a forward-thinking provider of online services. Sure it provides services that naturally lend themselves to the Internet as a service medium, but, Cisco has still been very focused on providing services of direct use to its customers, partners, and resellers.

It has taken its commitment to real-time customer service even further now with its help service "Cisco Live!" which offers synchronous browser sessions between e-customers having a problem with site navigation, user registration, and general Web site-related questions and a "Cisco Live!" representative.

Cisco's introduction to "Cisco Live!" is shown in Figure 7-1.

Cisco has also released "Cisco Interactive Mentor" (CIM), which combines CD-ROM-based functionality with Web site functionality to provide training through the simulation of network configuration and troubleshooting of network problems and interruptions.

In this case, the Web is used to complete a service by providing online community support for CIM participants.

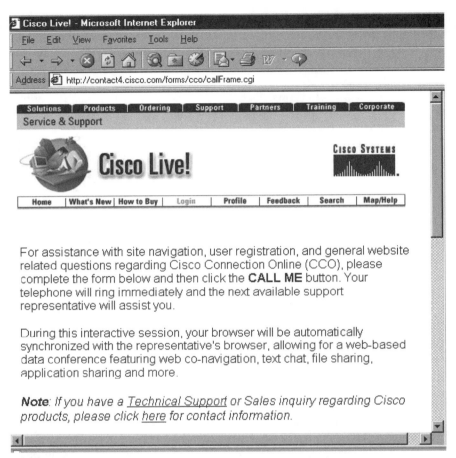

Figure 7-1 Cisco Live! takes interactive help a step further.
These materials have been reproduced by Prentice Hall with the permission of Cisco Systems, Inc. COPYRIGHT ©2000 CISCO SYSTEMS, INC. ALL RIGHTS RESERVED.

Cisco invites e-customers to:

Join other CIM users in sharing and creating knowledge ideas and resources. Help build the community, get on-line support, and enable future product development.

INDULGE.COM

Indulge.com promises an online shopping experience that engages the senses. It shamelessly recognizes, and facilitates, the indulgence of buying something luxurious.

"Online Personal Shoppers" are seasoned and knowledgeable shoppers who are there to support their e-customers' indulgence. Instant messaging is used to provide real-time chat with an online personal shopper who will offer advice on all the goodies that might be right for e-customers. Their "Personal Services" page appears as follows:

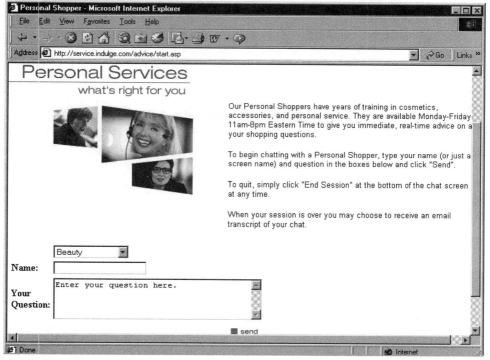

Figure 7-2 Instant messaging provides real-time chat for service.

And to make sure the tips e-customers receive are not lost, Indulge.com will e-mail e-customers a transcript of their chat session.

STATUSFACTORY.COM

StatusFactory.com is entirely dedicated to helping e-customers manage their bills. It has provided a Web site, and supporting functionality, that directly addresses the nightmare of bill-paying.

Cyberbills, the creator of StatusFactory.com, describes the site as a "lifestyle portal" and describes their approach as follows:

Cyberbills has developed technology to support a single interface that allows consumers to view, pay, and manage all of their bills over the Internet, whether the bills are sent [to StatusFactory] or in the traditional paper form.

CyberBills provides its service directly to the public through the StatusFactory.com portal. Businesses who desire to offer Bill Presentment and Payment Services to their own customers can choose from a selection of private, co-branded, reseller, or affiliate programs.

StatusFactory.com describes its e-service process in the online demonstration as shown in Figure 7-3

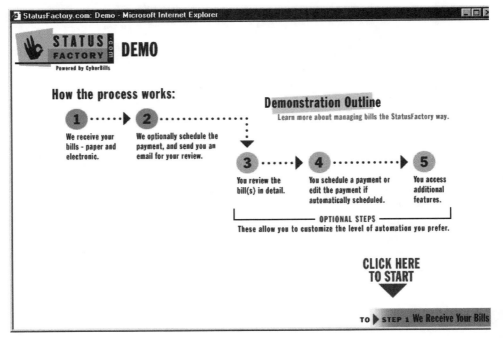

Figure 7-3 The StatusFactory process.
Courtesy of Status Factory.

StatusFactoy.com offers a number of service features that are useful to customers, such as:

- Providing electronic copies of bills online.
- Sending e-mail reminders when bills need to be approved.

- Sending StatusAlert e-mails when something happens, or doesn't happen, in relation to criteria e-customers set.

- Making up to twenty-four months of bill details available for online viewing.

- Allowing e-customers to prescribe different rules to different payees.

- Allowing e-customers to add a payee, where the payee could be anyone.

- Allowing e-customers to create reports online (against categories of expenses e-customers create) as well as request a CD of all their bill data at the end of the year.

StatusFactory has been very careful to give e-customers choice over the level of automation applied to their bill-paying process. E-customers can set up payments for each bill themselves, or they can request that StatusFactory automatically schedule payments against its payment rules.

And StatusFactory has matched service guarantees to the very hassles that e-customers are trying to avoid. I particularly like this one:

> You will cut down on the paper in your life, Status Factory Guarantees, or we will make a $25 donation in your name to the Rain Forest Foundation!

WEBSWAP.COM

WebSwap.com offers e-customers a new spin on the eBay idea of facilitating online trading between buyers and sellers. On WebSwap you can swap stuff as well as pay for it with cash.

WebSwap.com is simply built around "stuff I have" and "stuff I want" and customers don't have to have something to trade to look for stuff they want. WebSwap.com matches the data held by different e-customers to suggest swaps, or e-customers can look for swaps themselves.

The underlying process of "add," "match," and "swap" greets e-customers on download of the home page, as shown in Figure 7-4.

WebSwap.com offers a comprehensive tour of its site. This tour takes e-customers through the swap process step by step. E-customers also receive a "to do list" on their personal WebSwap page ("My WebSwap"), reminding them to do what they need to do, and continuing to help them with the swap process.

This e-service provides functionality that allows e-customers to equate two items they consider to be of equal value, and edit and approve suggested trades. The activity required for e-customers to "Review suggested swaps" is given in WebSwap's online tour, as shown in Figure 7-5.

Given its focus on a straight swap, the complexity of the auction process, such as that seen on eBay, is not required.

There are a few kinks in the site, which is in Beta, but the utility it offers, and the way it has been presented, is interesting.

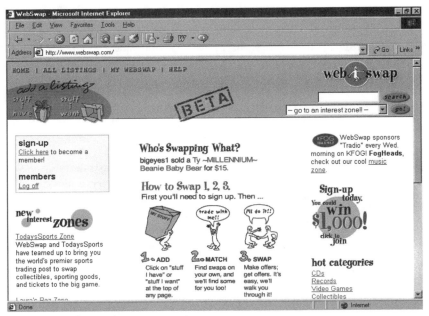

Figure 7-4 The WebSwap.com home page.

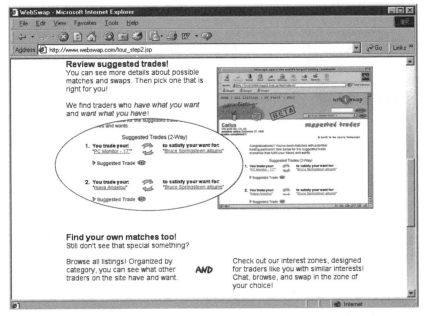

Figure 7-5 WebSwap.com functionality provides suggested trades
Courtesy of WebSwap.

AFTERNIC.COM

Afternic.com gives us yet another spin on the online auction. On this Web site, domain names are being bought and sold.

This Web site gives us a glimpse of the type of new enterprise that has sprung up as a result of the medium itself, but the site is also of interest because it provides core utility that allows e-customers to build and manage a portfolio though a "Personalized control center" called "My Afternic." E-customers are not only able to keep a summary-level view of their auctions and appraisals, they can also view their bids and complete the buy/sell process in "Closings."

In addition, e-customers can use "Tracker" to keep track of the status of domain names that interest them, but which they may not necessarily be involved in buying and selling. "My Afternic" can be seen in Afternic.com's online tour, as shown in Figure 7-6.

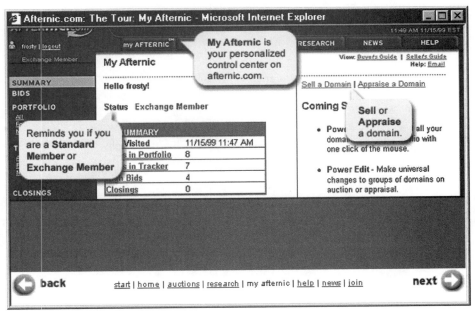

Figure 7-6 Afternic.com provides a personalized control center to manage and track auctions.
Courtesy of afternic.com.

Also of interest is Afternic.com's online help, which comes in three forms: context-sensitive, pop-up, and e-mail.

Context-sensitive help is available by clicking on help links available in the upper right-hand corner throughout the site. Pop-up help is available by clicking on a "?" whenever e-customers have a form to fill out, or may be in need of a definition.

The context-sensitive help links e-customers to FAQs directly relevant to the section of the site they are in at the time.

The links to FAQ information are shown in Figure 7-7.

Figure 7-7 Afernic.com's context-specific links to FAQs.
Courtesy of afternic.com.

In reality the "context-sensitive help" is part of the navigation and not dynamically context sensitive at a micro-level, but it does at least manage to layer and present FAQ information meaningfully throughout the site.

DIGITALTHINK.COM

DigitalThink offers e-learning to e-customers, and its Web site contains many components that harness the interactivity of the Web for the benefit of students, and the ability to participate within a community, in particular.

Students' experience is centralized around their personal locker where they access the various courses they're enrolled in as well as a menu of learning tools such as "scores," "resources," "tutor," "discuss," "classmates," "chat," and "messenger." The menu of help tools can be seen in DigitalThink.com's online tour as shown in Figure 7-8.

Students complete online exercises and quizzes to earn points. They can access "Scores" to find out how many points they have accumulated toward their course total and how well they are doing compared with other students.

Orientation is given through an online tutorial that takes students through core site and course elements. Additional support is provided by making course content available for download in PDF format under "resources" and encouraging direct contact with tutors under "Tutor."

Under "Discuss," community aspects are harnessed to encourage learning through threaded discussions related to shared questions and answers on course-specific topics. Online study groups can be held using online "Chat," and students have direct e-mail access to other students. Students can search, and e-mail, other students who are at the same point in the course as they are, under "Classmates." Students can also identify whether other students are logged into the course at the same time as they are, and e-mail them under "Messenger."

So often the potential of common, and relatively simple, functionality, such as e-mail, is not realized on Web sites. Not so with DigitalThink, whose Web site com-

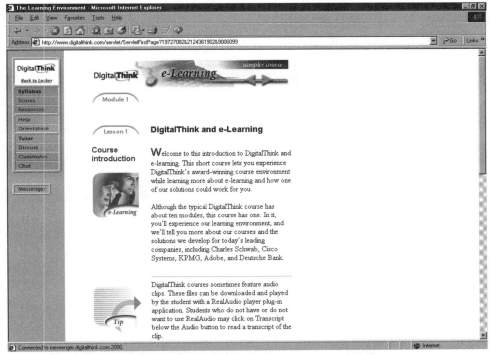

Figure 7-8 DigitalThink.com provide a menu for access to relevant utility components.
Courtesy of DigitalThink.

ponents use common functionality such as e-mail, threaded discussion, and online chat in ways that are extremely useful to students, as can be seen from the feedback DigitalThink has received from its students.

GARDEN.COM

Dedicated to garden enthusiasts, Garden.com, offers an online drawing tool that allows gardeners to design their own garden based on available designs, or from scratch themselves.

Once gardeners have designed their own personal garden, they immediately can buy all, or a portion of, the plants they used in their design online.

The "Plant Finder" is central to garden design, and can be used from anywhere in the site. E-customers use "Plant Finder" to select from plants that meet many different criteria such as sun exposure, soil composition, pH, moisture, color choices, season of bloom, and the level of care required. The garden design tool offers twelve tab functions, as can be seen in the "Planner Tutorial," shown in Figure 7-9.

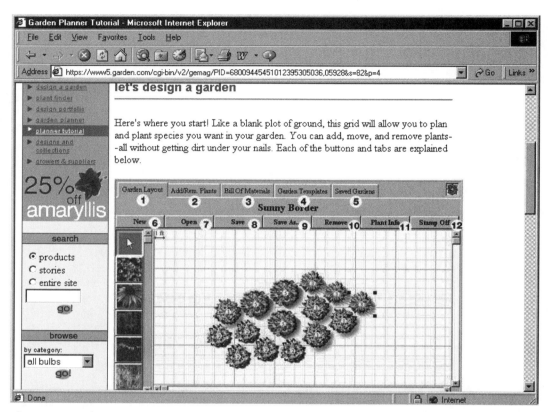

Figure 7-9 A drawing tool e-customers can use online to design their own garden.
Courtesy of garden.com.

The drawing tool has been designed to encourage experimentation, and this is supported through the ability for e-customers to save their designs and register in order to retrieve them on subsequent visits.

Garden.com has also added an interesting feature to the purchase process, in recognition of the fact the e-customers may be buying all of their gifts from the one store. Garden.com allows e-customers to send different products, bought at the same time, to different shipping addresses, by associating an address book with each order. An e-customer fills in the details of the address book and activates the details of different gift recipients in relation to each product. Personal gift messages can also be sent with each gift.

ALLSTATETERMLIFE.COM

Allstate Life Insurance provides a Web site that is very much oriented around things people are likely to want to do on their Web site, such as get a quote for insurance and either apply or save their quote for future use, check out the cost of term life insurance (as part of evaluating Allstate and competitive products), find out how much cover is needed, considering their liabilities and family situation, and find out about how term life insurance works (as part of evaluating different types of products that might meet their needs).

The various e-customer activities are clearly identifiable on the home page, as shown in Figure 7-10.

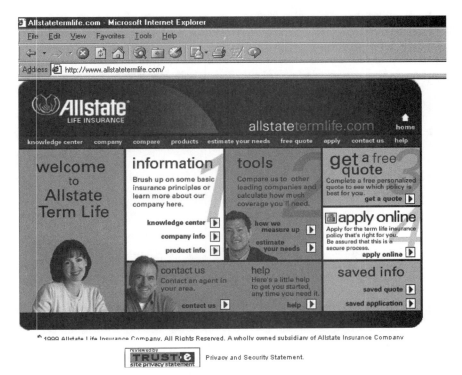

Figure 7-10 Allstatetermlife.com's home page.
Courtesy of Allstate Life Insurance.

Allstatetermlife.com offers "Tools" that allow e-customers to directly compare how Allstate measures up to its competitors. It is unusual to see this sort of direct comparison made, even though it's something e-customers are obviously trying to do by proxy. The invitation to "Compare" is shown in Figure 7-11.

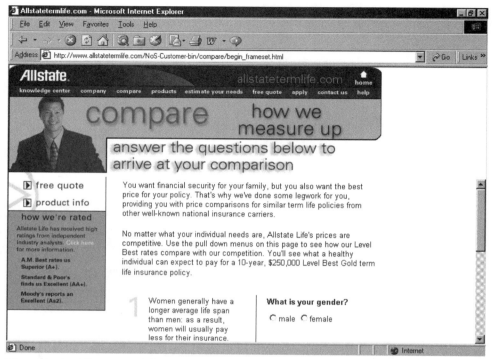

Figure 7-11 Allstatetermlife.com invites e-customers to "see how they measure up." Courtesy of Allstate Life Insurance.

Of course, this piece of utility is useful only as long as the content it returns is a valid comparison that e-customers find meaningful when evaluating different insurance providers.

ELEVEN SUCCESS FACTORS

Here are eleven success factors for providing utility on customer-effective Web sites:

1. If a company's competitive advantage is created by meeting a particular e-customer service need, all unrelated content and functionality are extraneous and should be avoided.

2. Leverage the best characteristics of the Web such as:
   - Ability for real-time information exchange between individuals and groups.
   - To create dialogue over time, to compare scenarios in real-time, and to dynamically provide information when it is needed the most.

- To provide information you couldn't create or find anywhere else.
- To shortcut processes that could be lengthy, and to create a seamless process where it might otherwise be fragmented.
- To simplify processes that might otherwise be complex.

3. Relate utility to the real-life service experiences and desires of e-customers. Utility doesn't exist for its own sake. It exists to serve e-customers better, smarter, and faster.

4. Relate utility to relevant e-customer actions and make utilitarian components visibly obvious and easily accessible.

5. Make the functionality intuitive by overtly structuring it around the e-customer's process (Statusfactory and WebSwap.com give good examples of this as seen in Figures 7-3 and 7-4 respectively).

6. Address common areas of customer frustrations and/or extend e-customer activities in new ways that are achievable only on the Web.

7. Don't overrate the utility you deliver (i.e., don't over promise). The phenomenon of not meeting expectations gets thrown into high relief if you use labels for utilitarian components that don't live up to the usefulness customers expect from the use of that label (e.g., "guide," "online consultant" and "personal assistant" are labels that can easily over promise).

8. Provide a comprehensive overview of how to use the functionality, step by step. The WebSwap tour is a good example of this.

9. Use common Web technologies such as e-mail and threaded discussion to directly support important e-customer activities (as opposed to using them as generic functions that serve no specific purpose).

10. Where application development is involved, combine other technologies (such as database functionality) with Web-based technologies via the Web site interface. In addition, apply creativity to combine technologies to create proprietary services that benefit e-customers.

11. Do not avoid complexity unnecessarily. Utility does not have to be simple. Complexity is OK if there is a reason for it and it can be worked through easily. Garden.com provides an eleven "page" tutorial on its sophisticated garden planner (which also includes an FAQ page)—this requires a five minute investment that may well be worth it for garden enthusiasts.

METAPHOR

Metaphor is a familiar concept to all of us; it's an integral part of our lives, without most of us even realizing it. In everyday speech we liken one thing to another because it makes it easier for people to understand what we are talking about.

When we use metaphor, we simply leverage a person's understanding of one thing, by applying it to another. Metaphor can, therefore, be important for learning as well as for communication.

We are exposed to a myriad of different metaphors in the world of technology. We are familiar with metaphors such as the ubiquitous realm of technology as "cyberspace," the Internet as "information superhighway," and the computer as a "tool," "assistant," "theater," and "ubiquitous resource."

Which metaphor, or metaphors, we subscribe to will influence our view of the world. A designer subscribing to the metaphor of "computer as tool" will be faced with fundamentally different design decisions as a designer subscribing to "computer as theater." A tool is important in performing tasks, while theater is important in creating scenarios and engaging the senses.

So too, Web sites use different metaphors to create different experiences for e-customers. And there are many metaphors that are common to Web sites. Ironically, most of the metaphors being used in Web site design are grounded in the physical world and are intended to give people orientation in, and comfort with, the virtual world. This practice has helped e-customers new to "cyberspace" to find their way around and get something done.

Common Web site metaphors include:

- Lobby—e-customers are greeted by a virtual representation of a physical lobby they are familiar with.

- Personal organizer and personal assistant—e-customers refer to the functions that a personal organizer or assistant performs to use various organizational tools on the Web site.

- Desktop—the physical desk gets represented virtually with different receptacles and tools for different functions e-customers perform at their desk (similar to the Windows desktop metaphor).

- Folder—many Web sites use folders as a way of allowing customers to collect different types of information and tools (e.g., into personal folders) and as a basis for navigation where information and tools are categorized into folders.

- Briefcase—the physical act of having a "carry-around" collection of important "stuff" is related to the collection and categorization of information and tools on Web sites.

- Store—many Web sites try to create the idea of physical aisles containing different items. This may be implicit in the way information is categorized or explicit in the way things are visually represented.

- Shopping cart—the physical shopping cart is virtually wheeled around to collect things that customers want to buy. Sometimes this gets creatively applied, such as in the case of Garden.com, where the shopping cart is a wheelbarrow.

- Gallery—e-customers can browse a virtual space as if it were a physical gallery space. Most Web sites that use the gallery metaphor struggle to simulate this type of experience (although this will change as multimedia capabilities become more achievable over limited bandwidth).

- Guide—a virtual guide can provide e-customers with advice on what suits them best and how to get around. While many Web sites try to leverage the idea of an e-customer being shown around by a guide, they fall short because of the difficulties of creating this type of dynamically generated, context-sensitive help.

- Neighborhood—individuals are collected into a community where they have a stake in, or a role to play as part of, that community.

Metaphors can be classified into three types, as follows:

- Organizational metaphors, which leverage the known organization of one concept to assist with the understanding of a new system's organization.

- Functional metaphors, which connect the functions you can perform in the source domain with those that can be performed in the target domain.

- Visual metaphors, which leverage visual recognition of known concepts in a new environment.

Many metaphors are purely visual, particularly in relation to navigation devices that use metaphoric devices to help e-customers find their way around; they do not offer any functional or organizational clues. However, many metaphors are both functional and organizational, such as in the case of the personal organizer/assistant metaphor, where functions and organization are implied.

It is useful to think about the type of metaphor being used to raise your awareness of what your metaphor is not doing for you (i.e., is it not providing visual, functional, or organizational clues?). This will help you avoid overestimating a particular metaphor's usefulness. It is quite common to see a visual metaphor used as if it did offer functional and organizational clues, for example.

WHAT WORKS?

The shopping cart metaphor is probably the most familiar, and yet, the shopping cart metaphor may actually be fraught with problems.

Problems arise when we "map" one concept onto another—but our mapping doesn't quite work. There may be things unique to the experience we're trying to create, and they don't correspond to the experiment we're referring to. Or there may be unique characteristics in the experience we're referring to, and these just don't relate to the experience we're trying to create. E-customers try to relate one thing to another, don't find a match, and get confused. There may be things they can do in the physical domain that they can't do in the virtual domain, and vice versa.

On Philosphe.com, Derek Sisson gives us his view on how errors occur when the physical shopping experience does not adequately translate to the virtual one. He gives us an idea of problems that may arise, as follows:

- A buyer requires authentication of the seller, but anyone can create an e-commerce Web site.

- The buyer requires courteous, professional helpful service, but e-mail is impersonal, especially when sent by autoresponders. In addition, context-insensitive help doesn't always help buyers.

- The buyer needs an obvious method for purchasing, but some sites don't make "checkout" obvious.

- The buyer needs to understand store policies for warranties, returns, exchanges, and refunds, but many Web sites don't give this information, or make it easily accessible, when it is needed.

- The buyer should be able to select what they want without having to give away personal information, but many sites require registration when it is not needed.

The article makes special mention of the authentication barrier and states that "if the user is not at the point where they are ready to lay down their money, experience tells them that there is no reason to prove their identity."

THE MAPPING PROCESS

To understand this better, let's talk about the idea of "mapping" a little further. Theorists describe the experience we're referring to as the "source domain" and the corresponding experience we're trying to create as the "target domain." The characteristics that make up our understanding of the known and referred experience, are called "slots." The process of equating the slots on one side (the source domain) to the other (the target domain) is called "mapping."

Theory notwithstanding, mapping is an important and simple exercise that helps us work out whether there are some mismatches that will confuse, frustrate, or disappoint e-customers. On the left-hand side we can list the characteristics ("slots") of the source domain and on the right-hand side we can list the slots of the target domain. We can then consider how well the left- and right-hand sides relate and how mismatches might confuse or frustrate e-customers.

Unless you go through a mapping exercise, you may not be aware of problems with your use of particular metaphor. Mapping can help identify inadequacies in the online execution of a metaphor as well as identify opportunities to minimize problems normally encountered in relation to the source domain experience.

An example

As an example of mapping, we will look at an online consultation process offered by clinique.com. On the left-hand side we will list the slots related to getting a physical, one-on-one consultation from a Clinique representative in-store (the source domain). On the right-hand side we will list the slots related to the online consultation (the target domain). We will then consider mapping the source domain to the target domain and discuss the issues that arise.

But first, let us familiarize ourselves with clinique.com's online consultation.

The Clinique consultation takes customers through the process of selecting answers to a list of questions to find out their skin type and skin tone. E-customers can then select a product category of interest from the general product directory and, once they have downloaded the page related to their selected product category, receive a list of particular products that match their skin type and skin tone.

Excerpts from the consultation are given in Figures 7-12 through 7-15

Figure 7-12 Clinique.com invites e-customers to an online personal consultation
Courtesy of Clinique.

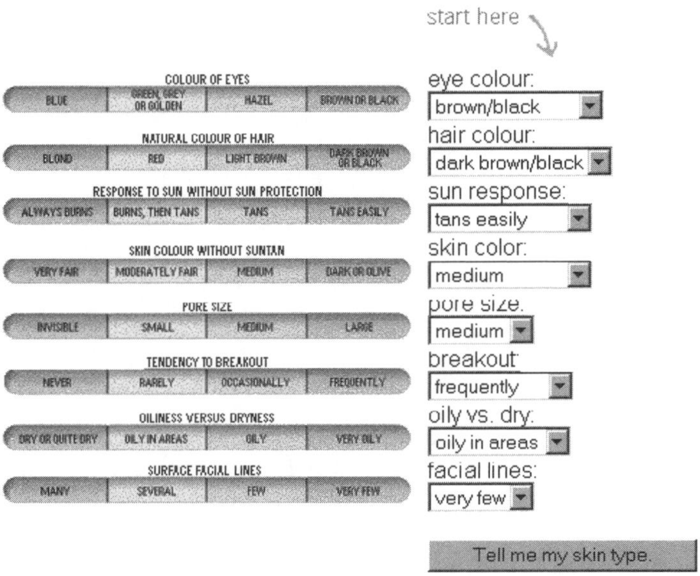

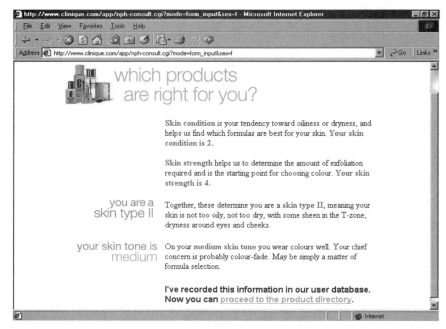

Figure 7-13 The e-customer answers a list of questions.

Figure 7-14 E-customers find out their skin type.
Courtesy of Clinique.

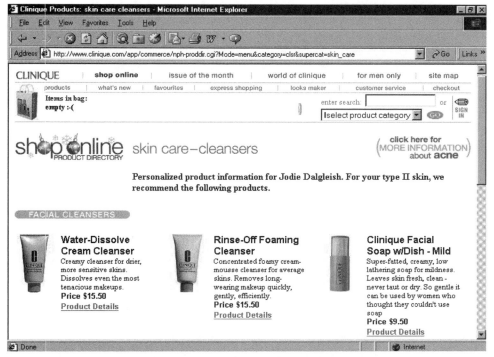

Figure 7-15 E-customers find out which products suit them.
Courtesy of Clinique.

Now, let's look at comparing a personal one-on-one consultation with the online consultation by mapping the source domain to the target domain in Figure 7-16.

It seems that the main benefits of the online consultation, when compared with the physical consultation, are:

- E-customers are not subjected to sales pressure.
- E-customers can store products as favorites.
- E-customers' skintype and favorites can be retrieved and reviewed on future visits. (This requires registration, which was listed above as a negative. Note that it is the timing of the registration that is the problem and not necessarily the registration in itself.)
- E-customers can receive product information by e-mail after the consultation.

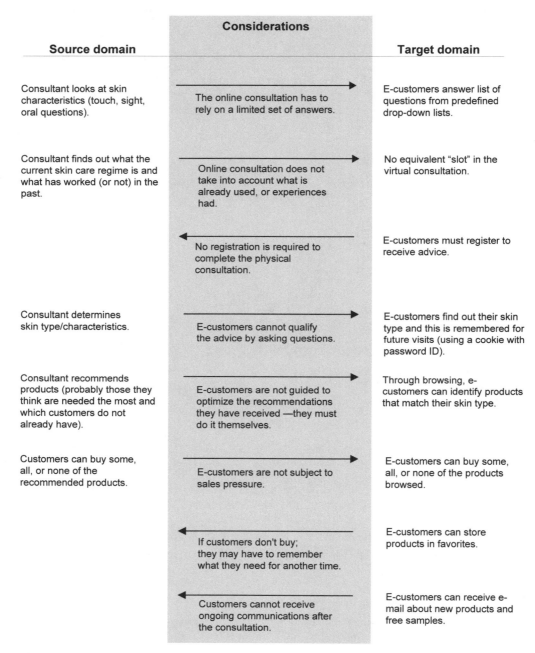

Figure 7-16 Mapping a physical personal consultation to the clinique.com online consultation.

The main limitations of the online consultation over the physical one are:

- The limitations of selecting answers from drop-down lists (i.e., this is a limited form of decision support).
- The online consultation does not take into account Clinique products the e-customer already uses, or has had experience with.
- Registration may act as a barrier to receiving advice.
- The online process does not directly recommend products. Suitable products are found as a result of browsing.

UNLEASHING THE POWER OF METAPHOR

By identifying the pros and cons of a metaphor (i.e., how the experience in the target domain is better, or worse, than in the source domain) we can start to tap into the potential of metaphor as a basis for learning and improved communication. Simply put, we must minimize the cons and maximize the pros.

When e-customers apply a metaphor they engage in a creative process—they engage their imaginations. The new experience is related to the known experience, but not limited by it. The Web offers characteristics, such as its immediacy, intimacy, and interactivity, that can be superior to physical characteristics. The Web also opens up a whole new realm of experience. To some extent "cyberspace" is a blank canvas on which we can paint. We do not need to be chained to our physical world when operating in a virtual world.

Think of the neighborhood metaphor and how it is executed. Many community sites draw strongly on the physical concept of neighborhood. Individuals are collected into locations each with its own Web page and allocated a location within the neighborhood. The neighborhoods get crowded and the individuals are presented as faceless, nameless entities—extrapolating the real-life difficulty of getting to know your neighbors. Diversity is inherently restricted and cliques develop. The cons of modern life have been transferred to the Web. But, the virtual world offers the transparency and intimacy needed for experiences to be shared and created. What new dimensions does this bring to the idea of a neighborhood? How does the Web allow us to create superior communities online? How can we use the Web to create new ways of thinking about, and doing, things? How can we make e-customers' experiences better, smarter, and faster?

As we start to create new experiences, they in themselves become metaphors for other new experiences, and so on. In this way, the real power of metaphor lies in remolding our experience.

EIGHT SUCCESS FACTORS

Here are eight success factors for the use of metaphor on customer-effective Web sites:

1. Be realistic in your choice of metaphor; it is too easy to overpromise and underdeliver.

2. Identify the key elements of the source domain that must clearly translate to the target domain. This provides shortcuts for e-customer learning.

3. Rather than accentuate the limitations of the virtual medium, accentuate its positives. The less a concept relies on physicality to be understood, the better it will map to the virtual medium.

4. Address the areas in the source domain that are problematic to e-customers. Make the target experience superior.

5. When choosing metaphors, think about your frame of reference. Have you limited yourself to the physical world? What metaphors already exist in the virtual world? If your e-customers have been on the Web for a while, the virtual world is also part of their frame of reference.

6. Don't overdo it. The more singular your metaphor is the easier it is for e-customers to work out what's going on. More than one metaphor can coexist and help customers in different ways, but they can also start crowding one another out and dilute the focus on what the e-customer is trying to do.

7. Don't use metaphor if it's not helpful or useful. Well-thought-through and presented experiences often don't need to refer to other known experiences to be understood.

8. Successful metaphors are dedicated to facilitating e-customers' pursuits. They are grounded in what e-customers are trying to achieve and their motivation for doing it.

PROVIDE DIALOGUE

All right, I have to admit that I'm going to climb onto a hobby horse. I don't understand why so many Web sites fail to deliberately guide e-customers through critical processes, such as an order process. I've seen how exacerbated e-customers get when trying to work out what's happening and why. I've felt embarrassed on behalf of the Web site creators who were so oblivious to e-customer needs. I believe that Web sites should provide dialogue that is useful to e-customers.

I think there are a number of reasons why e-customers end up frustrated when trying to complete a process that is important to them.

First, we can't predict the random behavior of e-customers, who will explore the Web site in whatever, linear or nonlinear, fashion takes their fancy. So we can't presume that e-customers will progress from one particular screen to another—they may do things in an entirely different order from what we expect and come in and out at points we don't expect. We don't want to provide dialogue that is irrelevant to where e-customers are at, where they've come from, or where they're going. Perhaps this has led to a complete lack of dialogue, where it is most needed, as well as the presentation of useful dialogue under "help."

Second, I think there has been a move toward, what I call "minimalist design" at the expense of providing the guidance that e-customers need. I believe minimalist design has been taken too far; it has led to the removal of vital text, for example, that e-customers need to effectively do the things they need to do. Web sites have tended to limit their cues to icons and labels—this leads to a nice clean, uncluttered design, but at what expense?

From talking to many e-customers across many industries, and in relation to many different e-services, I have concluded that e-customers like a design that isn't too cluttered—they want to be able to see what they can do quickly and easily. But this doesn't mean that e-customers wouldn't appreciate some more text-based dialogue to help them on their way, particularly in relation to high-involvement processes such as ordering.

Third, I believe that Web site design has been constrained by reference to the more established practice of GUI (graphical user interface) design. The Web offers a much richer and more interactive environment that should give us more leverage in how we design our interfaces. Web site design has tended to fall back into old paradigms where icons and labels have to stand on their own and encapsulate their entire meaning in a static entity.

So how can we provide dialogue that helps e-customers do what they need to do, better, smarter, and faster? Well, there are a few simple things we can do such as:

1. *Associating a label with an icon.* There is no need to make an icon stand on its own—and few will work hard enough for you anyway. And, always use language natural to your e-customers when deciding on labels.

2. *Using roll-over text and alttext to provide as much useful description of Web page elements as possible.* Roll-over text, being text that becomes visible when an e-customer rolls their mouse over an object, is a good source of additional textual information. For example, the dialogue boxes seen in Figures 7-18 to 7-21 would be roll-over text activated when e-customers roll their mouse over "Welcome", "Product", "Personal" and "Confirm". Alttext, being the text that tags what objects are before they download, is a good way of giving more clues to help e-customers understand the meaning and purpose of different objects.

3. *Explaining what a tool does (before it gets used) and what results from completing a certain process (before it is embarked on).*

And, if we take a customer-effective approach, we will know the key things e-customers are trying to do on our Web site, and why. We need to recognize that sometimes we do know the process an e-customer is embarking on, especially when that is controlled by the Web site.

When e-customers are faced with discrete processes, such as completing a search, soliciting recommendations, making a service request, or completing an order, for example, they need help and they need to know what's happened and what's going to happen, and why.

Why can't Web sites use elements such as interface content, navigation, and help together to intelligently and proactively guide e-customers through online processes?

Think of all the concerns e-customers bring to an order process and the things they need to know before they will progress to the next step (refer back to Figures 5-11 and 5-12, which presented an e-customer order process and a matching interface process). And, it's far from just order processes that suffer from lack of dialogue. Any process that requires interaction with e-customers should tell them exactly what's going on, what's going to happen before it happens (also refer back to customer directive number 2 "Tell me what I get if I do this" and the example of "blind registration") and what's going to happen next.

Amazon.com helps e-customers progress through their order process. It offers a navigation bar that presents the main steps of the order process, and it introduces discrete steps with introductory content that tells e-customers what's going on. These elements (navigation and content) combine to provide dialogue that is useful to e-customers. Amazon.com's screen presenting password requirements during the order process is shown in Figure 7-17.

Of course, Amazon.com also provides a shortcut ordering process with its one-click ordering. Once e-customers are comfortable with your order process, it is not necessary to provide the same level of guidance.

The idea of a guide is one attempt to provide the useful dialogue that e-customers need while using a Web site. Unfortunately, few guides are actually that.

Figure 7-17 Amazon.com provides some useful dialogue during the order process.

Most sites that purport to offer a guide really offer help only at certain points in an e-customer's experience. The label *guide* overpromises and underdelivers. A guide should show you around, not just be there once or twice. We simply don't have the dynamic intelligence of what e-customers are trying to do, and the context they are trying to do it in, to offer context-sensitive guidance—not yet anyway. When we are able to offer them, guides will be a useful feature.

AN EXAMPLE

If we were going to provide dialogue around an order process, maybe we could combine something like Amazon.com's navigation bar, access to help from each stage in the order process, useful introductory content at each step in the order process and roll-over text to create the screens shown in Figures 7-18 through 7-21.

Of course, these screen examples are abstract only and not indicative of any aesthetic treatment. In addition, the exact nature of your products and services will affect how your order process is structured. This order process assumes that products require some sort of set up (i.e., the e-customer needs to activate different product options). As less discrete products become available on the Internet, this type of product configuration will become more and more common.

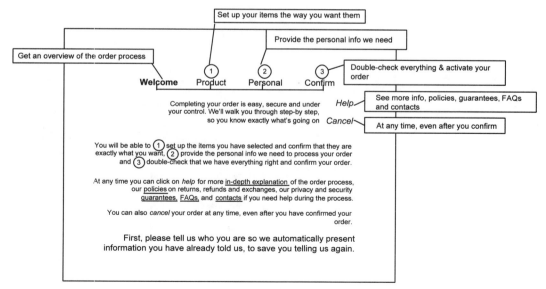

Figure 7-18 A welcome screen providing dialogue during an order process.

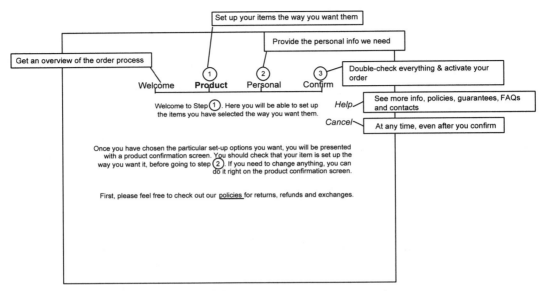

Figure 7-19 A "product" screen providing dialogue during an order process.

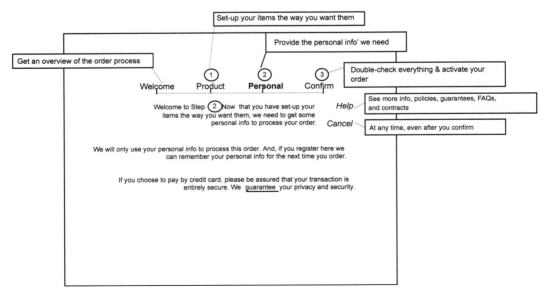

Figure 7-20 A "personal" screen providing dialogue during an order process.

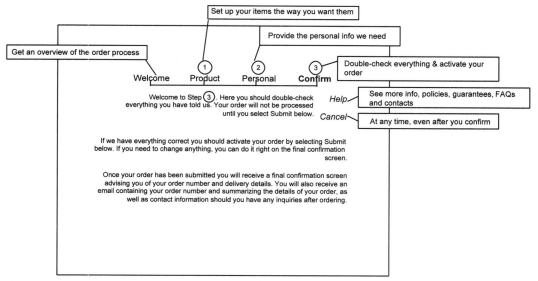

Figure 7-21 A "confirm" screen providing dialogue during an order process.

In developing dialogue around this order process, you would need to think about how help could really be helpful; FAQs and more in-depth explanation should be specific and relevant to what the e-customer is trying to do at the appropriate stage in the order process.

You would also need to consider the fit of this type of navigation with the rest of the Web site. If your order process can be handled discretely, and this treatment is not out of place on your Web site, then it could be favorable for the process to have its own navigation bar and help associated (of course, that help could easily be clicked into from any other relevant locations on your Web site). We will discuss navigation, in relation to e-customer processes, further in the next section.

NAVIGATION

A lot of books have already been written about information architecture and navigation, and it has become one of the most commonly discussed concepts in Web site design. My focus here is to discuss navigation specifically in relation to practices most required to create customer-effective Web sites.

Much has been made of "intuitive" navigation; in fact, it has become a dimension that Web sites are rated against by companies involved in benchmarking e-customer satisfaction. But what is "intuitive" navigation?

Ease of use seems to be one of the criteria against which intuitive navigation is judged. However, while some interfaces may use a consistent and understandable navigation system, that e-customers can easily find their way around, this doesn't mean that it is necessarily easy for e-customers to use it to do what they need to. Unless you talk to e-customers in a meaningful, "doing," context, you may not actually find out whether your interface is actually intuitive in the face of e-customer goals and activities.

Many designers and developers understand the importance of understanding e-customer goals when designing a navigation system and this needs to be formally represented in research and testing as well as in the measurement of e-customer satisfaction. (Refer back to Chapter 3 for a discussion of research and testing techniques for the e-service provider and the Web site development company.)

One of the key determinants of whether e-customers can use an interface easily to do what they need to, is the visibility and ease of access to key pieces of information and functionality; information and functionality aligned with e-customer activities, or "themes" (refer back to Chapter 6 for a discussion of e-customer themes.)

Deciding the relative visibility of functions and content related to e-customer themes is a key decision in the design of a navigation system. You will need to consider how to provide obvious paths to the utility your Web site offers e-customers and create a seamless path through an e-customer's process.

Let's consider some different approaches to navigation and then consider how easily e-customer themes can be represented in the context of these approaches.

TYPES OF NAVIGATION SYSTEMS

Generally , navigation systems are organized around certain content categories or "dimensions." These dimensions tend to be represented either vertically through frames or horizontally through navigation bars. Sometimes, frames and navigation bars are combined to allow organization against different sets of dimensions.

Some of the different dimensions navigation systems are organized around are as follows:

1. *By audience.* Some Web sites present content and functionality within discrete areas dedicated to different customers. E-customers are required to "self-select" themselves or maybe even authenticate themselves on entry to a Web site. This can work if your audiences are sufficiently different to warrant different categories and if e-customers are willing to be classified (refer back to customer directive number 8, "Be careful second-guessing my needs," in Chapter 3.)

   It is inherently more difficult to highlight core pieces of information and utility at the home page level because this page is probably dedicated to categorizing e-customers. However, this doesn't mean that navigation can't be intuitively modeled around e-customer themes subsequent to an e-customer's self-selection.

2. *By Information category.* Some Web sites aggregate different types of information and utility into categories related to the nature of that information and utility, "Products and Services," "About Us," "Contacts," "Help," etc. Often e-customers do not find out what the Web site can do for them until they have drilled into a particular information category.

   Inherently, the utility required to perform e-customer activities tends to take a lower profile in this navigation system and is often presented as content links within the navigation system.

3. *By product or store.* Some Web sites that are dedicated to the selection and/or purchase of products tend to organize their navigation system around types of products or "stores." Amazon.com, for example, offers "Books," "Music," "DVD & Video," "Auctions" and "zSHops" within a horizontal navigation bar. Such a navigation bar can be combined with other navigation bars or frames to also highlight core utility.

   However, you need to be careful of how many layers you use and how well they relate to one another. As with the use of metaphor, a singular system that captures what it needs to, is best. But, this does not mean that different navigation systems cannot be successfully combined within one Web site—it just presents more of a challenge for designers and, potentially, e-customers.

4. *By Web site function.* Some Web sites are structured around the core functions their Web site offers. This seldom forms the basis of the primary navigation system.

5. *By e-customer tasks and processes.* Few Web sites seem to structure around this dimension explicitly, although some Web sites offer some content and functionality, within the framework of the navigation system, under this type of categorization.

   Allstatetermlife.com is an exception. Allstate has provided categories such as its "Knowledge Center," "Compare," "Get a Free Quote" and "Apply Online," which are all directly related to e-customer tasks (see Allstate's home page in Figure 7-10). Allstate also offers a section called "Tools" related to e-customer functions including their "Compare" (see Figure 7-11) and "Estimate Your Needs" functions.

   Within the knowledge center, Allstate relates information to e-customer tasks in its "Insurance Basics," "Premium and Benefit Influencers," "Benefits of Applying Online" and "Glossary" categories.

   The "Knowledge Center" is shown in Figure 7-22.

   Given that this type of organization is most explicitly aligned with what e-customers are trying to do, it can lead to customer-effectiveness. Of course, the e-customer tasks and processes all have to be in tune with the e-cus-

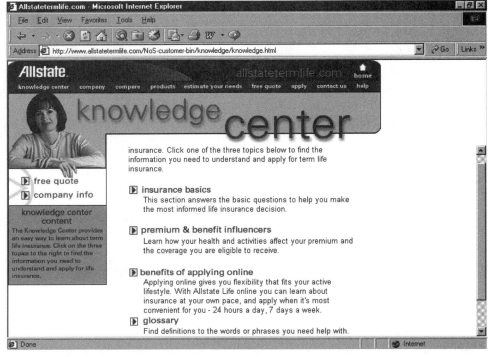

Figure 7-22 Allstatetermlife.com's knowledge center presents information categories related to e-customer tasks.
Courtesy of Allstate Life Insurance.

tomer, otherwise they will get in the way of what the e-customer is actually trying to do.

And nothing is ever simple. Categorizing content and functionality solely against e-customer tasks and processes may not be sufficient to capture unknown and emerging e-customer activities as well as activities the business wishes to create to meet specific business goals.

There is also a limit to how many categories can be presented in a primary navigation system, and you may not be able to visibly present every task e-customers wish to perform. Therefore, some sort of combination with other navigational dimensions may be required to provide the context for e-customer activities and the activities themselves. Consider Figure 7-23 where mks.com combine "Things to Do" (e-customer tasks) with "Information" and "Products and Services" within its primary navigation system.

As we can see, there are many types of navigational systems, and one system may not necessarily result in customer-effectiveness. You need to consider how the

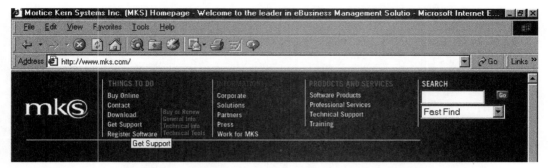

Figure 7-23 mks.com combines different dimensions within its navigation system.
Courtesy of mks.com.

navigation system seamlessly facilitates e-customer processes and how those processes are made visible.

In addition, during the contextual design process you will be considering how different processes relate to one another and can be grouped relative to common e-customer goals and functionality (refer back to the customer-effective design process in Chapter 6). The grouping of e-customer activities against themes, and the relationships between themes, should be overlaid on your emergent navigation system at this point.

Alternatively, you could use these themes and their relationships as the initial abstraction of the navigation system. But, if you do, remember that this may not necessarily be enough in itself—other dimensions may need to be provided to create the appropriate context and meet business goals.

ANCHORS

The importance of being able to find useful product information is reinforced in the GVU's (Graphics, Visualization Center of Georgia Technology Institute) tenth user survey. The survey showed that the most important attribute of Web vendor's sites is quality information. In addition, the greatest cause for customers to leave a site is not finding what they were looking for, followed by the site being disorganized and confusing.

Making it easy for e-customers to quickly and easily locate the information they are looking for is key to keeping e-customers on your site before they leave in frustration.

We provide "anchors" on our Web sites, and these help e-customers work out where to get the information they want. We can think of anchors as cues and functions that support e-customer behavior and goals. Anchors provide security and stability.

There are a number of anchoring Web site components; the navigation itself provides a support framework, the navigational devices such as icons and labels provide support within the framework of the navigation system, and hypertext becomes the syntax that anchors an e-customer's movement around a Web site. In addition, search functions provide interactive support for information retrieval.

All of these anchors need to intuitively fit with e-customer goals, activities, and natural language. We need to hold up every anchor for inspection in the light of what e-customers need. If we start to at least recognize these characteristics as anchoring, perhaps we will apply more rigor in getting them right on behalf of e-customers.

The importance of search functions in providing interactive information retrieval has been well documented. The degree of customer frustration with search functions has also been well documented. It appears that the importance of simple, customer-effective searching has been underestimated. Search is key to information retrieval on the Web.

We need to treat search as a discrete e-customer process, or "theme." As a theme, it requires context, dialogue and structure to make it understandable and seamless. In addition, we must recognize that search is a circular process where e-customers go backward and forward to refine their search on the basis of the results they get. In designing around the theme of search, we need to create a circular experience, as seen in Figure 7-24.

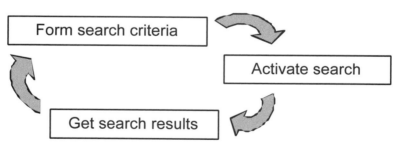

Figure 7-24 Search needs to be designed as a circular function.

One of the pitfalls in designing search functions is to provide the wrong anchors. A search must be done against criteria, such as a keyword, or a selection from one or more drop-down lists. Often, the criteria used just do not fit with what e-customers are trying to do, or the way they think about products, services, or providers. First, businesses don't know their e-customers well enough to identify meaningful search criteria, and, second, they use the business' language and not the e-customer's.

Another pitfall is to expect e-customers to be able to form complex search queries. Generally, e-customers will naturally think of keywords or phrases and are not experienced with formulating query structures, such as that required in Boolean search where e-customers must use rational operators such as "and," "or," and "not," between keywords to more finely define search parameters. This may change as people become better educated in searching, perhaps in an Intranet environment where they can get training and support. In the meantime, ineffectual and complex search functions may well be a barrier to some people's adoption of the Web.

And it's not just the search criteria that are anchors—search results are as well. Search results are high-touch objects that also act to orient and ground the e-customer.

Filters are also anchors (i.e., selections that allow results to be ordered or restricted, for example, by the number of results).

So we need to create the right anchors in our search criteria, and the filters that can be applied to results. Unfortunately, search criteria and results are often problematic.

If the scope of a search is not clear and there is no dialogue around a search function, e-customers may not know how to approach searching—they will not be able to form appropriate criteria. E-customers search in a context and they need triggers to help them search. Many Web sites provide these triggers by offering a number of prompted selections through drop-down lists.

It is not easy to provide the right criteria for prompted selections. E-customers should have control, but they also need guidance. As soon as we offer search criteria, against which e-customers select, we restrict their choices while offering some shortcuts and guidance that could make the search function more useful.

If e-customers' search criteria is well known to you, you can help e-customers make easy and targeted searches. To do this, you must match an e-customer's decision framework (i.e., the criteria by which they will decide what they want) with the criteria presented in the search function.

If you get the criteria wrong, you will actually heighten e-customers' inability to find what they're looking for. For example, say someone is looking for beauty products and the search function allows a search against a number of categories, one being "benefits." The e-customer can select from a drop-down list of generic benefits, such as "Exfoliating," "Firming," "Tanning," "Not Animal Tested" and "Long-lasting." How well will these benefits fit with real customer perceptions? From a marketing perspective, aiming at categorizing customer benefits requires a high degree of customer knowledge and intimacy. Businesses may be asking for trouble by trying to categorize products and their perception of e-customer benefits. It is better to work with lower-risk criteria that we know, than criteria we may not.

Consider another example. Say a professional is looking for a new job. What criteria will he or she be deciding against? Will it be location, salary, industry, skills, whether it's a contract or permanent position, salary, or something else? And of all of these, which one might be the most important to an individual and how should the criteria be combined to produce the optimal search results?

Many search engines anchor job selection against one or two simple criteria such as location and type of role (against some predetermined categorization of roles). E-customers end up having to manually scroll through pages and pages of jobs to manually filter results against their own important criteria. The anchors of location and role might be insufficient, or wrong, because they don't fit the decision framework of the job seeker.

Categorization of search criteria can work well when the product or service attributes are limited and well understood. In these cases, search can even become central to the functionality of the site.

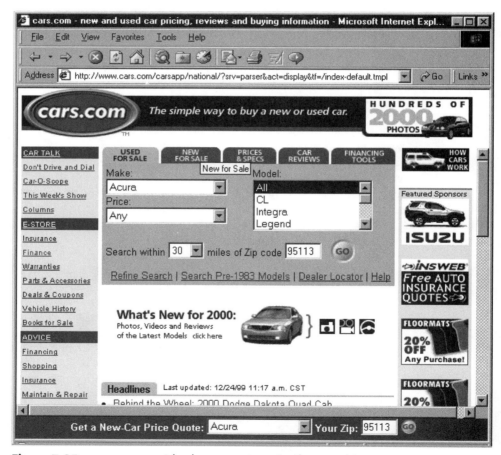

Figure 7-25 cars.com provides known categories for searching.
Courtesy of cars.com.

Cars.com is able to offer up-front support to e-customers looking for a new car. It can probably be pretty sure that the criteria will fall into the categories of "Make," "Price," "Model" and "Location." Their refined search, and "Criteria Search," also allow e-customers to search against other categories such as number of "Doors," "Transmission," "Body Style," "Horsepower," and "Mileage," etc. (see Figure 7-25).

When offering this type of categorized search, it is important to make sure that if e-customers are unable to make a selection within a category, or choose not to, this does not impact on their ability to find results against the categories they have selected against.

In addition, you should make sure search criteria are not mutually exclusive. If e-customers do not want to seek against multiple dimensions at once, an e-customer should not be forced to make a selection against your criteria; they should be able to select "Any" or "All" against a category if they do not wish to filter results against that particular category—for example, price (they may want to see a price range) or location (they want to see the different locations in case it's worth their while going further afield).

In addition, if multiple criteria are activated in one search you must make sure that the e-customer knows how the different criteria affect one another (e.g., if the search will fail without an exact keyword match, then the e-customer might leave this field blank and activate selections against other criteria provided).

And then when search results are presented, they should appear in a context that is relative to the search process and the Web site as a whole. E-customers need to know where the returned pages fit into the site. The search results page should provide dialogue to help the e-customer, and each Web page should carry reference to the site's navigational structure.

EIGHT SUCCESS FACTORS

1. Create intuitive navigation systems that fit an e-customer's mental model, support the seamless completion of important processes and use e-customers' language when labeling content and functionality. The e-customer will easily be able to learn by doing when interacting with an interface that makes sense to them.

2. E-customer themes must be supported within the navigation system. E-customers must be able to quickly identify where, and how, they can complete their online processes. While e-customer processes may not be the sole dimension on which a navigation system is based, they do need to have representation at an appropriate level, and that representation must remain visible throughout the process.

3. It is likely that a customer-effective navigation system will need to combine more than one dimension for categorization; for example, e-customer

processes and information categories, such as in the mks.com example (see Figure 7-23).

4. Where e-customer tasks aren't directly represented in the navigation system, they need to be distinctly represented in content and functionality, such as shortcut links or icons.

5. As with metaphor, don't overdo it. The more singular your navigation system, the easier it is for e-customers to work out what's going on. More than one navigation system can coexist and help customers in different ways but they can also start crowding one another out and dilute the focus on what the e-customer is trying to do.

6. Always provide a meaningful context for searching. This context should allow e-customers to intuitively form their own search criteria.

7. Provide triggers and selections such as drop-down lists, but never limit an e-customer's search. Always make sure that criteria presented for selection naturally fit the e-customer's context.

8. Relate all anchors to e-customer goals, activities and natural language; every anchor provides grounding in what the e-customer is trying to do on your Web site.

THEMING–PUTTING IT ALL TOGETHER

In Chapter 6, we discussed the customer-effective design process, which uses e-customer themes as a basis for design and development.

E-customer themes provide a contextual approach to Web site design. Contextual design inherently encapsulates, and directly relates design to, the e-customer's context—and this is the core requirement of customer-effective design.

Here we will further explore the idea of theming. We will explore it as a design discipline and refer to our discussion of metaphor, dialogue, navigation, and utility to explore it further. We will also drill down into the previous customer-effective design process to understand how design concepts are established during this process.

Theming requires us to inherently design around e-customer themes, or "threads" of activity within our Web sites, that allow e-customers to seamlessly complete an online process. In the Amazon.com example we identified ten specific e-customer themes "Find a Book I Know I Want," "Buy a Book I Want," "Browse Books I Might Be Interested In," etc.) and three generic e-customer themes ("Get Help," "Provide Feedback," and "Find Out What Is on This Web Site").

Embodying e-customer themes with components such as metaphor, dialogue, navigation, and utilitarian components results in a framework that allows e-customers to complete the online processes they need to.

We can think of these ten specific e-customer themes as horizontal "cylinders" traversing a Web site and encapsulating e-customers' experiences. And we can think of the three generic e-customer themes as vertical "threads" that run across the horizontal "cylinders." The resulting framework forms the basis for the following Web site concepts:

1. The core utility the site should offer (i.e., the pieces of functionality required to allow e-customers to complete their required processes).

2. The dialogue required to lead an e-customer through each process.

3. The type of content required to enable e-customer themes.

4. The basic navigation that arises from identifying horizontal and vertical themes, and the relationships between them. (Remembering that during the customer-effective design process we were involved in identifying categories of e-customer themes and components that were shared by more than one theme. Refer back to Figure 6-23 for the design process.)

We can represent this framework (with five specific e-customer themes and three generic) in Figure 7-26.

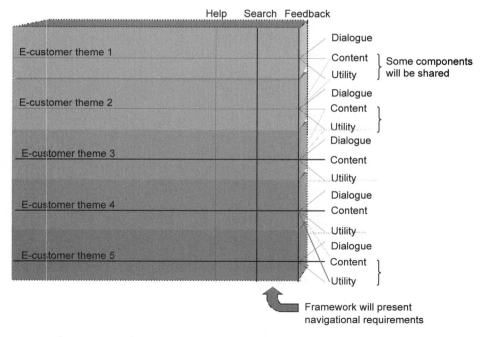

Figure 7-26 Theming results in a starting framework for a customer-effective Web site.

As discussed above under "Navigation," coming up with, and embodying, e-customer themes doesn't necessarily result in a complete customer-effective Web site. Sometimes, where the Web site is very utilitarian, or when a wider context is not required, theming will result in an almost complete Web site concept.

Generally, however, the theming framework will be a subset of the full, and final, Web site framework. An example of this is where additional navigational dimensions are required to encapsulate an entire Web site. For example, you might combine the dimensions of e-customer processes and information categories in your navigation system. This type of navigational system was discussed under "Navigation," and mks.com was given as an example in Figure 7-23.

Considering the relationship of the theming framework to the full, and final, Web site framework is useful because it will give us an idea of how easily e-customers will be able to locate, and seamlessly complete, their required processes.

The relationship of the theming framework to the full, and final, Web site framework can be represented in Figure 7-27.

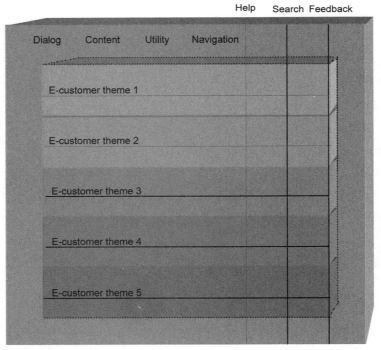

Figure 7-27 The theming framework will be a subset of the full, and final, Web site framework

The Web site may require additional dialogue to tie e-customer themes and other contextual components together, content and utility to perform functions that fall outside of e-customer themes, and navigational dimensions and components to complete the entire navigational system.

Of course, Figure 7-27 is an oversimplification of what might happen in real life. The full, and final, Web site framework may not simply extend the theming framework. The full, and final, Web site framework's navigation system may cut things quite differently from the straight horizontal and vertical representation we see in Figure 7-27. However, the completion of e-customer processes is at the core of the e-customer's required experience, and this may be embodied in some way, and the horizontal and vertical framework appeals as a way of achieving this.

Trying to depict the relationship of the theming framework to the full, and final framework, in two dimensions is a real challenge, as much as trying to depict any Web site framework themselves in two dimensions is a challenge.

Perhaps as we get more used to the multidimensionality of Web sites and have tools that effectively capture more than two-dimensions, we will become more adept at depicting Web sites. And as we become more familiar with the design discipline of theming, and better understand how this relates to full, and final, Web site designs, we may be able to better represent the relationship between the theming and final Web site framework. This is certainly something that I intend to continue to discuss and explore.

I would be keen to hear about experiences you have applying the theming approach. Together, with sharing and learning, we can all utilize the Web better for the benefit of e-customers.

CHAPTER 8

THE OPPORTUNITY

It is time to move past the fads and create connections with e-customers, for better business and a better quality of life.

THE QUICK AND THE VALUED

E-customers have put up with a lot on Web sites, but that is going to change as more and more new e-service providers come online. While it has been acceptable to lead e-customers into many new e-services, as customers become more and more Web savvy, they become less content with being led and form their own opinions on what e-services should be provided and how.

Those vendors and businesses that have come to the market early will find themselves having to continually review their products in light of e-customer feedback to stay competitive. Businesses that have sat back and watched others pioneer e-services are able to learn from their mistakes and do things better.

Never before has there been such an opportunity to learn from the pioneers and improve on their efforts. As e-service providers strive to create competitive advantage, e-customers should see a vast improvement in the relevance of online services offered and the customer-effectiveness of the Web sites that deliver them.

Businesses can gain immediate competitive advantage by improving Web interface design and development, and the content of this book will give them a head start on doing that. The Web interface is the manifestation of e-service strategy, and yet, often it devalues the service being provided. Think of online banking and online supermarket shopping, a great idea when they first came on the scene, but they were blessed with clunky interfaces shackled by adherence to physical metaphors that made finding and purchasing products a lengthy and unintuitive process. What will the next generation of online banking and supermarket shopping look like?

And there will be other improvements, that are much more than interface-deep—they will be based on new ways of thinking and new ways of doing things.

But we need to beware of the fads. It's as if we discover new aspects of the Web, aspects of its accessibility, intimacy, immediacy, and interactivity, and then flog them to death. In doing so, we miss the big picture. We miss the potentiality of the medium.

We will start to move beyond the fads.

We will move past trying to establish brand dominance on the Web. In a medium where equality reigns, value and credibility will be created by offering superior e-service rather than leveraging known brands.

We will move past the portal fad, where businesses have battled for some sort of "dominance" in creating a "window on the Web." In the context of a medium grounded in freedom of choice and limitless connections, the quest for the most significant amount of content will fade.

We will move past the (emerging) fad of personalization and customization for its own sake and realize that it's a key part of e-servicing—part of a bigger picture.

And maybe we will start to innovate. Maybe we will start to focus on the connections that can be made between e-customers and businesses and we will foster collaborative e-services that benefit e-customers, enhance business effectiveness, and create a better techno-social environment where individuals and businesses operate on an equal footing.

And it won't be a battle of content—it will be a battle of connections. Nor will it be a battle of the brands—it will be a battle of reputable e-service.

Neither will it necessarily be a matter of "the quick and the dead." It will be a matter of "the quick and the valued." Businesses can quickly jump on the bandwagon of the latest fad, but this will not create lasting value. A brief moment of reflection could go a long way in ensuring that businesses have a place in the cybercommunity of the future.

The e-services that most naturally fit around, and enhance, peoples' lives will survive. And the definition of what fits with, and enhances, peoples' lives will be constantly changing. An assumption that was made today may not stand tomorrow. Herein lies the potentiality of competitive advantage—to network with e-customers who are participants in online services, to *create* the change they require.

We will see new kinds of e-service providers emerging—those that understand the collaborative power of the Web and the effect it has on people's lives. E-service providers will realize that the Web is a medium that people live with, and that they need help to do that successfully. E-service providers will help people manage the anxiety that comes along with the information explosion and the demands of coping with constant technological change, for example.

ENDEAVORS

In getting to where we need to be, there are a number of endeavors we are likely to undertake.

Toward multiple dimensions

I have a vision in my mind's eye of a Web site that organically represents what e-customers are trying to do in three dimensions. It is not constrained by navigation that inherently reduces orientation to two dimensions. E-customers move through tunnels, enter chambers, create objects, change objects, and shift objects. Connections are Weblike and e-customers are a living part of that Web.

Is this virtual reality? Probably not. This is a Web site that escapes the shackles of two-dimensionality and creates its own meaning and experiences in multiple dimensions.

Will it require more efficient and sophisticated multimedia capabilities? Probably, but not necessarily.

One thing I know for sure: It will be the product of creative individuals who no longer see the Web page as anything, even slightly, akin to a physical page. They will see Web "pages" as spaces where interactions dynamically create e-service experiences for e-customers. E-customer themes are naturally embodied in an active medium.

Towards creativity

Collaboration requires creativity. The Web must develop as a medium where people go to create, as much as to review. Actually, the Web is already that medium; the gateways, such as browsers, are what present a barrier. Browsers allow you to read and review, but they don't allow you to edit.

Tim Berners-Lee, in his book *Weaving the Web*, states his desire to see creativity become a core part of the Web experience, as follows:

> We should be able not only to interact with other people, but to create with other people. *Intercreativity* is the process of making things or solving problems together. With all this work in the presentation of content, we still have really addressed only the reading of information, not the writing of it. There is little to help the Web be used as a collaborative meeting place.

In his frustration at not finding the tools needed to collaborate, Berners-Lee decided that it was best to try and create them. Berners-Lee talks of developing tools that allow participants to write and edit hypertext, and save the results on a server as particular versions.

Maybe Web browsers will start to take a leaf from Berners-Lee's book.

Toward customer integration

In Chapter 4 we discussed the key decisions businesses will have to make when developing their e-service strategy, and one of these was the extent to which the e-customer would be integrated.

Figure 4-1 illustrated the potential scope of e-customer integration as a continuum from one-way publication to two-way workflow. As e-customers become more integrated, the emphasis shifts from content to collaboration as activities become more real-time (symmetrical and synchronous).

Businesses will undertake the endeavor of integrating e-customers into business processes, and this will require a shift to working together to get business done.

And we need to bear in mind, as discussed in Chapter 1, and illustrated by Jim Sterne's diagram in Figure 1-1, e-customer expectations are raised as they become more and more integrated into the business.

It may be necessary for industry partnerships to be formed. These partnerships could enhance the integration of underlying systems and technologies and, in turn, the seamless integration of e-customers across end-to-end business processes. We are already starting to see partnerships forming as industries try to achieve the interoperability required to support the sharing and transference of data, for example.

Toward shared learning

As e-customers and businesses become more connected, and e-customers become more integrated, e-customers and businesses will be able to learn from each other to create new ways of working.

This will go beyond researching e-customers and building in their feedback throughout development. This will be the result of intercreativity (to coin Berners-Lee's phrase) because learning results from doing, and we need to do things collaboratively to learn from each other.

Toward application development

In addition, as e-customers become more integrated, and as the industry becomes more focused on providing utility (i.e., purpose-built functionality that serves e-customers' needs to get things done), development will become more application-centric.

In other words, development will apply Web-based technologies to specific e-customer needs.

But this doesn't mean that the wheel needs to be continually reinvented.

As utility becomes more and more commonplace on the Web, forward-looking vendors will start to develop Web-based applications that businesses can buy "off the shelf." These applications will be based on an understanding of the generic tasks that need to be performed by the users of that technology. Success here will depend on vendors' ability to build in the appropriate level of flexibility to allow different businesses to be customer-effective. It will no longer be acceptable for businesses to be driven by technology products rather than by their e-customers.

A CLOSING WORD

We are sitting on the verge of an e-service revolution. The Web can come of age as a service medium. But, if that is to happen, it's up to us to make it happen.

And it will happen only when we recognize our e-customers as equal partners in the revolution, and become customer-effective.

NETOGRAPHY

This book wouldn't be complete without a Netography, but please bear in mind that Web pages move and get deleted or replaced. Please refer to a parent Web site if you are unsuccessful in accessing a particular URL.

USER TESTING

Fleming, Jennifer, "User Testing; How to Find Out What Users Want"
http://www.ahref.com/guides/design/199806/0615jef.html

Graphic, Visualization and Usability Center's (GVU's) tenth user survey
http://www.gvu.gatech.edu/user_surveys/survey-1998-10/

Kehoe, Colleen M., & Pitkow, Jim, Surveying the Territory: GVU's Five WWW User Surveys, The World Wide Web Journal, Vol. 1, no. 3, 1996, p. 77-84
http://www.cc.gatech.edu/gvu/user_surveys/papers/

Nielsen, Jakob, alertbox on designing Sun's Intranet
http://www.useit.com/papers/sunweb/

Nielsen, Jakob, alertbox on severability ratings for usability problems
http://www.useit.com/papers/heuristic/severityrating.html

Nielsen, Jakob, alertbox outlining ten usability heuristics
http://www.useit.com/papers/heuristic/heuristic_list.html

Nielsen, Jakob, alertbox outlining usability inspection methods
http://www.useit.com/papers/heuristic/inspection_summary.html

PC Data Online Reports
http://www.pcdataonline.com/

Philosophe.com, "Types of Tests"
http://www.philosophe.com/testing/tests.html

Webmonkey, "Why User Testing Is Good"
http://hotwired.lycos.com/webmonkey/98/14/index3a_page5.html?tw=design

BUSINESS STRATEGY

"Business Strategies for the Digital Age"
http://www.contextmag.com/

PERSONALIZATION OF WEB SITES

Nielsen, Jacob, Alertbox for October 4 1998, "Personalization is over-rated"
http://www.useit.com/alertbox/981004.html

CONTENT CREATION AND OBJECT MANAGEMENT

The Cluetrain manifesto
www.cluetrain.com

Dart, Susan, "Webcrisis.com: Inability to Maintain"
http://www.mks.com/press/coverage/wi/crisis.htm

MKS, Web Integrity product
http://www.mks.com/products/wi

Quinn, Evan, and Heiman, Richard, "Web Object Management: Bringing Order to Opportunity"
http://www.mks.com/products/wi/wp/idc_wom.htm

Technology Deployment International, Inc., E-Business Management System Whitepapers. (You will have to request the whitepapers onlne.)
http://www.tdiinc.com/index.html?/tips/index.html

"The Web-Zine for Writers, Editors, and Others Who Create Content for Online Media"
www.contentious.com

WEB WRITING

Electric Page, "Writing for the Web, Part 1"
http://www.electric-pages.com/articles/wftw1.htm

Electric Page, "Writing for the Web, Part 2"
http://www.electric-pages.com/articles/wftw2.htm

Nielsen, Jakob, "Writing for the Web"
http://www.useit.com/papers/webwriting/

Sun, guide to Web style, content
http://www.sun.com/styleguide/tables/Content.html

BUSINESS PROCESS IMPROVEMENT

Boehringer, Robert, and King, Paul (Orion Development Group). "Process Mapping Gives Great Direction"
http://www.spss.com/software/allclear/techniques/promap.htm

Cohen, Phil (HCI Consulting), "Business Process Reengineering"
http://www.hci.com.au/hcisite/articles/businesspro.htm

Enterprise Integration Laboratory, Toronto University, Business Process Reengineering Advisory Group,
http://www.eil.utoronto.ca

INFORMATION ARCHITECTURE AND NAVIGATION

Nielsen, Jakob, Information Architecture/Navigation "Users first: how to structure your Web site," May 4 1999
http://www.zdnet.com/devhead/stories/articles/0,4413,2253058,00.html

Shiple, John, Information Architecture Tutorial,
http://hotwired.lycos.com/webmonkey/design/site_building/tutorials/tutorial1.html

van Ewyk, Onno (HCI Consulting), "Mapping Is The Key to Going Horizontal"
http://www.hci.com.au/hcisite/articles/mappingisthe.htm

Web page design for designers—navigation
http://www.wpdfd.com/wpdnav.htm

METAPHOR

Philosophe.com, "Metaphors & Schemas in Design"
http://www.philosophe.com/design/metaphors.html

Philosophe.com, "Ecommerce | Schemas & Concept Mapping,"
http://www.philosophe.com/commerce/schemas.html

Smilowitz, Elissa D. "Do Metaphors Make Web Browsers Easier to Use"
http://www.baddesigns.com/mswebcnf.htm

SEARCH

Nielsen, Jakob,"Search and you may find"
http://www.useit.com/alertbox/9707b.html

Philosophe.com, "Considering search: search topics"
http://www.philosophe.com/search/search.html

Shneiderman, Ben (Department of Computer Science and Human-Computer Interaction Laboratory), "Clarifying Search: A User-Interface Framework for Text Searches"
http://www.dlib.org/dlib/january97/retrieval/01shneiderman.html#framework

WEB SITE MAINTENANCE

Web Review on Webmastering
http://webreview.com/pub/Webmaster

WEBMARKETING

Good directories to get listed on
http://www.aia.net.au/success/good-directories.html

Virtual promote's links to guest tutorials on issues related to Webmarketing
http://www.jimworld.com/guest.html

Virtual Promote's list of "cool" sites
http://www.virtualpromote.com/hotsites.html

REFERENCE WEB SITES

http://www.afternic.com

http://www.allstatetermlife.com

http://www.amazon.com

http://www.bankofamerica.com

http://www.cars.com

http://www.cisco.com

http://www.clinique.com

http://www.digitalthink.com

http://www.ebay.com

http://www.garden.com

http://www.indulge.com

http://www.mks.com

http://www.philosophe.com

http://www.secretsites.com

http://www.statusfactory.com

http://www.useit.com

http://www.ventana.com

http://www.webswap.com

Note: the above URLs relating to suppliers are not supplier endorsements. They are, simply, good and useful reference materials.

BIBLIOGRAPHY

Baecker, Ronald, M., Grudin, Jonathan, Buxton, William A. S., and Greenberg, Saul. *Readings in Kuman-Computer Interactions: Toward the Year 2000* (2nd ed.). San Francisco: Morgan Kaufmann Publishers, 1995.

Berners-Lee, Tim. *Weaving the Web: The Original Design and Ultimate Destiny of the World Wide Web by Its Inventor.* New York: HarperCollins Publishers, 1999.

Beyer, Hugh, and Holtzblatt, Karen. *Contextual Design: Defining Customer-Centered Systems.* San Francisco, CA: Morgan Kaufmann Publishers, 1998.

Carroll, John, M. (ed.). *Scenario-based design: Envisioning Work and Tchnology in Systems Development.* New York: John Wiley & Sons, 1995.

Coyne, Richard. *Designing Information Technology in the Postmodern Age: From Method to Metaphor.* MA: Massachusetts Institute of Technology, 1995.

Fleming, Jennifer. *Web Navigation: Designing the User Experience.* Sebastopol, CA: O'Reilly & Associates, 1998.

Lakoff, George, and Johnson, Mark. *Metaphors We Live By.* Chicago: University of Chicago Press, 1980.

Norman, Donald A. *The Design of Everyday Things.* New York: Doubleday, 1998.

Rosenfeld, Louis, and Morville, Peter. *Information Architecture: Designing Large-scale Web Sites.* Sebastopol, CA: O'Reilly & Associates, 1998.

Siegel, David S., *Secrets of Successful Web Sites: Project Management on the World Wide Web.* Hayden Books, 1997.

Sterne, Jim. *Customer Service on the Internet: Building Relationships, Increasing Loyalty and Staying Competitive.* New York: John Wiley & Sons, 1996.

Sterne, Jim. *World Wide Web Marketing: Integrating the Internet into Your Marketing Strategy* (2nd ed.). John Wiley & Sons, 1999.

Stone Gonzalez, Jennifer. *The 21st-Century Intranet.* Upper Saddle River, NJ: Prentice-Hall, 1998.

Tufte, Edward R. *Envisioning Information.* CT: Graphics Press, 1990

INDEX

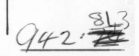

YORK

YORK
Peter Wenham

Illustrated by Douglas Phillips

Longman

LONGMAN GROUP LIMITED
LONDON

Associated companies, branches and
representatives throughout the world

First published 1971

ISBN 0582 15071 X

The map on p. 108 is reprinted by permission from Peter
Wenham's book *The Siege of York and Battle of Marston Moor
1644*, published by The Roundwood Press (Publishers).

*Printed in Great Britain by
The Camelot Press Ltd
London and Southampton*

CONTENTS

ERRATA

Page 33, line 35, should read:
Seven tenth-century burials

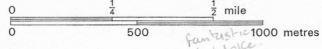

YORK CITY CENTRE

0   ¼   ½ mile

0   500   1000 metres

fantastic + bloke.

CHURCHES

a	All Saints, North St.	j	St Martin-cum-Gregory
b	All Saints, Pavement	k	St Martin-le-Grand
c	Holy Trinity, Goodramgate	l	St Mary, Bishophill Junior
d	Holy Trinity, Micklegate	m	St Mary, Castlegate
e	St Cuthbert	n	St Michael, Spurriergate
f	St Denys	o	St Michael-le-Belfrey
g	St Helen	p	St Olave, Marygate
h	St John	q	St Sampson
i	St Margaret, Walmgate		

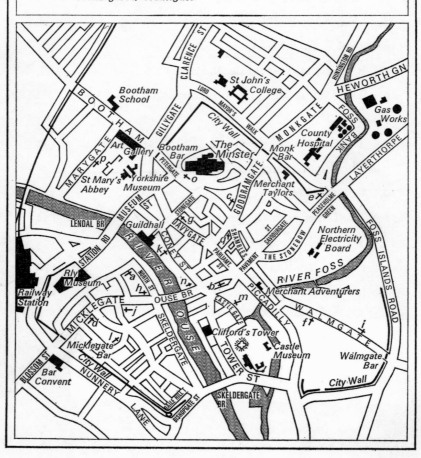

1. THE ROMANS – EBURACUM

York is one of the oldest cities in Britain. In its long history it has had many different names. To the Romans it was Eburacum; to the Anglo-Saxons, Eoforwic; to the Danes, Jorvik; nowadays it is York. Its beginnings are shrouded in the mists of history. The earliest written records about it are Roman, but flint artefacts dating from 3000 BC show there was a much earlier settlement. One of the trackways of these pre-Roman—Celtic—people was west of the city and took roughly the same line as the present York–Tadcaster road. This was built on a glacial moraine (a ridge resulting from the melting glaciers of the last Ice Age in Britain) which formed a dry causeway between the great marshy tracts now represented by the Knavesmire and Hob Moor.

The name of this Celtic, pre-Roman settlement was something like "Ebrauc". The Roman word Eburacum is the Latin form of the Celtic place-name. Etymologists interpret this as meaning either "the place of the Yews", "the place of the cow parsnip" or "the place of Eburos", Eburos being the name of some important person, perhaps a chieftain. By simply substituting an "o" for a "u" the Romans later made the name "Eboracum" or "the boar town". The boar became the symbol of the place. In AD 237 a rich merchant, Aurelius Lunaris, a magistrate of Eburacum, set out on a trading voyage to Bordeaux in the south of France. He had obviously made the journey before and knew the dangers his ship would encounter in the dreaded Bay of Biscay. He vowed that if he survived the ordeal he would erect an altar in thanksgiving to Dea Boudiga, a local Celtic goddess. He made the crossing safely and he fulfilled his vow, putting up the altar which now stands in

7

the Museum in Bordeaux. On one side of the altar is carved the
bust of a bearded man pouring water from a jug and on
the other, a boar. The former is the emblem of Bordeaux, the
latter of Eburacum.

When the Romans invaded Britain in AD 43 they found a
country divided into many independent kingdoms. The largest
of these was Brigantia, which covered the area between the
river Tweed—the present boundary between England and
Scotland—and the river Trent. It was ruled by Queen Cartimandua, a very clever woman. She believed that by remaining
friendly with the Romans she could keep her kingdom free
from invasion by the conquering legions. So Brigantia became
what the historians call a client kingdom of Rome. This policy
was successful for a number of years even though it was disliked by many of her own subjects who, like Yorkshiremen
today, were sturdy, independent folk. The Queen's husband,
Venutius, quarrelled with his wife and eventually became the
leader of this anti-Roman faction. On at least two occasions
these people rebelled against their Queen and her policy. On
both occasions the Romans sent troops to help Cartimandua
and crush the risings. After those disturbances it seems that the
Romans built a few forts in her kingdom, maintaining garrisons there. The sites of these forts are not known but early
Roman pottery found at York and Templeborough near
Rotherham indicates that these may have been two of them.

In AD 69 there was anarchy throughout the Roman world
following the suicide of the Emperor Nero. There were four
Roman Emperors in the space of twelve months! In Brigantia
Venutius seized this opportunity to organize yet another
rebellion against Cartimandua and her hated Roman allies. It
was successful. Cartimandua fled from Brigantia to seek refuge
with the Romans south of the Trent and disappeared from
recorded history.

In AD 71 Vespasian became ruler of the Roman world,
founding a new and great dynasty of Emperors. He built the
great amphitheatre in Rome known as the Colosseum. He
decided that Brigantia must be conquered. For this task he

appointed a new governor of Britain, his friend and relative, Petillius Cerialis from Pannonia (modern Yugoslavia). Cerialis led his troops in person. He marched the Ninth Legion with a number of other auxiliary regiments from Lindum (Lincoln) across the river Humber at Brough (the Roman Petuaria) via Malton (Roman Derventio) to Eburacum. Here they built a wooden fortress on a well-chosen site at the confluence of the rivers Ouse and Foss. York's recorded history now begins. From AD 71 until the present day we have documents telling us of its history and of the people who lived there. It is therefore most appropriate that, in AD 1971, the city and inhabitants should celebrate what is their nineteen-hundredth birthday.

What attracted the Romans to this particular site? A fortress built between two joining rivers had obvious advantages for defence. Until Naburn Lock, six miles south of York, was built in 1757 the rivers Ouse and Foss were tidal and Eburacum, seventy miles from Spurn Head, was the farthest point inland to which ocean-going galleys could penetrate. It was fairly easy to build a bridge at this point. The fortress was built thirty-five feet above sea level on one of the few sites high and dry above the great water-logged Plain of York, well above the danger level from flooding. As we have already noted it was also on a morainic ridge which carried an important pre-historic roadway from west to east, from the Pennines to the Yorkshire Wolds.

The first Roman building at Eburacum was the fortress. This followed the standard pattern, that of a rectangle with rounded corners. A Roman legion consisted of about 5,000 men who needed barrack blocks, storehouses, granaries, stables, latrines, a hospital, etc., together with a headquarters (*principia*) and a residence for the commandant (*praetorium*). This covered about fifty acres.

The fortress was occupied for 340 years—as long a period of time as from the outbreak of the Civil War (1642) to the present day. During that time buildings fell into disrepair or were damaged or destroyed by enemies of Rome. These had to be rebuilt. Nowadays when new building takes place in an English

city the first thing that happens is that bulldozers and workmen
clear the site of all previous buildings. The Romans did not do
this. They burnt the woodwork of the damaged building,
picked out any stones which could be re-used and then levelled
off the remaining rubble and built their new building on top of
this. If this happened more than once, building upon building
was constructed, one on top of the other. This is invaluable to
the modern archaeologist who, by carefully digging through
these layers and recording the coins, pottery and other finds
which are encountered, can date the various building periods.
This is exactly what happened in the fortress at Eburacum,

The river front of Eburacum

where we know there were five distinct phases of building and rebuilding. The fortress built by the Ninth Legion in AD 71 was of wood. Its defences consisted of an eight-foot high palisade, backed by an earthern rampart of about the same width and fronted by a V-shaped ditch six feet deep and six feet wide. About ten years later the fortress was rebuilt, again in wood, but with a higher palisade and wider rampart and a double ditch system. About AD 108, when Trajan was Emperor, the fortress was rebuilt in stone with outer walls fourteen feet high and five feet wide backed by a rampart about fourteen feet wide. About AD 200, under the Emperor Septimius

Severus, these defences, together with the internal buildings, were rebuilt in stone. Finally, about AD 300, under the Emperor Constantius Chlorus, the defences of that half of the fortress nearest the river (called by the Romans the *praetentura*) were rebuilt in a completely new style. For the first time the interval and corner towers projected beyond the outside wall. They were much larger than the earlier ones and made the river front of the fourth century fortress of Eburacum one of the most imposing in the whole of the Roman world.

The last two reconstructions of the fortress—those under the Emperors Severus and Constantius—seem to have been made necessary by destruction caused through enemy action. These enemies were either the Picts from beyond Hadrian's Wall or native tribesmen from the mountainous districts of Yorkshire who did not readily accept the civilizing influence of the Romans.

Four impressive remains of the Roman fortress still exist in York today. In Aldwark there is a corner tower, an interval tower and a 150-foot long stretch of the Severan wall, some of which is still standing to its full height of fourteen feet; only the parapet is missing. In the Museum Gardens there is the great corner tower of the Constantian rebuild known for generations as the Multangular Tower. It stands eighteen feet high. Joining it is a hundred-foot length of wall, sixteen feet high, and a partly preserved interval tower. In the cellars of the Mail Coach Inn in St Sampson's Square is part of a large bath-house built in the fourth century over earlier stables. Finally, in the Minster, the present excavations have uncovered important remains of walls, columns and floors of the headquarters building (*principia*). It is intended to incorporate these in an underground museum to be built under the great central tower. Part of a massive stone column twenty feet tall with a diameter of three feet, found during these excavations, has been erected not far from the south door of the Minster. Almost every day in York Roman remains are found ten to fifteen feet below the modern streets and houses by workmen digging deep trenches during building operations or drainage. They provide glimpses of the treasure-house of Roman history buried under the present city.

Many of the streets of modern York inside the fortress follow the lines laid down by the original Roman road builders. The present High and Low Petergate are the successors of the *via principalis*, the main street of the fortress leading from the gateway buried under Bootham Bar to another under King's Square. Stonegate follows the line of the *via praetoria* which ran from a third gateway under St Helen's Square to the entrance

to the *principia* near the Minster. Chapter House Street lies
some ten feet above the *via decumana* which went from the
back of the *principia* to the fourth gateway in the garden of
Gray's Court.

A curious ghost story is linked with the *via decumana*. The
Treasurer's House, which is built over part of this road, has a
number of cellars at different levels. Some years ago a plumber
and his mate—an apprentice—were doing some repairs in
one of these. When it came to the lunch-time break the apprentice was left alone eating his sandwiches. Suddenly he heard an
ear-piercing noise as if made by a brass band and—to use his
own words—he "saw a Roman legion march through one
of the walls of the cellar and out by another". He noted one
extraordinary fact about the soldiers—their feet and legs below
the knees were missing. A few years after this an excavation
was carried out in the adjoining cellar which revealed that the
cobbled floor there was a surviving stretch of the *via decumana*.
The top of that road was eighteen inches lower than the floor
on which the apprentice saw his "legion" marching.

About AD 124 *Legio IX Hispana* was replaced by *Legio VI
Victrix Pia Fidelis* which remained in Eburacum until all
troops were withdrawn from Britain about AD 406. It has long
been the view that the Ninth Legion was wiped out by bar-
barians in some sort of ambush just north or south of Hadrian's
Wall. Modern research shows that this is incorrect. The Legion
was transferred to the Continent where it remained for about
thirty years before being disbanded. The titles *Hispana* (Spanish)
and *Victrix* (Victorious) and *Pia Fidelis* (Loyal and Faithful) are
battle honours awarded to these two legions. *Hispana* does not
mean that the Ninth Legion was raised in Spain.

A military encampment as large as a legionary fortress soon
attracted numbers of civilians. Merchants, women, builders,
workmen, entertainers and such like people were attracted by
the presence of thousands of soldiers. At first these newcomers
lived in draughty, wooden houses built to no particular plan
in the area between the fortress and the rivers Ouse and Foss.
As their numbers increased this area became overcrowded

and they crossed the Ouse and settled in the Bishophill–
Micklegate area. This continued haphazardly until, about
AD 200, under either the Emperor Severus or his son Caracalla,
a completely new town was built there, surrounded by a
defensive wall, with a grid-like pattern of streets. In the
insulae—those are the square areas surrounded on all sides by
roads—the houses and public buildings were constructed.
Here were shops and workshops, fine town houses (many
with tessellated pavements), a forum or market place, public
baths, shrines and temples. One of the temples was dedicated to
Mithras, another to Bellona (goddess of war) and another to
Serapis (an Egyptian god). What the population was of this
town we do not know but it can hardly have been less than
10,000. It soon became a self-governing community. Tombstones have been found of *decuriones* (magistrates who governed
it) and of *seviri Augustales* (leading citizens responsible for
providing the annual ceremonies and entertainments connected with Emperor-worship). Tombstones and altars have
also been found of rich merchants, trading with such places as
Bordeaux and Bourges in the south of Gaul. Wine and olive
oil were imported from these places into Eburacum in return
for wool, jet, lead and hunting dogs.

Eburacum was a place of outstanding importance both as a
legionary fortress and a *colonia*. In Britain there were only three
permanent legionary fortresses and four *coloniae*, Eburacum
being the only place to be included in both categories. The
highest distinction that could be bestowed on a Roman town
was the title of *colonia*. Originally this meant the place to
which veterans retired on completing their twenty-one years
of service with the army. Later, the term lost its military
significance and became the equivalent of the modern term
"city".

Eburacum also had other claims to distinction. It became the
northern capital. Under either Severus or Caracalla the single
province of Britain was divided into Britannia Superior and
Britannia Inferior. Londinium (London) became the capital of
Upper Britain and Eburacum of Lower Britain. Two Roman

Emperors died in Britain: Septimius Severus in AD 211 and Constantius Chlorus in AD 306; *both* died in Eburacum. Cassius Dio, one of Severus' two biographers, wrote this about the Emperor's funeral:

> After this the Emperor's body, arrayed like a soldier, was placed on a pyre and was honoured by a solemn procession around it of the soldiers and of his sons; and as for soldiers' gifts those who had something at hand threw it on the pyre and his sons heaped up the fire. Afterwards the bones were put in a porphyry urn and carried to Rome and placed in the tomb of the Antonines.

Severus spent much of the last two years of his life in Eburacum. His other biographer, Spartianus, says he built a palace there. No Roman remains of this have been positively identified but it may have stood in the vicinity of All Saint's Church in North Street. Wherever the Emperor was, from there was the Roman world governed at that time. An imperial decree headed *ab Eboraco* (from Eboracum) has survived. Here would be the famous Praetorian guard, the Emperor's personal bodyguard; here would be the hundreds of officials and secretaries who composed and wrote the imperial decrees, and here also were the special messengers who carried these decrees from one *mansio* (posting station) to the next and on horseback along that wonderful network of Roman roads which centuries later were still to be admired by those who had none of the skills of the Roman engineers.

When Constantius Chlorus died, his son Constantine—Constantine the Great as he has always been known—was at his bedside. The legionaries of the garrison of Eburacum proclaimed Constantine Caesar there and then. He set out from Eburacum on his dazzling career. He it was who reunited the Roman world, he who built the new capital of Constantinople, and he who gave the Roman Empire a new state religion—Christianity. In the Yorkshire Museum is a head of Constantine, larger than life-size, which was found not far from the south door of the Minster. The statue to which it originally belonged probably stood by the gateway of the *principia*. Constantine summoned many councils to deal with the establishment of Christianity in his empire; one of these was at Arles in the south of France in AD 314. Three British bishops attended; one was the Bishop of Eburacum.

The Romans buried their dead in cemeteries alongside the roads radiating from their towns. Archaeological evidence from York has been the most important so far produced in the whole of Britain for our understanding of Roman burial practices. When they first arrived in Britain the Romans cremated their dead. In York over one hundred cinerary urns (the beakers containing the burnt bones of the dead) have been found together with part of a crematorium, the place where the funeral pyres were actually erected. This was found in Trentholme Drive, part of an extensive cemetery in the Mount area. It is interesting that coal as well as wood had been used there as fuel. In the third century cremation was superseded by inhumation. Hundreds of Romano-British skeletons have been recorded as being found in York during the last three hundred years, no fewer than 315 being uncovered in the Trentholme Drive cemetery alone. With burials the usual practice was to leave a pot or pots (often containing food such as a joint of meat, an egg, or a bird) with the body. In Trentholme Drive 150 such pots and over 100 animal remains, including one complete eggshell, were found.

While the excavation was being conducted in Trentholme Drive, a remarkable discovery was made in the garden of the house next door. An eight year old girl who lived there came home from school one day and asked if she might dig a trench in the front garden of the house. She dug a hole sixteen inches deep and returned half an hour later with a complete Roman flagon in her hand. She said she could see the remains of a skeleton just below where she had found it. Her parents wisely reported the discovery to the archaeologists who were working on the other side of the garden wall. They laid down trenches in the garden and dug it over carefully and scientifically. The family helped the archaeologists with the trowelling which was necessary once the topsoil had been removed. They discovered a complete skeleton and, from what the girl told them, established the fact that the flagon had been buried above its left shoulder. What was even more exciting was the discovery of a coin in its mouth. This showed that some of the inhabitants of Roman York believed—like the Greeks—that after death a person journeyed to the river Styx which he had to cross to reach the underworld. The only way across was by a ferry controlled by Charon, a miserly old man who had to be paid for his trouble. Relatives therefore put a coin in the mouth of the dead with which to pay Charon on arrival at the river bank.

This valuable discovery would have been damaged and probably even destroyed if the family had dug up the skeleton themselves. They had much more excitement and satisfaction in helping the archaeologists to dig it out carefully. All such finds should be reported to parents, teachers, museum curators or other responsible persons.

In Roman cemeteries richer people were buried in coffins which might be of wood, lead or stone. Over fifty coffins have been found in York, most of which are in the Yorkshire Museum. Many are magnificently carved and inscribed with the names, ages and particulars of the dead. Here is one found in 1956 in the Castle Yard close to Clifford's Tower. Flanking the inscription on either side were two *amorini*, winged male children, each holding a *pelta* (shield). The Latin is given above and the translation below.

D(IS) M(ANIBUS) ET MAEMORIAE IVLIAE VICTORIN(A)E QUAE VIXIT ANNOS XXVIIII MENSES II DIES XV ET CONSTANTIO QUI VIXIT ANNOS IIII DIES XXI MENSES XI SEPTIMIUS LUPIANUS EX EVOC(ATO) CONIUGI ET FILIO MEMORIAM POSSUIT

To the gods of the underworld and to the memory of Julia Victorina who lived for 29 years 2 months and 15 days and to Constantius who lived for 4 years 21 days and 11 months. Septimius Lupianus, a centurion recalled to the colours, put up this monument to his wife and son.

The phrase *ex evocato* indicates that Lupianus had served as an

By

other rank in the Emperor's Praetorian Guard. On his honourable discharge after twenty years he had continued to serve in the army, being transferred to Eburacum in Britain where he had been given the important military post of centurion in the Sixth Legion.

2. ANGLIAN YORK – EOFORWIC

Long before the Roman legions were withdrawn from Britain the country was raided by the Angles and Saxons from North Germany. At first it was mainly the south-east coasts which were attacked. To meet this danger the Romans built the so-called "forts of the Saxon shore" along the seaboard between the Wash and the Isle of Wight. Then the raids spread up the east coast into Yorkshire. To meet these, about the year AD 369, they built a series of signal stations, remains of which have been found at Huntcliff near Saltburn, Goldsborough, Ravenscar, Scarborough and Filey; others may have been destroyed later as a result of coastal erosion. Messages from these were passed by inland signalling stations to Derventio (Malton) and then to headquarters at Eburacum.

To strengthen this new defensive system, another military command was set up. This was the Dux Britanniarum (Duke of Britain), whose base was Eburacum. He commanded an army which consisted mainly of cavalry. They could move quickly to any threatened area and cut off the invaders before they got far inland. In 1959 a Roman road was excavated, running from Eburacum in the Stamford Bridge–Malton direction. It had originally been thirty feet wide, but had been extended twice until it was eventually fifty-two feet wide— wider than many first class roads today. Presumably these improvements had been made to ensure the rapid passage of the Duke and his forces.

All these precautions proved unsuccessful, and the departure of the Roman legions about AD 406 opened the floodgates to the enemy. Archaeology indicates that the Romano-Britons put up a determined resistance. Two excavations in particular show this. At the signal station at Goldsborough, the bodies of some of the garrison had been haphazardly and hastily buried in the ruined debris of the defences while at Malton a ditch and rampart had been hurriedly constructed between the Roman fort and the River Derwent, to try to hold up an enemy advancing from the east. Behind these defences crude forges had been hastily constructed to manufacture weapons and missiles.

Many such barriers were thrown up during this part of the Dark Ages, but they were in vain and the Angles spread steadily westwards, until at last Eburacum itself was under attack. The inhabitants of the town fled for protection inside the fortress, where conditions got worse and worse until eventually they had to surrender. The Romano-Britons were either enslaved or massacred, and soon even the very name of Eburacum was forgotten, and the new German one of Eoforwic took its place.

Written history tells us very little of this change, not even the date, but archaeology shows that it must have been about AD 450 or a little later. Recent excavations beneath York Minster show that part of the *principia* was occupied by squatters in the fifth century. There is evidence of their fires, and of the crude alterations they made to the Roman rooms there. Further evidence has come from the three Anglian cemeteries which have been found in York, on the Mount, near Heworth Green and on Lamel Hill. This last one dates from the later Anglian period, and contained inhumations, but the other two were very early, and that on the Mount was in fact inside the great Roman cemetery there. The Mount and Heworth cemeteries contained cremation burials, and the cinerary urns buried there were almost identical with some found in Germany around the River Elbe, the homeland of the York Angles. In the fourth century, before the Romans left York, one of the chief problems of the Roman military commanders was a shortage of soldiers. They met this difficulty by recruiting German tribes into the legion. Thus it may be that these two cemeteries were not merely early Anglian ones, but had catered for these allies or *foederati*, as they were called.

The departure of the Sixth Legion led to a breakdown of the political and economic life of Eburacum. Overseas trade came to an end, and the inhabitants of Eoforwic had to look after themselves like a beleaguered garrison in a hostile country. Extensive flooding of the Plain of York in the period AD 450–550 also contributed to the city's decline. This sudden rise in the water level is so far unexplained, but layers of silt, two feet thick in places, overlying the Roman remains of large areas in and around the city below the thirty-five foot O.D. contour, are found during excavations.

The Angles were country folk, used to building in wood, and they viewed with suspicion the heaps of stone and rubble from the ruined buildings and monuments which remained as evidence of Roman town life. During the early part of their occupation they avoided the fortress and *colonia*. Their early settlements were near York rather than in it, and the Anglian place-names of the villages clustering around York to this day bear this out: Clifton, Heslington, Fulford, Acomb, Stockton, Poppleton, Huntington, Murton and Askham.

The rate of conquest of the districts around the city varied greatly, and the Celtic kingdom of Elmet with its capital of Sherburn, some fifteen miles west of York, remained independent until as late as the beginning of the seventh century, when it was conquered by King Edwin. A part of the defences of Eoforwic has survived. In 1969 a stone tower built into a gap in the Roman fortress wall behind the Public Library in Museum Street was excavated. It is unique in Britain: nothing like it has so far been found on the Continent. It dates to about AD 600.

The new northern Anglian kingdom of Northumbria was the largest of the seven kingdoms, the so-called Heptarchy of Anglo-Saxon England. Northumbria consisted of what had originally been two smaller ones: Bernicia north of the Tees, and Deira south of it. Eoforwic was in Deira. The king of Northumbria had several royal residences at places of especial importance. Yeavering and Bamburgh in Northumberland were two of them; Goodmanham and Eoforwic in Yorkshire were two more.

One of the most well-known stories in the history of the Anglo-Saxon period is that of Pope Gregory the Great (who died in AD 603) and the English slave-boys in Rome. They came from Deira, so it is possible that they were even from Eoforwic itself. It is told by Bede in his *History of the English Church and People*:

> One day some merchants who had recently arrived in Rome displayed their many wares in the crowded market-place. Among other merchandise Gregory saw some boys offered for sale. They had fair complexions, fine-cut features, and fair hair. Looking at them with interest, he enquired what country and race they came from. "They come from Britain," he was told, "where all the people have this appearance." He then asked whether the people were Christians, or whether they were still ignorant heathens. "They are pagans," he was informed. "Alas," said Gregory with a heartfelt sigh: "how sad that such handsome folk are still in the grasp of the Author of Darkness, and that faces of such beauty conceal minds ignorant of God's grace! What is the name of this race?" "They are called Angles," he was told. "That is appropriate," he said, "for they have angelic faces, and it is right that they should become fellow heirs with the angels in heaven. And what is the name of their Province?" "Deira," was the answer. "Good, they shall indeed be de ira—saved from the wrath—and called to the mercy of Christ. And what is the name of their king?" he asked. "Aella," he was told. "Then must Alleluia be sung to the praise of God our Creator in their land," said Gregory, making play on the name.

A few years after this, in AD 597, St Augustine was sent on a mission to England by Pope Gregory, whose plan it was to organize the Church there, by establishing at London a metropolitan church with twelve bishoprics centred on it, and the same at York. In the south the scheme miscarried, and Canterbury, not London, became the ecclesiastical centre, but in the north it came about as planned. One of the reasons for the importance of York for the last 1,300 years is that it has been the chief religious centre of the north of England.

One of the greatest of the Northumbrian kings was Edwin, who reigned AD 616–32. At first he was a pagan. When he married Ethelburga, the daughter of Ethelbert, King of Kent, one of the conditions of the marriage contract was that she should be allowed to practise her religion, for she was a Christian. She brought Paulinus with her to York as her chaplain, and he used all his powers of persuasion to convert Edwin to Christianity. Eventually, in AD 627, he succeeded, and on Easter Sunday Edwin was baptized. Bede describes the occasion in these words:

> So King Edwin, with all the nobility and a large number of humbler folk, accepted the faith and were washed in the cleansing waters of baptism in the eleventh year of his reign, which was the year 627. . . . The king's baptism took place at York on Easter Day, the 12th April, in the Church of Saint Peter the Apostle, which the King had built of timber during the time of his instruction and preparation for baptism, and in this city he established the See of his teacher and bishop Paulinus. Soon after his baptism, at Paulinus's suggestion, he gave orders to build on the same site a larger and more noble basilica, which was to enclose his earlier small oratory.

In the crypt of the present Minster is a stone font which stands on the traditional site of Edwin's baptism. Painted on the panels of the cover are St Paulinus, King Edwin, Queen Ethelburga, St Hilda and James the Deacon.

From these humble beginnings grew the present Minster, one of the largest and finest cathedrals in Christendom. So far, excavations deep under the tower, nave and transepts have not produced any evidence of Paulinus's churches, but remains have been found there of eighth and ninth century buildings and gravestones, which are undoubtedly linked with the early successors of that first wooden chapel.

These first Anglian Christians in York had a bitter struggle to survive. Other kingdoms in the Heptarchy remained heathen. In AD 632 King Edwin was defeated and killed at the

The present Minster

battle of Heathfield, by Cadwallon, King of Wales, and Penda, King of Mercia. Queen Ethelburga, accompanied by Paulinus, fled to Kent. Only James the Deacon remained behind to preach the Christian faith in Northumbria. After a few years of paganism, a Christian, Oswald, became King of Northumbria, and restored that faith. He was succeeded by his brother,

Oswy, who presided at the famous Synod of Whitby in AD 664. This was the occasion when the Roman form of Christianity was adopted rather than the Celtic one which had sprung from the missionary work of monks from Ireland, Iona in Scotland and Lindisfarne, an island off the coast of Northumberland. The Roman case at this Synod was presented by St Wilfrid, an arrogant, overbearing individual. He was twice Bishop of York, AD 669–77 and 686–91. He claimed that the Bishop of York owed no allegiance to the Archbishop of Canterbury. This brought to a head the question of "primacy" in the English Church, a problem which led to quarrels between Canterbury and York until it was finally settled in Norman times. The ultimate compromise—embodied in the extraordinary formula which still persists to this day—was that while the Archbishop of Canterbury is "the Supreme Head of the Church in England", the Archbishop of York is "the Head of the Church in England".

The kingdom of Northumbria was famous throughout Europe for its learning, art and scholarship. Its greatest scholar was the Venerable Bede whose *History of the English Church and People* is the main source of our information about the Anglian invasions of England, the Anglian settlements there and the early history of Northumbria. Bede lived at Monkwearmouth (on the Wear) and Jarrow (on the Tyne) and, until he died in AD 735, those two monasteries were the chief centres of learning in England. One of Bede's outstanding pupils was called Egbert who, three years before Bede died, became Bishop of York. (In AD 753 he became Archbishop—the first of a long line stretching from that day to this.) He was a saintly, learned man and an excellent teacher. One of his first acts in York was to start a school and establish a library. To his school he not only attracted young boys training to become priests but also the sons of noblemen. At first Egbert himself taught in the school, then he put a kinsman called Æthelberht in charge. School and library soon became famous not only in Northumbria but throughout England and then further afield in Western Europe. Scholars flocked to York to read the books and listen to the teaching. One of the greatest tragedies in the history of York was the destruction of the library in 1069 by fire as a result of the Norman Conquest.

Æthelberht's most gifted pupil was Alcuin, a native of York. When, in AD 767, Æthelberht succeeded Egbert as Archbishop, Alcuin became master of the school. Under him it attained even greater fame while the library grew with gifts from all parts of Christendom. For about a century York was the cultural capital of Europe, as famous as Florence was to become in the fourteenth and fifteenth centuries. While on a pilgrimage to Rome Alcuin met Charlemagne, the Holy Roman Emperor, who was attracted by his wit, learning and scholarship. In AD 782 Alcuin accepted the Emperor's invitation to leave York and go to his capital Aachen (now Aix-la-Chapelle) to become Master of the Palace School there. Alcuin's task was to be a sort of Minister of Education, to frame and implement a scheme to educate Charlemagne's illiterate subjects. Alcuin never lost his love of York. He revisited it at least twice and kept up a steady flow of letters to his old friends in Northumbria. It is fortunate that many of these letters survive. He also wrote a long Latin poem in which he described the York he knew. This, too, has come down to us. He speaks of the ships from many nations anchored at its quays, of the wealth of its merchants and the splendour of their houses. He mentions ruined Roman walls standing to a considerable height. We know he was a reliable witness, for Roman walls standing six to twelve feet high are still to be found buried under modern York. He speaks, too, of his early days in York as a boy and tells how he wandered through the flowery fields around the city and fished in the Ouse.

This last great century (c. AD 730–830) of Anglian York was one of the greatest and most peaceful periods in the history of the city. We know little of how it was governed though the Archbishop and the churchmen associated with the Minster had great power and influence. There were also rich merchants in the city. Trade with the Continent was clearly considerable though we have only small, scattered references to the actual commodities imported and exported. Many Anglo-Saxon coins minted in York are found in North Germany and Scandinavia, while we know that Alcuin sent back wine and tin (to make church bells) from Tours in France.

3. VIKING YORK – JORVIK

Britain was attacked by the Vikings in the ninth century. Their invasion and subsequent settlement are very much like those of the Anglo-Saxons in the fifth century. At first there were isolated raids, followed by the setting up of a base from which the conquest could be carried out and finally the establishment of new kingdoms, ruled by the victorious settlers, extending over ever-increasing areas of the country.

The summer of AD 793 saw the first Viking raid on the north

York became Jorvik

A Viking raid

when the monastery of Lindisfarne was attacked and plundered; that of Jarrow suffered the same fate the following year. In AD 866 large numbers of Vikings swarmed over to England, and for the first time stayed here for the winter. The following year

they marched into Northumbria and attacked York. This was described vividly by Asser in his *Life of King Alfred*. He tells of civil war among the Christian Northumbrians, the overthrow of King Osbert by the usurper Ælla, "a tyrant", according to Asser, and not of royal blood. When they heard that the Vikings had taken York, "through divine counsel and the warning of the chiefs, for the sake of the common good the strife calmed down somewhat, and Osbert and Ælla united their forces, combined their armies and marched to the City of York". To protect themselves the Vikings hastily threw up a defensive wall, "for at that period the city had no firm and stable walls", but the Christians soon broke this down and entered the city. "The pagans, driven by desperation in their danger, wildly fell on them, slew them, put them to flight, laid them low, inside and outside the city." Both Northumbrian kings were killed, and the whole of their forces wiped out, except for a few who escaped and made peace with the pagans. Excavations have revealed parts of the earthen rampart which the Vikings threw over the ruined Roman walls to fortify their newly captured city.

Soon the whole of Deira was conquered, and the Angles who survived became their subjects. From AD 867 until 927 it was ruled by kings of Danish origin with Scandinavian names such as Ivar, Halfdene, Cnut Sihtric and Grithfrith. For most of that period York was, with Dublin, the joint capital of a kingdom which stretched across the north of England between the rivers Humber and Tweed, and included the Isle of Man and the eastern seaboard of Ireland. Under the kings were earls or "under-kings", some of whom lived and ruled in Jorvik, such as Beorn, Regnald and Eric Bloodaxe. This last is associated with one of the most remarkable stories of the Vikings in England. One of the Norse sagas which has come down to us deals with the adventures of Egil Skalagrimsson. He and Bloodaxe were members of two ancient Norse families, between which there had long been a bitter feud. Eric Bloodaxe had been exiled from Norway and after a series of blood-curdling adventures had settled in Jorvik, where he had gained the position of "under-king". One day, Egil Skalagrimsson set out across the North Sea on a trading expedition to England and was shipwrecked somewhere on the north bank of the Humber. In Jorvik he had a staunch friend called Arinbiorn and he decided to go there, despite the risks he knew he ran should he meet Bloodaxe. In disguise, he made his way to Arinbiorn's hall, or garth as it was called. This put Arinbiorn in an awkward position, for he was Bloodaxe's vassal, and could not shelter the sworn enemy of his overlord. After some hesitation he decided to make a clean breast of the whole affair, and take Egil to Bloodaxe's garth, trusting that the complex rules of Scandinavian hospitality, which forbade mankilling after sunset, would ensure that Egil survived the night at least. Bloodaxe was astounded and enraged to see his enemy, but as he could take no action that night, he ordered Arinbiorn to bring Egil to his garth early the next morning to take the consequences of his impudence.

So Arinbiorn took Egil home for the night, to try to find a way to save Egil's life. They decided that the only way to do this was for Egil, who was famous as a *scald* or poet, to compose a *drapa* or long heroic poem to show what a great seafarer and warrior Bloodaxe was. Egil went upstairs into the garret to do this. When, an hour later, Arinbiorn went up to see how he was getting on, he found that he had not written a single word. This was, said Egil, because a bird on the window-sill had twittered away endlessly, interrupting his thoughts. Arinbiorn recognized this bird as Bloodaxe's wife, Gunnhild, a reputed witch, in disguise. She had urged Bloodaxe to kill Egil on the spot, and was determined that no plot should be hatched to prevent her husband from taking revenge on his enemy. She knew that flattering him might have this effect.

When Arinbiorn had shooed the bird away, Egil set to work, and by dawn he had finished. The two friends went to Bloodaxe the next morning as they had promised. Gunnhild got in first and urged her husband to kill Egil at once, but Arinbiorn persuaded Bloodaxe to hear the *drapa*. Egil put on a magnificent performance, which so flattered Bloodaxe that, despite more hysterics from Gunnhild, and against his own better judgement, he spared Egil's life on the condition that he left Jorvik immediately and went south to the court of the Saxon king Athelstan. This Egil did.

Although the story is full of unlikely happenings there is no reason to doubt its essential truth. Scalds were highly respected and very important members of Scandinavian society. In an age when very few could read or write, they were regarded as the official record keepers and historians as well as entertainers. In any legal dispute, a scald's recital of a verbal agreement between two parties would be as binding as a legal document is today. Bloodaxe knew that if he let Egil live, so might his own fame. So, revenge and vanity competed for Egil's life. We are fortunate that vanity triumphed, and that this incredible story has been preserved, for it also gives an intimate insight into a period of York's history about which little is known. It shows us Bloodaxe and his vassal Arinbiorn each living in his own separate garth with his own following of soldiers and servants, each jealous of his own social standing, loyalties and rights. It tells us of the strange code of conduct concerning hospitality and feuding which cemented Viking society. We have a glimpse of the social classes hedged about by privileges and taboos. We see the feasting, heavy drinking and the minstrelsy.

Archaeological evidence of the Viking period gives a picture of the areas of settlement, and of some of the occupations carried on in Jorvik. We know there was extensive settlement in King's Square, Bootham, Hungate, Castlegate and Bishophill. In Hungate, alongside the river Foss, there was certainly a wharf. Castlegate has produced pottery, hones (for sharpening knives and weapons), knives and other metal instruments, wooden bowls, bone combs and weaving implements and the like. These finds suggest domestic dwellings and perhaps workshops. In King's Square, which used to be known as Coney Garth, part of a large house has been found, together with some pottery, combs and an ice-skate made out of the thigh bone of an animal. Other exciting finds came from an excavation near the church of St. Mary's, Bishophill Junior. The site of these discoveries is some 150 yards south of Micklegate, the main street of Jorvik. Two ninth century buildings were found, both built inside the ruins of Roman buildings. The Vikings had apparently done this to make use of the Roman conduits which still existed there and so get a cheap and efficient water supply. It speaks well of Roman engineering that, after a lapse of 500 years, part at least of the public water system of Eburacum was still in working order.

One of these buildings, seven feet below the surface of the garden on the north side of the church, deserves special mention as its history in the Viking period had been both long and unusual. Excavation revealed part of a large Roman apsidal-ended building at least forty feet wide and sixty feet long. Its purpose was not clear, but it might have been a temple or some other kind of public building. In the ninth century when the Danes first made use of it, the walls were still standing many feet high. In one part of the building they erected wattle and daub partitions to form a dwelling house; in another they dug into the Roman floor three roughly-circular pits five feet deep and five feet in diameter, which were kept filled with running water fed from a Roman culvert still working under the original floor. A few feet away from these pits was a room where herrings were cured. Lying on the Roman floor were thousands of the scales and bones of small herrings. Calculations showed that in an area of about eight square feet there had been at least 2,000 fish. Small post-holes in the floor showed where uprights had been placed, presumably to support shelves or lines on which the fish had been laid or hung for curing by drying in the wind and sun. The scales and bones on the floor were perhaps of small herrings which had been rejected and been trampled underfoot.

After being used in this way for about a century the building was no longer lived in, and the area had been turned into a cemetery. Seventeenth century burials were found during the excavation, many more may still be there. One of the skeletons, that of a woman, had a silver bracelet on its left upper arm. Another skeleton, a man's, was found with the buckle from his belt, and a whetstone and coin from inside the pouch he had worn. The coin was a St Peter's Penny struck at the Minster mint, which was set up by the Anglian archbishops about AD 790 and continued to be used by the Danes. The penny dated to about AD 930, and was one of the last to be minted in York.

Only two non-Roman buildings still stand in York which were built before 1066. One is the Anglian tower referred to on p. 21, the other is the tower of St Mary's, Bishophill Junior: it was built using Roman stones. Inside the church, under the tower, is a large Anglo-Saxon arch, one of the finest in England. Arch and tower could be as early as about AD 1000.

In one peculiar way York is still very much aware of its Viking history. Within the city walls, nearly every street name is of Scandinavian origin. Over forty end in "gate", the old Norse *gata* meaning street. Coney Street comes from the Viking *Kunungur* meaning "the king's street". Finkle Street, Blake Street, Ogleforth and Stonebow also hide their Scandinavian origin. Most of the "gates" fall into fairly obvious categories. There are those linked with churches and monasteries—St Saviourgate, Gillygate (St Giles), Marygate (St Mary's Abbey), Petergate (the Minster is dedicated to St Peter). The trades practised in them are remembered in many— Skeldergate (shieldmakers), Spurriergate (spur-makers), Colliergate (colliers, who sold charcoal). Some commemorate people—Goodramgate (Guthrum), Jubbergate (Jews), Davygate (in the eleventh century David-le-Lardiner lived there; he was the royal lardiner, or guardian, of the Forest of Galtres). Others are based on obvious topographical features—Ousegate, Fossgate, Castlegate; while the derivation of at least one— Whip-ma-whop-ma-gate—remains something of a mystery; it may be the street where vagabonds were whipped. Attention has already been drawn to the fact that the very name of the modern city is Viking: the Anglian "Eoforwic" became "Euerwic", which became "Jorvik", which is now "York".

Athelstan of Wessex, who reigned AD 924–39, was the first king to rule over the whole of England. It was Jorvik which

offered him the greatest opposition, and the inhabitants forti-
fied the city against him when he marched north with an army
and defeated them. This was in AD 927, an important date in the
history of York. For the first time since the Romans ruled
Britain, York was now under the control of a ruler from
southern England. These links with the south were to increase
as the centuries passed—particularly under the Normans and
the Tudors. On a subsequent visit, Athelstan's attention was
drawn to some humble religious folk, known as Culdees, who
looked after the sick and aged. The King gave them land and
endowments to found a hospital, which they dedicated to God
and St Peter. After the Norman Conquest this was re-endowed,
rebuilt and rededicated to St Leonard, and became the largest
medieval hospital in England. The ruins of it are still to be
seen in the Museum Gardens and in the Theatre Royal.

Following Athelstan's death there were further Danish raids
on England. From 1016 until 1042 the Danish kings Canute and
Harthacanute ruled England, but in 1042 the Anglo-Saxon
dynasty was restored in the person of Edward the Confessor.
He governed England through three great earls—Godwin in
the south, Leofric in the midlands and Siward, a Dane, in the
north. Siward governed from Jorvik, and lived in Galmanho,
an area of Bootham near St Mary's Abbey. Siward has left
his mark in literature as well as local history, for he is the Earl
Siward who, in Shakespeare's great tragedy, joined Malcolm
in crushing the tyrant Macbeth.

In the Anglo-Saxon Chronicle under the year 1055 is the
entry:

> In this year died Earl Siward at York, and he lies at Galmanho
> in the Minster which he himself had built and consecrated in the
> name of God and Olaf.

This "Minster" is the church now known as St Olave's, in
Marygate, close to St Mary's Abbey. On his deathbed, the
old earl is supposed to have said, "Shame on me, that after
missing death in so many battles, I must now die the death of
a cow." He bade his men clothe him in his shirt of mail, gird

on his sword, place his shield on his arm and his helmet on his head, that he might face death like a warrior. The tradition is that his heart was then buried under the high altar of St Olave's Church and his body in Siward's Howe, a mound off the Heslington Road near York University.

Edward the Confessor used Siward's death as a chance of strengthening his rule in the north, by appointing Tostig as the new Earl of Northumbria. Tostig was the son of Godwin, Earl of Wessex, who had died in 1053 and been succeeded by his brother Harold. Tostig was selfish, arrogant and cruel, and in October 1065, while he was away in the south of England, the citizens of Jorvik rose against him, slew his house-carls, deposed him, and elected as his successor Morcar, the brother of Edwin, Earl of Mercia. King Edward decided it would be wise to agree to these changes, and so he banished Tostig, who went overseas to his father-in-law, the Count of Flanders. Morcar was now officially the Earl of Northumbria, and the stage was set for the dramatic events of the following year.

About AD 1000 a visitor to York said this about it:

The city of York is the metropolis of the whole race of the Northumbrians, which city was once nobly built and strongly constructed with walls, but which is now abandoned to antiquity. [The reference is presumably to the ruined Roman walls.] It rejoices however in a multitude of inhabitants; not fewer than 30,000 men and women . . . are numbered in this city, which is filled with the riches of merchants coming from everywhere, especially from the Danish nation.

4. 1066 AND THE NORMANS

Few years in English history have had so many momentous events crowded into them as 1066. London and York were the two cities on which these events hinged. To understand the important part played by York we must know something of the national history of the time. Edward the Confessor had no children by his marriage to Edith, daughter of Earl Godwin. Who would succeed? There were at least five claimants. Eadgar Atheling, the grandson of Edward's half brother Edmund Ironside, had the best hereditary claim, but in 1066

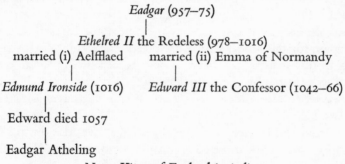

Eadgar (957–75)
|
Ethelred II the Redeless (978–1016)
married (i) Aelfflaed   married (ii) Emma of Normandy
| |
Edmund Ironside (1016)   Edward III the Confessor (1042–66)
|
Edward died 1057
|
Eadgar Atheling

Note: Kings of England in italics

he was only twelve years old. Another hereditary claim was held by Sweyn, King of Denmark, as the nephew of Canute. Harald Hardrada, King of Norway, had a very dubious claim through a treaty made between Harthacanute and King Magnus of Norway in 1038. Hardrada, the greatest warrior of his time, "the last heroic figure of the Viking age", could be expected to launch an attack on England simply because he loved war and adventure. William, Duke of Normandy, claimed that the Confessor had promised him the crown and

37

that Harold Godwinson, Earl of Wessex, had solemnly sworn to support him. In 1052 William had visited England and been given a most cordial welcome by the English king. Nothing is recorded of what passed between them, but the Norman tradition that William then received formal recognition as the heir presumptive is a strong one. Finally, there was Harold Godwinson himself. For sixteen years since 1053 he had virtually ruled the country as the Confessor's adviser. He was acknowledged to be a fair ruler, a good soldier and was generally popular in the south, the seat of power in England at this time. He had two advantages over all the other adult claimants; he was English and he was on the spot.

On 5th January 1066, Edward died. He was buried in Westminster Abbey the next day and a few hours later Harold was elected King and crowned by Ealdred, Archbishop of York. The *Anglo-Saxon Chronicle* summed up his reign thus: "Little quiet did he enjoy the while that he wielded the kingdom." He spent the spring of that year travelling to various parts of his realm trying to win support for himself and to prepare for the ordeal which lay ahead. He was in York when his troubles started in May. A few weeks before he arrived Halley's Comet had first appeared in the sky and was to be seen in the city all the time he was there. It was taken as an omen of disaster.

Harold had to face no fewer than three invasions during his short reign. Two—those of his brother Tostig and of Hardrada —he successfully beat off; the last, launched by William of Normandy, overwhelmed him. First, Tostig crossed the Channel with a fleet of sixty ships from Flanders where he had been in exile, harried the east coast, and was eventually defeated in Lincolnshire. He fled with his remaining twelve ships to Scotland, where he plotted another invasion with Hardrada.

Meanwhile, William of Normandy had been preparing for his invasion, so in June Harold mustered the English fleet to await the attack. The wind, however, remained against the Normans, and by September the English troops were tired of waiting and wanted to go home to get in the harvest. Reluctantly Harold called his fleet back into the Thames. Hardrada took this opportunity to launch his invasion. Tostig's and Hardrada's combined fleet of 330 ships sailed down the east coast from Scotland and up the Humber, driving before it the small number of English ships which had been sent out against it. Hardrada anchored at Riccall, ten miles below York, in September, and the English ships fled before him up the Wharfe to Tadcaster.

As soon as the news of the invasion reached Harold in London, he set out for the north with as many soldiers as he could muster. Meanwhile Hardrada advanced from Riccall to York on 20th September and was met by the northern Earls Edwin and Morcar at Fulford, now a suburb of York. Little is known of this battle; the fullest account of it is given in the Heimskringla Saga:

Then King Harald went to the Humber . . . and landed. The earls Morcar and Edwin his brother, were in York with a huge army. King Harald was lying in the Ouse when the army of the earls came down. King Harald went ashore and arrayed his army. One wing lay forward of the river, the other extended up inland to a dyke. It was a deep, wide marsh full of water. The earls allowed their army to concentrate down near the river with the whole body. The king's banner was near the river. He had a dense array there; it was thinnest by the dyke and least reliable there. The earls attacked down the dyke. The Norwegian wing that extended to the dyke gave way. The English thought that the Norwegians were in full flight and pursued them. The banner of Morcar advanced there.

But when King Harald saw that the English formation had advanced alongside the dyke, he had the attack signal blown and encouraged his army heartily, had the banner Landwaster borne forward, developed such a fierce attack that all gave way before it. There was great slaughter in the earls' army. The troops soon took to flight, some ran up along the top of the dyke, but most ran out over the dyke. The slain lay so thick that the Norwegians could go dry-shod over the marsh. Morcar died there . . . Earl Edwin and those who escaped fled to York. Casualties were very heavy. The battle was on Wednesday, the day before St Matthew's day.

Hardrada's men in action

Some historians have expressed surprise that Hardrada did not then plunder York. The explanation may lie in the fact that he had come to conquer England not merely to carry out a raid. He knew, probably from information supplied by Tostig, that York and Yorkshire with its largely Scandinavian population had little love for its southern neighbours. Not only was it a good base for an advance south, but properly handled, some of the northerners might even join his army.

Before moving south Hardrada called for hostages from the Northumbrian thegns and arranged to meet them at Stamford Bridge on 25th September. On that fateful Monday, Hardrada, Tostig and some two-thirds of the Norwegian army left Riccall to march to Stamford Bridge at about the same time that, all unbeknown to them, Harold Godwinson left Tadcaster on the last stage of his remarkable march north. Harold went through York and arrived at Stamford Bridge about noon, taking the Norwegians completely by surprise.

The most colourful account of the ensuing battle occurs in the Heimskringla Saga. The story begins as the Norse army leaves Riccall.

> The weather was exceptionally good, with hot sunshine. The soldiers left their mailshirts behind, but went ashore with shields and helmets and spears and girded with swords, and many had bows and arrows as well and they were quite happy.

Soon after they reached Stamford Bridge

> . . . they saw a cloud of dust and beneath it bright shields and glittering mailshirts . . . and the force was bigger as it drew nearer and it was like looking at an ice-field, so shining were the weapons.

Tostig urged Hardrada to retreat to Riccall and refrain from fighting until the whole of his army could be brought into action. Hardrada refused but sent "three bold fellows" on the fastest horses available to Riccall to summon Eystein Moorcock and the remainder of the Norwegians to Stamford Bridge. Hardrada arranged his army in two large circles, one around himself and his banner Landwaster, the other around Tostig

and his banner. When the English army was drawn up opposing them a parley took place between Harold and his brother.
Harold offered to restore to Tostig his earldom of Northumbria together with a third of England. Said Tostig:

> "Now if we were to take that choice, what will be offered
> King Harald for his labour?" Then said Harold . . . "Seven foot
> space of English soil or longer as he is taller than other men."

The battle then began. After fierce hand-to-hand fighting
the Norwegian shield wall was broken.

> But when King Harald Hardrada saw that, he advanced in the
> battle to its heart. Then there was the fiercest of fights and many
> fell on both sides. Then King Harald was so angry that he ran
> forward from the ranks and hewed with both hands. Neither
> helmet nor mailshirt could withstand him. All those nearest
> him fled. It was in the balance whether the English would turn
> in flight . . . King Harald Hardrada was wounded by an arrow
> in the throat. That was his death wound.

Hardrada's death ended the first phase of the battle and Tostig
then took command. There was a lull while both sides re-
formed. Again Harold offered a truce to his brother and again
it was refused. In this second phase Tostig was killed. Eystein
Moorcock then arrived with the reserves from Riccall. He
took Landwaster and rallied the invaders a third time. After a
long and bitter fight the Norse ranks broke for the last time.
Survivors fled as far as Riccall closely pursued by the English.
At Riccall the Norse made a final stand during which some of
their ships were burned. Olaf, Hardrada's son, finally surrendered and Harold allowed him and his men to depart on the
condition that they would never return to England. So many
had been slaughtered that thirty ships were sufficient to carry
the survivors home across the North Sea.

On 28th September—three days after the English victory at
Stamford Bridge—William of Normandy landed at Pevensey.
The news reached Harold on 1st or 2nd October; tradition has
it that this was in York where he had been frantically trying
to restore some sort of order. Harold immediately marched to

London with what was left of his army. On 14th October he was killed on the battlefield at Hastings. England had been conquered for the last time in its history. Soon the whole of the country—and York and Yorkshire in particular—was to know the ruthless character of its new master, William, Duke of Normandy, who on Christmas Day 1066 was crowned in Westminster Abbey.

The capture of York gave William the Conqueror more trouble than any other English city. In 1067 the Northumbrians, under a leader called Gospatric, revolted against the Normans. They proclaimed Eadgar Atheling, who has been mentioned already, as King. When William marched on York the citizens' enthusiasm evaporated and they made their peace with him. William had a wooden castle erected on Baile Hill: the *motte* (earthen mound) remains to this day. Leaving a garrison of 500 behind to man this castle the Conqueror moved south. Early in 1069 the news was brought to him that Northumbria was again in revolt. In Durham the royal representative, Robert de Commines, was murdered, while in York the new castle was destroyed and its garrison killed. William returned to the north, rebuilt the castle on Baile Hill and built a second one on the other side of the river Ouse, later to be known as Clifford's Tower.

In August of that year the long-expected invasion by King Sweyn of Denmark took place. A fleet of some 240 ships carrying an army of 10,000 men sailed up the Humber and threatened York. The citizens threw in their lot with the invaders and again attacked the Normans, who set fire to houses near the castles to create a diversion. This got out of control and the Minster, the magnificent library attached to it, St Peter's hospital and many parish churches and houses were destroyed. The castles were captured and the garrisons killed. William returned to York a third time, vowing that he would now teach the city and Northumbria a lesson they would never forget. His troops plundered what little was left of the city, slew those inhabitants who had not fled and then ravaged the countryside between York and the river Tees. Thousands were slain and hundreds of villages were put to the fire, during what is recorded in history as the "Harrying of the North". Sweyn retreated across the North Sea, and York made its final peace with William.

The castles were rebuilt yet again, the defences of "Clifford's Tower" being strengthened by the addition of a moat. To keep this filled with water a weir was built across the river Foss below the castle. This raised the level of the river to such an extent that no fewer than 120 acres, including arable land, meadows and gardens, together with two new mills, were flooded. This, called the King's Pool or Fishpool, remained waterlogged until it was finally drained in the nineteenth century. It is now built upon but retains the name of Foss Islands. At the same time the Normans strengthened the city defences by heightening the rampart, surmounting it with a wooden palisade and fronting it with a ditch filled with water. A stretch of this ditch, now dry, may still be seen in Lord Mayor's Walk.

York had learnt its lesson. It gave no further trouble to the Conqueror. In fact it soon recovered and entered into a period of expansion, prosperity and ever-increasing foreign trade.

5. RELIGION IN THE MIDDLE AGES

In the history of England the Middle Ages is generally regarded as stretching from 1066 to 1485. This period is often called "the Age of Faith", because the Roman Catholic Church played such an important part in every aspect of life—very different from the present. The daily life of people, their ideas and even their business activities in the Middle Ages can only be understood against this background of religion. One obvious example of this was the great number of religious buildings which existed, only a few of which survive today. In York these included the Minster, parish churches, monasteries, hospitals, and other religious houses.

York has long been famed for its Minster—by far the largest building in the city and the third largest cathedral in Britain. Generation after generation of Englishmen have left money and property so that the Minster could be built and rebuilt, altered and added to, furnished with monuments, treasures and beautifully carved woodwork. It was not until about 1500 that it finally attained its present size and magnificence. In 1435 Æneas Sylvius Piciolomini, later Pope Pius II, passed through York. He described the Minster as "templum . . . et opera et magnitudino toto orbe mirandum" ("a shrine . . . in structure and size the wonder of all the world"). One of the best known people associated with the building of the Minster is Walter de Gray (Archbishop 1216–55) who was responsible for the south transept. A remarkable discovery during the recent excavations in the Minster was that of his coffin in the south transept. On the lid was painted a life-size effigy of the Archbishop.

On a hot, sunny summer's day there is no more refreshing

experience than to enter the Minster. It is cool and shaded and the pictures and colours in the stained glass of the windows stand out vividly in the sunshine. There are 125 such windows containing half the medieval stained glass in the whole of Great Britain. In date it ranges from the twelfth to the eighteenth century. There is only space here to refer to two of the windows, both of which are world famous.

The Five Sisters' window in the north transept dates from the year 1260. It is made up of five lancets (narrow, pointed windows), each one fifty-six feet long and four feet wide. The window, made of grisaille glass, contains no "pictures" as such but is a series of geometric patterns on a grey-green background. In his novel, *Nicholas Nickleby*, Charles Dickens wove a delightful story—entirely fictitious—about this window. It is well worth reading.

The other famous window is the great east window, one of the largest in the world—larger than a tennis court. In it are 117 panels, each three feet square and each containing a complete little picture. It covers the Bible story from the Creation, through the Old and New Testaments, to the Last Judgment as described in the Revelation of St John the Divine. At the very top in the tracery is a figure of God with an open book before Him on which are the words "Ego sum Alpha et Omega" ("I am the Beginning and the End").

The man who designed this vast window was John Thornton of Coventry. It was begun in December 1405 and finished in 1408. The Dean and Chapter agreed to pay him four shillings a week with a £5 bonus at the end of each year and a final one of £10 if the work was completed within three years.

It may seem strange that a glass painter from Coventry had to be imported into York to design this window as the city was already famous for its stained glass and the craftsmen who made it. The dearth of such craftsmen may have been the result of the Black Death of 1349 when it is estimated that the population of York declined from about 35,000 to less than 12,000. The Archbishop of York at this time was Richard le Scrope. From 1386 to 1398 he had been Bishop of Lichfield and Coventry; perhaps he knew of Thornton's work in the midlands and recommended him to the Dean and Chapter when no local men were available.

A window of this size and magnificence cost an enormous sum of money. A wealthy patron, Bishop Skirlaw of Durham, presented it to the Minster. His portrait is depicted in the window in the base of the central panel of the bottom row. Thornton's own device and the date 1408 occur at the top of the tracery, telling us when it was finished.

Thornton stayed in York after this work was completed and in 1410 was made a member of the glaziers' guild. He was probably responsible for windows elsewhere in the Minster and in other York churches, though none is known for certain. It has been suggested that the fine window, "The last fifteen days of the world", in All Saints' Church, North Street, was his work.

In the Middle Ages everybody was expected to go to Mass in his parish church every Sunday. So, in a great city like York, there were numerous parish churches, each with a priest in charge; by the end of the Middle Ages there were nearly fifty, only eighteen of which have remains still standing today. These are:

> *All Saints, North Street
> †*All Saints, Pavement
>   Holy Trinity, Goodramgate
> †*Holy Trinity, Micklegate
> †*St Cuthbert, Peasholme Green
> *St Denys, Walmgate
> *St Helen's Square
>   St John, Ousebridge
>   St Lawrence, Lawrence Street
> *St Margaret, Walmgate
>   St Martin-le-Grand, Coney Street
> †St Martin-cum-Gregory, Micklegate
> *St Mary, Bishophill Junior
> †St Mary, Castlegate
> *St Michael-le-Belfrey
> *St Michael, Spurriergate

*St Olave, Marygate
St Sampson, Church Street

Of these St Lawrence has only the tower remaining and just eleven—marked above with an asterisk (*)—are still used for regular services.

We only know the actual foundation date of one of these churches. This is St Olave's which is mentioned in the Anglo-Saxon Chronicle as being built by Earl Siward in 1055. Eight churches are mentioned in Domesday Book (1086) of which five—noted in the above list with a dagger (†)—still exist today. One of these—St Mary's, Castlegate—is of particular interest as its dedication stone was found there during restoration work between the years 1868 and 1870. It is partly in Latin and partly in Old English. Much is indecipherable but its general meaning reads something like this:

> Efrard and Grim and Aese built this minster in the name of Our Lord Jesus Christ and of St Mary and of St Martin and of St Cuthbert and of all the Saints. It was consecrated in the year . . .

The inscription dates to the eleventh century, just before or after 1066. As pointed out earlier, St Mary's, Bishophill Junior, with its Anglian tower, is also pre-Norman. By 1100 there were fourteen parish churches, by 1200, thirty-seven, and by 1485, forty-six. Those which now remain are worth visiting, because of their architectural features, tombstones, furniture, stained glass, brasses, parish registers, etc.

Some men and women in the Middle Ages wanted to dedicate their lives to God and so entered monasteries or nunneries. These covered many acres and were founded by wealthy people who asked that the monks and nuns should pray for their souls, the souls of their ancestors and all the faithful departed. A great church was therefore the largest and most lavishly decorated single building in a monastery. In addition to prayers and church services, the members kept schools, copied manuscripts, gave daily alms to the poor and needy, gave hospitality to travellers, sometimes looked after the aged and engaged in business enterprises—especially sheep farming—

through which they played a most important part in the social, cultural and economic life of the time. York had at least two great monasteries and two nunneries. In 1078 Alan, Earl of Richmond, gave the church of St Olave, together with four acres of land adjoining it in Bootham just outside the city walls, to a Benedictine monk called Stephen who became the first Abbot of St Mary's Abbey. Land, property and money were showered on this house by royal and other benefactors so that at the time of the Dissolution in 1539 it was one of the richest monasteries in England. Much of its wealth was spent on embellishing it internally and externally: the present scanty ruins give only a glimpse of its original size and grandeur.

The second great Benedictine house in York was that of Holy Trinity, Micklegate. This was founded before the Conquest, possibly in the reign of King Oswald (971–92). After the conquest it became the property of Ralph Paganel, High Sheriff of Yorkshire, who gave it to the Abbey of St Martin at Marmoutier in France. Until the fifteenth century the monks in this priory were known as Alien Benedictines because they owed obedience to a monastery in a foreign country to which they paid annual subsidies and by whom their priors were always appointed. In 1426, when England and France were at war, an Act of Parliament was passed severing all such foreign links. From then until it was dissolved in 1538 it was independent.

Religious enthusiasm waxes and wanes, rises and falls. In the medieval monastery so much depended on the leadership of the Abbot. If he was saintly, self-sacrificing, and unselfish the monks under his care were likely to follow his example. Equally he could set a bad example by being worldly, lazy, lax in his attendance at Mass and at prayers and a frequent absentee. The Normans founded many monasteries in England and, during the first century after the Conquest, monks and nuns were, as a general rule, well disciplined. As time went on they became more careless and by about 1200 the monasteries throughout Christendom had fallen into disrepute. A new religious idealism was injected into the church by St

DY

Francis of Assisi (1182–1226) and St Dominic (1170–1221). They founded two orders of friars—the Franciscans (Grey Friars) and the Dominicans (Black Friars). In their early days the friars differed from the monks in that they did not live in fixed communities but wandered about the country as preachers living by the labour of their own hands or on alms given to them by people who admired their austerity and devotion. Later, as they became more and more popular and as more and more money and property was showered on them, they adopted a way of life little different from that of monks. They built friaries which in their plan and size were not unlike monasteries. In the thirteenth century four such friaries were built in York. The Dominicans landed in England in 1221 and eventually established houses in Yorkshire at Beverley, Doncaster, Hull, Pontefract, Scarborough, Yarm and York. They arrived in York in 1228 and built their friary on the site of the Old Railway Station in Toft Green. Their community consisted of a prior and some forty-five to fifty brethren. The Franciscans, or Friars Minor, landed in England in 1224 and built six friaries in Yorkshire at Beverley, Doncaster, Pontefract, Richmond, Scarborough and York. This last house was built about 1230 sited between the castle and the river Ouse; part of the precinct wall of it still remains in Friar's Terrace. Their house was ruled by a prior and, throughout the Middle Ages, their number varied between forty and fifty. Two smaller orders of friars were the Austin Friars who were established in York some time before 1270, and the Carmelites who came to the city some time before 1253. The house of the Austin Friars was in Lendal near the site of the present Post Office and their property extended down to the River Ouse. Their numbers varied between twenty-five and forty. The Carmelites' first house was in the Horsefair near Gillygate. About 1300 they built a new house on the land between Fossgate and Stonebow Lane. The house never numbered more than thirty. All four orders of friars continued in the city until their houses were dissolved in 1538 .

In the Middle Ages man was constantly trying to express his

religious feelings in different ways—sometimes, as we have seen, it was in buildings, sometimes by separating himself from the world in monasteries, sometimes by taking to the road as a preacher as the friars did in the early days, sometimes by shutting himself off from his fellow men as a hermit or an anchoress (there were six of these in York). In the fourteenth and fifteenth centuries he used another device. He founded chantries. He left money or property to pay the stipend of a priest who, every day, said Mass for his soul and the souls of his wife, parents and anyone else he nominated in his deed of foundation. These chantries might be in a specially constructed chapel or, more likely, in some already existing church. In 1485 there were sixty-three chantries in York Minster and seventy-four in various parish churches of the city. Sometimes the parish priest or his curate was also priest of one or more chantries; sometimes the chantry priest was master of a school as well; but often he did nothing else but say Mass each day at the altar dedicated to his founder. Consequently many priests had very little to do. Those connected with the Minster lived in various houses in the city, often as lodgers, and did not always conduct themselves in as seemly a manner as their vocation demanded. Eventually the scandal became so bad that in 1436 the Dean and Chapter built St William's College where these priests had to live in a community, obeying rules and regulations and keeping regular times for eating and retiring to bed, rather like monks and friars. A few years ago an excavation took place on a piece of ground adjoining St William's College when the medieval kitchen, with its well, salting pits, ovens and hearths, was uncovered. Just outside it was found a superb jet crucifix, presumably lost by one of the priests who lived in the house.

A York man who founded not one but five chantries was Nicholas Blackburne, one of the wealthiest of the fourteenth century merchants in the city. His portrait, that of his wife Margaret and one of his eldest son and his wife are to be seen in the glass in the east window of All Saints' Church, North Street. This is a magnificent window and depicts St

Anne teaching her daughter the Virgin Mary to read from a medieval horn book. Blackburne founded two chantries in St Martin-cum-Gregory Church, Micklegate, one in St John's Church, Ousebridge, and another in St William's Chapel on Ousebridge. The fifth chantry was in St Mary's Church in Richmond, Yorkshire. He also left money for the repair of the bridges of Catterick, Thornton near Helperby in the North Riding and Kexby, £13 as alms to the poor and £100 to deliver debtors from gaol. He is a typical example of how a rich man might be affected by Christian teaching in the Middle Ages and feel under an obligation to help those less well off than himself. He was buried in the Minster.

A building connected with the Minster was the Bedern built in 1252. Here were housed thirty-two Vicars Choral, the deputies of the Minster Canons. To understand this situation we must look at the reforms of Thomas of Bayeux, the first Norman Archbishop of York (1069–1100). When he arrived in York in 1069 he found the Minster a blackened ruin; he rebuilt it and put it under the government of thirty-six Canons of whom four—the Dean, Precentor, Chancellor and

Ousebridge 1807. Remains of medieval bridge on left and St William's Chapel on

Treasurer—were the most important. Each Canon held what was known as a prebend—that is he was also the priest in charge of a church somewhere in the diocese from which he drew the revenues. He rarely visited his parish and paid a chaplain to perform the services. He himself took turns at saying the services in the Minster. Eventually even this became irksome and the Canons appointed deputies—the Vicars Choral—who took the services for them. The Bedern was a kind of small "monastery", though with a freer discipline: the Vicars could certainly go in and out of the city as they wished. They had a pleasant garden, surrounded by separate apartments for each of the

inmates, a chapel and refectory. All that remains today is part of the chapel.

In addition to the religious buildings mentioned there was the great hospital of St Leonard adjoining St Mary's Abbey and numerous small chapels in various parts of the city. The most striking of these was the chapel of St William on the old Ouse Bridge. This famous bridge, like old London Bridge, had houses and shops built upon it; it was demolished in 1809. On the north side at the east end was the Common Hall with the notorious city gaol beneath it and at its south end, where Messrs Boyes shop is now, was St William's Chapel. This was built in the thirteenth century and was dedicated to St William, the patron saint of York, who was a nephew of King Stephen.

The cult of a patron saint was a notable feature of the medieval religious scene. Some saints, such as St John of Beverley, St Thomas of Canterbury, St Cuthbert of Durham and St Wilfred of Ripon, were world famous and, because of the miracles which they were reputed to perform, attracted pilgrims from far afield. York was late in the field in acquiring its own saint and St William never attained the popularity of those mentioned above. He was Archbishop of York (1143–7 and 1153–4) and was buried in the Minster where his shrine became the centre of pilgrimages. During his lifetime he was reputed to have performed miracles, the most notable of which occurred on Ouse Bridge, in 1154, when he re-entered the city after his restoration as Archbishop. He was being welcomed in York by a great crowd. Part of Ouse Bridge, then built of wood, collapsed and many onlookers fell into the river. All were saved, due, it was believed, to the intercessions of the saint. He died thirty days later, poisoned, so it was said, by his enemies. In 1226 he was canonized. This miracle led to the building of a chapel at this particular place.

One of the treasures in the Yorkshire Museum is a set of alabaster carvings found in 1962 in Hungate. They probably formed part of a reredos (altar piece) of some nearby church and were deliberately buried at the time of the Reformation to prevent them from being destroyed. They are superb. They portray a series of scenes in the life of St William, showing his birth, death and various miracles, including the one at Ouse Bridge.

The Mystery Plays

Story-telling and acting, the two ingredients of drama, are as old as man. In the early days of the Christian Church, drama had been frowned upon as a heathen custom, but during the Middle Ages it was adapted and used extensively for religious purposes. In most towns of any size it became usual for Bible plays in English to be enacted on religious festivals in churches, in the adjoining graveyards or elsewhere, sometimes by the clergy, sometimes by laymen and sometimes by both. By the thirteenth century such plays were well established, particularly after religious drama became associated—exactly when and under what circumstances is unknown—with the craft guilds. These plays became known as "Mystery" Plays, being performed by members of the "misteries" or crafts and, when grouped together into a succession of linked plays, were known as "cycles". The commonest of these cycles was a varying number of plays on subjects connected with the Creation, the Old Testament, the New Testament, scenes from the life of the Virgin Mary and the Last Judgment. Many of the large towns in medieval England developed their own Mystery Plays but the texts of only four have survived to the present time: York (a cycle of forty-eight plays), Coventry (forty-two), Wakefield (thirty) and Chester (twenty-five).

At an early date these plays became linked with the Feast of Corpus Christi. This feast was instituted in 1264 by Pope Urban IV in honour of the sacrament of the body of Christ. The date—the Thursday following Trinity Sunday, in the middle of June in high summer—became quickly associated with festivals, processions and religious plays. The York plays were always performed on this day.

More is known of the York Mystery Plays than of any others in England, and their modern revival in the setting of the ruins of St Mary's Abbey in York in 1951, and at three-yearly intervals since, has done much to re-awaken interest in them, to emphasize the beauty of their language, their vivid dramatic force and their value as a medium of religious instruction. The text of the plays has been revised and rewritten in a more modern form by a York Scholar, the late Rev. Canon J. S. Purvis, from an original manuscript belonging to the Corporation of York and now in the British Museum.

The York plays, which date from about 1340, are anonymous but there are reasons for supposing that they were the work of three authors at three different periods, their first one perhaps being a monk of St Mary's Abbey, York. The plays are written in a varied metre and there is some attempt to match the metre to the particular character speaking: the words of the shepherds in the Nativity Play, for instance, are forthright, simple and in dialect. A few stage directions—in Latin—have been added to the York copy and mostly relate to directions for singing. The plays vary considerably in length. The shortest is a monologue of eighty-six lines, spoken by God, describing the first five days of creation, while the longest —545 lines—deals with the Entry into Jerusalem. The number of actors taking part in each play varies also. The Entry into Jerusalem has sixteen, the Trial scene—of some 300 lines— has seventeen. The average seems to have been between seven and eight but there may well have been many more supernumaries—angels, devils, lost souls, crowds, etc.

Humour, drama and tragedy were cleverly intermingled. Some of the characters (e.g. Noah's wife and Herod) became traditional figures of fun. Herod, was a pompous, bullying, raging figure with a black face, who wore an elaborate crest or helmet of gilt and a gown of blue satin and buckram. He was normally accompanied by an attendant, a boy, whose duty it was, if Herod showed any signs of mildness, to beat him into a condition of fury again with a bladder attached to a stick. The most amusing of all the stage directions appears alongside this play in the original document—*hic Herod pompagit*—"here Herod shall pomp".

The stage on which the plays were enacted was the pageant

wagon (*pagina*), a contraption crowned with pennants and banners. The wagons were trundled about the streets by human agency and in the Bakers' accounts for 1584 we are told that fourpence each was paid to six labourers to push, while in 1472 the Mercers spent twopence on "sope" for the wheels. Each play had a separate wagon and, when not in use, these were kept in sheds built on Toft Green which was anciently called Pageant Green.

Most of the actors were guildsmen and amateurs. There are, however, hints that in the late fifteenth century professionals from outside the City were being employed in the more important roles. In the Chester cycle some of the women's parts (such as the Virgin) were played by women, but in York all the evidence points to only youths taking these parts. A high standard of acting was expected and heavy fines were levied by the Corporation on those who did not know their parts or who played them in a slovenly manner. Normally one guild was responsible for each play and the guild had an obvious and appropriate link, e.g. the Butchers were responsible for the Crucifixion.

As far as the costumes of the actors were concerned no attempt was made to imitate those of the Old and New Testaments; contemporary medieval ones were used. It appears, however, that these were expected to be new and colourful and those who wore shoddy ones were fined. Certain characters in the plays—angels, devils, Adam, Eve, lost souls, saved souls, etc., wore "traditional" costumes: Adam and Eve close-fitting leather tights, saved souls white leather coats and hose, lost souls black and yellow or red and yellow (representing the flames of hell which were already upon them); devils had their coats ornamented with hair and feathers as in the window at the end of the south aisle of St Michael's Church in Spurriergate, archangels like Michael and God himself wore garments of leather and buckram heavily gilded and often had gilded faces as well.

Judged by modern standards the properties and scenery were crude and limited. Horses and asses were dummy figures made of hoops and canvas: small boxes like modern sentry boxes represented important buildings such as the Temple, the Synagogue and Herod's Palace. In the case of some of the larger plays it is clear that the wagon itself was too small and the street alongside the pageant must have been used as well.

The expenses of the plays were borne by the guilds. Most of the ordinances of the York guilds which have come down to us have a clause detailing the annual amount of "pageant silver", as it was called, which its members had to pay. It is curious to note that many guilds were still receiving this payment from their members as late as 1771, nearly two centuries after the plays themselves had ceased to be performed! As explained earlier, sometimes a single guild was responsible for a play, sometimes a number banded together to perform it. The biggest number joining together seems to have been six— the Cutlers, Bladesmiths, Sheathers, Scalers, Buckle-makers and Horners combined one year to produce the play of Pilate. The smaller guilds frequently changed from one play to another in different years; for instance on one occasion the Water-leaders united with the Bakers to produce the Last Supper and on another with the Cooks for the play about the Thirty Pieces of Silver.

On the day before the plays took place—that is, on the eve of the Feast of Corpus Christi—the plays were formally proclaimed around the city by a herald on horseback. He commanded everyone to go unarmed the following day, while the guilds performing the plays were ordered to provide "good players, well arrayed and well speaking" with "every player that shall play" ready "in his pageant at convenient time that is to say at the mid hour betwixt 4 and 5 of the clock in the morning, and then all the other pageants fast following each other one after the other as their course is, without tarrying".

The plays were performed at various places—"pageant stations"—in the city. The number and situation of these varied. At first there appear to have been nine—three on the Micklegate side of the Ouse and six on the other—but this later became sixteen, the number subsequently varying between nine and sixteen. From the fifteenth century onwards it appears that the city used the plays as a means of augmenting revenues, for citizens were allowed to bid against each other for the privilege of having the plays presented in front of their houses. In 1454 the city collected £6 3s 4d in such "rents", in 1486 £4 13s 4d, in 1522 £1 5s 6d and in 1561 £1 14s 0d. In 1551 the stations were limited to ten because of the plague. In the sixteenth century one station—often in Petergate—was free, being reserved for the "Lady Mayor" and other ladies variously described as "her sisters" or as "other Aldermen Wyffi's (wives)". Each pageant wagon was trundled from one station to the next. As soon as a performance was finished it moved on and its place taken by the following one. The first station was always at, or near, the gateway of Holy Trinity Priory in Micklegate. Here the first wagon—the Barkers playing The Creation—would draw up about five a.m., soon after daybreak. It would reach its last station (usually in Pavement) about noon, at which time the last play—the Judgment performed by the Merchant Adventurers—was playing at the first station in Micklegate. This wagon would reach Pavement (barring accidents, which must have been frequent!) between eight and nine in the evening.

One of the most celebrated of all the performances of the York Mystery plays took place in 1397 when a most exalted spectator in the person of King Richard II watched them from a specially erected box opposite the Priory gateway in Micklegate. It must have been a magnificent occasion. We know that the wood used to build the box cost £21; that the box was decorated with a new banner, new pieces of painted cloth, rushes and flowers costing £18; that extra porters were employed to speed up the passage of the wagons (they were paid eightpence each); that £28 was spent on beer, bread, wine, meat and fuel (perhaps the day was cold!); that tips were given to the King's Minstrels, and that no less than £88 was expended on new liveries of red and white for the servants waiting personally on the King.

The York Mystery Plays were one of the many casualties of

The Mystery Plays

the Reformation. There was a strong feeling amongst the Protestant clergy that they contained "superstitious doctrine" and savoured too much of the old Romanist religion. Despite the protests of the churchmen and growing doubts among some of the more Puritan of the civic authorities they continued to be performed until 1572. In the following year all copies of the play were called in by the Elizabethan Archbishop Edwin Sandys for correction. None was ever returned and we must assume that the Archbishop ordered their destruction. One complete copy did, however, survive and, after many wanderings, found its way into the British Museum where it is now.

6. THE MIDDLE AGES,
GOVERNMENT AND TRADE

It was over a century before York recovered from the effects of the Norman Conquest. The damage caused by the Norman attacks on the city was aggravated by another great fire which devastated it in 1137. The Minster and nineteen churches, together with hundreds of houses, were destroyed. Two documents—Domesday Book (1068) and the so-called "White Book" of Southwell Minster (1106)—enable us to build up a fairly comprehensive picture of what York was like during this century. In 1066 "in the time of King Edward" (i.e. before the Norman attack on the city) there were some 2,000 "mansiones" in the city. A "mansio" was a property containing at least one house. In 1086 there were only about 1,500 of which 540 were empty and 400 not "regularly" occupied. Assuming a family of between four and five per house, this gives a population in 1066 of between 8,000 and 9,000 and of less than half that twenty years later.

Domesday Book says that in 1066 York was divided into seven "shires" or, as we should now call them, "wards". One of these belonged to the Archbishop and was the area surrounding the Minster, later to be called the "liberty of St Peter". We do not know the exact location of the other "shires" though one was later cleared to build the castles, another was in the Micklegate/Bishophill/Clementhorpe area and a third was in the Walmgate/Layerthorpe area straggling alongside the river Foss. The Archbishop had complete jurisdiction over his "shire" and collected all the "customs" (taxes) from it, but the other shires seem to have been controlled by either the King's sheriff or by "burgesses" (some sort of city council), while the

Archbishop also received a third of the "customs" from the Walmgate/Layerthorpe ward. We know that ships berthed at the wharves there with fish from the Hebrides and corn from the East Riding.

According to Domesday Book, the largest landowner in the city, after the King himself, was the Count of Mortain, William the Conqueror's half-brother. He owned fourteen "mansiones" two of which were "in macello" (the market), together with the church of St Crux. There were many other property owners. The Bishop of Durham had a house and the church of All Saints, Pavement, and Odo Balistarius (the Crossbowman) had three houses.

Domesday Book also mentions four "judices" (justices) who enjoyed privileges over and above those of a burgess. It is assumed that they represented what remained of a group of twelve such men who had been responsible under the Danish kings for the maintenance of law and order. They presumably presided over a borough court of justice. This is important in showing that York had some sort of self-government during the pre-Norman period. The court continued after the Conquest and eventually led to the development of a Corporation headed at first by a Mayor, and then by a Lord Mayor. During the period 1100 to 1212, however, the King's sheriff, with Clifford's Tower as the seat of his authority, was the chief power in the city. He was responsible to the King for the maintenance of law and order and for supervising the collection of the *firma burgi* (the annual tax due from the city to the King) and seeing that it was duly paid into the Exchequer at Westminster. In King Edward's time this tax was fixed at £53; William the Conqueror increased it to £100; then it was raised to £120 in 1200. It is difficult to convert these amounts into modern equivalents but £100 in 1086 would be worth at least £100,000 today.

The Normans were great builders. Besides the two castles they rebuilt the Minster and many churches. St Denys' and St Margaret's in Walmgate still retain fine Norman doorways. (The latter was moved to its present position from the church of

St Nicholas outside Walmgate Bar which was so badly damaged in the siege of York in 1644 that it was demolished.) Ingram's Hospital in Bootham has another: it came from the demolished church of St Giles in Gillygate. Other important Norman buildings were the Archbishop's Palace, a little of the arcading of which still stands in Dean's Park, the original Treasurer's House, now incorporated into Gray's Court in Chapter House Street and the so-called "Norman House" in Stonegate.

The bars (gateways) and walls of the city were built about 1230. They were necessary to protect the citizens from attacks by the Scots. In Edward II's and Edward III's reigns these were frequent. Edward I, the so-called "Hammer of the Scots", had almost succeeded in conquering Scotland. His son and successor showed none of his father's military ability; he had thrown away this advantage and been ignominiously defeated at Bannockburn in 1314. After this the Scots raided England almost as they pleased. In 1319, for example, they advanced into Yorkshire and, when the Archbishop of York raised an army— in which there were many York citizens—he was defeated at the Battle of Myton-on-Swale. The walls of York had been hastily strengthened as the city was one of the few barriers preventing the Scots advancing further south into the midlands towards London. Both Edward II and Edward III paid many visits to ensure that the city defences were adequate. In 1327 Edward III came to York on such a visit, bringing with him some mercenaries led by John, Lord Beaumont of Hainault. The citizens of York disliked these foreigners and fighting, leading to bloodshed, broke out.

In 1328 Lord John went home only to return the following year with his niece Philippa, daughter of William, earl of Hainault, Holland and Zealand. The Council responsible for the government of England during the King's minority assigned to the Bishop of Lichfield the task of selecting a bride for the King. Five girls of noble birth were considered, one of whom was Philippa. "The piercing eye of the bishop observing . . . the lady Philippa to be of a good sanguine complexion agreeing with that of the king's, he secretly advised his colleagues that she was the lady most likely by her sweet disposition, to please the king their master." Soon afterwards the young couple were married in the Minster by William Melton, Archbishop of York. The event was celebrated in the city by three weeks of jousting, revelling, feasting and dancing.

These festivities were marred by renewed quarrels between the Hainaulters and the citizens and the climax came when the former set fire to one of the suburbs of the city. The citizens challenged the foreigners to a fight and a miniature battle took place somewhere in the city. As a result, 347 Hainaulters and 242 Englishmen were drowned in the river Ouse. Despite these unhappy omens the marriage was a happy one and Philippa proved to be an excellent wife. Twenty years later she showed qualities of high statesmanship. In 1346 Edward III crossed to France with an army to start another campaign in the so-called Hundred Years' War which was to result in the great victory of Poitiers. On leaving England he appointed the Queen as his regent and deputy. A major crisis occurred when the Scots under King David II crossed the border, ravaged Northumberland and quickly reached the outskirts of Durham. Philippa hurried to York, made it her headquarters and set about raising levies to repel the invaders. The Archbishop of York together with the two great northern lords, Neville and Percy, took command of these forces and met the Scots at Neville's Cross. This battle, fought on 24th August 1346, was a remarkable one. It took place so close to the city of Durham that the monks of the abbey (now the cathedral) clambered on to the top of the central tower where they had a grandstand view of the fight. They saw the Scots king hit by an arrow which became so deeply embedded in his cheek-bone that it could not be wrenched out. After desperate fighting David was captured by Sir John Copeland, the King's seneschal of the royal castle of Bamburgh on the Northumbrian coast. During the hand-to-hand fighting the King had hit Copeland across the face with his gauntlet, knocking out two teeth. Copeland took the King to Bamburgh. News of the victory and of the

EY

King's capture was sent to Philippa at York. The Minister bells greeted the English success. The Queen sent two York barber-surgeons, William de Bolton and Hugo de Kilvington, to Bamburgh "to extract the arrow and heal him [King David] with despatch". They operated on the King's cheek, extracted the arrow and attended him until the wound was completely healed. They were paid £6 from the royal exchequer for their services. A curious book has been published called *Arcana Fair-faxiana* (The Recipe Book of the Fairfax Family) which lists recipes and cures dating back to the Middle Ages. One which might well have been used by the two barber-surgeons at Bamburgh was as follows:

> To take corns from the feet and also to extract broken needles or arrowheads from the flesh.
>
> Take one oz. of wax, $\frac{1}{4}$ oz. resin and one oz. of both *Aristolochia Rotunda* and *Aristolochia Longa*. Melt the wax and the resin and then add your powder, finely beaten up and sifted, and stir well until the whole is cold. Lay it on as a plaster to any injured part, morning and evening. It has been tried and is a quick healer.

Aristolochia rotunda and *Aristolochia longa* are plants with a long root like a radish.

In 1347 King David of Scotland was taken to London where he was imprisoned in the Tower of London; he passed through York on his way south. His ransom was fixed at the enormous sum of 100,000 marks to be paid in ten annual instalments. Scotland was too poor a country to pay this and when the King was released after spending twelve years in captivity the balance of the ransom was still unpaid.

Edward III and Queen Philippa have two other links with York. Philippa bore Edward seven sons and three daughters. William of Hatfield, the second son, died young and was buried in the Minster. This royal tomb, the only one in York, shows an alabaster effigy of the boy, arrayed as a knight, with a mantle thrown over his shoulders. When the Queen died in 1369—eight years before her husband—her richly embroidered bed was sent to the Minster as a reminder of her link with the city. The fine bed clothes were converted into copes and other vestments for the clergy.

Reference has been made above to the Barber-Surgeons Guild. More is known of this than of any other York Craft Guild. Members of the guild performed a number of curious services ranging from hair-cutting to surgical operations. This old rhyme recalls some of these:

> His pole with pewter basins hung
> Black, rotten teeth in order strung
> Ranged cups that in the window stood
> Lined with red rags to look like blood,
> Did well his three-fold trade explain,
> Who shaved, drew teeth, or breathed [cut] a vein.

We can follow very closely the training which an apprentice underwent in this guild here in York. Medical science—such as it was in those days—taught that most diseases could be cured by bleeding. A surgeon had to know exactly where and when to bleed his patient—it was no good bleeding him just anywhere. The red and white pole and bleeding dish displayed outside the barber's shop were not only the symbols of his trade but were also of practical use. When the patient was undergoing the operation of phlebotomy (bloodletting) he grasped the pole to make the veins in his arm (if that was where the bleeding was being done) stand out prominently and so help the blood to flow more freely. As this pole was liable to be stained with blood it was painted red. When not in use barbers suspended it outside their doors with a white bandage twisted round it. When placed there it indicated that the barber was now free to be consulted by another patient. In later times when the pole became a mere symbol, permanently displayed, it was normally painted red and white. Sometimes a brass or pewter basin was hung from it; this was the receptacle into which the blood was shed. The dish was often graduated inside so that the quantity of blood to be taken—a pint or half a pint—could be precisely gauged. One of these barber's poles with a dish attached is on display in the Castle Museum in York.

The apprentice had to learn by heart the bleeding spots in the body. A York document has survived showing a body marked with thirty-three such bleeding points. To each of these is attached a note explaining what particular diseases could be relieved by cutting at that particular place. The apprentice memorized a long doggerel verse which started like this:

Every man has thirty and three
Listen and I shall tell them thee.
Some are above and some beneath
Listen and thou shalt know them each,
Behind his ears find thou two;
If thou let blood from these
His sight shall never fail;
They heal as well turnsick [giddiness] and scale [skin disease]
The two in the temple shall only be made
For aches and for stinging in the head.
In the midst of the forehead find thou one
For leprosy and saucefleme [inflammation/swelling] to be done.

The apprentice also had to learn which were the unlucky days in the calendar. There were thirty-one of these "perilous" days in each year. To take blood on these was "nought good but great peril". In addition the apprentice had to learn to set limbs and perform operations. One type of operation was for the removal of stones from the bladder. This was a serious and dangerous operation and, in an age when there were no anaesthetics, excruciatingly painful. In 1394 such an operation was performed in York. John de Cartwell, a barber-surgeon, knew that he required an operation for a stone. He approached another of his craft called John Catlewe and asked him to do this. Catlewe gave the matter some thought and then said he would only do it if both Cartwell and his wife Alice signed affidavits (legal documents) declaring that, no matter what the outcome of the operation, they would in no way damage his professional reputation or take legal action against him even if death resulted.

The Barber-Surgeons Guild was one of about sixty such

guilds which controlled the trade and industry of York for most of the Middle Ages. All the guilds were organized in the same way though their numbers varied according to the demand for their wares or services. Obviously there were far fewer barber-surgeons than there were butchers, tailors or labourers. The members of a guild were either masters, journeymen or apprentices. Apprentices served a master for at least seven years learning their craft. A parent or guardian signed an indenture and paid a premium (sum of money) by which a master agreed to train a boy while the boy agreed to serve his master faithfully, obey him and not betray his trade secrets. A boy was normally apprenticed at the age of twelve. He was given free board and lodging in his master's house and was given the equivalent of a little pocket money each week. At the end of his apprenticeship he took a test arranged by the guild and, if he passed, he became a journeyman. He was now paid for his work. The word journeyman comes from the French *journée* and means that he was paid on a day-to-day basis. The journeyman could either stay and continue working for his old master, transfer to another master or set up a business of his own. If he did the last he had to take a further test arranged by the guild which involved making a "masterpiece"—some special product connected with his particular trade. If he passed this he was accepted as a full member of the guild and— after paying the customary fees—became a freeman of the city of York. His name was now solemnly added to the list of the freemen of the city kept in the Guildhall by the Clerk to the Corporation. This list was started in 1272 and has continued to the present day.

Every new freeman became a member of the particular guild which controlled his craft. Each year the guild members met together to elect their officers for the year: these were the Master, or Warden, and the Searchers, two or more in number. The Searchers had the task of visiting the shops of the guild members to see that the guild rules were being obeyed. These rules were drawn up to ensure that the quality of the goods was maintained, that only those prices fixed by the guild were charged and that only the permitted hours of working were observed. This latter rule, in an age when artificial lighting—except for candles and oil lamps—was unknown, was necessary in a trade such as that of the tailors who, if they started work before it was fully light, would produce inferior goods. The tailors were not to start work until one hour after sunrise.

A document which gives a vivid insight into the economic life of York in the fourteenth century is the Lay Poll Tax Return of 1381. The collection of this tax, which was granted to the King (Richard II) by Parliament, had momentous consequences in English history. In Kent and the adjoining counties, it sparked off the popular rising known as the Peasants' Revolt though in York and the north it had no such repercussions.

The document is written in Latin. A tax of one shilling per head was to be levied on all lay persons except beggars—hence its name—over fifteen years old. However, the collectors were instructed to levy the tax according to the ability of the individual to pay, so that whilst each parish in York paid as many shillings as it had persons rated for tax, the rich paid more than a shilling and the poor less, though no one paid more than twenty shillings nor less than fourpence. A man and his wife were rated as one unit, that is to say they were not both called upon to pay. Other members of their household—children, relatives and servants—if over fifteen were required to pay. The names of those who paid are listed under the ecclesiastical parish in which they resided, and are grouped in household units. The particulars of each one are listed in four columns: the name of the householder, his family and other dependants living with him—if over fifteen; his trade or craft; relationship of other members of the household to the householder, i.e. "his wife" (Latin—*uxor eius*), "his servant" (Latin—*serviens eius*), or "relative" (Latin—*famulus* or *famula eius*); the amount of the tax paid.

Parts of the returns relating to the city are missing and parts are so perished as to be indecipherable. Nevertheless, the titles of twenty-eight of the York parishes have survived. While the return is too defective to give an accurate picture of the population of the city, it does supply most valuable information about the various crafts, their relative importance and their location. There are 126 crafts listed. An analysis of the trades in each parish shows that some industries tended to be concentrated in a particular area of the city while others were widely dispersed throughout it. Of the former the following are the most striking: all ten cutlers were in, or near, the parish of St Michael-le-Belfrey; ten out of the twelve pinners (pinmakers) were in St Crux in Pavement; twelve of the thirteen lorimers (leather-workers) were in parishes near Ousebridge; of the nineteen girdlers, thirteen were in parishes in, and around, the street called Girdlergate; all but three of the forty-four tanners were in the parish of All Saints, North Street; eighteen of the twenty-three saddlers were in parishes adjoining what is now Coney Street, Spurriergate and Castlegate; the parchment-makers were all located near Monk Bar. The crafts dealing with food were, as might be expected, the most widely dispersed, though the greatest concentration of butchers was to be found in the parishes of St Crux in Pavement and of Holy Trinity in King's Square, that is, the parishes in which the street called the Shambles is situated.

Nearly 1,000 persons are named in all. The largest single craft was that of the labourers (numbering 203—about twenty per cent of the total). The next were the weavers (75) and the tailors (73). The five most important groups of associated trades were:

Textiles	approximately	25%	of the total
Leather	„	15%	„
Food	„	13%	„
Metal	„	11%	„
Building	„	8%	„

This stresses the fact of the importance of wool, the wool trade and associated crafts in York in the fourteenth and fifteenth centuries. In Tudor times the decline of this trade was one of the causes of unemployment and distress in the city.

Markets have been held in York as in other ancient cities and towns from time immemorial. In Roman, Saxon and Danish times York was one of the most important markets in the north of England. The earliest mention of the markets after the Norman Conquest is in the charter of 1203 granted by King John to the city.

There were two main market-places—one in the Pavement called in the Middle Ages "Market-Shyre" and the other in St Sampson's Square called "Thursday Market"; though, as we shall see later, other localities were used as well. The Pavement market was for the sale of corn, food and drink and was held on Tuesdays, Thursdays and Saturdays while the Thursday

A market scene

market (actually held on Thursdays and Saturdays) was for the sale of cloth and hardware. One ancient document implies that up to the reign of Edward II (1307–27) the sale of victuals and merchandise had also taken place in open market on a Sunday. Though forbidden in this reign it appears that the veto was not complied with, for as late as 1416 we hear of the parishioners of St Michael-le-Belfrey complaining of the noise of the market held in the adjoining churchyard and of the annoyance caused by the stamping and neighing of the horses tethered there which interfered with their worship.

Here are some of the other places in the city where particular commodities were sold:

Sea fish	Foss Bridge
Fresh fish	East end of Ouse Bridge in what was called "Salter-greeses"
Malt	Coney Street
Butter	In front of the church of St Martin-cum-Gregory in Micklegate
Swine	Peaseholme Green
Corn	East end of All Saints' Church, Pavement
Hay	Haymangergate (? near the Shambles)

Regulations for the control of markets were detailed and strict. Changes to the existing regulations were announced publicly by proclamation in the markets. Price control was one of the most important. Stallholders were only allowed to sell at the prices fixed by the civic authorities. The reason for this was obvious. The Craft Guilds of the city had the prices of their commodities fixed by guild regulations; they were extremely jealous of the "strangers" and "foreigners" from outside who sold in the markets and so were constantly on the alert to see that they were not being undersold. A long list of prices charged in 1392 has come down to us. In the following table, which is based on this, the comparative prices of various animals, commodities, etc., of 1392, 1736 and 1970 are listed. The descriptions in the first column are taken from the four-teenth century document.

Description	Prices								
	1392			*1736*			*1970*		
	£	s	d	£	s	d	£	s	d
Carcase of choice beef	1	0	4	9	10	0	90	0	0
Carcase the next sort		14	0	7	0	0	76	0	0
Carcase Scotch beef		12	0	3	10	0	105	0	0
A Scotch cow		10	0	2	15	0	86	0	0
Carcase of best mutton		1	8	1	2	0	34	0	0
For a worse sort		1	4		15	0	10	0	0
A carcase of best veal		2	6	1	0	0	10	0	0
For a worse sort		1	6		15	0	5	0	0
A lamb			8		8	0	8	10	0
A hog or pork, the best		3	4	1	15	0	14	0	0
For another sort		3	0	1	1	0	12	0	0
A capon, the best			4		1	9	2	5	0
A capon, a second sort			3		1	1	1	10	0
A hen			½			7		10	0
A pullet			1			6		18	0
Good bread made according to the assize, wheaten and of good boulter—four loaves for			1			—		8	0
Beer well brewed, good and strong, according to the assize, the best sort per gallon			1½		2	0		20	0
All sorts of white wine			6		6	8	1	0	0
A fresh salmon, the largest and best		2	0		10	0	5	0	0
Twelve pigeons			3		1	3	1	10	0
A partridge			2			8		8	0
A plover			½			6	Not available today		
A woodcock			½			9		6	0
A teal			½			9		12	0
Twelve fieldfares			2		1	6	Not available today		
Twelve larks			½			6	Not available today		
A wild duck			4		1	6		10	0

Other regulations covered such matters as these:

(i) Place of sales. All articles were to be sold in the open market at the properly appointed places and not hawked around the streets "nor withdrawn into shops, houses or elsewhere". As a corollary to this the Corporation ordered that no guildsman of the city was to sell his wares on any stall in the market place but only within his shop, on pain of a fine of 6s 8d.

(ii) Time of sales. No one was to start selling before the market began and no one was to continue selling after it was closed. Different markets seem to have opened at different times, the opening time normally being fixed by the striking of the clock in the nearest church. In 1513 it was ordered that the malt market was to start at ten a.m. and, until noon, sales were only to be made to citizens and after that to anyone. The victual market, on the other hand, seems to have opened in the summer as early as six a.m. and closed at six p.m. when the bell in St Michael's Church at Ousebridgend (now St Michael's, Spurriergate) rang for evensong.

(iii) Weight and quality. These were to be according to the Assize (that is, as ordered by the Corporation) and Searchers were appointed to examine weights, measures and goods to see that the approved standards were observed. Two interesting examples of the enforcement of this have survived. In 1585 four fishmongers were sent to prison for five weeks because they had "practysed and used steepe stocke fysshe in water mixed with a quantitie of lyme to seem fayre and white to sale which is also thought not only deceiptfull but alsoo dangerouse to the health of the queene's people". In 1553 Bernard Horner, a butcher, was brought before the Corporation for exhibiting for sale "corrupt and stynkynge fleisshe" and was committed to prison. At the same time the two Searchers of the Butchers Guild were also sent to prison for their "neglygens and slakness" in allowing this meat to be offered for sale.

(iv) Forestalling. This was the practice of selling and buying goods before they reached the markets. There were many objections to this: toll had not been paid; the goods had not been "searched", i.e. approved for quality, weight, etc.; there was no check on the price; if the goods were in short supply it could lead to buyers "cornering the market" and placing themselves in a position to command an abnormally high price.

(v) A regulation in a Corporation minute of 1484 sounds an incongruous note in this present age when strikes are a daily occurrence. This ordered that the bakers of the city should be fined five marks because "of late" they had baked *no* bread "within their houses to be sold to the commoners of this Citie, to the grate hurt of the same".

As noted previously in this chapter one of the principal aims of the guild system in medieval cities and towns was to create, as far as possible, a monopoly of trade for the local craftsmen. Guild regulations were drawn up so as to make it difficult, if not impossible, for outsiders—"strangers" or "foreigners" as they were often called—to share in the local trade. But some "outside" trade was both necessary and, indeed, welcome. Luxury goods, particularly those from abroad, had a special attraction. Some local extra-mural products were also encouraged—farm products, such as vegetables, meat, butter, cheese, eggs, fish, etc., are obvious examples—and these could often only be supplied from manors and settlements outside, and independent of, the towns. Hence the necessity for fairs and markets.

In connection with both of these the influence of the Church is at once apparent. The market *cross*, the corn *cross*, the barley *cross*, etc., were the visible and material structures around which the chaffering, buying and selling of particular commodities was conducted. Further, the cross stood as a reminder of the "peace of the church" which was vital if commerce was to exist, let alone flourish. All contracts, however simple and small, required some sanction, some witness, some certainty that the bargain made would be honoured. In an age when respect for the law was much less than it is today, the morality thus implied had its basis in religion.

It is not, therefore, surprising to find that so many fairs of medieval England were associated with particular saints' days: St Botolph at Boston in Lincolnshire, St Ives at Huntingdon, St Giles at Winchester and St Bartholomew at Smithfield, London. The fact that these fairs—and hundreds of others throughout the length and breadth of England—were held on particular saints' days, year after year, made it easy for people to remember them, but it often hid another significant fact. In some cases the fairs themselves were controlled by the ecclesiastical authorities (we shall see that the earliest York fair was of this sort) and, through the collection of tolls, formed an important source of revenue. But other factors are also involved. Fairs frequently grew up in centres which had notable religious shrines; that of St William of York, for instance, had more than a purely local reputation. Consequently business at a fair could be coupled with a pilgrimage and—to use a modern term—a "holiday". These were the reasons which encouraged people living a long way from a city to decide that the cost, the inconvenience and the peril of a visit to a distant fair was worth the annual effort.

The actual origins of most English fairs are shrouded in mystery. A few fairs may have survived which began before the Norman Conquest but most of them, especially in Yorkshire, seem to date from after 1066. Between 1227 and 1514 the charters of no less than 157 fairs in Yorkshire are known. A book published in 1770 lists ninety-seven Yorkshire towns and villages as holding fairs during the year. Further, as many of these places had more than one fair—some as many as five or six during the course of the year (York had five in 1770)— 300 fairs in Yorkshire in the late Middle Ages may not have been an exaggerated figure. It should also be borne in mind that very few fairs lasted one day, the majority were for at least two, some as many as seven or eight and one—at Kingston-upon-Hull—for no less than thirty days.

Throughout most of the Middle Ages there was only one fair held annually in York. This was the Lammas or St Peter's Fair of the Archbishop beginning on 31st July, the Vigil of the Feast of St Peter-in-Chains. It ended three days later on 2nd

August. The patronal feast of the Minster would therefore be celebrated on the middle day of the fair and doubtless attracted large crowds. The date of the origin of the fair is unknown; it is first mentioned in 1279 but had clearly been in existence some time before that date. In 1449 (one) and again in 1502 (two) further fairs—all three controlled by the city and nothing whatever to do with the Archbishop—were authorized by royal charter. The first of these was held on Whit Monday and the five days following while the other two began, respectively, on the Monday after Ascension Day and continued for six days, and on the Feast of St Luke (18th October) and continued for the same period. Documents have survived which give us a vivid and detailed account of the procedure and ceremonial which marked the opening of the Archbishop's Lammas Fair.

As the bell of St Michael's Church, Spurriergate, commenced ringing for vespers (three p.m.) on 31st July, the Archbishop's steward or deputy, accompanied by two or more other gentlemen, the beadle of Wistow and thirteen jurymen also from Wistow, met the city sheriffs, their notary or clerk, together with other civic members, in the Council Chamber on Ousebridge. The steward presented to the sheriffs a document—"Patent" as it was called—being the Archbishop's authority to hold the fair. This was read to the assembled court by the clerk. The city sheriffs then delivered their rods—the staves or wands which were the symbols of their office and of their authority—to two of the Archbishop's representatives who were appointed by him or his steward to act as Sheriffs of the Fair for the three days that it was held. In this way complete control of the city was formally handed over to the Archbishop who, through his representatives, now superseded the civic authorities as the source of law and order. At this same ceremony the keys of Ousebridge Gaol were handed over to the steward who took "possession" of it by having the door formally opened. After the party had partaken of wine supplied by the Archbishop a procession was formed in this order:

Beadle of Wistow with his white rod of office
Two halberdiers
Seven of the Wistow jurymen
The Archbishop's steward
The two new (Archbishop's) sheriffs
Other gentlemen (if any)
Six of the Wistow jurymen

They proceeded to near the Minster and, "at the high end of the Bowling Green against the Bishop's Prison", a proclamation opening the fair was read. This began by ordering everyone to keep the King's peace, listed the "true" weights and measures to be used, enjoined that all food sold "must be good and wholesome for man's body" and commanded that the Sabbath day was not to be broken by buying and selling nor "by sitting, tippling or drinking in any tavern". It also instituted a Court of Pie Powder, ordering that all offences committed during the time of the fair should be determined by it. It ended thus: "Therefore now at 3 o'clock begin in God's name and the King's, and God send every man good luck and this fair good continuance."

The party then proceeded from the Bowling Green in the same order "to ride the fair", reading the proclamation a second time in Thursday Market and a third time in the Horsefair (now Gillygate).

A word on the Pie Powder Court and its jurymen from Wistow. Every fair had its Pie Powder Court, a corruption of the French *pieds poudres* ("dusty feet"). Many of the people who frequented fairs either as buyers or as sellers were strangers, here today and gone tomorrow. The only way to ensure that law breakers could be brought to justice was to have a court always in session for the duration of the fair. Most of the cases to be heard would be petty ones which could be settled by a fine or a few hours in the stocks, pillory or prison. The Pie Powder Court had very limited authority and could only sit during fair time.

Wistow is a village three miles east of Selby and in the Middle Ages was a manor belonging to the Archbishop of

York. The jury was always impanelled from among its inhabitants presumably because, living thirteen miles from the city of York, they would be less biased in any judgements they might have to make than residents of York. A fortnight before the fair opened the beadle "pricked" (nominated) the jurymen who had to commence their duties, as we have seen, on Ouse-bridge at the time of the beginning of the fair. Following the proclamation on the Bowling Green the jurymen were sworn in by the steward—the foreman separately and the remaining twelve in three groups of four each. The following words were used:

> You shall diligently inquire and true presentment make, of all such matters and things as shall be brought before you, or given you in charge during this Fair. You shall present no man for malice or hatred nor spare none for favour or affection but in all things to the best of your knowledge shall present the truth, the whole truth and nothing but the truth, so help you God.

The jurymen were paid for their services—half a crown a day in addition to three meals daily with ale. Where the Courts of Pie Powder were actually held during the Middle Ages we do no know; from 1755–99 they were held in the George Inn in Coney Street and from 1800–1812 in the York Tavern in St Helen's Square. The last Court appears to have been held in 1812.

The Archbishop's primary purpose in holding and organiz-ing the fair was, of course, to make money. He did this from the tolls which he collected on all goods coming into the city to be sold and on those going out of the city after having been bought. A sixteenth century list of these tolls has survived, including:

Every beast to be sold	1d
Every led horse and mare to be sold	2d
Every twenty sheep	4d
Every pack horse carrying wards	4d
Every load of hay	4d

> Every other thing to be sold in any
> wallet, basket, cloth, bag or port-
> mantua (portmanteau) to the value
> of 12d   IS

Earlier, in the Middle Ages, one assumes that the tolls were somewhat smaller. Besides tolls there was a charge for setting up a stall or for using a stall already set up. This was called "stallage": the usual charge appears to have been twopence for a seven-foot stall.

One of the reasons why, during the fair, the city was "handed over" to the Archbishop was to ensure that these tolls could be collected. The gates or bars of the city—Micklegate, Bootham, Monk and Walmgate—and the posterns—Fishergate, Castlegate, Skeldergate, Layerthorpe and North Street—together with the staithes along the river banks, were manned by the Archbishop's collectors. In this way—as far as was humanly possible—the city was "sealed" from the outside world and all traders coming in or going out could be taxed appropriately.

The Archbishop's fair seems to have ended at three p.m. on the third day. No records have come down to us of any closing ceremony but clearly there must have been one by which authority was transferred back again to the civic authorities by the Archbishop's steward.

York, like all British cities today, is largely responsible for governing itself. This is a right which has been gained slowly and with difficulty during the long centuries since the Norman Conquest. We have seen how, during the years 1066–1200, York was under the control of sheriffs appointed by the King. A body known under a variety of names—bailiffs and burgesses, aldermen and councillors and today as the Corporation—gradually acquired more and more power so that eventually it replaced the sheriff as the source of local government. Their leader, first known as Mayor and later as Lord Mayor, was a man of great authority and dignity. The first Mayor of York is recorded in 1213 and the first Lord Mayor about 1450. By 1365 the Mayor was always accom-

Fy

Micklegate Bar

panied by a sergeant bearing a mace, the symbol of his office.
In 1393 a second sergeant was added to carry the city sword.
This sergeant also wore a special hat called the Cap of Mainten-
ance. Cap and sword were given to the city by King Richard
II. The sword is still carried before the present Lord Mayor
on all official occasions and is one of the most treasured posses-
sions of the city. The swordbearer still wears a cap of mainten-
ance. The one in current use was given to the city by King
George V in 1915. The city still possesses the cap of 1580.
Richard II had a special affection for York. We have already

seen how he watched a performance of the Mystery Plays in 1393. The sword is a very ancient one. It belonged to the Emperor Sigismund of Germany (1368–1437) who gave it to Richard who gave it to York. The city arms date from the same time. The correct way to blazon (describe heraldically) these is: argent, on a cross gules five lions passant guardant or. This means that, on a silver shield, is a red cross on which are superimposed five golden lions. The red cross is that of St George, the patron saint of England, while the lions are royal emblems appearing on the royal standard. The arms are simple and dignified and most appropriate for York, a city which, since medieval times, has ranked as second in hierarchy and prestige only to London.

7. TUDOR YORK

On 22nd August 1485, Henry Tudor, Earl of Richmond, defeated and killed Richard III at the battle of Bosworth. Soon afterwards he was crowned king and, for the next 118 years, he and his Tudor successors ruled England.

Henry VII was a usurper, that is to say he had no rightful claim to the throne; he seized it by force. His predecessor, Richard III, has been one of the most maligned of English kings. Shakespeare's play of that name portrays a monster, physically deformed, who committed almost every sort of crime. Tudor contemporaries who wrote about him paint a similar picture, doubtless because the new ruling house would have taken drastic measures against anyone showing Yorkist sympathies. Modern research, however, proves this to be a distortion of the facts. Richard had few, if any, of the foul vices ascribed to him and was well built; the indications from the two short years that he reigned suggest that he might have made a very good king. Certainly many of his subjects liked him and his government. Nowhere was this more true than in York. In the Corporation Housebooks—what we would nowadays call the Corporation Minute Book—is this moving tribute to him on the day following his death:

> King Richard, late lawfully reigning over us, was thrugh the grete treason of the Duc of Northfolk, with many othyr lords and nobilitie of thes North Partes, was pitiously slane and murderd, to the grete hevyness of this Citie.

Henry VIII became King in 1509. His reign and that of Queen Victoria three centuries later did more to alter the character and appearance of the city than any other after the

84

Norman Conquest. In 1509 York was at the summit of its architectural splendour. The Minster, recently completed, dominated a city which had two other large monastic buildings —St Mary's Abbey and the Priory of Holy Trinity, Micklegate. St Mary's was magnificent with a church which, in any other city, might well have become a cathedral. In addition there were forty parish churches, six hospitals and almshouses, two friaries and two nunneries together with half a dozen chapels, the Bedern housing the Vicars Choral and St William's College, the residence of the Minster chantry priests. All these in a city with its walls, nearly four miles in length, still intact— pierced by four great gateways or bars with barbicans and portcullises and five smaller posterns. Clifford's Tower still dominated the tongue of land between the rivers Ouse and Foss and hundreds of timbered houses lined the old streets. Among these were the civic buildings—the Guildhall on Ouse- bridge and the "new" one in Lendal. Then there were the guildhouses belonging to the craft guilds—the Merchant Taylors in Aldwark, the Butchers in Shambles, St Anthony's in Peaseholme Green, while on the banks of the river Foss in Fossgate was the great hall of the Merchant Adventurers' Company. There were a few stone-built mansions such as the Treasurer's House but most of the houses were half-timbered. The Shambles, Petergate, Stonegate and Goodramgate still retain enough of these today to enable us to imagine what the city was like.

Henry VIII's religious changes swept away the monasteries, hospitals and some chapels. Only the truncated parish church of Holy Trinity remains of the Priory in Micklegate and the pathetic remains of St Mary's Abbey and St Leonard's Hospital supply but a glimpse of what were two of the largest and finest buildings in York. An Act of Parliament of 1547 made the city join together some of the smaller ecclesiastical parishes, as a result of which sixteen parish churches were pulled down.

In Edward VI's reign, with the "official" disuse of the chan- tries (the Corporation of York had seized most of them twenty years earlier), St William's College passed out of the control

The Shambles

of the Minster into lay hands; it is only in the present century that it has come again under the control of the Church. It is now the meeting-place of the Northern Synod.

The destruction of these ecclesiastical buildings not only changed the physical appearance of the city, it also affected the economic life. While the monks and nuns from the destroyed religious houses were pensioned off or given other ecclesiastical offices and while the number of the lay persons employed in them has probably been exaggerated, nevertheless the religious communities brought a great deal of trade to the city, such as the purchase of foodstuffs and luxury goods, while the month-by-month repairs necessary to buildings as huge and as old as the monasteries and friaries supplied work to numerous York craftsmen.

Other factors which caused the decline of York during the Tudor period were the numerous plagues, the decay of the wool industry, the development of Hull as a rival port and the problem of fuel.

The most important of these were the recurring plagues. The stinking streets and houses built too close to one another harboured vermin of every description and with each hot summer epidemics spread unchecked through the poorer classes. These annual visitations were aggravated by the more deadly bubonic plague. The worst attacks were in 1538, 1550–2, 1570 and 1579. In 1552 stringent regulations were issued by the Mayor that food was to be conveyed to houses affected by the plague and left on the doorsteps and that red crosses were to be put on the front doors. In the following century there were further major outbreaks in 1604 and 1631. It is not surprising that these plagues occurred so frequently when we consider the abominable hygienic practices of so many of the citizens. In June 1607, for instance, George Hobson who lived in Stonegate was sent to gaol for three months because "about a month since he cast filth out of a pott forth of a Chambre window in his house into the Strete on the daie tyme which lyght on the heades of certain countrie men who were filling their waynes [wagons] at the said widow Waslinge dore . . . some whereof did lyght on the said widow Waslinge".

During the sixteenth century the infant mortality rate was, by modern standards, appalling. The parish registers of St Michael-le-Belfrey record that, during the years 1572–85, out of a total of 461 burials 155 were of infants under the age of two. The population of York at this time was probably about 8,000, 3,000 less than it had been two centuries earlier. In 1334 York was listed second largest among the provincial cities of England; in 1523 it was fifteenth.

The increase in the size of ocean-going ships meant that fewer vessels could get up the fifty miles of river from the mouth of the Humber to York. Therefore the city's overseas trade declined during the Tudor period. More and more ships berthed at Kingston-upon-Hull, discharged their cargoes there and, if these had to be sent on to York, it was done in small river craft called lighters. Naturally Hull demanded payment on all such goods and a bitter quarrel ensued between the two cities. York claimed that Hull "is and evermore was but port town of the said City of York". Hull rejected this and its Corporation was far from tactful in the ensuing correspondence with York. For instance, in 1558, requesting help to equip ships for the Queen's navy, the Hull Corporation gave as a reason—"forsomuch as you are one of the chief members belonging unto the same port of Hull". York indignantly replied "that is not true . . . for it is a city of itself and no member".

Nowadays when only a small proportion of the goods coming into York is carried by barges on the rivers, it is easy to overlook the importance of the Ouse and Foss in time past. The construction of Naburn Lock seven miles below York in 1757 made it impossible for ships larger than barges to get up to the city.

From earliest times the river had also been an important source of food. The thousands of oyster and sea shells found on Roman and medieval sites such as Malton, Brough and York came from the lower reaches of the Humber. In the Middle Ages when people were compelled to eat fish on Fridays and during periods of fasting such as Lent, fish was a considerable source of profit. People such as the Archbishop, the Bishop of Durham and local landowners, as well as the Corporations of Hull and York, had fishing rights in the Humber, Ouse and Foss. Fishgarths—permanent wooden structures on which nets could be hung—were built by these people. Others were built illegally by interlopers ready to face the risks involved. There were constant quarrels, brawls and lawsuits amongst the people concerned. These fishgarths proved a constant danger to shipping and every year the Mayor of York went down the river in his magnificent "official" barge to establish the Corporation rights and order the destruction of any fishgarths illegally erected.

Another reason for the decay of York in this period was the decline of the wool trade. We have seen that in the fourteenth and early fifteenth centuries York was one of the greatest cloth producing centres in England. Its cloth of scarlet was famous and a quarter of its citizens got their living, directly or indirectly, through its manufacture. Ten years ago in an excavation in Petergate in York some fragments of this cloth of scarlet were found; they could be dated to about 1370. From 1475 onwards the decline in the wool trade was catastrophic. The Tudor monarchs were notorious for insisting on the payment of every penny due to them and the fact that they all exempted the York weavers from paying their taxes shows how bad the situation was. In 1517 weaving is not listed among the thirteen most important crafts in the city; in 1561 there were only ten weavers; a few years later there were none.

The reasons for this decline are easy to see. With the application of water power to fulling, it was quicker and cheaper to make cloth in places like Halifax, Leeds and Wakefield where the streams and rivers from the Pennines had sufficient force to turn the water wheels which generated the power. Further, these "new" towns were not subject to guild regulations such as existed in York. This freedom from interference by outside bodies is a characteristic of what is called capitalism.

This was the new economic system which fostered the Industrial Revolution.

Inventors were encouraged to experiment constantly to find new processes by which production on an ever-increasing scale could be performed by means of machines, rather than by hand, and in factories rather than in small workshops. The system of craft guilds with its emphasis on uniformity—each craftsman producing his goods to a set standard, a particular length and width, to sell at a fixed price, during certain carefully defined working hours—was anathema to the new capitalists. The centre of the cloth industry passed from towns such as York and Beverley to the West Riding of Yorkshire where it is still firmly implanted today.

A further reason for the decline of York at this time was the problem of fuel. Ever since Roman times coal had been used in Yorkshire but in small quantities, obtained almost entirely from outcrops. Forests spread over vast areas of the north so that wood was plentiful and cheap. Wood and charcoal (obtained from wood) were thus the chief fuels and not coal. Wood was also the main building material. Medieval man regarded the forests as inexhaustible and cut them down ruthlessly. North of York was the great Forest of Galtres stretching forty miles to the river Tees. Every day dozens of carts brought wood and charcoal into the city from this forest: every day the distance covered by the wagons got longer and longer. By the end of the Middle Ages it was considerable—ten to twenty or even thirty and forty miles. This increased the cost. In the West Riding coal was now being mined on a large scale and was considerably cheaper. Coal was brought to York but, because of the distances involved, it was more expensive than in the new wool towns of the West Riding.

Tudor England was a period of poverty and unemployment. Pauperism affected every town. No real effort was made to solve the problem until Queen Elizabeth's Poor Law Act which Parliament passed in 1601. It detailed different treatment for the "sturdy beggars" who were capable of working but would not and the "true beggars" who, through disease, illness or injury were incapable of working. York had been operating on these lines fifty years earlier. In 1515 the Corporation issued badges to be worn "upon his shoulder of his overmost garment" to the deserving poor who were then allowed to beg while "sturdy beggars" were flogged and put out of the city. But this did not solve the problem. York, like every large city, acted like a magnet to down-and-outs and ne'er-do-wells. By 1530 master beggars were appointed in each ward whose task it was to report to the authorities the arrival of new and strange mendicants. These master beggars were even issued with a special gown on which was sewn the city's coat-of-arms! They were also issued with birch rods by which they asserted their authority! In 1550 the Corporation imposed a weekly poor rate on each parish in the city. Each Sunday the constables, assisted by the master beggars, distributed these monies to the needy poor.

The dissolution of the lesser monasteries in 1536, the rise of Protestantism and the hatred felt by many people for the new religious changes in England led to the so called Pilgrimage of Grace in that year. This rebellion was centred on the northern counties; Robert Aske, a Yorkshire lawyer, was the leader and York played a leading part in the events. On Sunday, 15th October, the rebel army, numbering about 30,000, arrived outside the city. Aske and 4,000 horsemen were allowed inside and were welcomed into the Minster by the clergy. The leaders went to the high altar where Aske left a rich gift. During the three days the rebels were in the city the small dissolved monastic houses were restored. On 20th October the whole army passed through the city on its way to Pontefract. To emphasize the religious character of the rebellion the rebels forced the Abbot of St Mary's Abbey to head the procession carrying his finest crozier. Eventually the rebellion was crushed and Aske was condemned to death. His sentence was a fearsome one: to be hung in chains from the top of Clifford's Tower. He was put there on 21st September 1537; four days later he was still alive!

Clifford's Tower

In its long history Clifford's Tower has witnessed many gruesome events. Another occurred much earlier, in 1190 in the reign of Richard I, when the crusading spirit was high in England. At that time there was a small but very wealthy Jewish community living in the city. On 15th March the citizens began sacking their houses and murdering some of them. The Jews fled for protection to Clifford's Tower, locking themselves inside. The wooden tower was set on fire. One contemporary account says that this was done deliberately by the Jews who preferred death in this way to the atrocities which they knew would be meted out to them by the Christians if they surrendered. After this the tower was rebuilt in stone very much as it is today. In 1661 George Fox, founder of the Quaker movement, was imprisoned there for two days.

Robert Aske had drawn up a manifesto stating the grievances which he and his followers had against Henry VIII's government. Among these they said that kings of England had, for a long time, neglected the north and had seldom visited it. They stated that the dissolution of the monasteries removed a source of wealth and would make the north even more poverty-stricken than it had been before. They pointed out that, compared with the south, there were few merchants and consequently little trade. Further, the northerners were lawless, wild people quite as prepared to ally with the Scots, their neighbours, as with the King, their Sovereign.

King Richard III had understood the north and its problems better than most of his predecessors and he had formed a Council to govern the north based at Sheriff Hutton. This had been of little importance under the Tudors before Aske's rebellion. In 1537 this Council of the North was removed to York and firmly centred on the King's Manor—the Abbot's quarters of the dissolved Abbey of St Mary—in the city. Its members were appointed by the King, paid by him and responsible only to him; it practically ruled the north in his name. Its head, the Lord President, was one of the most powerful men in England. For a hundred years York was in fact, as well as in name, the capital of the north.

Under the Lord President were numerous councillors, lawyers, clerks, servants and others. One important department dealt with justice. In civil cases the York courts followed the Star Chamber proceedings. Litigation was cheap, as fees were fixed; it was also quick and effective and so, in general, popular. The King's Manor as the seat of civilian justice in the north and the Minster as that of ecclesiastical justice made York of great legal importance in England. The Council dealt with between 1,000 and 2,000 cases every year. It brought trade to the city and gave York "a pleasant feeling of self-importance". The most famous of the Lord Presidents was Thomas Wentworth, Earl of Strafford, who lived in the King's Manor from 1628 to 1633. The Council was abolished by the Long Parliament in 1641.

In the autumn of 1541, four years after Aske's death, Henry VIII and his fifth wife, Catherine Howard, visited York: they stayed in the King's Manor, which had been specially prepared for them. The huge cellar which exists there was built for this occasion to ensure that the King and his courtiers were well supplied with wine. The city viewed the King's visit with apprehension since many of its citizens had rebelled with Robert Aske against him. The King entered the city from the direction of Selby and at Fulford Cross, the city boundary; he was met by the Mayor, recorder, aldermen, the "twenty-four" (the Corporation councillors) and 120 of the "most discreet" citizens wearing new gowns of fine "sadde tawny". On the King's approach all fell on their knees and the trembling recorder read a long speech of welcome. He said that the city repented of the part it had played in the "traitorous rebellion" and the citizens "from the bottoms of their stomach repentant" promised the King anything he desired. They then gave him and the Queen two cups of "silver double gilt". The King's contained £100 in gold and the Queen's £40.

York had learnt its lesson. Never again did it offer any opposition to either the Tudors or the Stuarts. It is noteworthy that not one of Henry's Tudor successors—Edward VI, Mary or Elizabeth I—even deigned to visit the city.

While officially York supported the policies of Henry VIII and his successors, individual citizens were not so docile. In religious affairs the Tudor period was one of ferment. The monolithic Roman Catholic Church of the Middle Ages was no more; different Protestant sects were preaching conflicting views while the monarchs themselves set highly contradictory examples to their subjects—Henry VIII was Catholic, Edward VI (or rather his "Protectors" the Duke of Somerset and the Earl of Northumberland) was Protestant, Mary was Roman Catholic, while Elizabeth was Anglican or Church of England.

The first recorded Puritan in York was a man called Gilbert Johnson, a Dutchman and "carver". In 1528 he was tried in the Archbishop's Court and eventually abjured (renounced) his errors. He had said that Catholic doctrines, such as the following, were wrong: confession, prayers for the dead, holy bread and water, fasting, the supremacy of the Pope and the power of priests to forgive sins. He also denounced the wealth of priests and refused to pay tithes. As a punishment he had to go in four processions round the city being flogged by the clergy at certain prominent landmarks.

Another Puritan, Edward Freeze, was born in York and apprenticed to a painter there. He later joined a monastery in Essex but ran away and settled down in Colchester where he married "and lived like an honest man". He became a Protestant and one day, when painting an inn sign, introduced into the design texts from the Bible which left no doubt as to his views. He was thrown into Colchester jail and later moved to the Tower of London. John Foxe in his *Book of Martyrs* describes his ordeal. He and the other prisoners there

> were fed with fine manchet [a kind of bread] made of sawdust, or at least a great part thereof. . . . Some had horselocks on their legs, and some had other irons. This painter would ever be writing on the walls with chalk or a coal, and in one place he wrote, "Doctor Dodipall would make me believe the moon were made of green-cheese". And because he would be writing many things, he was manacled by the wrists so long that the flesh of his arms was grown higher than his irons. By means of his manacles he could not comb his head, and he remained so long manacled that his hair was folded together.

Eventually he was brought to trial and

> they kept him three days without meat before he came to his answer. Then, what by the long imprisonment and much evil handling, and for lack of sustenance, the man was in that case, that he would say nothing but look and gaze upon the people like a wild man; and if they asked him a question, he would say nothing but "My Lord is a good man".

It is clear that, as a result of his ill treatment, he had been driven insane. His brother Valentine and his wife were also Puritans. They were both burned to death, chained together, on the Knavesmire, York.

A Catholic martyr of York in this same century was Margaret Clitherow. She was married to a butcher and lived in a house in the Shambles which has now been converted into an oratory by the Roman Catholics. She was a devout, god-fearing woman and allowed Catholic priests to hide in her house in the reign of Queen Elizabeth I, at a time when the Catholics, largely because of the threat of an invasion from Spain, were not allowed to practise their religion and when Catholic priests were forbidden to enter the country. In 1586 she was arrested for harbouring "Jesuits and seminary priests" and, when brought to trial, refused to plead either "guilty" or "not guilty" to the charge against her. In such cases the law of England enacted that the person concerned should be subjected to the "*peine forte et dure*". This dreadful punishment, as pronounced by the judge on Margaret Clitherow, ran thus:

> You must return from whence you came, and there, in the lowest part of the prison, be stripped naked, laid on your back next to the ground, and as much weight laid upon you as you are able to bear, and so continue three days without any food except a little barley bread and puddle water, and the third day to be pressed to death, your hands and feet tied to posts, and a sharp stone under your back.

She met her death in this frightful fashion on 17th March 1586. She was revered by the Catholic Church and in November 1970, along with thirty-nine other martyrs who, between 1535 and 1679, died in England because of their faith, she was canonized in Rome by Pope Paul VI. One of the most treasured relics in the possession of the Bar Convent in York is what is believed to be the hand of the saint.

Nowadays there are four road bridges and a footpath (on the Scarborough railway bridge) across the river Ouse and the closing of any one of these, while delaying and inconveniencing travellers and vehicles, would not stop them altogether. Lendal Bridge was opened in 1863, Skeldergate in 1881 and Clifton in 1960. Until little more than a century ago all traffic had to cross the river either by Ouse Bridge or by the ferries at Lendal and Skeldergate. The collapse of part of Ouse Bridge in the winter of 1564-5 caused consternation in the city. Its eventual repair was expensive and difficult. The episode is dealt with in detail here because it gives a vivid insight into the way in which the Corporation of York worked in the Tudor period.

In January 1564—a year before the bridge collapsed—the City Council "agreed that the reparation of ousebrige in masonrie shall with all convenient spede be sett apon". Suitable stones from the ruined chapel on Foss Bridge and of Holy Trinity Priory in Micklegate were to be set aside for the work. Three months later it was decided, on account of the cost involved, to appoint certain skilled men to view the existing wooden bridge and "if therapon they can perceyve that it will hold and contynew still as it is without great jeopardy then the sayd worke to stay unto an other tyme". These experts decided that the bridge could safely be left as it was—an ironical decision in view of what followed.

Ouse Bridge was vital to the city and its communications. The bridge is first mentioned in a charter dating to about AD 1200. Throughout the Middle Ages it was made of wood— until 1566 entirely so. In that year, as we shall see, the central arches were replaced by a stone one. In 1810 the bridge was pulled down completely and the present one built.

The medieval bridge had six arches; only under the two centre ones was the river deep enough for navigation. Periodically through the centuries of its long life it had been in danger of falling down and piecemeal repairs had frequently been necessary. In 1307 the Archbishop of York had appealed for money to repair it. In his appeal he added that its falling down would involve the destruction of property and loss of life, which indicates that already houses and shops had been built upon it. In 1435 there were some twenty-three shops on the north side and twenty-nine on the south: in 1563 the figures were twenty-one and twenty-six.

At the Skeldergate corner of the bridge was the Toll Booth

GY

where the toll collectors stopped traffic by putting a chain across the road; for the year 1280 the tolls amounted to 77s 9d. The Council Chamber stood on the north side and here the business of the city was transacted. Near it was St William's Chapel, demolished in 1810, which was the civic chapel. Beneath it were both the Lord Mayor's and Sheriff's prisons, notoriously filthy places and both divided into two sections to accommodate the different sexes. The civic clock stood in the tower of St William's Chapel and set the time for the civic meetings and for the opening and closing of markets, while the bell in the clock also marked the "official" beginning of the York day—4.15 a.m. in summer and 5 a.m. in winter—and the end of it—8 p.m.

Except for the ferries which plied across the river, this narrow, congested bridge was the sole link between that part of the city on the south bank and that on the north of the Ouse. It also carried the through traffic from the west and south of York and the East Riding. It was essential.

The winter of 1564/5 was a hard one. There were heavy snowfalls and long periods of frost when the river was partly frozen over. A rapid thaw in the first week of January caused a great flooding of the Ouse. The ice on the river broke up and piled against the piers of the bridge. The central one collapsed under the strain and two arches fell into the river, the houses and their occupants with them. The story of the dilemma facing the civic authorities as a result of this disaster may be traced in the reports on the deliberations of the Corporation as published in the *York Civic Records*.

On 9th January 1565, Robert Maskewe and John Wilkynson were granted the right of controlling the ferry which was set up alongside the bridge. "All franchised men inhabityng within this Citie" were to have free passage at all times for themselves, "their horse and cariage", while "strangers or foreyners" were to pay—for a man and horse a penny, for a footman alone a halfpenny; the return journey was free.

The civic fathers now turned their attention to the much more serious problems of rebuilding the old bridge and of raising the necessary money for these repairs. On 16th February they ordered that the parish constables of the city were, before "Monday next", to bring to the Lord Mayor a list "fayre wrytten" of the names of every householder in their parishes with the amount "what every of them will frankly gyve towards the seyd reparacons". As might be expected the response was virtually nil and the Council finally decided that "a competent somme of money for the reedificing the sayd brig agayne of stone with all convenyant spede be taxed and levied of every the inhabitants of this sayd Citie and suburbs of the same by discrecon of my Lord Mayour and Aldremen". The sum required was £400—the equivalent of £8,000–£10,000 nowadays—to be employed on "reedyfying of Ousebrige and other charges for clensyng the ryver of Ouse". Collectors were named for each of the parishes in the city. It appears that every householder was assessed according to his means. The levy was to be paid in four equal parts, before the dates—25th May, 25th June, 25th July and 25th August.

The next task was to proceed with the actual bridge building. There were to be two stages. First a caisson or, as it is called in the *Records*, a "gytty" or "gyttie", had to be sunk alongside the damaged pier to assess both the depth and the extent of the foundations which would have to be sunk into the river bed, and also to provide protection to the workmen during the actual rebuilding or, as the *Records* quaintly put it, "for avoydyng of the watter . . . so that the masons shall work dry". Secondly, the plans for rebuilding the bridge had to be drawn and the work put in hand.

Leonard Craven, a carpenter, apparently a local man, was given the task of constructing the caisson and in June reported that the work was progressing and that "he hadde no dowbte to fynyshe the same" soon. To ensure this "more spedy expedicon of the common work and reparacons of Ousebrig", and doubtless to ensure that the city's money was not being wasted, the Council agreed in July "that one Alderman or his sufficient deputie within his ward shall dayly see to the work folk at the sayd brig by turne begynyng on Monday next first at the most auncient Aldreman and soo in ordre so long as the said common work be in hand".

With regards to the second problem—the drawing up of plans for the new bridge—advice was sought in London. At this time one of the most prominent Aldermen of that city was Sir Martin Bowes, a native of York; he eventually became Lord Mayor of London. Many references to him occur in the Civic Records at this time and he was clearly a staunch friend to the city of his birth; in 1545 he had given it the State Sword, still one of York's most treasured possessions. On 7th July 1565, he wrote to the Lord Mayor and Corporation of York telling them that he was "verie sorie" to hear of the disaster to the bridge. He had heard of this through "Maister Hall and Maister Swordbearer . . . sewtars unto me", which implies that they were sent from York by the Council to ask for advice and help. Sir Martin had been "an earnest sewtar to my L. Mayor and his Bretherne here [London]" and, as a result, it was agreed that one Thomas Harper, "the most expert workman that aperteyneth to London bridge and (as we thynk) within the realme for such bridge work", and "Maister Laurens" be seconded for one month from their employment in London to give advice in York. Harper was to be paid no wages but "his chardges to and fro you must beare and his chardge for bedd and boarde whilst he remayne with you; and that you will gyve unto hym let it be in recompense at his departure, otherwise not". His assistant was to receive 2s 6d a day plus "meat and drynk and lodgyng and bootes to stand in the water". Sir Martin ends by reiterating that Harper "cannot be absent above one moneth. And moche adoo I had to gett that space for hym to helpe you."

We are not told what advice he gave, but whatever it was it must have carried great weight for on 6th August—a month after his coming to York—the Lord Mayor wrote to Sir Martin Bowes to thank him for his help and spoke most enthusiastically of Harper and his assistant "the connyngest men that could be gotten for amendyng of our decayed brig of York, specially their head man Maister Harper . . . we founde theym very expert and peynfull men; and especially Maister Harper, a man of excellente conynge. . . . Sorie were we so soone to depart with theym." As Harper would take no wages the Council voted him £5 "becyds xˢ to his costs homward ageyne".

It was largely on the advice of the two Londoners that it was decided not to replace the two central arches which had been destroyed but to build only a single new one of stone and so avoid the difficulty of making foundations for new piers in the deepest part of the river. The actual rebuilding did not start until 10th April 1564—the period before this and subsequent to Harper's departure in early August was taken up in completing the caisson or caissons, erecting the necessary scaffolding and woodwork and collecting stones necessary for the actual new arch or "bow" as it was called. This last difficulty is a curious one. It might have been expected that stone would be plentiful in a city where only thirty years before something like twenty monasteries, friaries and churches had been pulled down. It is clear from the records that only with the utmost difficulty were the stones obtained. For instance on 13th May 1566, "it was thought mete that the mansion hows called Saynt George Chapell nigh the Castell Mylnes shalbe taken downe and all the free stone of the same to serve towards present reparacon of Ousebrig; and all the resydew of tyle, tymbre and stuff therof to be husbanded by the Chamberleyns to the most profit of the Citie". Twelve months later the bridge was completed and for the next 250 years it became once again the vital link between the two halves of the city.

8. THE STUARTS AND THE BATTLE OF MARSTON MOOR

York and Yorkshire played a decisive part in English history during the so-called Stuart Period (1603–1715). On 24th March 1603, Queen Elizabeth I died at Sheen near London. It took three days for the news to reach York. James VI of Scotland was immediately proclaimed there as King James I of England. The proclamation was read first in Pavement and then on the steps of the south door of the Minster. The new King set out on a slow progress from Scotland to London. He reached York on 16th April, entering the city at Micklegate Bar. Blossom Street just outside the Bar was widened and straightened in honour of the occasion. At the Bar the traditional ceremony of delivering the keys of the city to the King was performed by the Lord Mayor. The King spent the next day in the city staying at the King's Manor where he was presented with a great silver cup.

In August 1617, James was again in York, this time on his way north on a visit to Scotland. He dined in the Long Gallery in Gray's Court where, after the banquet, he knighted eight Yorkshire gentlemen. The following day he attended Matins in the Minster and afterwards touched seventy persons there for the "King's Evil" (scrofula).

In 1604 and again in 1631, York was affected by the plague; during the former year no fewer than 3,500 people died. Some of the precautions taken to stop the spread of infection sound curious to the modern ear. The sick were urged to eat sage, sorrel or garlic with their bread, to mix ginger and burnt wormwood with their drink and to perfume their houses with vinegar, rosemary or bay leaves. Houses were to be fumigated with tar, resin or juniper wood. "Lodges"—wooden huts called "pest houses"—were erected at Tang Hall and Hob Moor where the infected were taken. One man who lived on Toft Green and was removed to the pest house at Tang Hall had two cows. They were driven to the Knavesmire and made to swim in the water there to ensure that they were free from infection!

The Roman Catholic religion was never suppressed in England despite the violent persecution under Edward VI and milder persecution under Queen Elizabeth. York was always a centre of recusancy as we have seen from the tragic fate of Margaret Clitherow in 1586. In 1603 there were at least fifty recusants in the city. The Roman Catholics throughout England had high hopes that the new King, the son of a Roman Catholic mother, would relax the laws against them. They were bitterly disappointed when it became clear that James intended to do nothing. Some of them entered into a plot to overthrow the government by blowing up King and Parliament in November 1605. This wild, rash plot is famous in history as the "Gunpowder Plot". One of the leaders, Guy Fawkes, was born in York. The actual house is not known, though Young's Hotel in Petergate claims to be the place. He was baptized in the nearby St Michael-le-Belfrey Church on 16th April 1570; the entry in the Baptismal Register is plain and clear. He went to St Peter's School in York. His father died when he was nine and his mother took as her second husband a staunch Roman Catholic. Guy's family and friends were mostly Roman Catholics and his schoolmaster at St Peter's was also sympathetic to the old faith. In fact four other Old Peterites took part with Fawkes in the Gunpowder Conspiracy and were eventually executed. Fawkes was arrested when one of the conspirators betrayed the plot to a member of Parliament. He was actually seized in the cellars of the Houses of Parliament while guarding the powder kegs and after suffering frightful tortures on the rack he, together with eight other conspirators, was tried and condemned to death. The conspirators were executed on 31st January 1606, at Westminster, by the barbarous method of being hanged, drawn and quartered.

Charles I visited York on a number of occasions. The first two were happy ones. In May 1633 he broke his journey to Scotland by spending a weekend in the city. He stayed at the King's Manor. His arms and initials which were carved on a stone panel to mark the occasion are still to be seen there. He attended a horse race somewhere in Acomb. He came to the city again on 30th March 1639, and stayed a month. He "kept his Maundy" while he was there. This ancient custom is still performed by English sovereigns; in 1968 Queen Elizabeth II distributed her maundy in Selby Abbey and some of the recipients on that occasion came from York. The ceremony is held each year in the week before Easter, when the monarch distributes money to the poor and needy. The number of the latter is always the same as the age of the monarch. Charles I was thirty-nine in 1639, so thirty-nine old men assembled in the Minster. The Bishop of Ely washed their feet in warm water and dried them with a linen cloth. The King then gave each man a new gown, shirt, stockings and shoes, one purse containing twenty pence, another containing thirty-nine single pennies, a wooden platter on which was some salt fish, a loaf and a cup of wine. The next day the King touched 200 people in the Minster for the "King's Evil", at the same time placing about their necks a white ribbon on which hung a gold coin called an angel. On Easter Sunday he ordered £70 to be distributed in the city to the poor and on the following Tuesday and Wednesday he touched another 200 people for the evil.

The next year the King was back again in York on account of the war which had broken out with Scotland. Early in that year the King, badly advised by William Laud, Archbishop of Canterbury, had ordered the Scots to use a new prayer book in their churches. Ever since the days of John Knox the Scots' religion had been an extreme form of Protestantism called Presbyterianism in which the services were very simple and very plain, without ceremony and vestments. In England,

Laud—with some success—was attempting to return to the sort of church service which had existed before the Reformation. In Scotland such changes were greeted with horror and abuse and twice—in 1639 and again in 1640—the Scots raised armies and invaded England rather than accept these changes.

On both occasions Charles came north to lead his armies in person and made York the headquarters for his operations. For security reasons he brought with him the Mint and its craftsmen from London. They carried on their work near Bootham Bar in what is still known as Mint Yard. Here they coined half-crowns, shillings, sixpences and threepences. These are beautiful coins. On the reverse they bear the Latin inscription which, translated, reads "I reign under the auspices of Christ" while on the face they show the King on horseback with the letters "Ebor" (Eboracum) below.

By 1642 the relations between Charles and his Parliament— the famous Long Parliament—had reached another crisis. Charles was again in York. Fearing that Civil War was imminent, he brought his printing press (it was set up in St William's College) and, as London was strongly Puritan, he made the much more loyal York his new capital. In June Charles tried to rally support for his cause by summoning the nobility and gentry of Yorkshire to a great meeting on Heworth Moor— now one of the suburbs of York. A vast crowd assembled, some of whom were openly or secretly opposed to the King. One of these was Sir Thomas Fairfax. As a native of Yorkshire he was only too aware of how divided loyalties were in the county and how the common people hated the very thought of war. A moderate himself, he wanted, if possible, to reach some understanding with the King. He and many gentlemen who had similar ideas drew up a petition stating their disagreements with the King's policy and suggesting a compromise. Sir Thomas took upon himself the task of presenting this petition in person to the King. So many people crowded around the King's charger that this was not easy. Eventually Sir Thomas got alongside and placed his petition on the saddle-bow in front of Charles. At that very moment the horse reared in fright and Sir Thomas was nearly trampled under its hooves. Although the King was clearly annoyed that he had met with such an unfriendly reception there is no reason to suppose that he intended any personal injury to Sir Thomas. However, the general feeling was that he had tried to ride Fairfax down. Fairfax was acclaimed as a popular hero. The Royalist cause had suffered another blow and the King had made another enemy who, as events showed, was to prove one of the ablest generals to emerge from the ranks of Parliament.

In August 1642 Charles left York and went to Nottingham where he raised the royal standard. The Civil War had begun. He left Sir John Bellasis in York as Governor. In February of the following year Queen Henrietta Maria, Charles's wife, arrived at Bridlington from Holland with a convoy of ships loaded with munitions of war, including thirty-two cannon and 10,000 muskets. A few days later these were transported to York in 500 carts and some of them were then used to strengthen the city's defences while the rest were taken south to the King in Oxford. This is how a seventeenth century York historian described the preparations:

> . . . the city was everywhere strongly fortified, and above twenty cannon, great and small, were planted about it. Two cannon were planted upon old Baile Hill . . . two at Micklegate Bar, two at Monk Bar, two at Walmgate Bar out of which last was a strong bulwark erected. At several lanes ends, within the city, were ditches and banks made and cast up, with hogsheads filled with earth for barricadoes. By the general's orders the magistrates were to find eight hundred men to work daily at the repairs of the walls, and securing the ditches of the city.

The magazines were filled with gunpowder, lead and ammunition, the storehouses with grain, meat and beer, together with fodder for horses and cattle. The hub of the city defences was Clifford's Tower; platforms were built on it to support cannon which commanded long sectors of the walls and the fields beyond. Finally, at least four emplacements (sconces) were constructed outside the city about 300 yards from the walls. Their purpose was not only to protect the road approaches to the city but also to act as a screen for the open fields which lay between them and the walls, where cattle could be pastured to ensure a source of fresh meat for the garrison.

On 1st January 1644 the Scots, who had allied with Parliament, entered England with an army of 20,000 men. The northern Royalist army under the command of the Marquis of Newcastle marched north to meet them. South of them in Yorkshire was a small Parliamentarian army raised in the West Riding by Lord Ferdinando Fairfax and his son, the Sir Thomas we have already met on Heworth Moor. In March the Fairfaxes planned to march north to assist the Scots by attacking Newcastle's Royalist army in the rear. A letter outlining their plan was captured by a Royalist who took it to Bellasis in York. Bellasis decided to surprise the Fairfaxes near Selby and on 11th April marched out of York with the garrison and attacked them there. His army was hopelessly defeated and he was himself captured. York was now at the mercy of the Fairfaxes. When the news of this disaster reached the Marquis of Newcastle near Durham he marched his army south to save York from falling into Parliament's hands. He arrived in the city just ahead of the Fairfaxes, and the Scots, who, as soon as they realized he had retreated, followed him south. On 16th April the Marquis entered York. Six days later the two Parliamentarian armies surrounded the city; "the great and close siege of York" had begun.

These two Parliamentarian armies in themselves were too small to surround the city effectively. They asked Parliament for help and the army of the Eastern Association commanded by the Earl of Manchester (with Oliver Cromwell as its second in command) was ordered to join the siege. This army arrived on 4th June. The city was now entirely surrounded and the stage was set for the real siege to begin. The besiegers pressed home their attacks fiercely and relentlessly. The Scots attacked the three Royalist sconces to the west of the city, capturing two after bitter fighting. The third one was only saved when the

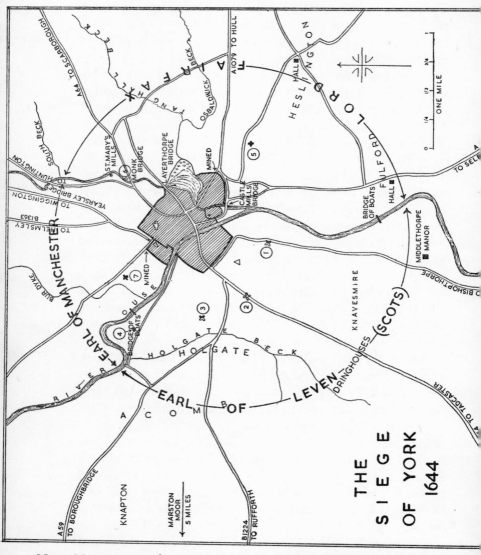

Note: Nos. 1–3, 5 and 7 are sconces (gun emplacements) erected around the city

Royalists sent a relief force out of the city through Micklegate Bar to reinforce it. Fairfax erected a battery on Lamel Hill, a dominating landmark some 300 yards outside Walmgate Bar. Having no cannon of his own he obtained some from the Scots' ordnance depot at Middlethorpe. One of the guns "carried a Sixty pound Bullet" and was, by the standards of 1644, a most formidable weapon. It was nicknamed the "Queen's Pocket Pistol" and did great damage to the city and its garrison. The garrison sent out parties to destroy the suburbs, the aim being to deny cover to the besiegers where snipers and miners could work. Finally, the besiegers started digging mines under the city defences in two places. Fairfax's men dug under Walmgate Bar, while Manchester's dug under St Mary's Tower. One of the soldiers working under the Bar was captured and after being questioned in Clifford's Tower, divulged what was going on. The Royalists counter-mined by digging a hole above this tunnel and flooding it with water. The other mine, under St Mary's Tower, just outside Bootham Bar, was never discovered by the garrison and the blowing up of the tower, together with the attack on the King's Manor, constituted the most dramatic event of the entire siege.

It took place on 16th June: Trinity Sunday. Tunnelling under St Mary's Tower had begun very soon after Manchester's army took up its position in this sector. The work had been under the direction of Lieutenant-General Laurence Crawford, one of Manchester's subordinates. About noon on the 16th, while many of the Royalists were still at Matins in the Minster, Crawford exploded the mine. Part of the tower was blown up and, as the wall fell outwards, some 600 of his men, waiting with their weapons, ladders and other scaling equipment at the ready, entered the breach. The garrison was taken completely by surprise. The attackers rushed through the garden, orchard and bowling green of the Manor and some reached the Manor itself. The garrison, however, rallied and a resolute counter-attack not only halted the Parliamentarians but soon drove them back. The attackers were hampered by the high walls surrounding the garden, orchard and bowling green;

some of the garrison climbed on to these and fired down on them. Another Royalist force went out of the walls through Lendal postern, along the river front and up what is now Marygate to seal off the breach on the outside and thus cut off the Parliamentarians from their own lines. The attack was a complete failure, over 300 of Crawford's men being killed or captured. The Royalists lost perhaps thirty men, including four officers. We have this sad account written by a Parliamentarian of the aftermath of the attack:

> On Munday morning (being the day following) some of our Souldiers betwixt nine and ten a clock, approaching towards the place where the Tower stood, heard in the rubbish a very dolefull cry, some calling, Help help: others, Water, water. Their lamentable complaints moved our men to resolve their relief: so they digged out one dead in the rubbish, and brought two alive: but from the Town such fierce opposition was made by the merciless enemy against our Souldiers while they were labouring to save their friends lives, that they were compelled to leave many poore distressed ones dying in the dust.
>
> Upon Wednesday or Thursday we obtained an hours time to bury our dead.

After the assault on the Manor there were no more major episodes connected with the siege until the arrival of Prince Rupert with his relieving force on 1st July. The besiegers were dispirited after the failure of 16th June; illness seems to have been rife among them ("Very many of our Scotts sojours were fallen sick") and they were short of ammunition, while the growing expectation of Prince Rupert's coming caused a rise in confidence amongst those inside the city. In fact on 24th June the Royalists took the initiative and sallied out of the city through "the little sally port at Monk Barr". About 600 men took part in this counter-attack which was timed for daybreak —four o'clock in the morning. They "furiously assaulted" Manchester's forces. They were, however, driven back after a "sharp conflict", suffering at least forty casualties.

On the evening of Sunday, 30th June, news reached the besieging armies that Prince Rupert, marching to raise the siege, was near Knaresborough, some fifteen miles west of York. Expecting him to march direct on the city and wishing to place their united forces between him and his goal, the Parliamentarian generals raised the siege and concentrated their armies west of the river Ouse in and around the villages of Long Marston, Tockwith and Hessay. Manchester's army crossed the river by a bridge of boats in the Poppleton–Clifton area and Fairfax's by another in the Fulford–Middlethorpe area. The besieging armies moved off so quietly during the night 30th June–1st July that the Royalist garrison had no certain knowledge of their departure until well after daylight. In the afternoon of 1st July the Parliamentarian allies were drawn up in battle formation on Marston Moor.

But Prince Rupert did not advance directly on York. He detached a force of cavalry along the Knaresborough–York road and, by seizing Skip Bridge, controlled the crossing of the river Nidd. This misled the Parliamentarian commanders into thinking that it constituted the advance guard of the entire Royalist army. In fact, by a brilliantly executed forced march, the Prince moved his army northwards via Boroughbridge (to cross the river Ure) and Thornton Bridge (to cross the Swale) down the east bank of the Ouse so that on the evening of 1st July it was somewhere in the Skelton–Clifton area, only a few miles north of York. He followed this up by capturing the bridge of boats in the Clifton area before the "Regiment of dragooners" left behind by Manchester as a guard could destroy it. The Prince himself did not enter York. He sent his second-in-command General George Goring to present his compliments to the Marquis of Newcastle and to order the latter and his garrison to be ready to march against the enemy at four o'clock the next morning. But at dawn the next day the Marquis and his troops did not appear and the Prince, not wishing to lose the chance of attacking his opponents while they were still baffled by his movements, took his army over the bridge of boats captured the night before and marched towards the enemies' rendezvous on Marston Moor.

Rupert's brilliant manœuvre had bewildered the Parlia-

mentarians and they could only guess at his immediate intentions. They thought he might move south, in which case he
would have to cross either the river Ouse or Wharfe. The
former was bridged at Selby and the latter at Tadcaster. To
deny him these crossings the united army was ordered to
march south-westwards. So, at daybreak on 2nd July the infantry, with the Scots in the van, moved off in that direction.
Some 3,000 cavalry remained behind near Marston to protect
the rear and to watch the enemies' movements.

From daybreak onwards Rupert passed his army—first the
cavalry and then the infantry—over the boat bridge at Clifton.
By nine a.m. 5,000 soldiers had reached the Marston area.
The Parliamentarians realized that the whole Royalist army
was building up against them and that, with their own infantry
strung out along the eight miles to Tadcaster, they were in a
dangerous position. Messengers were hastily sent to command
the marching troops to halt and return immediately to the
positions they had left at Marston. The Scots were only a mile
or two from Tadcaster when the message reached them. The
next three hours were critical for the Parliamentarian forces.
On the moor itself they were outnumbered and not deployed
in battle order ready to receive any attack which Rupert might
launch against them. If only the Marquis of Newcastle had
brought the York garrison on to the field by six a.m. as Rupert
had ordered, the Royalists would have been able to force a
battle any time before noon with the scales tipped in their
favour. The Marquis and some of his staff did arrive at Marston
about nine a.m., being greeted by the Prince with the words,
"My Lord, I wish you had come sooner with your forces,"
but his troops did not start to arrive there until five hours later.
Prince Rupert fumed and fretted as he saw the opposing force
build up while he waited for the York garrison to join him.
As the morning and early afternoon passed his advantage slipped
away. It was after four p.m. before Newcastle's men finally
took up their positions: long before that the Parliamentarian
armies had been in battle array. The initiative, so long with
Rupert, had passed to them. At five o'clock the sound of their

psalm singing was wafted across to the listening Royalists. Two hours later the battle began.

The battlefield stretched from the village of Tockwith on the west to that of Long Marston on the east, a distance of nearly 2¼ miles. Both armies were drawn up, about 400 yards apart, with the cavalry on the wings and the infantry in the centre. The Royalist forces were arranged thus: Rupert's cavalry, some 2,600 strong, was on the right, while that on the left wing, numbering slightly less, was commanded by General Goring. In the centre were the infantry, numbering about 11,000. Here was the York garrison, Newcastle's "Lambs" or "Whitecoats", so-called because their jackets were of undyed woollen cloth. In front of the entire army, lining the ditch which ran across the battle front, were musketeers, the so-called "forlorn hope". Their job was to harass and impede any attack as long as possible before falling back on the main body.

On the Parliamentarian side the cavalry on the left wing facing Rupert was commanded by Oliver Cromwell. It was arranged in three companies; the first two, under Cromwell's personal command, consisted of his famous "Ironsides" and numbered about 2,500, while the third, of about 800, consisted of Scots commanded by David Leslie. The cavalry on the right wing was commanded by Sir Thomas Fairfax. In the centre the Scots and English foot were massed under Lord Leven, Lord Fairfax and the Earl of Manchester.

The Parliamentarians had some twenty-five guns on the ridge behind their forces; the Royalists had far fewer and these were placed near the ditch. Both sides began firing in a desultory manner about seven p.m. without doing any appreciable damage. The baggage of both armies was at the rear of their respective forces, the Parliamentarians' being near what is now called "Cromwell's Plump", and the Royalists' near Wilstrop Wood.

The Royalist army was drawn up on Marston Moor proper. This consisted largely of open ground where cavalry could manoeuvre easily, except on the east side where the moor

H*y*

was broken up by shallow ditches, rabbit holes and furze bushes. The moor is now enclosed and has long been under the plough so that it is quite misleading to think that, in 1644, it looked as it does today. The ditch between the two armies marked the end of the moor. South of it, where the Parliamentarian armies were drawn up, the land looked much as it does today, being under the plough and enclosed with fences. In fact on 2nd July 1644, it was carrying a crop of knee-high rye which was wet and slippery as a result of heavy showers during the day. The Parliamentarians had the advantage of the slight ridge but this was offset by the ditch which masked the whole front and which was, in places, deep and wide and a formidable obstacle to horsemen trying to cross it.

Soon after seven p.m. Rupert decided that there would be no battle that day and he retired to the rear of his forces to eat his supper. The Marquis of Newcastle also withdrew to his coach to smoke a pipe. Half an hour later, to the accompaniment of peals of thunder and the biting lash of a sudden hailstorm, the whole Parliamentarian army began to advance. The surprise was such that the Royalist "forlorn hope" lining the ditch was over-run and four guns there were captured. Soon the infantry in the centre of both armies met head on and bitter and confused fighting ensued.

On the flanks, events took a more dramatic turn. On the Parliamentarian left, Cromwell, leading the charge of his "Ironsides" in person, drove the Royalist front line before him. Some of the fleeing horsemen were rallied by Rupert who, on hearing the noise of battle, rushed to his post. "Swounds, do you run? Follow me," he cried. For a moment it seemed that his counter-charge might halt the "Ironsides" and rally the Royalists. However, after both sides "stood at the sword's point a pretty while, hacking one another . . . at last Cromwell broke through them, scattering them before him like dust". Soon Rupert's cavalry—and the Prince with them—was "flying along Wilstrop Wood as fast and as thick as could be".

On the Parliamentarian right their cavalry under the com-

mand of Sir Thomas Fairfax had met with disaster. They found
the rough ground there a much more formidable obstacle
than anything Cromwell had encountered on the other wing.
Fairfax only managed to get some 400 of his cavalry over the
ditch and there, after fierce hand-to-hand fighting, they were
either killed or forced to flee. Sir Thomas found himself isolated
and surrounded by enemy horse. Snatching the white handker-
chief from his head—the distinguishing mark of the Parliamentarian army—he rode forward through the Royalist lines,
being mistaken for one of their cavalrymen, and took part in
the final dramatic charge which snatched victory for Parliament.

But to return to the earlier phase of the battle. Goring,
commanding the Royalist cavalry opposing Fairfax, sensing
that the initiative lay with him, charged as resolutely and as
successfully as Cromwell had done on the Parliamentarian
left. One section of his forces—under his personal command—
swept through the horsemen opposed to him, charged up the
hill and plundered the Parliamentarian baggage in the rear.
However, unlike Cromwell, Goring could not then regain
control of his horsemen, halt them and bring them back to the
field of battle. Their success, striking though it was, was not
decisive: they had won a charge but not a battle.

Another detachment of Goring's cavalry, commanded by
Sir Charles Lucas, wheeled right and engaged the right wing
of the Parliamentarian foot consisting of two regiments of
Scotsmen. A violent fight ensued. Three times the Royalists
charged and three times it was touch and go whether the
Scots would break. However, by kneeling down, with the
butts of their sixteen-foot long pikes wedged in the ground
and resolutely thrusting the points at the throats and flanks
of the horses driving against them, they held these furious
onslaughts and the Royalists withdrew. Lucas himself was taken
prisoner.

In the centre of the battlefield the infantry on both sides
remained locked in an inconclusive struggle. At first success
seemed to be with the Royalists. Some Scottish regiments

fled and with them went the Earl of Leven. It was some time the next day, in either Bradford or Leeds (the contemporary accounts differ) that he—as senior commander of the allied forces—was informed of "his" victory! Lord Fairfax also fled (he got as far as Cawood, where the story is that he went straight to bed) and the Earl of Manchester also left the battle-field some time though he seems to have returned before mid-night. At one time during the fight not one of the five com-manding officers—the Royalists: Rupert and Newcastle, and the Parliamentarians: Leven, Fairfax and Manchester—was actually present on the field.

At this stage in the battle the balance was nicely poised. The issue depended on some determined and decisive act. It was supplied by Oliver Cromwell. The discipline which had earned his men their nickname now paid dividends. After he had swept Rupert's cavalry off the field, he retained control over his men. Somewhere near Wilstrop Wood, Thomas Fairfax contacted him and informed him of the disaster on the Parlia-mentarian right. In the gathering dusk Cromwell, accompanied by Fairfax, led his men round the rear of the Royalist infantry until he occupied almost the same position as that originally held by Goring at the beginning of the fight. Here he re-formed and charged. First he drove the remnants of the Royalist cavalry off the field and then he attacked their foot in the centre.

The last desperate resistance of the Royalists came from Newcastle's "Whitecoats". Though repeatedly called upon to surrender they scorned quarter and fought to the death. Only thirty were eventually taken alive, the rest died in the ranks in which they had fought. Their last struggles took place near White Sike Close and it was there that these gallant north countrymen were buried in a mass grave the next day.

Soon after ten o'clock the battle was over, having lasted little more than three hours. The victorious Puritans sang a psalm of thanksgiving and then camped down on the battle-field for the night. Food was short. As we have seen their baggage was plundered during the fight and for the second night running they had to rely on any odd scraps for food and on pools and puddles for drinking water. The next day they exercised their gruesome privilege of stripping the enemy dead. Huge burial pits were then dug by local countrymen to take the naked bodies. The Royalist dead numbered over 4,000; some of the nobly born were taken to their homes for burial, a few were buried in York Minster. The Parliamentarian dead numbered only about 300. Some 1,500 Royalists were taken prisoner; over 6,000 muskets were captured, together with all the Royalist cannon, powder and baggage and nearly one hundred standards. Among the baggage were the personal papers and private possessions of Prince Rupert. They were in boxes loaded on his "sumpter", or pack-horse.

Like thousands of his men Rupert fled from the battlefield to seek protection behind the walls of York. Tradition has it that on the way he had to hide in a beanfield to elude his pursuers. This incident afforded contemporary pamphleteers with a wealth of satirical material which they seized upon with glee.

During the battle, "Boy", Rupert's favourite dog and constant companion, was killed. The Parliamentarians regarded "Boy" as the personification of the devil himself. Its loss was, therefore, a psychological blow to the Royalists and a cause of jubilation to their enemies.

The night of the battle was one of horror and terror in York. All night long wounded and dispirited soldiers who had managed to escape from the battlefield wended their way back to the city. One Parliamentarian tract alleges that their "fore troops did execution to the very walls of Yorke". Micklegate Bar, being nearest to the approach roads from Marston Moor, was thronged with soldiers clamouring for admission. The following morning after "warme words" had passed between the Prince and the Marquis of Newcastle—"after their Rout; they charging each other with the cause thereof"—the former left the city for Richmond, forty miles to the north, with what cavalry and foot soldiers he could muster. The Marquis, together with "some twenty more of good Ranke" went to Scarborough where they took ship for Hamburg in Germany.

Oliver Cromwell in York after the Siege

Newcastle did not return to England until after the Restoration. His authority in York was delegated to Sir Thomas Glemham who, a fortnight later, surrendered the city.

A contemporary tract entitled *The Articles of the Surrender of the City of Yorke* gives in detail the terms of the surrender. Glemham was to hand over the city together with "the Forts, Tower, Cannon, Ammunition, and furniture of Warre belonging thereunto" on the 16th July while his troops were allowed to "march out of the City on Horse-back and with their Armes, flying Colours, Drums beating, Matches lighted on both ends, bullets in their Mouths, and with all their bag and baggage, that every Souldier shall have 12 charges of Powder". They were to be allowed to go unmolested as far as Skipton "or the next Garrison Towne within sixteen miles of the Prince's Army". Other clauses laid down the treatment to be afforded to those who remained behind in the city and such like matters. The terms were lenient.

It took the garrison six hours to leave the city, as they were hampered by their baggage, by sick and wounded and by many women—their wives and relatives. A Parliamentarian tract describes the incident thus:

> The fourth part of them . . . who marched out of the Town were women, many very poor in their apparell, and others in better fashion. Most of the men had filled, and distempered themselves with drink; the number of the Souldiers, as we conjectured, was not above a thousand, besides the sick and wounded persons . . .
>
> When the enemies were departed, our three Generalls went together into the Citie, attended with many of their Officers. The first house they entered was the Minster-Church, where a Psalm was sung and thanks given unto God by Master Robert Duglas [Douglas] Chaplain to the Lord Leven, for the giving of that Citie into our hands, upon such easie terms.

So ended the siege of York. With the loss of the second city in England the King's cause suffered a mortal blow. The significance of the siege and the battle cannot be overestimated in any history of the Civil War. The damage to the city was tremendous. A Parliamentarian among the besiegers, writing to a friend in London, said: "Beloved. Had thine eyes yesternight with me, seene Yorke burning, thy heart would have been heavy. The Lord affect us with the sad fruits of wasting warres, and speedily, mercifully end our combustions, which are carried on with high sinnes and heavie desolations. Truly, my heart sometimes, is ready to breake, with what I here see."

9. THE STUARTS: AFTER MARSTON MOOR

Frequent mention has been made in the previous chapter of Ferdinando and Thomas Fairfax. In a sense the history of the Civil War in the north of England is the history of this family, a very ancient one which had lived in Yorkshire for many centuries. The name is Anglo-Saxon and means "fair hair". There have been many branches of the family in Yorkshire and they owned property at Steeton, Bilbrough, Nun Appleton, Denton, Gilling near Helmsley and York. As we have seen, when the Civil War broke out the Fairfaxes reluctantly took up arms for Parliament and Lord Ferdinando became Commander-in-chief of the Northern Army. His son Thomas who, with Oliver Cromwell, played such a decisive part in the Parliamentarian victory at Marston Moor, emerged as one of the outstanding generals of the Civil War. Following the Battle of Marston Moor and the surrender of York, Lord Ferdinando was appointed Governor of the city. In the York Art Gallery is a fine portrait of him by the York artist Edward Bower. It depicts a handsome, kindly, cultured man. York owes much to him as he managed to prevent the victorious Puritans from damaging many of the ecclesiastical treasures in the city, especially the medieval stained glass in the Minster. But in some of the parish churches he was not so successful. In the Walmgate/Fossgate area in particular the new Puritan ministers who replaced the Anglican clergy there were extremists and despoiled many of the fine windows. Today St Margaret's and St Denys' Churches have only a small part of their medieval glass.

With the surrender of York a new order of things was introduced. Not only were the Royalist mayor and aldermen replaced by Parliamentarians but also most of the clergy were replaced by Puritans. An assembly of many ministers was appointed which sat weekly in the Chapter House of the Minster to advise and assist Lord Fairfax "for the casting out of ignorant and scandalous ministers and putting in able and faithful ministers into places vacant and to receive petitions and complaints and make orders for that purpose".

The most distinguished of these Puritans was Oliver Bowles, one of the four put in charge of the Minster. He was also chaplain to the Fairfax family and was present at the Battle of Naseby. It was he who broke open the King's cabinet after the battle and took out of it letters which he sent to Parliament. Parliament rewarded him with £200 with which he bought a piece of silver plate on which he had inscribed the words "Remember Naseby". Bowles had a curious link with George Fox, the founder of the Quakers or Society of Friends. In his *Journal* under the date 1651 Fox wrote as follows:

> I was commanded of the Lord to go to the great Minster and speak to Priest Bowles and his hearers. Accordingly I went, and when the Priest had done, I told them I had something from the Lord God to speak to the priest and people. "Then say on quickly" said a professor that was among them, for it was frost and snow and very cold weather. Then I told them, this was the word of the Lord God unto them, that they lived in words, but God Almighty looked for fruits among them. As soon as the words were out of my mouth they hurried me out and threw me down the steps, but I got up again without hurt and went to my lodgings. Several were convinced there.

Fox visited York five more times. The last one was in 1680 when he visited many friends imprisoned in the Castle "for truth's sake".

York became one of the most important centres of Quakerism in England. Prominent Quaker families in the city have been the Tukes, Rowntrees and Terrys. All have been renowned for their philanthropy and business acumen. The two great chocolate factories which bear the names of Rowntree and Terry are examples of the latter; the Retreat, Bootham

School (founded 1828) and The Mount School (founded 1831) are three examples of the former.

After the siege of York Sir Thomas Fairfax besieged Helmsley Castle which he eventually captured, though not before he was himself severely wounded. Then, in 1645, he was appointed Commander-in-chief of the New Model Army which he led to victory at Naseby later that year in what was the last important battle of the Civil War. Fairfax was now the most powerful man in England. The next three years were taken up with the tedious negotiations between King, Parliament, the Army and the Scots. York has important links with these.

In 1646 King Charles fled from Oxford and joined the Scots, who were at that time allied with Parliament. After protracted negotiations the Scots agreed to surrender the King to Parliament for £400,000. It was arranged that when half of this sum had been paid the Scots would hand over the King. York was fixed as the place where this first instalment was to be paid. The money was packed in some two hundred barrels and sent from London in a convoy of horse-drawn wagons under heavy guard and was handed over to the Commissioners in the Guildhall in York early in 1647. The Scots insisted on opening every barrel and counting the money. It took twelve days. To commemorate the occasion the Corporation has recently had this notice carved on the panelling of the inner chamber in the Guildhall:

> This room, formerly called the Inner Chamber, was erected at the same time as the Guildhall (between 1448 and 1458). According to tradition it was here that £200,000 of the arrears due to the Scots for assisting the Parliamentary forces in the Civil War was counted early in January 1647. Half of it was paid to them at Northallerton and the remainder on the north side of Newcastle. Arrangements were subsequently made for the English Commissioners to receive the person of Charles I from the Scots at Newcastle.

On 27th January 1648, Charles I was brought to trial in Westminster Hall, London. Many Puritans as well as Royalists were appalled. Sir Thomas Fairfax's wife was a spectator at

Sir Thomas Fairfax

THE STUARTS: AFTER MARSTON MOOR

the trial and, when her husband's name was called out as one of the judges, she protested and said he would never take part in such sacrilege. Soon afterwards Sir Thomas resigned as Commander-in-chief of the army. Cromwell was appointed in his stead, the first step to his ultimately becoming Protector and dictator of England. Until 1648 Thomas Fairfax appears to have been in sympathy with Cromwell and the other Parliamentarian leaders, but when he became convinced that their policy would lead to the downfall of the monarchy and the death of the King he drifted further and further away from them.

On 30th January 1648, Charles I was beheaded on a specially constructed scafford outside one of the windows of the Palace of Whitehall. At least three York citizens were powerfully affected by the execution—Sir Thomas Herbert, Thomas Hoyle and Jane Stainton.

Thomas Herbert was born, in 1606, of an old York merchant family who owned and lived in a house on the site of the one still known as the Herbert House in Pavement. The present house was built about 1616. His early life was spent in most exciting journeys to Asia and Africa. Later he entered the diplomatic service. When the Civil War broke out he first supported Parliament. In 1647, when the King was imprisoned in Holmby House, Herbert was sent to attend him as a personal servant, in reality to keep an eye on him on behalf of Parliament. Writing in 1736, Francis Drake, the York historian, described what happened.

Being thus settled in that honourable office, and having a nearer view, as it were, of his majesty, he soon discerned the real goodness of the king, dispelled of all those clouds of aspersions his party had endeavoured to blacken him with. From this moment he became a convert to the royal cause, and continued with the king, when all the rest of the chamber was removed, till his majesty was, to the horror of all the world brought to the block.

Herbert stood with Charles I on the scaffold. Just before he was executed the King gave him his watch and cloak. In 1665

Herbert returned to York and lived in No. 9, High Petergate, where he died in 1681. He was buried in St Crux church in the remains of which a memorial inscription to him is still to be seen.

Thomas Hoyle—a prominent Puritan alderman—became Lord Mayor of York on 3rd September 1644, when Edmund Cooper, the Royalist mayor, was compelled to resign. Hoyle was also one of the two Members of Parliament for York and it was while he was in London on his Parliamentary duties that, unable to appease his troubled conscience over his opposition to the King, he committed suicide. Christopher Hildyard, a seventeenth century York historian, explained the circumstances in these words:

> January the 30th 1650 much the same houre of the day that our late Soveraigne was murdered the year before, Thomas Hoyle . . . became his own Executioner, by hanging of himself in his house at Westminster and was there found dead by his Lady.

Jane Stainton came of a well-to-do York family. Her father had been Rector of St Cuthbert's Church, Peaseholme Green, and her step-father and many of her relatives were members of the Corporation, some being aldermen and Lord Mayors. All were staunch Royalists and many were members of the Merchant Adventurers' Company. Jane never married. Like thousands of English men and women she considered King Charles a martyr and each year kept the anniversary of his death as a day of prayer and solemn remembrance. She died in 1692 and was buried in St Cuthbert's Church "under the blue stone between the minister's seat and the clerk's". She drew up her will a month before she died. Among other bequests she left property in Coppergate to the Mayor and Corporation on the condition that they paid "fifteene shillings per annum to the Minister of All Saints in the Pavement for an anniversary sermon the thirtieth day of January for ever with the desire that the subject matter of discourse may be to put his auditors in mind of their latter end".

This payment has been honoured from that day to this and

is still made to the Rector of All Saints. Each year on the Sunday nearest to 30th January, he preaches a sermon in which he reminds the congregation of "their latter end". This service is attended by the Lord Mayor and Corporation and the Governor and Brethren of the Merchant Adventurers' Company. It is a colourful and impressive occasion and is but one of the many traditions which York delights to maintain. Jane chose the 30th January because that was the day on which Charles I was executed. She was thirteen years old in 1649 when this happened; she was fifty-six when she died. The King's last word on the scaffold is reputed to have been "Remember!" One of his York subjects observed this instruction faithfully for forty-three years while the City of York has now done so for two hundred and seventy-eight years.

While York played only a minor part in the events of the Commonwealth and Protectorate, it played an outstanding role in the Restoration of Charles II in 1660. In 1658 Oliver Cromwell died and his eldest son Richard succeeded him as Lord Protector of England. Richard was a nonentity and abdicated a few months later. In Scotland General Monk, who commanded a Parliamentarian army of 7,000 men, realizing that popular opinion favoured the return of the Stuarts, decided to bring about the Restoration. He marched his army south to find his way barred by another Parliamentarian army of 10,000 commanded by General Lambert. He sought advice from Thomas Fairfax. Fairfax promised that, if necessary, he would himself raise a supporting army. On 3rd January 1660, Fairfax met some of Lambert's army on the battlefield of Marston Moor where he won them over to the cause of Charles. On 11th January, Monk entered York. He was flanked by two "Presbyterian teachers", one of whom was Oliver Bowles. During the next five days Fairfax, Monk and Bowles met many times either in York or at Nun Appleton and between them planned how the Restoration was to be brought about. Then Monk continued his march to London and summoned the Rump—the remnants of the Long Parliament—which decided to restore the monarchy. Six peers and twelve commoners, with Fairfax at their head, were sent to The Hague in Holland where Charles was in exile to ask him to return to England as King. Bowles went with them. On 11th May 1660, Charles landed at Dover and on 29th May, entered London. The magnificent white horse which he rode on both occasions was a gift from Thomas Fairfax, being bred and reared in the Fairfax stables at Nun Appleton eight miles west of York.

Bowles soon regretted the part which he had played in the Restoration. He was dismissed from his office in the Minster. "I have buried the good old cause," he said, "and am now going to bury myself." He died in 1664 and was buried in All Saints' Church, Pavement, where, during the Commonwealth, he had delivered weekly sermons to packed congregations.

Francis Drake described the Restoration celebrations in York in these words:

> May 11. The lord-mayor, aldermen and twenty-four, on horse-back in their proper habits, preceded the cavalcade on foot in their gowns. These were attended by more than a thousand citizens under arms, and lastly came a troop of country gentlemen, near three hundred, with Lord Thomas Fairfax at their head, who all rode with their swords drawn and hats upon their swords points. When the proclamation was read at the usual places, the bells rung, the cannon played from the tower, and the soldiers gave several vollies of shot. At night were tar-barrels, bonfires, illuminations, &c. with the greatest expressions of joy that could possibly be testified on that happy deliverance.
>
> May 29. The king's birth-day, and the day of his publick entrance into the city of London, the loyalty of our citizens was in a more especial manner expressed. The effigies of the late tyrant and usurper Oliver Cromwell cloathed in a pinked satten suit, with that of that base miscreant and unjust judge John Bradshaw habited in a judge's robe, as likewise the hellish Scotch covenant and the late state's arms, which were erected in the common-hall, were all on the same day hung upon a gallows set up for the purpose in the Pavement; and at last put into three tar barrels and burnt, together with the gallows, in the presence of one thousand citizens in arms, and a multitude of other spectators.

Since 1385 it has been customary for the second son of the reigning monarch to be dubbed Duke of York. This is a compliment to the city which William Camden, the Elizabethan historian, in 1586 called "The Second City in England"; which John Leland, the antiquary, fifty years earlier had called "The Queen of Northern Britain"; and which, in 1685, Sir John Reresby, then military Governor of York, described as "The first city next to London". One of these Dukes of York was James, the second son of Charles I. He had a chequered career.

He returned to England after the Restoration and, because Charles II had no legitimate children, was heir presumptive to the throne. He was for a time Lord High Admiral of the British Navy and was responsible, in 1667, for sending to North America the squadron of the fleet which captured New Amsterdam from the Dutch. The place was renamed New York in his honour and has grown into one of the largest cities in the world. In the Guildhall in York are three flags—one the Stars and Stripes, another that of the County of New York and the third that of the city of New York. They replace flags destroyed in the fire of 1942. With them is the original plaque which reads:

> To the Ancient and famous City of York whose storied monuments and living chronicles enshrine so great a part of the history of the English race this tablet is affectionately inscribed as an expression of friendship and goodwill from her god-child in America, the City of New York. July 18. 1924.

As an ardent Roman Catholic, James, Duke of York, was unpopular in England and in 1678 Titus Oates and other Protestant fanatics concocted a plot alleging that Catholics intended murdering Charles II and placing James on the throne. There was panic in England and James was sent to Scotland to avoid trouble. On his way north he stayed in York. In Gray's Court is a brass table with this inscription:

> James Duke of York and Maria Beatrix of Modena his wife, afterwards King and Queen, lodged in this house Nov. 6th 1679.

Iy

This so-called Popish Plot led to the persecution of Roman Catholics in England. In York, Thomas Thwing, a Catholic priest, was condemned to death. He was hanged, drawn and quartered on the Knavesmire on 23rd October 1680, the last person to be executed there on account of his religion.

Thwing had been arrested in a house in Castlegate together with some nuns belonging to the order of the Institute of the Blessed Virgin Mary. They were imprisoned in York Castle from 1680 to 1685, being released when James became King. In the following year they were given a house at the junction of Blossom Street and Nunnery Lane. From this humble beginning grew the Convent and School long known as the Bar Convent. For three hundred years the nuns have been highly respected in York and their school has attracted girls from all parts of England.

The founder of this order, Mary Ward, was a remarkable woman. She was born at Mulwith near Ripon in 1585 and died at Heworth Hall, York, in 1645. Her reputation—even greater in Germany and Italy than in England—rests on the fact that she was a pioneer in girls' education. Because of persecution in England she went, as a young woman, to Flanders where she became a nun.

Amidst prejudice, opposition and persecution, she persisted in her life's work of establishing schools where Roman Catholic girls could be educated. During her lifetime ten such schools were established in five different countries in Europe; today there are about three hundred in different parts of the world. This is not the place to recount her career in detail. The last few years of her life are however of interest, as they were linked with York. She returned to England for the last time in May 1639. At first she lived in London but, with the approach of the Civil War, she moved north, first to Hutton Rudby and then to Heworth on the outskirts of York where she lived in the Hall. In 1644 she was compelled to seek refuge with her followers and the few possessions which they could carry, within the walls of York. For six weeks she was numbered among the Royalists besieged in the city. When the city surrendered to Parliament she returned to Heworth Hall where she died on 20th January 1645. The Puritans were now in complete control. She was such a well known Roman Catholic that at first no clergyman would consent to bury her in his churchyard. Eventually the Vicar of Osbaldwick was bribed and she was buried in the churchyard there. A large tombstone, now in the church, was erected over her grave. The inscription reads:

> To love the poore Persever in the same Live dy and Rise with them was all the ayme of Mary Ward who Having Lived 60 year and 8 days dyed the 20 of Jan. 1645.

At first the grave was a place of pilgrimage for the nuns in the Bar Convent and then for various reasons the grave became neglected, the gravestone removed and the site forgotten. In 1965 when extensions were being made to the church, permission was obtained by the nuns of the Bar Convent to examine parts of the churchyard to see if they could find the grave. They asked the writer to supervise the excavation. A grave and skeleton were found which possibly belonged to Mary Ward. What may be her bones now rest in the Bar Convent among the nuns whose order she founded about 350 years ago, and by whom she is still greatly revered.

10. GEORGIAN YORK

In the reigns of Queen Anne and the four Georges—the so-called Georgian period—York was the fashionable social capital of the north of England. The gentry of Yorkshire took their families into the city to enjoy the summer and winter seasons there. The summer one centred around the Assizes, when the criminals condemned to death were publicly hanged on the Knavesmire. A more civilized event was the Race Meeting, held first on Clifton Ings before being moved to the site of the present racecourse, on the Knavesmire. It was an age of elegance. The men wore wigs, inhaled snuff and drank port. The women wore silk dresses, and used powder and patches. Concerts, plays, balls and card parties were well attended. The cockpits, coffee houses, Assembly Rooms and the Theatre Royal were popular meeting places. The streets were still mostly unpaved and filthy and the well-to-do, to avoid soiling their rich clothes, travelled in sedan chairs, borne by two bearers and accompanied by footmen and torchbearers. When the cavalcade reached its destination the torches were placed in iron brackets which hung on each side of the doorway. Three extinguishers, with which the torches were snuffed out, still remain in York today.

In the early eighteenth century parties were held either in the King's Manor or in private houses. It was then decided to build the Assembly Rooms, a magnificent example of Georgian architecture, designed by Richard Boyle, third Earl of Burlington. Originally it had a semi-circular portico but this was removed in 1828 and the present entrance added.

One of the features of Georgian York was the rebuilding which took place. Many of the medieval half-timbered build-

The Mansion House

ings which had been damaged during the Civil War were replaced during this affluent period by elegant red brick ones, many of which still grace the city today. Bootham, Micklegate and Castlegate have some superb examples. Of the "public buildings" constructed at this time, surviving examples are the Mansion House in St Helen's Square (1730), the Assize Court (1777), the Debtor's Prison, now part of the Castle Museum (1780) and Bootham Park, first built as a lunatic asylum (1777).

The greatest York architect at this time was John Carr (1723–1807) who built many houses still standing in the city. A famous family of woodcarvers were the Ettys, father and son, whose work survives in Gray's Court and the Queen's Hotel, Micklegate. Grinling Gibbons was apprenticed to them for a time.

Deliberate attempts were made to beautify the city at this time and the results of at least three of these are still with us today. In 1719 Lord Mayor's Walk was widened and planted with elm trees; soon afterwards the Fulford area of the river Ouse was replanned and the New Walk was opened there as a promenade, while in 1746 Cumberland Row was built in New Street. This was so-named to commemorate both the suppression of the Jacobite Rebellion in that year and also the fleeting visit paid to the city by the Duke of Cumberland—the victor at the Battle of Culloden—on his way south from Scotland to London on the evening of 23rd July 1746. He was entertained in Gray's Court where he was given the freedom of the city. A few months after his visit seventy-five Jacobites who had fought at Culloden were tried in York. Of these, forty-three were executed on the Knavesmire and the heads of two of them were placed on poles on Micklegate Bar—the last time that this was ever done. They remained there for seven years before they were secretly removed. The culprit was found, fined £5 and imprisoned for two years.

By an Act of Parliament in 1763, houses had to be provided with downfall pipes to channel water from the roofs. Before this the rainwater had cascaded down without any control or direction, drenching anyone unlucky enough to be passing at the time. The new pipes were rectangular in shape with ornamental heads on which it was fashionable to put the crests and initials of the owners and the date of the building. Many of these can still be seen in York.

Every householder was responsible for paving and keeping in good repair the pathway in front of his own house and for keeping clean the street there. Both these duties were irksome and cost money and it was rare that anyone did anything about them unless threatened by the overseers of the highways—

men appointed by each parish to superintend this—with a
fine or imprisonment. The Corporation employed a paver to
look after the pavements in front of their own properties and
also a scavenger to deal with the rubbish there. These two
men represent the ancestors of the present public works
department of the city.

This period saw an enormous increase in traffic in the city.
The congestion caused by public coaches and private carriages
led to street improvements and road widening. Many of the
unpaved streets were cobbled at this time. St Helen's Square—
originally the graveyard attached to St Helen's Church—
was opened up in 1780, Museum Street in 1791, Duncombe
Place, replacing the much more romantically named Lop
Lane, in 1784, while in 1753 John Carr had altered Micklegate
Bar by adding two more arches to it so that traffic could pass
more quickly through it.

York became the main coaching centre of the north of
England. It was at the intersection of two main traffic routes—
from Hull and Scarborough on the east coast to Manchester
and Liverpool on the west and from London in the south to
Newcastle and Scotland in the north. The George and Black
Swan Inns in Coney Street, the Starre in Stonegate and the
White Swan in Pavement were famous York coaching houses.
From 1706 onwards there was a regular coach service between
Newcastle and London via York. The London coach left the
Black Swan in York at five a.m. on Mondays, Wednesdays
and Fridays, taking four days to reach the Black Swan,
Holborn, in London. The coach for Newcastle left York on
Mondays and Fridays and took two days to complete the
journey. Each passenger was allowed to take fourteen pounds
of luggage; the single fare from York to London was eight
shillings.

Sometimes coaches were stopped by highwaymen and the
passengers robbed. Two highwaymen—John Nevison and
Dick Turpin—are famed for their links with York. Turpin was
hanged on the Knavesmire on 22nd March 1739, and buried
in St George's churchyard. During the night "resurrection

men" (grave robbers who removed newly buried corpses and sold them to surgeons for dissection) removed the body and hid it in a garden in Stonegate. When some citizens heard of

The London–York Coach at the Black Swan in Coney Street

this they were enraged, found it, placed it in a coffin containing lime (to hasten the decomposition of the corpse), and carried it in procession through the streets to St George's churchyard where they reburied it. Grave and tombstone remain there to this day.

Every York boy and girl knows of the alleged exploits of Dick Turpin, particularly how he was supposed to have ridden from London to York on Black Bess in fifteen hours. This is, of course, physically impossible. In reality Dick Turpin was a despicable thug. The romantic "legendary" Turpin was the invention of William Harrison Ainsworth who, in his novel *Rookwood*, published in 1834, told a story which is quite unhistorical and quite misleading.

The penalties imposed on wrong-doers at this time make strange reading today. Sentences of death were imposed for what, nowadays, would be treated as trivial offences. In 1763, a man was condemned to death for stealing £4 and a woman for stealing £19. Also in 1763 a man found guilty of perjury

was condemned to stand in the pillory (which was in Pavement) for one hour, while a year later a woman was publicly whipped through the streets for the same offence. In 1757 a man accused of starting a riot in the city was transported for life to the West Indies. In 1729 a ducking stool was placed alongside the river in St George's Field; scolding and nagging wives were placed in it and ducked in the water.

To the wealthy the Georgian period in York was one of luxury and pageantry. Each year when the Lord Mayor was sworn in he had to declare on which two days each week he would keep "open house". He was expected to feed and entertain citizens. In practice these seem to have been drawn only from visiting gentry, aldermen, councillors and leading city freemen, perhaps about 150 in all. In addition he had to pay and feed a large household staff of about sixty servants ranging from the town clerk to the chambermaid. To help meet these expenses he received an annual allowance of about £600 from the Corporation; the remainder he had to find from his own pocket. The Corporation kept a pack of hounds which hunted twice a week, and owned a magnificent barge which the Lord Mayor used for his ceremonial journeyings up and down the Ouse.

The eighteenth century saw the beginnings of newspapers as we know them today. The first York paper—the *York Mercury*—was published by Grace White in Coffee Yard, Stonegate, and many followed in the next hundred years, some of which survived for only a very short time. The daily *Yorkshire Evening Press* and the weekly *Gazette and Herald* are the modern successors to these Georgian beginnings. The early newspapers—particularly the items relating to parliamentary and foreign affairs—formed the basis of many a long and animated argument in the numerous coffee houses which sprang up during this period. In these same coffee houses and the local inns men discussed such publications as Francis Drake's monumental *History of York* (1736) and best selling novels such as Laurence Sterne's *Tristram Shandy*. Sterne was Vicar of Coxwold near York and a constant visitor to the city.

There was, however, another side to the elegance, culture and learning of Georgian York. Between 1700 and 1750 the population was about 12,000 and in 1800 about 17,000. Over half of these people lived in slums which disgraced many parts of the city—especially in the Bedern, Walmgate, Fossgate, Gillygate and Bishophill areas. Here unemployment, disease and misery were rife. Epidemics such as smallpox, measles and influenza occurred every year. The filth and rubbish which lay uncollected in the streets and the unfiltered water spread dysentery, cholera, "putrid fever" and "sweating sickness".

A long, harsh winter was an ordeal to the poor. It is romantic to read of the winter of 1704 when the Ouse was frozen over and roast chestnut booths were set up on the ice and football matches were played there. We forget the poor and aged shivering in draughty, decaying houses, sitting over inadequate fires and racked by rheumatic aches and pains unrelieved by modern medicine. The Barber-Surgeons Guild still flourished —all barbers and all surgeons were obliged to belong to it just as they had in the Middle Ages. A new regulation had been introduced into their rules whereby apprentices had to perform dissections on actual corpses before they completed their training but, in general, medical training had improved very little. Children were still sent up to London at the city's expense to be touched by the King for scrofula, the so-called "King's Evil", and quacks still made a good living. In 1768 a "professor" Hilman advertised in the *York Courant* of his ability to cure the blind in a matter of minutes!

However, there were glimmerings of better things. The York County Hospital (1746) and the Lunatic Asylum at Bootham Park (1777), both of which still flourish, were founded, while the Dispensary, which provided the poor with free medicine and medical treatment, was opened in 1788. One of the "revolutionary" new treatments practised there was the inoculation of children against smallpox. Almost at the end of the century in 1796, William Tuke, a York Quaker, founded the Retreat, which had the distinction of being the first hospital to practise the humane treatment of the insane.

The hospital, still under the management of the Society of Friends, continues today.

The Georgian period saw a further decline in the industries of York. Though ships were still being built there as late as 1771 and though York was one of the leading markets in the north of England, especially for grain and cattle, there were no trades comparable with the great wool and cloth industries of the late Middle Ages. A century was to pass before the humble grocer's shop opened in 1725 in Castlegate by Mary Tuke blossomed into the great chocolate and cocoa manufacturing firm of Rowntrees, or the small confectionery business started in St Helen's Square in 1767 by a family named Terry grew into a similar undertaking.

Poverty and unemployment breed crime as well as disease. We have already noted some of the punishments meted out to criminals in York—hanging, the pillory, imprisonment, whipping and transportation. The city gaol was still housed under Ouse Bridge while a new House of Correction in St Anthony's Hall had a treadmill as a means of punishment. Fortunately some more enlightened citizens of York, as in other cities at this time, tried to combat some of this misery. Almshouses were founded of which the Hewley foundation (1700) and the Mary Wandesford foundation (1739) in Bootham still survive today. Each parish appointed overseers of the poor whose responsibility it was to keep lists of the "deserving poor" and to levy a poor rate on those who could afford it from which a dole of between fourpence and two shillings a week was given to each family. In 1770 there were 170 receiving relief in Monk Ward, 150 in Walmgate, 90 in Micklegate and 80 in Bootham. This system worked so badly that later in the century it was planned to set up a workhouse in each parish (or in a group of parishes) where the able-bodied could be put to work. One was opened in an old cotton factory in Marygate in 1768. It was still in use in the nineteenth century.

A distinguished visitor to York in the early Georgian period was Daniel Defoe, the novelist, who had this to say about the place:

No city in England is better furnished with provisions of every kind, nor any so cheap in proportion to the goodness of things; the river being so navigable, and so near the sea, the merchants here trade directly to what part of the world they will; for ships of any burthen come up within thirty mile of the city, and small craft from sixty to eighty ton, and under, come up to the very city.

Defoe summed up his opinion of York by describing it as "indeed a pleasant and beautiful city". It is perhaps not surprising that when he came to write his famous novel, *Robinson Crusoe*, one of the best selling novels of the eighteenth century, he fixed on York as his hero's birthplace. The novel begins with the words, "I was born in the year 1632, in the city of York."

11. THE NINETEENTH CENTURY

In 1801 the population of York was 17,000. There were only a few houses outside the medieval walls. York was still a small compact city, little changed from the Middle Ages. In the next hundred years a population explosion took place and the city boundaries were pushed further and further into the countryside. Places such as Clifton, Heworth, Holgate and Dringhouses, which had been isolated villages near the city, were absorbed into it. In 1851 the population was 40,000; in 1901 75,000; in 1951 105,000; while today it is 110,000.

Considerable though this growth was, it was small compared with that of other Yorkshire cities such as Leeds and Bradford. The Industrial Revolution made little impact on York. In fact, the first forty years of the nineteenth century were sad ones in the history of the city. It was no longer the northern metropolis it had been in the Georgian period. Fashions had changed; the gentry no longer flocked to York for the races, theatre, balls, concerts, cock-fighting and coffee houses. There were few new industries in the city. The workshops were generally small and rarely employed more than thirty to forty men so that unemployment was considerable. To quote a contemporary document, the poor "not being properly supplied with work are become highly burthernsome". In an age when the modern welfare services were unknown and the poor depended entirely on private charity, beggars, vagrants, down-and-outs and petty thieves were an ever-present problem. York was still important as an ecclesiastical centre, as a market for cattle and foodstuffs, as a coaching centre and for small handicrafts. The manufacture of confectionery by Rowntrees, Terrys and Cravens was growing, but the general character of the city was one of stagnation.

In the opinion of contemporaries the cause was the high cost of coal compared with places such as Leeds and Bradford, but it went deeper than that. York's economic life was still basically medieval. Only freemen could trade in the city and this stifled enterprise and initiative. The city was controlled by a Corporation which was self-perpetuating. When a councillor died or resigned his office, the remaining councillors elected his successor. It was therefore impossible for young men with progressive ideas to have much influence on local affairs.

There were a few exceptions and one York firm in particular had a national reputation. This was Walkers, the ironfounders, established in 1800. Some of the work they did for Queen Victoria at Sandringham still survives, as it does also at such unlikely places as the Botanical Gardens in Mauritius. In 1850 Walkers got the contract for supplying the gates and railings around the British Museum in London. These are most impressive. Little of their work remains in York except for the railings in front of the Judge's Lodgings in Lendal.

The character of the city was considerably altered in 1835 and 1840 by the two greatest changes of the nineteenth century: the Municipal Reform Act of 1835 and the coming of the railways. As a result of the first of these the city was governed by a Corporation of about forty elected councillors and nine aldermen elected by the Corporation. The city was divided into six wards, each of which returned councillors who held office for three years. All ratepayers had a vote. The Corporation had the right to levy rates and was made responsible for sanitation, water supply, lighting and law and order. To enforce the latter it could raise a police force. It is no accident that one of the main responsibilities of this new Corporation was hygiene. The appalling conditions which existed in York at this time are shown in a report drawn up in 1844. Here are some extracts from it:

The houses of the higher classes and all the more respectable houses recently built have water-closets which empty into drains or cesspools. In the newly built ranges of cottage tenements, one privy is appropriated to from four to eight, twelve, and even fourteen families; sometimes, however, there is a privy to each house. . . . The soilholes are usually open, and run over and flood back courts. . . . During wet weather, the privies have to be emptied by buckets into the open channel in the middle of the street. In the Water-lanes there are several houses without privies, so that the inhabitants have to use those of their neighbours by stealth or go into the street. The pigsties attached to numerous cottages and yards constitute a most unnecessary and unpleasant nuisance.

The courts and alleys inhabited by the poorer classes are cleaned by appointed scavengers. The night-soil is retained, giving off its impurities, until a sufficient quantity is accumulated, when it is removed from the yard during the night in barrows (and this is the method also in private houses), and put into the street; from thence it is carted away to large dung-hills within the city. There is an immense heap of this kind at the side of the river Foss, close to Layerthorpe bridge, and the inhabitants all around complain loudly of the stench. . . . The night-soil of the city is usually sold to the proprietors of these dung-hills, who are manure merchants by trade. . . . A load and a half is on the average taken from each house annually, and the cost of getting out and loading is about 2s. per load; so that the city pays at least £900. per annum for this labour. The annual value of the manure of all kinds made in the city cannot be less than £8,000. to £10,000. In addition to the night-soil there is the manure of pigsties, cow-houses, and stables, all of which are found in great number in the courts and yards, especially of the poorer classes.

Houses are built both in wide streets and in narrow courts. To some cottage tenements lately built there is no drain or sewer in the street, it is also unpaved and so full of ruts and ashes and all kinds of filth as to be quite impassable to pedestrians or even to persons on horseback. The road is higher than the adjoining yards, and the filthy mud flows into the back premises and even houses in the next street. The City Act gives no control over the builders of houses, nor can they be compelled to sewer, drain, or prepare the ground in any way for the health and convenience of the inhabitants except as their own judgment dictates. The consequence is, that several new streets in York are unpaved and undrained, full of deep holes, ruts, and mud, and traversed with difficulty even by carts.

... Of 98 families living in the Bedern quarter, 67 have only one room for all purposes, 18 two rooms, and 13 three rooms or more. One entire building is let off in single rooms, the stair-case windows are so made that they cannot open, the rooms are low and confined, the light of day almost excluded, and the walls and ground damp and undrained. The building is occupied by 16 families, two abominably filthy privies being appro-priated to all, and situate, with their accompanying "ash-hole" or "bog-hole", in a little back court. As might be expected the smell in rooms of this kind is most disgusting and oppressive. Against the back wall of a cottage there is sometimes a dung-hill, the fluid of which soaks into the house. Indeed, this circumstance is repeatedly complained of by poor people.

The general state of the air in the dwellings of the poorer classes ... is bad; the courts and yards are confined, the inhabitants numerous; the privies, sewers, and drains defective, the latter, indeed, generally wanting; and yet there is usually an evident desire to keep all clean and neat as possible, even under circum-stances the most unfavourable to personal and domestic cleanliness. There were some instances of extreme poverty. . . . In St Mar-garet's a family of seven were found in one room with no other bed than a few shavings in a corner.

The quantity of soot which falls is very great. Some idea of the amount may be learnt from the fact that a drawing-room window not having been opened for two or three months, the soot had collected between the bars just as in a chimney, the current of air passing from without into the room being loaded with and depositing the soot there as it passed through the bars.

The state of the parochial buying-grounds of York must have a considerable and noxious influence on the atmosphere within the churches, and on that of the city generally, and on the water. The greater number of these grounds are of extreme antiquity, and must have been buried over very often. In fact, many of them are raised above the street level from the accumulated remains of generations. That of St Michael, Spurriergate (now closed), is at least three feet above the floor of the church. A few years ago the ground of St Helen, Stonegate, was raised three feet by fresh soil in consequence of the great number of bodies placed there. York having now an excellent cemetery, a strong feeling is very generally expressed against the continued use of these grounds for the purposes of interment. Graves are dug in the public thoroughfares and putrescent human remains exposed; nor is it an uncommon circumstance to see bones lying about. The analysis of the water from wells near St Cuthbert's and St Sampson's churchyards, shows that the wells are tainted by the drainage from these burying grounds, and there can be no doubt the air is also polluted, not only by the direct emanations, but as well from the drainage from these bodies into the public sewers. Indeed, individuals have stated that they perceive the stench as they pass along the city street.

Water is supplied to the city from wells and cisterns, but principally, for all purposes, from the river Ouse, by a company first established in 1677, and subsequently by Act of Parliament.

The causes of the unhealthiness of York, as compared with the country, have in some degree been indicated. Bad sewerage and drainage, bad water, bad air, not only from the decomposition of refuse animal and vegetable matter, but from the crowding of the artisan class into a confined space. In addition to these noxious agencies, their employments and their workshops are often unhealthy; sickness makes them poor, and their food and clothing are consequently scanty. It is difficult to estimate the influence of all these causes on the health in York. The city is divided into wards and parishes, and in those good streets and bad streets, open thoroughfares and gardens, and densely populated badly ventilated courts, are closely intermingled.

The report adds that calculations based on 26,000 entries in Parish Registers indicate that the average life span of a York citizen was twenty-eight years in 1770, twenty-nine in 1801 and thirty-two in 1841. These figures were so low because of the appalling infantile mortality rate. In 1770 thirty-eight per cent of all deaths in the city were of children under five, in 1801 the figure was thirty-five per cent, and in 1841 forty-two per cent. There were numerous outbreaks of epidemic diseases in York in the nineteenth century. One of the worst was the cholera outbreak in 1832 which caused nearly 200 deaths. Some of the victims were buried in St George's churchyard and others in a new one which was opened in Thief Lane just outside North Street Postern. Part of this remains with its tombstones still standing as a traffic island near the Royal Station Hotel.

In the new Corporation elected in January 1836 there were twenty-one Whigs and fifteen Tories. Two years later the Tories had a majority which they retained until 1850. Their leader was George Hudson, one of the most remarkable and influential men in the long history of York. Hudson lived in Monkgate and had a draper's shop not far from St William's College. In the 1830's he realized the importance of the role which the railways were to play in the development of transport and he started to buy railway shares. These increased in value very quickly and he became a rich man. He set up companies to build new railways and, between the years 1835 and 1859, established a network of railroads of which York was the centre.

Hudson ensured that only Tory M.P.'s represented York in Parliament. The leader of the Whig or Liberal Party in York was George Leeman. Enmity grew between Hudson and Leeman as the years passed. Hudson controlled a local paper, *The Yorkshire Gazette*, and was director of numerous companies including the York Union Banking Company and the York Union Gas Lighting Company (one of the companies responsible for bringing gas lighting to York). In 1837 and 1838 and again in 1844 and 1845 Hudson was Lord Mayor of York and from 1845 to 1859 was M.P. for Sunderland. He was rich, powerful and feared; he controlled the Corporation of York, had a voice in Parliament and was admired as one of the financial "wizards" of his time, being known far and wide as "The Railway King".

In the early 1840's railway shares rose to astounding prices and those who "played the market" shrewdly and successfully made fortunes in a very short time. This state of affairs could not last and in 1848 there was a slump, as a result of which hundreds of investors had to sell their shares for less than they gave for them. They were ruined. They looked for a scapegoat and blamed Hudson. In 1849 his affairs were investigated and irregularities were found that led to his downfall. He, too, was ruined and when he died in 1871, aged seventy, he left only £200 in his will. From being the beloved idol of his native city he became the most hated of men. Hudson Street was renamed Railway Street and his portrait as Lord Mayor was removed from the Mansion House. (It has since been replaced.) The man who did much to ruin Hudson was George Leeman. When Leeman died in 1875 a statue, paid for by public subscription, was erected in Station Road; it is still there. There is no public monument in York to Hudson. The centenary of his death falls this year (1971). The Corporation proposes to rename Railway Street "George Hudson Street" in honour of this occasion.

The building of railways in the nineteenth century was a haphazard affair, being undertaken by dozens of different companies. Nowhere is this better illustrated than in York. The first line—from York to Normanton—was laid down in 1840 by the York and North Midland Company (controlled by George Hudson). A year later the Great North of England Company (controlled by Hudson) linked York with Darlington and Newcastle. In 1845 the York and North Midland Company built the Scarborough line and two years later the branch line to Market Weighton; the extension to Beverley was added in 1865. In 1848 the East and West Yorkshire Junction Company (controlled by Hudson) opened the line to Knaresborough and finally in 1913 the Derwent Valley Light Railway Company laid down the track to Cliffe Common near Selby.

These early railway companies gradually amalgamated. In 1854 the North Eastern Railway Company was formed, in 1923 the London and North Eastern Railway Company came into being, while in 1948 all the railways in Britain were joined together to form British Railways—an exception being the Derwent Valley Light Railway Company which is still run as a private company. York became the headquarters of the North Eastern Company and in 1906 the large building still known as the Railway Offices was erected on Station Rise.

At the same time important carriage works were opened in the Holgate area on the present site. In 1928 the Railway Museum in Queen Street was opened.

The first York Railway Station, opened in 1841, was in Tanner Row. It was pulled down in 1966, though the booking office and waiting rooms still stand. This station was inside the city walls, through which new arches were made to allow a passage for the trains. The siting of this station proved to be a mistake, as there could be no through flow of traffic. Consequently a new station—the present one—was built in 1877 outside the city walls. This is a magnificent example of Victorian engineering. It is a huge, curved building covering eight lines for through traffic. The main platform is 500 yards long and when first built was the longest in Britain. In 1840 the train journey from York to London took fourteen hours, in 1841 ten hours and in 1848 six hours; today it takes just over three hours.

The railways, of course, brought an end to the coaching era. In 1830 York was one of the most important coaching centres in England and hundreds of men and women were employed as coachmen, ostlers, stableboys, postmen, innkeepers, serving men and women. In 1830 coaches carried over 36,000 passengers from the city to Leeds, 18,000 to Hull, 76,000 to Selby and 23,000 to London, the total being over 150,000. In addition carts and wagons conveyed over 7,000 tons of goods to Leeds alone. By 1850 all this was taken over by the railways.

Hudson is typical of one aspect of Victorian York—the desire to make it a progressive industrial city. There were other forces at work which wanted it to retain its old world character by preserving the Minster, walls and ancient buildings which were its chief charm. Tourism was a word unknown at this time, though in the twentieth century it was to constitute one of York's major industries and in 1969 the city appointed its first Tourist Officer. William Etty (1787–1849) is one of the Victorians who ensured that, long after he died, York had preserved enough of its architectural heritage to make it a worth-while visiting place for travellers from all over the world. He had no easy task. Etty was the seventh child of humble parents. His father was a miller, baker and confectioner, well known for his tasty gingerbread. William's education was short, finishing at the age of eleven when he was apprenticed to a printer in Hull. His ambition was to be a painter and in 1807, assisted by an uncle and brother, he went to London. He entered the Royal Academy where he showed exceptional promise. His style and interests were influenced by visits to the Continent where he saw the works of French and Italian painters. In 1824 his work was recognized when he was elected an Associate of the Royal Academy. He and Robert Flaxman

First railway station in Tanner Row, 1841

(1755–1826) are the only York citizens to receive that honour. Etty is famed as a painter of both portraits and nudes. He had a passionate love for his native city. It was a great grief to him in 1829 and again in 1840 to hear in London of the disastrous fires to the Minster. On both occasions he returned to York and by his gifts of money, his example, leadership and enthusiasm, he raised funds so that restoration could go ahead.

In 1825 there was a plan to pull down Clifford's Tower to extend the gaol there. Etty was one of those who prevented this. In the eighteenth century the walls of York had been hopelessly neglected and, in places, were falling down. In 1808 Skeldergate Postern was pulled down, followed, in 1825, by the barbican of Monk Bar, in 1826 by Castlegate Postern and the barbican of Micklegate Bar, in 1829 by Layerthorpe Postern and in 1831 by the barbican of Bootham Bar and a

section of the wall there to make way for St Leonard's Place. In 1832 there was a move to demolish Bootham Bar entirely. Etty protested against what he called "the Vandals" who were prepared to see these unique features of York destroyed. He headed a subscription list and Bootham Bar and the walls were saved. In 1840 he protested when the Railway Company breached the walls in Queen Street. Two years later the Corporation proposed to remove Walmgate Bar. Again by letters, protests and donations Etty led the fight to preserve this —the only one of the four bars or gateways which retains its barbican and so shows to the modern visitor exactly what the defences of a medieval city gate were like.

In 1848 Etty retired to York and died there in the following year. He had wished to be buried in the Minster but in his will had made no provision for the payment of the necessary fees. His fellow citizens—preoccupied with the financial worries connected with the downfall of George Hudson—failed to launch a public subscription to meet these. He was buried instead in the churchyard of St Olave's church where his tomb may still be seen.

It was not until 1911 that York paid tribute to one of its outstanding artistic sons. In that year his statue was erected in front of the City Art Gallery where over sixty of his paintings —the biggest collection in England—are housed. Perhaps the greatest single service Etty performed for his native city was his work in establishing the School of Design, or York School of Art as it is now called. It was opened in 1842 in Blake Street, later it moved to Minster Yard and in 1890 it was re-housed in its present premises adjoining the Art Gallery. In this school hundreds of young men and women are taught art. They visit the Art Gallery and study Etty's works. They may take inspiration from this tribute paid to him by one of his biographers: "Never was a more assiduous student the whole of his life than William Etty, R.A. Never, so long as his health lasted, did he miss a single night at the night school, where his studies from the nude were the wonder and admiration of his fellow-students, young and old."

Queen Victoria died on 23rd January 1901, after a reign of sixty-three years, the longest of any British monarch. Her death marked the end of an era. That same year saw the publication of a book about York which was to have a profound effect on British social history. *Poverty, a study of town life* was written by Seebohm Rowntree, a member of the family of chocolate and cocoa manufacturers in the city. It dealt with the living conditions of the working people in York. As a Quaker, Rowntree had long been interested in working class problems, and the publication of a book by Charles Booth on contemporary social conditions in London shocked him into carrying out a similar investigation in York to see if the same depressing conditions existed there. During 1899-1901 he and his helpers visited 11,560 families in the city, drawing up an account of the income and expenditure of each household. In eighteen instances they compiled detailed lists of their expenses.

In order to assess exactly what was meant by "poverty" Rowntree worked out how much money a family needed to pay for the bare necessities of life—food, fuel, clothes and rent. He concluded that a single person needed seven shillings a week; a man and wife 11s 8d; a family with two children 18s 10d and one with four children 26s. In case anyone should accuse him of being too generous he explained carefully what this did *not* include.

The family must never spend a penny on railway fare or omnibus. They must never go into the country unless they walk. They must never purchase a halfpenny newspaper or spend a penny to buy a ticket for a popular concert. They must write no letters to absent children, for they cannot afford to pay the postage. They must never contribute anything to their church or chapel, or give any help to a neighbour which costs them money. They cannot save, nor can they join sick club or Trade Union, because they cannot pay the necessary subscriptions. The children must have no pocket money for dolls, marbles, or sweets. The father must smoke no tobacco, and must drink no beer. The mother must never buy any pretty clothes for herself or for her children. . . Should a child fall ill, it must be attended by the parish doctor;

should it die, it must be buried by the parish. Finally, the wage-earner must never be absent from his work for a single day.

Rowntree's conclusions were that in York 1,465 families, or nearly ten per cent of the population, were living below the "poverty line". Rowntree then analysed the causes of this poverty. The popular belief among well-to-do Victorians was that it was due to improvidence—because the father was lazy and work-shy and the mother was a feckless spendthrift, careless in her household management. In other words "the poor" were thriftless folk whose misery was largely their own fault. Rowntree disproved this. He showed that well over half of those below the poverty line were poor despite the fact that the husband was in regular employment and that the wife was careful and efficient in running her house. The main cause of poverty was appallingly low wages. Another was lack of provision of unemployment or sickness benefit to help the family, should the breadwinner—through sickness or old age—lose his job.

The book is of great interest to us today as it gives a vivid picture of the life of the ordinary man and woman in York in 1901. Here is what Rowntree wrote about one of the families which he visited:

Carter   Wages (regular) 20s.

The father drives a lorry; he is now in regular work, but was out of work for six months last year. During that period the family incurred a heavy debt, which Mrs. D. is now striving to clear off. Questioned as to how they lived during these six months when Mr. D. was earning no regular money, Mrs. D. replied that she didn't know; her brother was very kind to her and bought shoes for herself and the children, her mother gave her odd things, and for the rest they got into debt.

There are two children, a boy aged 5, and a little girl aged 2. The children do not look very strong, and are just recovering from the whooping-cough.

The mother lacks method, and always apologises for the house and children being dirty. Although the house in which the family live contains only three rooms, it is three storeys high. From the living room you go upstairs straight into the bedroom, and from that by means of a ladder into the attic. The only place for keeping food in is an unventilated cupboard under the stairs. There is a water-tap in the living room, in a corner behind the entrance door, but as there is no sink or drain the droppings from the tap fall on to the floor, which consists of red bricks, badly broken and uneven. The floor is partly covered with a piece of linoleum, in addition to which there are several woollen rag mats about. The fireplace is usually untidy. A square table (generally covered with dirty cups, saucers, plates, etc.) occupies the centre of the room, around the sides of which there are two wooden easy-chairs, a sofa covered with American cloth, and a large chest of drawers. Under the window stands a table on which many house-hold treasures are displayed—fancy vases, glass slippers, photo-graphs, etc. There are several framed photographs on the wall, and an unframed almanac or two. The house is situated down a narrow cobbled thoroughfare, and being faced by a high brick wall it gets very little sun. The rent is 3s. per week.

The meals are fairly regular, Mr. D. coming home for them. One day when the investigator was making a call on Mrs. D. the little boy came running in to his mother with 2½d. in his hand, and the message, "Father will be home at 12 o'clock and wants something good for his dinner, and here is some money to buy it with." Mrs. D. appears to do her principal shopping at the end of the week, and deals at the Co-operative Stores. She makes her own bread. She is glad to do a day's charing, or will do plain sewing at home, but her needlework is not very good, so that it is difficult to find work for her, as she has no sewing machine. Although Mrs. D. lacks method she has great ideas of keeping her house, etc. nice, and always imagines that when they "get round a bit" it will be easier to do so.

STATEMENT OF INCOME AND EXPENDITURE FOR EIGHT WEEKS

Income:						
	Eight weeks' wages at 20s.			£8	0	0
	Overtime.				4	6
	Mrs. D.				10	0
				£8	14	6
Expenditure:	Food, including beverages	£3	19	0		
	Rent and rates	1	4	0		
	Coals and firewood	1	1	3		

Oil, matches, candles		2	8
Soap, etc.		1	5½
Sundries		2	3½
Sick Club		8	3
Life Insurance		6	5
Clothes		8	9½
Boots		5	10½
Doctor's Bill		9	9
Repayment of debt		5	0
	£8	14	9
Deficit	0 0	3	£8 14 6

PURCHASES DURING WEEK ENDING FEBRUARY 22, 1901

Friday:	2 bags of coal..........	£0	2	6
	1½ stone flour..........		2	0
	yeast.................			1
	4 lbs. sugar............			7
	½ lb. tea..............			4½
	1 lb. butter...........		1	0
	3½ lbs. bacon..........		1	5
	firewood..............			2
	½ lb. lard.............			2½
	baking powder........			1
	6 eggs................			6
	candles..............			1
	matches..............			½
	1 lb. soap............			2
	starch................			1
	soda.................			1
Saturday:	Doctor's bill..........		1	3
	frying pan............			6½
	2 teaspoons...........			1
	1 tablespoon..........			2
	½ st. potatoes.........			5
	cabbage..............			2
	3 lbs. pork...........		1	7½
	1 lb. onions..........			1
	1 qt. oil..............			2½
	½ lb. rice.............			1
	milk.................			1

$\frac{1}{4}$ lb. coffee   3

kippers   2

2 tins condensed milk . . .   5

Monday: Insurance   11

Club   1   3

Doctor's bill   1   3

Tuesday: Debt   1   0

1 lb. figs   5

	Breakfast	Dinner	Tea	Supper
Friday	Bread, butter, tea.	Bread, butter, toast, tea.	Bread, butter, tea.	
Saturday	Bread, bacon, coffee.	Bacon, potatoes, pudding, tea.	Bread, butter, shortcake, tea	Tea, bread, kippers.
Sunday	Bread, butter, shortcake, coffee.	Pork, onions, potatoes, Yorkshire pudding.	Bread, butter shortcake, tea.	Bread and meat.
Monday	Bread, bacon, butter, tea.	Pork, potatoes, pudding, tea.	Bread, butter, tea.	One cup of tea.
Tuesday	Bread, bacon, butter, coffee	Pork, bread, tea.	Bread, butter, boiled eggs, tea.	Bread, bacon, butter, tea.
Wednesday	Bread, bacon, butter, tea.	Bacon and eggs, potatoes, bread, tea.	Bread, butter, tea.	
Thursday	Bread, butter, coffee	Bread, bacon, tea.	Bread, butter, tea.	

At this time Britain was the richest country in the world and the head of a vast empire. Until these statistics became available few people would believe that one-tenth of the population lived in such poverty that they could not afford the bare necessities of life. Booth's report on London—the capital city—and Rowntree's report on York—a typical provincial town—had a profound effect on public opinion, on the Liberal Party in Parliament and on statesmen such as Asquith and Lloyd George. Ultimately they did much to bring about the emergence of the modern Welfare State.

12. TWENTIETH CENTURY YORK

Since 1900 the three confectionery firms of Rowntree, Terry and Cravens have been the largest employers of labour in York. They have made amazing growth this century and now export to all parts of the world. In 1901 they employed nearly 2,000 persons, in 1911, 4,000, in 1939, 12,000 and in 1970, 15,000. The second largest group is the railway. This employed 5,500 in 1938 and 8,000 today. These two groups between them employ about half the working population of the city. The only industry of any appreciable size to be established this century is the British Sugar Corporation which set up its plant at Acomb to process sugar-beet grown on the rich farmlands of the plain of York. Messrs Cooke, Troughton and Simms—precision instrument makers—were established about 1870. Today, the other important employing bodies are the distribution trades (shops and stores) and government services (national and local). York still has a flourishing weekly market attended by farmers from far afield. In 1970 over $3\frac{1}{2}$ million cattle, sheep and pigs were bought and sold there. It has long been an important centre for the sale of Irish cattle, which are shipped from Ireland to Liverpool, brought by train to York and there sold to farmers who fatten them for the slaughterhouses of the West Riding cities.

As the city expanded to take in the surrounding villages and as new municipal building estates have been developed, especially in the Acomb and Dringhouses areas, so people have had to travel longer and longer distances to work. So the problem of local transport has increased. The earliest form of public transport in York was provided in the eighteenth century by chairmen (carriers of sedan chairs) and hackney

The horse-drawn trams

coachmen. In 1763 they were licensed for the first time and their charges fixed. About 1835 horse-drawn omnibuses were introduced, being later replaced by horse-drawn trams. In 1879 the York Tramways Company took these over and eventually introduced first steam and then electric driven trams. In 1909 this company was taken over by the Corporation. Trams were never a success, as the problems presented by the narrow streets, the walls, bars and bridges and the steep incline of Micklegate Hill were considerable. Even when the trams were electrified, horses still had to pull them up Micklegate! In 1915 petrol-driven buses were introduced and these gradually replaced the trams. In 1934 an arrangement was reached by which the Corporation and the West Yorkshire Road Car Company jointly ran the transport services. In the following year the trams were abolished.

The wars of the twentieth century have left their mark on York as on all other European cities. Two War Memorials—

one in Station Rise and the other in the garden off Leeman Road
—stand as sentinels to the memory of the dead of World War I
(1914–18) and World War II (1939–45). In the second of these
wars death and destruction actually took place in the city
after a space of 300 years.

The night of 29th April 1942 was clear and bright. York
Minster lay bathed in brilliant moonlight. The city of York,
which in its long history had undergone attacks by land and
by river, was about to experience another, this time by air.
(There had been Zeppelins over the city during the First World
War when they did a little damage.) About midnight air-raid
warnings sounded and a few minutes later German aircraft
were over the city dropping flares. They were closely followed
by some twenty bombers which dived low to drop their loads.
One York newspaper described it thus: "Showers of incendiaries
were dropped, followed by high explosives and the raiders
dived and machine-gunned blazing buildings and streets."

While York had expected such a raid, the defences were
woefully inadequate. A few searchlight beams raked the sky

The German raids on York

but anti-aircraft fire and air cover were virtually nil. Even the air raid warning siren failed to sound owing to defective mechanism! Soon numerous fires blazed in the city, far too many for the fire-brigade, fire-watchers and civilians to cope with. The biggest fires gutted two of York's oldest and most historic buildings—the church of St Martin-le-Grand in Coney Street and the Guildhall only 150 yards away. Both buildings had stood in York for over 500 years; they were burnt out in less than five hours. One of the glories of St Martin's Church was its great west window containing rare medieval stained glass depicting the life of its patron saint, St Martin of Tours. Fortunately the glass had been removed to a safe place before 1939 in anticipation of just such an attack. The church is now restored; the window has been moved to a new position and the glass replaced in it. It is breath-taking in its size, detail and magnificence.

There was a particularly ironic twist to the destruction of the Guildhall. When the air raid took place a renovation scheme costing £12,000 and necessitated by the ravages of the death-watch beetle was within three weeks of completion. It

had been in progress for three years! When the fire was finally extinguished the steel scaffolding which had been used in the repair work stood mockingly above the ashes.

The following day a York newspaper describing the event had this to say: "The Germans say the raid on York was a reprisal for 'the British air attacks on the civil population of Cologne'. They claim 'good results' were achieved with high-explosive and incendiary bombs." This statement gave rise to the belief—still held by many York people—that the Germans had intended to destroy the Minster and that this was a so-called "Baedeker Raid". The name arose in this way. Before the war the German firm of Baedeker published guidebooks of towns likely to be of interest to Germans visiting Britain. It was British propaganda to argue that, in retaliation for Allied raids on historic German cities such as Cologne, the German High Command thumbed through these guides selecting towns with famous cathedrals such as Coventry, Canterbury and York, which were to be systematically destroyed.

As far as York was concerned this was not true. German documents captured after the war and now housed in the restored York Guildhall consist of maps of the city on which the targets for this particular raid are ringed. The places scheduled for bombing are Lendal Bridge, the Railway Station and the adjoining marshalling yards—all "legitimate" bombing objectives. Clearly the German bombers—probably harassed by the anti-aircraft fire which they encountered—misjudged their targets.

After the war it was decided to rebuild the Guildhall exactly as it had been before 1942 except for minor details such as the lighting. Clearly it was impossible to replace the Victorian glass in the windows. Except for the west window, which is filled with modern stained glass, the other windows now contain plain glass. The building is supported (as it was originally in the Middle Ages) by twelve huge wooden pillars each twenty feet tall and four feet in diameter, each hewn from a single oak tree. The new ones came from Lord Feversham's estate at Duncombe Park near Helmsley. The rebuilding began in 1958 and was completed two years later when the opening ceremony was performed by Her Royal Highness Queen Elizabeth, the Queen Mother.

In order to foster better international relations after the war York "twinned up" with the French town of Dijon and the German one of Munster. Each year the civic dignitaries of these cities exchange visits. Civic leaders from Munster were present at the opening ceremonies of the new Guildhall on 19th June 1960. In the course of his speech of welcome the Lord Mayor of York (Alderman William Ward) said:

> It was fitting that they [the Germans] should be there for the re-opening of the restored Guildhall as some York people had been for the re-opening of Munster's Rathaus [Guildhall]. . . . Both of our peoples played their part in the destruction of these. We are glad now and happy that we can instead live in that peace and harmony which we all so much desire.

When planning the new Guildhall it was decided that the west window should depict scenes and persons from York's past and present. The various subjects were chosen by the late Dean of York (Rev. Eric Milner-White) while Harry Harvey of York was commissioned to design and make the window. It is a magnificent example of the modern glazier's art. As a lecturer in history at St John's College in York, I find it a first-class teaching aid, being, in miniature, a pictorial history of the city. It has supplied the material for many a history "lesson". Each September when I meet my new students for the first time I take them on a tour of the city. The final visit is to the Guildhall where we study this window in detail. The window consists of five main lights or divisions. Above these, set in the tracery, are twelve small panels, two of which contain heraldic shields and ten the figures of important people.

The first light is concerned with architecture and shows the Minster, the Merchant Adventurers' Hall, together with the four bars or gateways of the city—Bootham, Micklegate, Monk and Walmgate. The second light records the military history of York. Three cavalrymen remind us that from AD

71 until AD 410 Eburacum was one of the most important places in Roman Britain. A Viking longboat recalls the Danish attack on York in AD 867 and the Danish kingdom centred on the city for the next two hundred years. The Siege of York of 1644 during the Civil War is shown by Royalists defending the walls against Parliamentarians. The last scene in this light is of the west window itself, on fire as a result of the German air raid of 1942.

The centre light deals with civic affairs. Below the arms of the city is a modern civic procession with the Lord Mayor, aldermen and councillors wearing their robes of office. They are accompanied by the mace-bearer and sword-bearer. Another scene shows a herald on horseback proclaiming the opening of the Mystery Plays. With him is one of the pageant wagons in the form of Noah's Ark as the particular play being enacted is that of the Flood. Onlookers are shown dressed in both medieval and modern dress to remind the visitor of both the medieval beginnings of these plays and also of their modern revival as the central feature of the York Triennial Festival.

The fourth light features aspects of York as a centre of commerce and transport. Below a medieval market scene is a sailing ship of the type used by the Merchant Adventurers in the later Middle Ages. The coming of the railways is represented by an early locomotive, while the significance to York of the river Ouse is shown by a picture of the old Ouse Bridge with its five arches and houses built upon it.

The religious and cultural history of the city is portrayed in the fifth light. The baptism of King Edwin by Paulinus in AD 627 in the first Minster is shown. St Hilda, King Edwin's niece and the foundress of Whitby Abbey, is one of the congregation. Below this is Alcuin teaching in the Minster School and below that a couple in Georgian attire dancing in the Assembly Rooms.

The first and fifth lights are surmounted by three white Yorkshire roses, while the second and fourth are surmounted by the same number of red and white Tudor ones. Above the five lights, in the tracery, are two rows of emblems and figures.

In the top row are the arms—those of the Glaziers Guild and of the Merchant Adventurers' Company—while the figures are those of John Thornton, designer of the great east window of the Minster, the Emperor Constantine who started his dazzling career as ruler of the Roman world here in Eburacum, King Athelstan, the first Anglo-Saxon king of *all* England and founder of St Leonard's Hospital in York and finally the York painter William Etty. On the lower row in the tracery are portrayed Archbishop Walter de Gray holding in his hands a model of the Minster, Thomas, Lord Fairfax, Parliamentarian General in the Civil War, King Edward III and his wife Philippa of Hainault who were married in the Minster, Robinson Crusoe who was "born" in York and finally Richard, Earl of Burlington, the architect of the Georgian Assembly Rooms.

The twentieth century saw the fulfilment of a long-time dream—the foundation of a university. On a number of occasions since the golden days of Alcuin in the eighth century the foundation of a university in York was mooted. Not until 1963 did this actually take place. Two of the men who had much to do with its foundation were the late Dean of York, Rev. Eric Milner-White, and the late Mr J. B. Morrell. The latter purchased the Elizabethan mansion, Heslington Hall, on the outskirts of York, and presented it to the University. During the last few years a vast amount of building has been done on the site adjoining the Hall and the university now houses over 2,000 students.

Mr Morrell was also instrumental in founding another major cultural attraction in York. During his lifetime (1869–1940) the late Dr John L. Kirk of Pickering collected many "bye-gones" which were in danger of being lost or destroyed. These ranged from timber-framed buildings, which he dismantled, to fire-engines, hansom cabs and more mundane objects such as chairs, ornaments and kitchen utensils. In 1935 these were presented to the City of York and housed in the Female Prison near Clifford's Tower. They constituted the nucleus of the Castle Museum, one of the finest folk museums in the world.

In 1969, 762,000 people visited it. In the summer months long queues of schoolchildren from all parts of the north of England are to be seen passing through its period rooms, its famous "street" reconstructed from demolished buildings—and its shops and work-rooms.

York has two other fine museums—the Yorkshire Museum in the Museum Gardens and the Railway Museum in Queen Street. The former houses a large collection of geological, prehistoric, Roman and medieval material while the latter is the mecca of all those interested in the early history of the steam locomotive.

The present century has made four notable contributions to the architecture of York. The extensions to the various factories and the huge re-housing schemes in the city have produced almost no buildings of any merit. The university complex, the telephone exchange in Hungate, the extensions to the Theatre Royal and the Yorkshire Insurance Offices in Rougier Street are the only exceptions—and they, too, have their detractors. On the other hand buildings in Stonebow and

Part of York University

Goodramgate are a disgrace to the city and have aroused considerable anger and criticism.

One of the outstanding changes in life in the present century is the greater facilities for travel. This, in turn, has led to tourism becoming a major industry. York's glorious Minster, its ancient churches, Roman remains, walls, Guildhalls, museums, its picturesque streets such as the Shambles, Stonegate and Petergate, timber-framed buildings, Georgian houses, Treasurer's House and the Mansion House—to name but a few of its treasures—are becoming known to ever-increasing circles of British and foreign visitors. However, the city is still not fully aware of its potentialities in this sphere. The York Civic Trust, an independent body of York citizens, is anxious to do everything it can to preserve what is good of the past and to use these as a magnet to attract the tourist. However, the Corporation and the shopkeepers are not yet convinced that it is in this sphere that the future of York lies. In 1966 Lord Esher was invited by the Government to make a survey of the city and to report on ways and means that its exciting physical heritage might be preserved and the area inside the walls restored as a place where people live and work as in the great days of the past. So far York has been slow to respond to his suggestions. There are few cities in Britain where so much of the past survives. The late King George V went so far as to say, "The history of York is the history of England". A building, once destroyed, can never be replaced. It is the duty of this generation to conserve and treasure what remains.

What of York today? It is still the seat of the Archbishop and the centre of Church activity and administration in the north of England; the assize town for the Ainsty—the area immediately around York—and the North and East Ridings of Yorkshire; a vital link in the main railway communications between London and Edinburgh; the scene of the weekly market; headquarters of Northern Command of the Army; the centre of a new, adventurous and thriving university; a commercial and industrial centre, small by comparison with the neighbouring giants of Leeds and Bradford, but prosperous, successful and with branded manufactures essentially its own.

York's central situation and good transport facilities by rail and by road mean that seaside resorts such as Scarborough, Bridlington and Filey, the glorious dales and moors of north-east Yorkshire, together with the stately homes, ruined abbeys and ancient castles for which Yorkshire is famed are within easy reach of its citizens. Leeds, part of the vast industrial conurbation of the West Riding, is only thirty miles to the west.

The river Ouse has always been important to York. Not only did it provide one of the strategic reasons for the siting of the original city, but it has provided a valuable highway ever since, sometimes a highway for war as in the original Anglian and Danish invasions, but usually for peaceful trading purposes. The prosperity of the medieval York Merchant Adventurers was due to the use of the river for their trade with the towns of the Hanseatic League in the Baltic Sea, and though York is no longer a "staple" town, many of its modern factories still get much of their raw material by barge from Hull. The City Council is still responsible, as it has been since the Middle Ages, for the navigation of the Ouse until it becomes the Humber. In another way the river is absolutely vital to the life of the city—it provides a never failing water supply, some ten million gallons being pumped daily from it into nearby reservoirs.

The city is also a focal point for shopping, entertainment and education over a wide area. Within its walls are to be found shops to suit all tastes—department stores, supermarkets, craft and antique shops and those offering the specialized services that only small, privately owned establishments can offer. It is to be hoped that before long the suggested scheme of making certain streets, especially Stonegate—described as the "finest street in Europe"—into shopping precincts, prohibited to vehicular traffic, will be implemented.

In the realm of sport, York Races, held since 1731 on the Knavesmire, are among the most picturesque, best organized and best patronized in England. The city has two professional football teams: one plays in the Northern Rugby Football League while the soccer eleven plays in the Fourth Division of the Football League. In 1959 the latter, "the Robins" to their supporters, achieved fame when, as a lowly Third Division club, they reached the semi-final of the F.A. Cup.

The Theatre Royal in St Leonard's is one of the cultural centres of the city. Its resident Repertory Company is one of the most progressive in Britain and many of its former players such as John Barrie, John Alderton and Althea Charlton are nationwide celebrities on television and radio. The theatre is an interesting building. Most of what is visible today is nineteenth century built on eighteenth century foundations but, incorporated into it are stone walls and vaulting belonging to the twelfth century Hospital of St Leonard.

The school population of York is now about 18,000, education being provided by forty-two primary schools, thirteen secondary modern schools, four maintained grammar schools and four special schools. The Central College of Further Education, the School of Art, the York Settlement, Marygate Centre of Further Education and other institutions of adult education provide a variety of vocational and recreational courses for young people and adults. The city also has a number of well-known independent schools, including St Peter's— the lineal descendant of Alcuin's ninth century Minster school —Bootham School for Boys, the Mount School for Girls and the York College for Girls.

York has long spread far beyond the city walls. Acomb which, a century ago, was a picturesque country village, frequently visited by citizens for "a day out" in summer because its elevated position made it cool and breezy, is now linked to the old city by streets lined with brick and stone houses and constitutes the largest suburb of modern York. Greater York extends two to three miles in all directions beyond its walled core.

York has always been an important traffic centre—pack-horses and wagons in the Middle Ages, coaches in the eighteenth and early nineteenth centuries and now buses, coaches, cars and motor cycles. The city is notorious as a bottleneck for road transport. This is one of its major problems today. The solution lies either in the building of new bridges, the construction of ring-roads or the total prohibition of cars in certain areas within the city. It is at night, when the commercial traffic of the day has gone, when the shops are aglow with their neon lighting, when the Minster's great central tower is floodlit, that the true glory of York can be appreciated. It is then that its ancient buildings come again to life and its ghosts walk. It is then that the full meaning of this passage by the York historian Charles B. Knight is best appreciated:

But the greatest attribute of all she ever possessed, she still possesses. Nothing can take it from her, nothing can belittle, nothing overshadow, the peerless record of [nineteen] centuries of vivid life, or dishonour that ancient fame which all York men can justly appropriate as their own proudest boast. The history of York falls somewhat short of being a complete epitome of English history; but it is almost a complete index.

The active and leading part the city played in the making of the English realm and the English nation; her streets and halls time and time again the scene of events whose significance and effect have influenced the course of the nation's history: the long list of names which adorn England's roll of fame—of kings, nobles, ecclesiastics, statesmen, soldiers, merchants—whose feet have trodden her ancient ways and who within her walls have planned and brought forth some of the most notable schemes, for good or ill, in English story; the memory of generation after generation of those whose names have not endured, but who in their day upheld the honour and fame of the city in intellectual and artistic attainment, in craftsmanship, or by force of arms diversely in England, Scotland, in a Breton harbour, or in South Africa— all these are hers; gloriously, surely, irrevocably. Who among her sons today does not feel his heart burn within him as he calls these things to remembrance, or experiences no thrill of pride at sharing in so great a heritage?

The Minster and City Walls from Station Rise

FURTHER READING

GEORGE BENSON, *York*. Three volumes 1911, 1919 and 1925 (Republished by S. R. Publishers Ltd, 1968).

A. L. BINNS, *The Viking Century in East Yorkshire* (East Yorkshire Local History, Series no. 15, 1962).

A. L. BINNS, *East Yorkshire in the Sagas* (E.Y.L.H.S. no. 22, 1966).

F. W. BROOKS, *The Battle of Stamford Bridge* (E.Y.L.H.S. no. 6, 1963).

F. W. BROOKS, *Domesday Book and the East Riding* (E.Y.L.H.S. no. 21, 1966).

The City of York. The Victoria County History of England, ed. P. M. Tillott (O.U.P., 1961).

FRANCIS DRAKE, *Eboracum* (London, 1736).

Eburacum, Roman York. An inventory of the Historical Monuments in the City of York (Royal Commission on Historical Monuments, 1962).

Georgian Houses in York (York Georgian Society, 1969).

CHARLES B. KNIGHT, *This is York* (Herald Printing Works, 1951).

PETER WENHAM, *The Great and Close Siege of York 1644* (Roundwood Press, 1970).

PETER WENHAM, *Eboracum*. Ginn History Patch Series, The Romans (Ginn, 1971).

PETER WENHAM, *Gray's Court (St John's College) York* (Ellesmere Press, 1966).

York. A summary 1959. Published by the Local Executive Committee on the occasion of the meeting of the British Association in York, 1959.

PETER YOUNG, *Marston Moor 1644* (Roundwood Press, 1970).

INDEX

WHY ERP?

A Primer on SAP Implementation

WHY ERP?

A Primer on SAP Implementation

F. Robert Jacobs
Indiana University

D. Clay Whybark
University of North Carolina

Boston   Burr Ridge, IL   Dubuque, IA   Madison, WI
New York   San Francisco   St. Louis
Bangkok   Bogotá   Caracas   Lisbon   London   Madrid   Mexico City
Milan   New Delhi   Seoul   Singapore   Sydney   Taipei   Toronto

McGraw-Hill Higher Education

A Division of The **McGraw-Hill** *Companies*

WHY ERP? A PRIMER ON SAP IMPLEMENTATION
Copyright © 2000 by The McGraw-Hill Companies, Inc. All rights reserved. Printed in the United States of America. Except as permitted under the United States Copyright Act of 1976, no part of this publication may be reproduced or distributed in any form or by any means, or stored in a database or retrieval system, without the prior written permission of the publisher.

This book is printed on acid-free paper.

3 4 5 6 7 8 9 0   QPF/QPF   0 5 4 3 2 1 0

ISBN 0-07-240089-7

Vice president/Editor-in-chief: Michael W. Junior
Publisher: Jeffrey J. Shelstad
Executive editor: Richard T. Hercher, Jr.
Marketing manager: Zina Craft
Project manager: Jim Labeots
Manager, new book production: Melonie Salvati
Coordinator freelance design: Mary L. Christianson
Compositor: Electronic Publishing Services, Inc., TN
Typeface: 10.5/12.5 Times Roman
Printer: Quebecor Printing Book Group/Fairfield

Library of Congress Card Number:
99-068246

http://www.mhhe.com

Contents

Preface to Why ERP?

This is a book about ERP systems, enterprise resource planning systems. Now you see why we have done the book. We had to ask too, especially with all the press such systems are getting! ERP systems are large computer systems that integrate application programs in accounting (i.e., accounts receivable), sales (i.e., order booking), manufacturing (i.e., product shipping), and the other functions in the firm. This integration is accomplished through a database shared by all the application programs.

When you first see an ERP program, the application programs are similar to those with which you are already familiar. So the production scheduling, billing a customer, processing a payroll, and other tasks are done in ways that should be pretty familiar to those of you who have worked with these applications over the years. So what is the big deal? Integration! ERP systems tie these, usually separate, applications together. When a customer service representative takes a sales order it is entered in the common database and in the other applications where it is needed, for example, in the manufacturing backlog, the credit system, and the shipping schedule. No more carrying little pieces of paper back and forth. Or writing translation programs to get the information from one function to another. Sounds great, right? Read on!

ERP systems work in real-time, meaning that the exact status of everything is always available. Further, many of these systems are global. Since they can be deployed at sites around the world, they can work in multiple languages and currencies. When they are, you can immediately see, for example, exactly how much of a particular part is on-hand at the warehouse in Japan and what its value is in yen or dollars. This is a pretty amazing accomplishment. Sound too good to be true? Well, that is one of the reasons you should read this book. All this doesn't come free.

That was another reason for doing this book and for you to read it. It is not just about how these systems work, although there is that. In addition to the technical details, the way the hardware and software are organized, and technically how the logic of the system functions, there is another aspect to understanding ERP. It is the management and implementation issues associated with the systems. We focus much of the book on these concerns, in our view the most important of all. Whether you are considering the use of ERP, are faced (forced?) with implementation, or are just generally concerned about the management issues involved in using ERP systems, we feel you should understand some of the tradeoffs involved.

We are all concerned about keeping up with new technology and the challenge that this poses. The pervasive promotion and use of ERP systems suggest that, for this technology, we need to understand the scope of these systems and have a basic knowledge of how they work. Fortunately, learning about ERP is not so much learning all-new concepts and ideas, but rather learning about new ways to do things that we already have been doing and the ERP terminology associated with them. This means, whether you are a general manager, information system executive, an accountant, or a student, you already know more about how ERP works than you think you do, but you still need to learn the managerial issues associated with the degree of integration they support.

This book uses SAP R/3 as an example ERP, but the issues are the same whether you are talking about BAAN, JD Edwards, PeopleSoft, Oracle, or any of the other 30–40 ERP offerings. In terms of deployment it has been estimated that SAP R/3 is used at more than 20,000 sites around the world, making it one of the most widely implemented comprehensive business software systems to date. Many of the largest companies in the world use the package. Oh, before you ask, we know that we have used different releases of R/3 for the figures in the book. We choose the release that produced the most readable figures for the examples being shown.

We realized early on that this could be an extremely tedious, boring topic. So, to make it more interesting for you and us we decided to write a novel instead of a textbook. The main character is Billy, a manufacturing manager at a furniture plant in North Carolina. He faced what some of you have faced, are currently facing, or will face: a mandated consideration of an ERP implementation. Other important characters are Prof, a professor from the local university who acts as a sounding board for Billy's ideas and provides advice from time to time, and Ruth, who owns the local café and keeps the coffee flowing as Billy tries to figure out what to do.

In the first part of the book, Billy learns about ERP systems like SAP R/3 and some of the issues that are associated with buying and installing them. Billy's boss, Mr. McDougle, who owns the company, has an opportunity to expand the business by buying his brother's furniture manufacturing plant in Ohio. As luck would have it, the plant in Ohio is already using SAP

R/3 and Mr. McDougle wants to get some efficiency by running the same software at both plants. While this sounds like a great idea there are more than a few problems in the details and, of course, Billy feels his plant is operating just fine with its existing software systems, thank you.

In the second section of the book, Billy goes to an SAP training seminar and you will be sitting right next to him all along. Billy attends the seminar to learn more about the system and to determine whether it is appropriate for his company. He is introduced to ERP concepts, the SAP R/3 software, some of the functionality, how the hardware is configured and a technique to help with the implementation. We hope that Billy asks some of the same questions that you would have or will in a similar situation.

In the third section, Billy is charged with evaluating the SAP R/3 installation in use at the Ohio plant. The implication is that he will end up being charged with implementing the software in North Carolina. He travels to Ohio and learns about how that plant works and compares it to what he knows about the plant in North Carolina. He ends up with all kinds of questions about transferring the software from the Ohio plant to the North Carolina plant. In the end, Billy has to present his boss with his recommendations and, in the process, develops some guidelines for how ERP systems should be implemented. You may be interested in what Billy actually decides to do. We wonder whether you will agree with his decisions.

We sincerely hope you enjoy reading the book.

F. Robert Jacobs, Bloomington, Indiana

D. Clay Whybark, Chapel Hill, North Carolina

October 1999

Acknowledgments

We start with apologies to lawmen and gunslingers worldwide and to Wyatt Berry Stapp Earp in particular for the outrageous corruption of his name in titling this book. A number of people and institutions have made this book possible and to them we do owe a debt of gratitude. First off the Kelley School of Business at Indiana University and the Kenan-Flagler Business School at the University of North Carolina supported us in this effort. Particular thanks go to Deans Dan Dalton and Bob Sullivan for their encouragement. Thanks to George Hettenhouse at the Kelley School who provided the initial incentive to start this project.

The text was improved greatly by the comments of a number of reviewers. We would like in particular to recognize Urban Wemmerlöv at the University of Wisconsin for his careful reading and insightful comments. In addition, we had valuable feedback from Al Segars of the University of North Carolina and Jake Simons of Georgia Southern University. Several anonymous academic reviewers also contributed comments that improved the material.

A number of non-academics commented on the text, including Sam Anand of Glaxo Wellcome, Curt Helfrich of Bayor Corporation and Brian Swift of PeopleSoft, from our executive MBA programs. Their input was quite valuable. Thanks to Gloria Chou of Ford Motor Company for her great ideas on an early draft. Among the consultants who provided feedback, Ian Ward of the DynPro consulting company, Chapel Hill, North Carolina, was particularly helpful, as was Ron Silver and Richard Martin, independent consultants in Greensboro, North Carolina, and Bloomington, Indiana. Special thanks go to Gini Bright, whose encouragement lifted us over a tough spot.

At the McGraw-Hill Companies, Jeff Shelstad deserves a medal for putting up with our machinations and responding creatively and quickly to our requests. Dick Hercher took his share of lumps from us, but managed the project throughout. Thanks to both of them and the supporting cast in Burr Ridge, Illinois.

Finally, two great ladies, Jeanne Jacobs and Neva Whybark, patiently gave up their husbands for a few days, the phone for several evenings, and lots of time listening to us argue over text and laugh at Billy's various difficulties. Their feedback on the book was not only helpful to the text, but invaluable to keeping the project enjoyable. We love you both and you will get your dinner out.

Introduction to ERP   **I**

1. The vacation is over—What is ERP?

The car radio was on his favorite station as Billy Armbruster pulled out of his driveway and headed off to Ruth's Café. After two marvelous weeks of vacation with his family on the Carolina coast, he was looking forward to a cup of coffee and a bagel before heading back to work. As the song ended and the ads started, he was vaguely aware that the announcer was saying something about "providing solutions for small and medium size businesses in partnership with SAP."

"Jeez! I just can't seem to get away from it," he said as he punched the radio button for National Public Radio and listened to a segment of Morning Edition before he saw the red and white neon sign that was the magnet for the Café.

It was a little after 6:00 a.m. when Billy pulled the car into the parking lot at Ruth's Café. Whenever possible, he would stop here for breakfast before going to work as the manufacturing manager for a local furniture company. It was not just the coffee; he usually would see his friend, Professor Peter Kellsdorf, who taught in the business school at the local college. Stepping out of the car, he was much more aware of fall in the air than he had been last night on the family's return. Looking around the parking lot, he was disappointed not to see the professor's car. "Too bad," he thought, "Prof might know something about this SAP stuff."

"Hey, Billy, how was the vacation?" yelled Ruth from behind the counter.

1

"Great! Now all I have to do is pay the bills! How's it been around here? By the way, where's Prof? I thought for sure that I'd see him here this morning."

"I haven't seen him for a couple of days. He must be working for a living for a change. Still black?" she asked as she poured a cup of coffee.

"Yeah, but I'm changing the rules on you, Ruth, I'd like a raisin bagel this morning instead of garlic. I might have to talk to a lot of people at the plant today."

There were only three other people in the restaurant and Billy recognized two of them as morning regulars. After they exchanged greetings and insults about vacation, Billy began to think of the day ahead of him. He liked to be at Ruth's on the early side so he could get to the plant before the shift started. It gave him a chance to organize the workday and do a little paper work before chaos broke out. This day, he knew there would be a lot of material on his desk, even though he had checked in with the plant several times during the vacation.

Just then the door opened and Billy heard a voice behind him, "Hey, Billy, welcome back. How was the trip?"

As Billy turned around he saw Professor Kellsdorf come in the door and immediately responded, "Hey, Prof, come over here and sit down. Ruth's been spreading mean rumors around here about your having to work. Tell me it's not true. It would ruin your image. Besides, I need to get your opinion on something and it wouldn't be right for me to go into the plant without having a chance to swap lies with you."

Prof came over and sat down at the table and gave Ruth his order. He then turned to Billy and asked "How was your vacation, anyway, Billy?"

"It was really great! We had a good time with the kids and the weather held for us. I'm kind of sorry I had to come back and start work again."

"Well, you could always get a teaching job and stop working, you know. Ruth was wrong, I haven't taken on a real job yet. I'm still plodding along as Mr. Chips, just teaching my classes and keeping out of trouble with the Dean."

"Yeah, sure, I've seen what you do. I don't know if I want to put up with that kind of stuff. But I really do want to get your insights into something. While I was down on the coast, I attended a Rotary meeting and met a bunch of other tire-kicking, production geeks. All they could talk about was SAP and ERP and I felt out of it. What is this stuff? Is it just MRP in bigger font? Some of those guys talked like it was a silver bullet solution to all their problems, while others told horror stories. It sounded like the software from Hell."

"Hold on! Time out! Stop!" interjected Prof, "You sound just like the group we had in our executive program last week. They were buzzing about this ERP thing as well. Billy, I wish I had time to talk more about this now, but I need to get to the office. We've got a grant deadline today. Before we go, let me leave you with a few things to think about. Is it a silver bullet? Do you want to buy some beachfront property in Phoenix, Arizona? Come on, you know that no software can manage the company regardless of what the salespeople say. Managers manage the company. Now go away and practice your craft. I'll see you tomorrow."

2. At the plant—A new opportunity

Usually, when Billy arrived at the plant, he was the only one in the parking lot, other than the night watchman. Sometimes one of the other managers would also be there to get an early start on the day's work. He was surprised this morning to see both the finance and sales managers' cars in the lot. He wondered if he might have missed something during the last couple of days of his vacation. He resisted the temptation to say something to them and went directly to his office to confront the e-mail messages and paper piles.

The plant and corporate offices were housed in a single-story building on the outskirts of town. The building had been expanded and added to over the years, but recently had been treated to a major renovation that improved product flow in the factory, consolidated some of the administrative offices, and modernized the facility. The company, McDougle Furniture, had been in the McDougle family for several generations and produced a line of very fine handcrafted furniture for residences and offices. The company was founded in the foothills of the Smoky Mountains in western North Carolina in order to take advantage of the high-quality hard woods and labor force in the area.

McDougle's had always produced wood products and almost always had some furniture in the product line. During World War II, the company produced items to support the war effort; products like wooden ammunition crates, portable cot frames, wooden shipping containers, and the like. After the war, the pent-up demand for furniture was obvious and the family began to design and produce residential furniture. Since that time, furniture had come to dominate the company's products.

Their products achieved a reputation for high quality and their designs garnered many awards for innovation and style. As they did so, the stature of the company grew. The company's designers began to work with individual families and corporate customers to create exclusive pieces of furniture and suites for houses and offices. The business grew, but slowly. The McDougle family had always been concerned about providing employment for the work force and did not want to expand the business to the point where they might risk having to lay off people or find other ways of using the capacity. They had succeeded in managing demand by constantly improving the quality of their furniture, setting prices to control the backlog of orders and moderating the number of new customers that they took on.

At the current time the company produced custom products, mainly office furniture and furnishings for reception areas, for several large corporations with offices in the eastern United States. Although some of these companies were European and Asian, there were few export sales. In the residential market, several architects and interior decorators worked with the firm's designers to produce custom furniture for expensive homes in the southeast region of the U.S. McDougle Furniture also sent furniture to the High Point market, one of the industries' most important. This huge exhibit is where the company displayed furniture for some exclusive stores and contractors to see. Sometimes McDougle displayed furniture that was being developed for a customer, but mostly they would show speculation pieces and new designs to get customer reaction to their concepts.

The factory employed a very experienced and highly skilled work force. The McDougles had always treated their employees well and paid a premium over the local market for their people. They prided themselves on the apprentice-like system that's still in use on the factory floor. They contacted promising students from the local high school shop courses and hired them for summer jobs to see if they would work out for permanent positions. For each successful new hire in the plant, the company estimated it took something like 10 to 15 summer employees. There was something about finding people who had the "feel" of the high-quality furniture they were producing and who were willing to "sit at the feet of the masters" already there. The atmosphere in the factory was informal and the people would help one another out when there was a problem. It would be stretching it to say that there was a family feeling among the employees, but there was a real sense of camaraderie.

The company had installed a material requirements planning (MRP) system several years ago to help manage the production process. Basically it scheduled the purchase or production of all the pieces needed to make the furniture for a customer's order. The system had been tweaked to meet some of the unusual needs of the plant, particularly those involved with the long period of design and customizing practices. The time from initial conversation to delivery of a customized suite for a large reception area or an executive's office could be as much as eight months. During this time there might be several changes suggested by the customers and/or designers. The software had been tailored to allow bills of materials to be adjusted as these changes took place, even after the order had been released to the shop. It could still coordinate manufacturing, capacity, and delivery promises as the changes occurred. The company worked hard at estimating capacity requirements in order to minimize overtime and slack time in the plant. Admittedly, many of these adaptations to the software were based on the experience of the work force and managers. Although it was becoming a little dated, the software pretty well met the manufacturing needs of the plant.

Despite the informality and flexibility of the workforce, there was the usual tension between sales and manufacturing. The sales force wanted to accommodate the wishes of the customer in the design of the pieces, regardless of manufacturing difficulty, and was much more tolerant of late-breaking change requests. From a sales standpoint, forecasting was extremely difficult, since they never really knew which deals they might land. The production people had developed their own forecasting system as the basis for planning the long lead time items and managing capacity. Good wood, for example, was often difficult to get, so planning six to nine months into the future was very important.

As Billy entered his office he saw right away there were some changes since the last time he had checked. A couple of orders that he thought had already been shipped were still on the floor. One of these orders was a custom desk for an Atlanta lawyer—a big $20,000 order.

It looked like a large amount of raw material was stacked in the return area. In scanning the sheets for the previous week, he saw that some overtime had been used in trying to get caught up. He knew that two key people had been out sick and this apparently had caused some of the problems. He skimmed through the pile of papers on his desk and his e-mail to see if there was any crisis that needed attention. Nothing seemed to be badly out of control, but a couple of new complicated orders had just been loaded into the MRP system and he knew he'd have to follow up on those. The most important note he saw, however, was an e-mail that had been sent to most of the management team on Friday asking them to meet in the boardroom at 10:00 this morning.

Billy went around and said hello to a couple of the other managers before going out to check on the factory floor activities. They were not sure what the meeting was all about and didn't know of any crisis or major plans in the company. Billy went out to the shop, greeted the workers, and began to get caught up on what was going on in the factory. He managed to stay quite busy until the time of the meeting.

At the meeting Mr. McDougle, the CEO and Chairman of the Board, looked at each person in the room and then said, "I wanted all of you to know about a couple of things before the rumor mill starts working. I have been talking with my brother about his company up in Ohio. He is thinking about retiring and wants us to have right of first refusal on the business. Now this is all very much in the air, but my sister-in-law has let it be known that she wants him to start slowing down and so the rumors have already started up there. I will keep you informed about what is happening, but at the moment if you are asked, you can say that you know that my brother wants to retire but that nothing has been decided.

"The other topic is quite different. My brother has been asking me about our computer systems, how we like our MRP system, and whether we have been considering some of the new ERP systems. Yes, I know! I had to ask too! Enterprise resource planning systems. Coincidentally, I was invited to a function last week where I met the CEO of a company that is implementing such a system developed by Baan, apparently a leading supplier of the software. He said that it was more difficult than he had expected, but that they projected significant benefits, including better clerical efficiency, some reductions in overhead costs, and much better information for running the business. Later I heard an ad on our local station for another system called SAP. I'm not sure what these things are, but I feel that we need to learn about them. Billy, I'm going to ask you to help us do that. Can you stay a couple of minutes after the meeting?"

After a couple of questions about Mr. McDougle's brother's health (no problem) and some comments about things that various people had heard about SAP (a mixed bag), the meeting broke up. After talking a bit with Mr. McDougle it was clear to Billy that he didn't have a formal assignment and certainly wasn't going to be pulled out of his current job. He was, however, to learn about ERP systems in general and to make some assessment about whether they should be seriously considered for the company. As he left the boardroom, Billy got a sick, nervous feeling. He stopped at the vending machine and purchased a tube of Rolaids.

3. The next morning—It's sinking in

"Well, it's happened! I am trapped and being held captive by ERP and I don't even know what it is. Ruth, I need a cup of coffee!" moaned Billy at the Café the next morning. When Prof came in, Billy nearly knocked him down to get him to a table where they could talk.

"You won't believe what happened at the plant yesterday. The boss said that he wanted us to look at ERP systems for our plant because his brother asked him about whether we were considering them. He picked me to look into it, but didn't say anything about what I was to do while I did this. He did mention some company other than SAP that sells the software. Baan I think it's called. And to add insult to injury I called that 800 number that is advertised on the radio here and the line was busy. It seems to be the story of my life."

"Are you through?" asked Prof.

"Yeah! I still have all those questions from yesterday, but I really need the answers now. What do you mean that software doesn't manage the company?" asked Billy.

"Where should I start?" responded Prof. "Maybe I should start at the beginning. ERP. Enterprise resource planning. Billy, these systems are simply integrated information systems for the company, the enterprise."

"What do you mean integrated?"

"Well, first off that means that the accounting system talks to the sales system, which talks to the production system and so on. You and I have discussed this before. Remember that time you told me that you didn't bill a customer for the last shipment of his order? It went off your system, you sent the paper over to the accounting folks, they lost it and the customer conveniently didn't remind you that he owed you money. Well, your material requirements planning system didn't, I guess still doesn't, communicate with the accounting system, so you depend upon having an accountant reenter the information into their system in order to get the bill to the customer. But integration means that all the systems talk directly to each other. Some firms are even integrated with their suppliers' and customers' systems."

"You seem to be saying that there are other things that are implied in the integration."

"Well, yes. Integration does have another aspect. It means that the information that everybody uses is common. By that I mean there is one inventory number for an item, there is one value for monthly sales, there is a single production schedule, and only one accounts receivable amount. I'll bet that if you ask different groups in your company what last month's sales were, you'd get different answers. Sales in the accounting department would be the amount of income received while the sales people think of it as booked orders and you guys in production think it's shipments.

"I think," Prof continued, "that you can see that ERP systems provide the means for having a common, unique database for everybody to use. One other thing about this aspect of integration is that the data are made available in real time in most modern systems. The information is updated as changes occur and the new status is available for everybody to use to manage their part of the business."

"It does sound like the silver bullet idea. I can see enterprise, but where do the words resource and planning come from?"

"I don't know. Maybe from material requirements planning. Remember that some people now say that MRP stands for manufacturing resource planning. Since MRP seems to form the heart of the production system in these approaches, it's plausible. Other people have the idea that the resources correspond to business functions as we talk about them today. For example, there are parts of an ERP system that correspond to the Human Resource function, the Accounting function, the Purchasing function, and so on. I guess these would be like people, money and material resources. The planning aspect is a mystery to me. I don't see much planning capability except where MRP is used in the production area. The easiest way to think of ERP is as a big information system that everybody has access to."

"Billy, the phone's for you!" Ruth was yelling across the room. "It's Jerry from the plant."

As Billy left to answer the phone, Ruth started to pour some coffee for Prof, but he protested and said that he needed to get to the office. "It doesn't look like Billy is going to be able to talk any more anyway. Say, who is Jerry? Do you know?" asked Prof.

"Yeah! Jerry is Jerry Mancora, the sales manager for McDougle's Furniture. I'm sure you have met him." replied Ruth.

"Sure enough," Billy came back and said, "I need to get over to the plant. It seems that we've lost somebody's desk and Jerry is really steaming. He tried to call me at home last night while we were out. Sheesh! It's going to be a long day."

"Let me make it longer." said Prof. "While you're in the plant find out how many different forecasts you have for next month. Also, how many people are involved in putting a customer order into the computer? I want to talk to you about that next time we get together."

4. Information crisis—The missing desk

"Okay, Jerry, what's up?"

"I'll tell you what's up! $20,000 is what's up. We've lost the desk for that lawyer in Atlanta. You remember the one that was supposed to ship a couple of weeks ago. He called me yesterday and said enough is enough. He reminded me of all the delays we had since he first placed the order. I reminded him of all the changes he wanted made. He reminded me that the last notice he got after the final change was that the desk would be there no later than last week. Well, he didn't believe us so he postponed some big cocktail party until this week so the desk would be there. I stopped reminding him of stuff and said I'd find out what was going on." Jerry was not happy.

"What did you find out?"

"Nothing. I went out in the shop yesterday evening and couldn't find the darn thing. I tried to call you at home but I guess you didn't get enough vacation."

"Wait a minute, going over to the in-laws to swap the pictures of sand we each took at the beach isn't exactly an extended vacation. How the heck can we lose a lawyer's desk?" Billy was not happy.

"I don't know and neither did the two guys I talked to from the shop. They said it was still sitting there yesterday. What is going on anyway?" asked Jerry.

"Well, I remember now. There was a delay because of the last minute change in some of the hardware that the guy wanted. Remember we found out the vendor couldn't ship that until last week and then we needed some time to make sure the finish was okay. When we ran the MRP system to check the schedules, I learned that desk wouldn't ship until late last week, but it didn't go. It must have gone yesterday, late. I'll check and let you know."

Back in his office, Billy pulled up the record for the desk and found the order was closed out. He went back to the history file and learned that it indeed had been shipped late yesterday and that it was off the production books. Why the salespeople didn't know it had shipped was a mystery to him. He called the trucking company and asked them where the shipment was. Expecting to be told they would check and call back, he was pleasantly surprised to be told immediately that the shipment was picked up late yesterday, had gone to Raleigh where another Atlanta bound shipment was picked up and that the truck was now on the outer beltway of Atlanta. The clerk apologized and said that it might be midday before the delivery could be made. They had to drop off the other shipment first. Finally, the clerk took Billy's number and said he would call if there were any delay in getting the shipment to the customer by noon.

"Why can't we do that?" wondered Billy.

He called Jerry and told him to tell the lawyer to go ahead with his party. Then he asked why the shipment never got picked up in the sales system. Jerry replied, "It looks like it never got entered yesterday. It's probably still on someone's desk. I'll check and see, but I'm really more worried about our not knowing of the delay two weeks ago when you did."

"I wonder if this is a problem that comes from lack of integration," mused Billy as he set about learning about how many forecasts the company had for next month.

5. The truth is out—It's not the software!

"Well, what did you find out?" asked Prof.

"First I learned that we hadn't lost the lawyer's desk. It had been shipped and the shipment never got entered into the sales system. The paperwork was sitting on somebody's desk in sales. Worse yet, the last change of ship date was sitting on the same desk under a pile of unrelated papers. I think I see the integration thing you were talking about yesterday. If our systems had been communicating, the instant the record closed out in our system the sales guys would have known it.

"The desk was delivered almost before we could call the lawyer back to tell him it was on the way. The trucking company was great. They not only knew when it was picked up, they knew the routing and where the truck was. They could tell me when it would be delivered and said they would call if anything changed. Now that is what Jerry would like us to be able to do."

"Well, good," interrupted Prof, "at least you see part of the theory of integration now. Of course, that's a key element of an ERP system. But let's go back and talk about management for a bit. What did you learn about customer orders and forecasts?"

"Do we have to talk about this? You know the answer already! There are three forecasts for monthly sales and I couldn't reconcile them. Accounting uses some kind of dollarized forecast for cash planning purposes, but I couldn't figure out how they got the numbers and they weren't very happy that I was asking about it. The sales guys are using their Quija boards and other sorcery to figure out what deals they'll close. Meanwhile, we use historical averages to plan material and production stuff in the shop. You know that it takes us a long time to get some of the wood from overseas. And customer orders! Wow! I stopped counting when I got to five different people or groups that did something with those orders. What has this got to do with management?"

"Remember that we talked about there being one number for sales, one number for inventory, and so forth. Well, which number are you going to use? Who gets to enter the forecast that everyone is going to use? Is that a problem that software is going to solve? No! You need to make a whole bunch of decisions like that before you can use an ERP system. You need to solve the management problems and get the relationships between functions sorted out before you can fire up the system."

"Oops, there goes the silver bullet," said Billy. "I'll bet this is the time you're going to tell me a whole bunch of other bad news. Is this why there are all the horror stories about implementation that I heard out on the coast?"

"Partly. It's pretty clear that the software doesn't make those kinds of decisions. Some firms think they can hire a consultant for decisions like these, but you can't really delegate them to someone who doesn't have a real good understanding of what the company is like. If your Rotary Club friends thought installing the software was going to answer the tough questions, they'll probably believe buying a word processor will write their letters for them.

"There are other reasons for the horror stories as well, but let's stay with the management stuff for a while. Remember that these systems are designed for all kinds of firms so you have to configure them to match your company. Since it is an integrated approach, everything ties to everything, which leads to great complexity. So this means there is another bunch of decisions about information flows that have to be made in order to get the appropriate information to the right place to manage the firm. Sometimes even small companies can't make these decisions or they make the wrong ones.

"I also have to tell you that the ERP software houses have a view of the enterprise that may not match that of some of their customers. It may be too restrictive, or appear to be, to some managers. Some managers may not want to bring in the formality that is required either. You know that entering the data, especially since it is done only once, requires extensive formal procedures."

"Man, you're no fun! What do you mean 'formality'—you know how informal we are in the plant," said Billy.

"Let me guess that when you put in your MRP system, you still had a lot of people with little notebooks that ran the plant. In fact, let me guess that is what still goes on. Think about that trucking company that told you about the desk you didn't lose. Suppose that the dispatcher simply put a guess in the system that the clerk was using. How long do you think the clerk would believe the system? How good do you think the information would be that you were told? Would you use it to talk to your customers? As it is they probably pick the truck position off a satellite and feed it right into their computers. That is a management issue, not a system issue. You know: Garbage In, Garbage Out.

"Just like your MRP system, if the job isn't in the system, it doesn't exist—right? The same is true for an ERP system, but everybody is involved. They have to be convinced that it will help them do their jobs. As long as I'm on the pulpit . . ."

"Hold on a minute," interrupted Billy. "If I do all this stuff, why do I need ERP? Can't I just run with the MRP system? Well, I'd like to chat with you some more about this but I've got to get to work and you've given me a headache to start the day."

As Billy turned to go out the door, Prof said, "You ought to go to one of the seminars these guys put on. That way you could beat up on someone else for a change."

"You're right—sorry! It's just that I feel pressured to come up with an answer that says that an ERP system is going to be the answer to all our problems, that somehow 'truth' will automatically appear on our screens and that our coffee will always be fresh. It seems I've got to be learning something all the time about the computer. Anyway, we're happy with our material requirements planning system and I guess that's as smart as I want to get. Hey, I haven't even asked you about the grant you're working on."

"It's to study ERP systems!"

"I should have guessed. Ciao!"

6. Ohio has SAP—Off to school

Back at the plant, Billy spent some time on the shop floor checking on some orders, talking with the workers, and looking over some paper work. There didn't seem to be too many problems and he sarcastically muttered under his breath, "The ERP system must be working." In addition to the usual paperwork in his office there was a message asking him to set up a meeting with Mr. McDougle that afternoon. He called Mr. McDougle's secretary, Mary Lou Ledbetter, and set the meeting for just after lunch.

Mr. McDougle started, "How is the ERP study coming, Billy? I trust you are finding out some things that will be useful to us."

"I'm learning a little bit from one of the professors over at the college. The key thing that I'm finding out is that there is a great deal of management work needed before you can implement one of those systems, and it is the kind of work that you really can't delegate to someone who doesn't know the plant intimately. The systems are apparently complicated to configure. To do so, they require a clear specification of the relationships between functions, common definitions of the data, and a good understanding of how business is done in all the departments. I was even asking why we would want to install a system after we had gone all through the company, made all those tough decisions, and had new ways of doing business all in place."

Billy was interrupted by Mr. McDougle, "Well, I'll give you a reason, but you'll have to keep it under your hat for a while. I don't want the information out until it is really necessary."

"What's up?"

"It's my brother and the plant in Ohio. I told you that he was interested in getting out of the business. Well, it's stronger than that. My sister-in-law has said that they want to sell the plant and use the money to travel. We don't want the business to go out of the family, so we're trying to work out a way that I can buy it and run the two businesses together."

"Wow. I'll keep my mouth shut, but what has this got to do with my learning about ERP?" asked Billy.

"Everything. The Ohio plant has implemented SAP or, at least, is implementing it. If it makes sense, I want to make sure that the systems are compatible in the two facilities. That would make it so much easier for accounting to consolidate the reports. It would also mean that we might get some synergies out of the system and maybe our operations. I'm trying to keep an open mind. I don't want to commit until we're convinced that it will be okay for us here."

"So I guess one implication of this is that I should focus on SAP in particular—is that what you're suggesting?"

"Yes, and I think you need to get some formal exposure to their approach. Why don't you sign up for one of their seminars?"

Billy complained, "Geez, I just learned how to forward my e-mail and now you want me to go back to computer school. Are you thinking that you want me to be the guru on this? Who is going to run the shop while I'm gone?"

"I'm not sure yet that you should be the point person, but you do have a successful MRP installation. Besides, you seem to have a healthy skepticism that might keep us honest in this process. You also won't let me do anything stupid."

Mr. McDougle continued, "I don't know why you are worried about the plant. It didn't collapse while you were on vacation did it?"

"No, but we thought we lost a $20,000 desk."

"Jerry told me about that. It was just a paper problem, right? The paper work got to sales, but didn't get into the computer? Anyway, the information systems guy up at the Ohio plant tells me that this is just the type of problem that SAP is designed to avoid. He is the guy responsible for implementing the system there."

Billy responded, "Did he also tell you that sales and production would have to agree on a bunch of stuff before the system would do that? It isn't the SAP software that solves those problems, it's the way that people work with the information. The software doesn't manage the people."

"That's exactly why I want you to go to an SAP seminar for us. You'll ask the right kind of questions. There is one other thing you should do also. You should order the book *Why ERP?* by Jacobs and Whybark from Amazon.com. It's supposed to be the best quick management overview. At least that's what the people up in Ohio tell me. Now get yourself signed up for some schooling and keep me posted."

7. ERP implementation?—A new reason!

The next time he was in the Café, Billy lamented, "Help, Ruth! Pour me a cup of coffee and you'll be responsible for saving my life. I've just been told to go away to school again. I've almost decided I hate computers."

When Prof came in, Billy immediately said, "You've been talking to Mr. McDougle, I know you have. It's your fault."

"What are you talking about?" asked Prof. "Ruth, what did you put in his coffee this morning?"

"Nothing, but he's been complaining like an overloaded Ford pickup all morning. Maybe you can shape him up. If you can't, just let me know and I'll pour some ice water on him," replied Ruth.

"Prof, I need help! Come sit down for a few minutes and let's see if you can help me overcome my latest insurmountable opportunity." Billy pulled Prof over to a corner table and asked Ruth to keep the coffee cups full.

Billy started out, "The boss told me to go to school, that's why I blamed you for calling him. It's entirely your fault! You see the family plant up in Ohio is using SAP and the boss wants our plant to be compatible with it. So he tells me to go to SAP school. Now I'm going to have to learn more about SAP than I ever wanted to know."

Without indicating the family part of the deal, Billy explained the situation as best he could. He explained that the information systems manager at the Ohio plant led the SAP implementation. He also said it sounded like Mr. McDougle was trying to keep an open mind but really thought SAP would perform some kind of a management miracle for him by enabling the family to more effectively integrate the accounting for the two facilities.

About this time the Prof put his hands up in the classical time out fashion and said, "Whoops, this sounds like a new reason to implement ERP. First of all, let me tell you a little bit about what I've learned about why people implement enterprise resource planning systems. As silly as it sounds, some companies implemented very expensive ERP systems to solve the Year 2000 problem. This was roughly equivalent to buying Big Ben and trying to move it to your living room when your clock battery has run down. It attacked an important problem, clearly, but it didn't attack the problem with the appropriate solution. I think that most firms that had this limited view of what they were doing and why they were using the software were doomed to have problems anyway. I'll ignore that reason.

"It seems there are three other reasons that firms implement ERP systems. Of them, only one makes much sense to me. To start with some firms will adopt them when they learn of their integrative aspects and they realize all their legacy systems aren't integrated. There are often a large number of legacy systems. You know, the old, sometimes homegrown, sometimes purchased systems from different vendors that are used to manage accounting or personnel or sales or inventory or forecasting, whatever it may be. They're sometimes very slow and difficult to maintain. Some managers will try to implement ERP to sweep out these legacy systems and integrate the various functions of the business or force a badly needed organizational change.

"Once again, it seems to me the issues, the fundamental issues, of integrating the organization and the functions is a problem that is not going to be solved with the software. The organizational issues need to be tackled by management if it's to be appropriately done. Again, firms that don't look at the organizational issues clearly are going to fail in the implementation and the system will be blamed for the failure.

"The second reason is one that won't affect you guys, until you try to integrate with the Ohio plant. Firms implement ERP systems when they have a large number of plants and facilities scattered around the country or the world. They are looking for better communication and integration among these facilities. Once again, the reason is a noble one that may or may not have to do with legacy systems, although most often they're involved. But again, it's the issues of people, organization, functions, and business objectives that need to be addressed before the system can be used. One manager who I interviewed about a failed implementation told me he knows of no software that will solve these people problems.

"Finally, some firms are implementing enterprise resource planning systems because they recognize that the organization does need to change to be positioned to exploit future communication and computing technology for E-business and other applications. They address the organizational issues, they assess where their needs are, they look carefully at which legacy systems can still serve their companies, and then implement the enterprise resource planning systems in those areas where the integration is essential. These companies are more likely to have a more successful implementation than others."

"Wow," said Billy. "I don't know that we're in any of those categories, but that doesn't prevent the boss from wanting me to move ahead. I think he feels that he can get common information, common management systems, common data, and common reports from the system. After that, the family can simply use the same kind of management in both places."

"Well, I'm not sure that will work," said Prof. "But you better go to school and learn some of the details of the SAP approach before you make up your mind. I'm not worried about your being tainted by an aggressive SAP salesperson."

The SAP School   **II**

8. First impressions—Donuts!

The seminar started with all participants quickly introducing themselves and their companies. There were some 20 people and as Billy listened to the introductions, the diversity of the group struck him. There were two people from a Los Angeles–based chocolate company, two from a chemical company in Saudi Arabia, an individual from a major software consulting company, an individual from a pharmaceutical company based in Germany, an individual from an insurance company, two employees of an oil company, and others. He was surprised that such a mix of companies from around the world would all gather in Chicago for an SAP seminar!

> *How could one program product be this flexible, wondered Billy? How could it be useful to all of these different types of companies? We've got process firms (oil and chemical), discrete manufacturing (chocolates and pharmaceutical), and service companies (insurance and consulting) all represented. Even with this variety, I'm the only furniture industry representative.*

Having already checked out the break room, Billy found the pastries were awesome. This was no low-budget operation. These companies were spending big money and the representatives at this workshop were serious about learning more about the SAP software. Prof had warned Billy about the food. Work for an hour and a quarter, take a 15-minute break, work another hour then break for 15 minutes, lunch in a great little restaurant on the first floor. You could easily put the pounds on during the weeklong program.

"I'm delighted to see such a mix of industries and people," began the SAP instructor, Amanda Chisak. "I am looking forward to working with you over the next few days. Let me start by outlining the seminar. I'll describe

19

both parts even though some of you will be leaving us after a couple of days. That will give me a chance to show you all the good stuff you'll miss if you leave.

"Essentially, the two sections divide into covering basic, general material in the first two days and more technical material in the rest. You'll have a chance to see what the system does in both parts, but we will dig a little deeper in the second. At the start I'll introduce you to SAP's R/3 software and show you a bit of what it can do for you. I'll show you how R/3 is based on contemporary business practices and how they are documented in the processes that are used in the software. We'll discuss some of the advantages of using the system and what it takes to do so. Some of you who won't be here at the end are concerned about implementation, so I'll make sure we have time to look at a product that is designed to expedite implementing the system before you go.

"In the second part we'll get to the fun stuff. Sorry about that for those of you who won't be here. We'll look in more detail at how SAP defines business practices, the processes that underlie all the programs. We'll discuss the roles that people play in using the system and do more demonstrations of the software. Finally, I'll describe the structure of the software and hardware.

"Let me start with a bit about SAP. In English, the acronym SAP stands for Systems, Applications, and Products in Data Processing. The company is headquartered in Walldorf, Germany, but has offices and customers all over the world. The product that we are going to describe in this seminar is SAP's R/3. You will find many people who use the terms SAP and R/3 interchangeably, but they are different. I will tend to use SAP R/3 or just R/3. SAP is the company and is much better known than R/3. R/3 is an SAP product that integrates the information throughout an organization, providing the benefits of single data entry, immediate access, and common data. All users have the same 'Windows-like' interface with the system and all processes are integrated with the same data. Since the data are the same and the computer screens look the same to everyone, when the accountant is in the sales office, the screens and information are familiar. Data are updated in real time, meaning that when data are entered into the system, the changes are immediately available to everyone else using the system."

Yeah, sure, thought Billy! This is the stuff that Mr. McDougle has been hearing. She hasn't said a word about all the work you've got to do to get this to happen. She makes it sound like magic.

"Here is an example of what I mean by integration and immediacy. Suppose that I just completed a production order in a factory in Germany and posted it to finished goods inventory. Immediately the sales office in Los Angeles could see that the item was available, the accounting department in

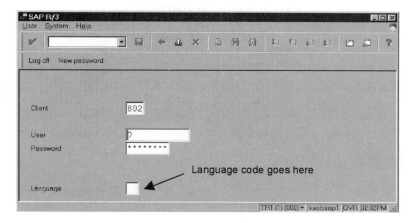

Figure 1: SAP R/3 Opening Screen

Chicago would see it go from work-in-process to finished goods, and so forth. Now that is global integration, both from an information and from a process viewpoint. There is no redundant information, the data are kept in one place and made available for everyone in the company to use."

That's interesting, but not very relevant. I'm not worried about Germany and Los Angeles; I'm just worried about keeping Jerry off my back!

"Okay, let's look at what the computer screens for R/3 look like. I'm going to turn down these front lights and project some examples onto the board here, although I'll sometimes use the overhead projector. First, I'll log onto the system (Figure 1). If there are any purists in the room, I'll admit right now that I'll be using examples from two different versions, releases, of the program. I haven't gotten them all converted to the latest release yet.

"We'll get to that Client code number later, but for now notice that, in addition to the usual User Name and Password, the software wants to know what language should be used. SAP R/3 is a multi-lingual software package. The system also understands different currencies. United States users see costs and prices in dollars, German users see these amounts in deutche marks, Japanese users in yen, and the system handles all of these conversions automatically."

This may be an example where it really is automatic. If the rates are in there, the program and not the people can do the conversions. Maybe there is something here. But I wonder how the exchange rates get into the system.

"Let's begin to get this a little closer to home. When people think about their organization, they usually think in terms of functions. Functions tend

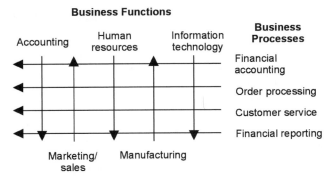

Figure 2: SAP R/3 is organized around business processes, which cut across business functions.

to be the way we organize the people. We have people who work for the Vice President of Sales, for example. SAP has chosen some names for functions like sales, product development/marketing, supply chain planning, production, and human resources and has even changed them from time to time.

"This is one of the topics on which we find confusion. Don't worry if you have other names for the functions in your organization, R/3 can accommodate those differences. The next thing that you should know is that SAP R/3 is designed around business processes. Some major ones are sales order handling, quality management, material requirements planning, and recruitment. These processes are usually not how people are organized and they cut across functional areas as you can see here (Figure 2). I'll use the terms function and process frequently. But you can now see why integration without integrated software is so hard."

We only have some of these functions. Do we need to reorganize to use this? I wonder what she means when she says that processes cut across functions. Is that the problem we had with the lost desk?

What is SAP R/3?

"There is some other terminology that I'd like to introduce, simply because it's in use. SAP R/3 is an ERP system where ERP stands for enterprise resource planning. But what does it mean? First, keep in mind that this is all about integrating the resources of the entire 'enterprise' from an information standpoint. The idea is that if information is completely common, and the processes are integrated, then organizational integration is possible. Moreover, duplication of information is eliminated, saving time and improving the efficiency of operations. Of course, it is not really that simple, if we use information to integrate the organization, we will probably need to change the way people do things—change their jobs."

Hey! She finally said something about the management issue. I hope we don't have to get up and confess that we have multiple forecasts in our plant.

"For example, if in the past the marketing folks kept their own demand forecasts, and this was different from the forecasts used by the production planning group, integration would imply that only a single forecast is made. Clearly, the way forecasting is done must change. Marketing and production will have to consolidate their efforts and even agree on the approach used. What are the benefits of this integrated approach? If nothing else, there should be less duplicated effort.

"SAP R/3 provides efficiencies and increases in productivity through integration of information and processes across the entire firm. Information that a company deals with—such as client data and manufacturing data—enters the system at one time and in one place. This strategy cuts down on the number of times information enters the system, as well as on the error rate associated with multiple entries, and assures that all divisions of the company are dealing with current and identical data."

How did she find out about our forecasting systems? I wonder if she knows the clerk in sales who was supposed to enter that shipping date change? If we entered the information only once, what would that clerk do?

"So how can SAP R/3 be defined? Many experts view R/3 as a turbocharged version of manufacturing resource planning—MRP for short—modified and strengthened to help manufacturers face the challenges of the new millennium. But there are major differences. R/3 goes beyond material, labor, and production-centered manufacturing systems to integrate all functions of the business, whatever they are called. From hiring, training, and firing decisions to running the sales campaign to tracking the portfolio of assets owned by a company, R/3 provides integrated software support. R/3 can be viewed as a software image of the major business processes of an organization."

Turbocharged MRP? ERP? I still don't see where this is enterprise resource planning. Information certainly. Enterprise, maybe. Resource, maybe. Planning no way!

"As we've discussed, SAP R/3 can support the operation of multiple international sites, global sourcing of parts and services, global distribution, and provide appropriate performance metrics for operations around the world. For instance, a company's U.S. sales office may be responsible for marketing, selling, and servicing a product assembled in the U.K. using parts manufactured in Germany and Singapore. R/3 enables the company to understand and manage the demand placed on any of these facilities. It allows a global enterprise to use the most suitable metrics for measuring efficiency in its operations."

Here she goes again! I wish that the phone wasn't busy when I tried to reach that 800 number from our radio station. I wouldn't have to be learning geography as well as SAP R/3.

"SAP R/3 in a global, multi-plant enterprise is very different from a single shop in Indiana trying to tie its accounting department and distribution together. We can use the R/3 system for both of these, but will need to scale the program to the real-world needs of the enterprise. One of the big jobs in using R/3, then, is to match the system to the organization. That effort is called configuration."

Gee, this is some of the stuff that Prof was trying to explain. Amanda really has added a lot of international things that we don't have to put up with, but there are a lot of international firms here. Maybe she's trying to connect with them. Anyway, this is better coffee than Ruth's and I am getting some insights from her.

What resources are managed?

"When we talk about the resources of an enterprise, what do we really mean? Resources are those assets of the company that are required to carry out the activities needed to stay in business. These include the buildings and equipment owned by the company. The employees of the company, although not owned by the company, are resources that need to be managed as an integral part of business. In addition, the materials and supplies needed for ongoing operation need to be managed.

"The world doesn't stand still, so managing these resources over time as things change is also important. The dynamic nature of business means that a critical aspect of management is responding to the peaks and valleys of the business cycle with the appropriate resources. Anticipating needed changes based on past history and planned future activities is essential."

"There is also a spatial dimension to managing resources. They can be spread across the globe. Products specific to unique local markets, production facilities tailored to special products and people working within different countries and time zones must all be managed.

"This global dimension is possibly the most unique capability of the R/3 software system. Due to the extensive global deployment of the system, business practices unique to the United States, Europe, and Japan are built into the system. Accounting practices, government tax requirements, human resource management practices, and even manufacturing practices that are unique to different regions around the world are incorporated in this single system.

"Consider the switch to the Euro currency in parts of Europe. To handle the new currency, new conversion rules, as established by the European Union, were integrated into the software. These conversion rules covered the different European currencies that were ready to adopt the Euro on January 1, 1999. At that time the system automatically could maintain accounts in the new Euro currency.

"There is still a complication, though. For a period of time, there will be a dual currency phase, which the software must accommodate. During this unique period, customers will be able to perform certain tasks, such as generating price lists or submitting official reports to authorities in the public sector, both in Euros and their local currency."

This is the first time that anybody has really talked about the number of resources that needs to be managed. Even Prof didn't see all those things.

9. Introduction to R/3—It looks familiar

"Let's get back to the computer and see what R/3 really is about. I know that many of you are asking, 'What does it look like?' 'How difficult is it to use?' Well, anyone familiar with Windows will find the point-and-click approach used in R/3 familiar. But be assured, even though the program is easy to use, there is much complexity beyond the screens and menus you'll see.

"Okay, I'll finish logging on and we'll go to the screen that is at the top of R/3 and from which you enter the programs that you use in your work (Figure 3). This menu is what all users see when they log on the system. Before you ask, this is the way that SAP thought about organizing all the business processes when they wrote R/3. It is probably neither the way that you would name things nor the way you would collect programs together. You can create your own menus and the submenus to fit your situation, but we're going to use the ones that are here.

"We will first be concerned with the 'Office' option. Each of the menu items at the top of the screen: Office, Logistics, Accounting, etc. gives you access to a number of other menu items that eventually communicate with the R/3 program. When we select 'Office,' for example, we have access to the programs that support our e-mail, an appointment calendar, the meeting scheduler, and the other functions common to life in the office that you see on the screen.

"The user navigates between screens in the system using several special buttons (Figure 4). The 'enter button' is used to tell the system that you have completed entering the appropriate data on the screen and want to have the

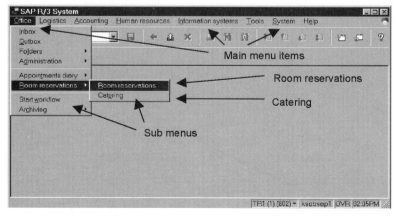

Figure 3: R/3 Main Menu

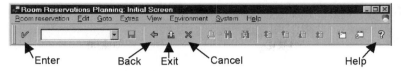

Figure 4: R/3 Navigation Buttons

system accept the new information. The 'cancel button' erases all entries on the screen. The user can quickly return to the prior screen, or move up a level in the menu structure, with the back and exit arrow buttons."

Hey! I think I can get the hang of this. It's a lot like the Windows programs I have back home. But my big worry is still Jerry's clerk.

10. A first use of R/3—Room reservations

"Okay now; let's go through an example so you can actually see how R/3 works. I'm going to work 'live' from the Office menu. For our example, we'll take a look at scheduling a meeting. Even though it is a simple task, it is common to every one of your organizations. We will schedule a noon lunch meeting to be held in our Walldorf, Germany, facility.

"We begin by selecting Office from the menu items, and then the room reservations menu (Figure 3). As you can see from the submenu options, the program can even handle the catering of the meeting. The system is comprehensive, in that we can also bill the room to an outside client, or to an internal customer, if that is desired.

"After selecting room reservations with a click of the mouse, we are presented with a form (Figure 5) to provide information needed to reserve the room. The use of these types of screen forms is basic to R/3. It is imperative that everything that needs to be completed on the form is entered. The trick is that some of the fields are required and others are optional. If all the required fields are not completed on the first try, the system tells you what is needed—one missing item at a time. This can be a tedious process."

Do I really need to know this? When am I going to book a meeting in Germany? Ohio, maybe. But not Germany!

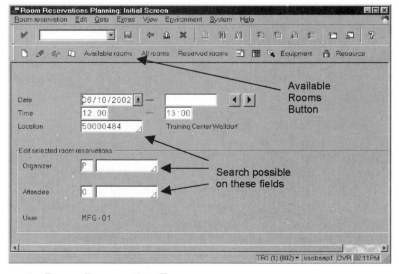

Figure 5: Room Reservation Form

"Our meeting will be from noon to 13:00 on the 10th of June 2002 in Walldorf. For our form, we have indicated the date and the time. The location number 50000484 corresponds to the training center located in Walldorf. R/3 has a number for everything. I will call these numbers codes. Actually, R/3 calls them 'match codes,' but I prefer the shorter version, codes.

"Notice the little triangle to the right of the number 50000484 in the location field. This indicates that a search can be done to find the proper code for the data required here. This is another standard feature of the system. The codes for such items as user ids, part numbers, plant numbers, etc. can be found using this standard search feature. The system automatically entered my user ID code, MFG-01, as the person making the reservation. Remember when I logged on? I entered this information then."

Man, I can't even remember my wife's birthday, I'm glad they've got those little triangles!

"After entering the date, time, and place for the meeting, we check to see what rooms are available by clicking on the 'Available Rooms' button at the top of the screen (Figure 5). The system responds with a list of rooms that can be scheduled (Figure 6).

"From this list, we can select our room by double clicking on the room that we want to use. We selected the TR Bogota room for our lunch meeting. The system responds with the completed room reservation form (Figure 7). Notice that the 'room' field has now been completed and that the booking information has been supplied for our room.

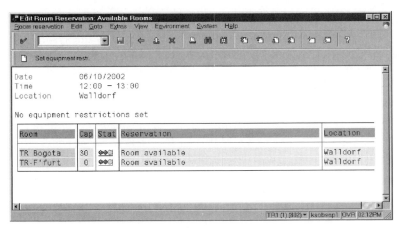

Figure 6: Rooms Available for Reservation

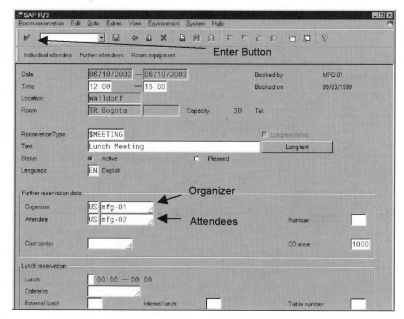

Figure 7: Completed Room Reservation Form

"The final thing needed to reserve the room is to indicate who is organizing the meeting, and who the attendees will be. For our example user MFG-01 has been entered as the organizer and I entered user MFG-02 as the attendee. If you have groups that meet frequently, it can be like your e-mail, you can set up groups of individuals to speed the data entry.

"All of the information entered so far is required by the system. At this time, we can click the enter button, the 'check mark' up at the top, to schedule our meeting. The system responds by sending e-mail messages to all of those involved, establishes an account number for the meeting, and warns purchasing of any food that needs to be bought."

Who's in charge here? It looks like I would even have less control of my time. Is this progress? I don't even know who is coming to my meetings. How can I enter their names? I guess they would be blank. We need a break!

11. "Best" practices—Business processes

Man, I better not grab that comfortable seat over there. If she lays global integration with Europe stuff on us again as she did before, I'll fall asleep.

"Okay, I'm going to break in here and explain a bit more about what is inside R/3. The R/3 designers have incorporated contemporary business practices or processes in the software. SAP calls these processes 'best practices.' Remember we saw before how the processes cut across the business functions (Figure 2). SAP has documented these 'best practice' processes and bundled together they are called the R/3 Reference Model.

"Earlier we saw, through a series of screen selections, the process involved in reserving a conference room for a meeting. R/3 describes this process in their reference model using the process flow diagram shown in here (Figure 8). Impressive isn't it!

"On the right side (Figure 8) the entire process flow diagram is shown, and on the left we have focused on a portion of it. The symbol in the circle represents a logical AND to indicate that all of the items above and below must be completed prior to the next operation. Other symbols (Figure 9) represent the OR and exclusive OR (XOR) logical operators. The difference between these OR symbols is that in the case of exclusive OR, only one of the items

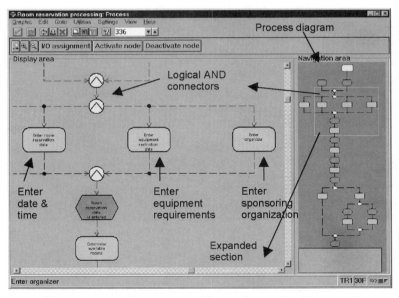

Figure 8: Flow Process Diagram for Reserving a Conference Room

Figure 9: Process Flow Diagram Symbols

can be completed, whereas the non-exclusive OR can have one or more of the items completed."

What is all this logical stuff? If that was "Exclusive Oar," I'd think of a restaurant on the coast. I guess ands are bad and ors are good, and if we can be exclusive about it, that's great.

"Where you see a function in the flow diagram, you must enter data on a screen form. In the case of our conference room schedule, the room reservation date and time must be entered (Figure 8), together with equipment requirements and sponsoring organization. After entering this information, an event marking the completion of the entry of room reservation data occurs.

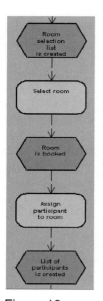

"Following this, the next operation is started to check the availability of rooms. This results in a list of available rooms followed by a function to select a room. Entering the participants and the creation of a list of participants (Figure 10) follows the booking of the room.

"The process continues by creating name tags and organizing for catering food or coffee. Notice that in the process flow diagram detail (Figure 11), the name tags and the catering events are connected using an AND connector. The coffee service and the lunch arrangements are connected using the OR symbol indicating that either or both of the paths could be followed. Following the bottom AND symbol is a single event marking the end of the Room Reservation Process."

At home I just call Mary Lou. If she has to do all this, she'll quit.

"Every one of the hundreds of processes supported by the SAP R/3 system is documented. You can see that the system is comprehensive. Every process is just like the room reservation process. You might think this is tedious, but the benefit of doing things the R/3 way is that all of

Figure 10

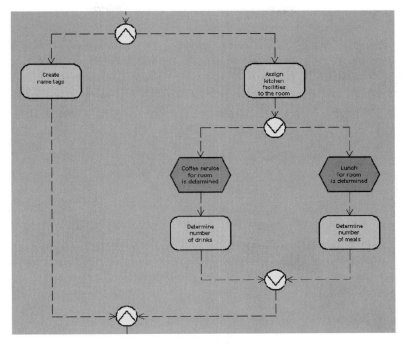

Figure 11: Room Reservation Process Detail Continued

the linkages to the other functions in the system are maintained. The food, for example, is billed to the right cost account; the order is entered for the food with the food vendor, and so on. Changes to processes can be made, but the program might not now include all of the dependent linkages required. Further, this can be time consuming, requires programming, and might not be compatible with any upgrades to the R/3 software."

I wonder if they catered the donuts into this seminar this way. Is "best practices" having donuts and name tags at every meeting? Sounds good to me! The real problem, though, is how do you get this thing implemented? The resistance if we try to implement R/3 will be incredible.

12. The war stories—Why implement SAP?

"Welcome back," said Amanda. "Now that you know how to reserve a room in Germany, you can have your company parties there. I know that it was a simple example, but you should at least now see how comprehensive the processes are in the R/3 system. Many of you are still saying that you don't see the advantages of having to go through all of that work. After you have finished your donuts, I'll try to give you a feel for that. Incidentally, you have single-handedly wiped out the capacity of the local donut shop to ship emergency orders to us.

"Okay. How many of you have had a customer service problem recently. Wow! Joe, you're the only one who doesn't have a hand in the air. Now Joe, that's not fair. I think we should throw him out. Okay, I was just kidding! You can stay, but I'm going to call on someone with a problem."

That certainly isn't fair. That's one of the guys from the candy company. Of course he doesn't have any customer service issues. He is just establishing a new division in Portland and doesn't have any customers yet. But he is the only one. If they just started up the division, I wonder why he is thinking of SAP? One of the consultants has her hand up. Those consultants always want to talk!

The lady from the consulting company described a problem they had. Recently some clients on the East Coast complained that several consultants were late in getting out to the clients' sites. The consultants had made commitments to meet with the clients on a particular day and had to postpone at the last minute. It was embarrassing because some of the clients brought people into town just to meet with the consultants! At one site, there were other complaints. The catering company showed up with the breakfast snacks and, to make matters worse, someone forgot to cancel lunch. At least that client ate well that day.

She explained that the problem arose because the consulting company was working on a huge job for a key client in the Midwest and was running late. The Midwest client wanted them to finish and the consultants agreed. They didn't want to come back for just a couple of days of work at a later time. Some of the people that were supposed to be in the East Coast meetings were held on the job in the Midwest. The East Coast office didn't know about it in time to reschedule the meetings, even though they knew in plenty of time in the Midwest.

Man, you'd think she was billing a client by the word.

"Well, R/3 could have helped with that problem by making the schedule of those consultants visible to you in the East Coast office. On the other hand, you all know that the problem was not just an information system issue.

Why do you suppose that I would say that it is not just an information system problem?

"Right! Someone has to enter into the system the changes in the consultants' schedules. Also it would have been nice if they would have sent an e-mail or picked up the phone to tell someone about the changes."

> *I know how those phone calls work. Mary Lou gets the call on her way out of the office and forgets to tell anyone. e-mail may be the answer, but do we need SAP to upgrade our e-mail?*

The jobs may change

One of the people from the oil company explained a problem they had recently faced with an internal customer. Two of their divisions were trying to bring some crude oil into their refineries. This required ocean tanker delivery capacity. It turned out that, unknown to each other, both divisions were bidding for the same ship. This, of course, ran up the price of the charter. It also delayed delivery for the division that "lost" the bid. They had to locate and bid on other capacity and that meant the delivery to their internal customer, the refinery, was late. The speaker wondered how R/3 could have helped.

"Well, you certainly have widely spread facilities and activities that could benefit from coordination. R/3 could help you have the information available and visible to all divisions. If you had R/3, the divisions might have cooperated with one another—but maybe not. In order to have it happen, you would have to make sure that the management roles were appropriately defined, the performance measures were correct and the incentives were right. Another approach to be sure, would be to make the information available to a central department that had to supply crude oil to all the refineries. They could have made the best choice for the company in terms of which capacity they chartered for each refinery. I see you shaking your head."

The petroleum people explained that they seemed to constantly be in the process of centralizing or decentralizing and weren't sure they wanted to initiate another swing of the pendulum. They simply wanted to control their own destiny and not be subject to some group in corporate who just could not understand their local problems and priorities. They concluded by saying that they simply wanted to do their jobs better.

"You have come to the real nub of the issue—do your jobs. I'll get a bit more into this tomorrow, but you can see already that some of the jobs may need to change to get the most out of SAP R/3. For now let me just say that having the information available in both divisions might have helped your problem, but only if one of the divisions would have agreed not to bid for that ship."

I think I'll tell her about the desk. It might be good to get her reaction to a problem from a small company.

After Billy described the problem, Amanda replied, "Sounds like I would like one of those desks. So it wasn't really lost, only the paper work was lost. You've hit on a major advantage of R/3. Part of your organization already knew the details on the status of the desk; it just didn't get transferred to another part of your organization. Wouldn't it be nice to know that as soon as the first clerk finished entering the update information, it was immediately distributed to all the other parts of the company that needed it? That is an important part of what R/3 does.

"We've only scratched the surface of the advantages of having an integrated, common information system. One of the benefits we have discussed here relates to the integration aspects of the system. That is everyone who needs to know of a change that could affect them is immediately notified. We've also talked about the advantage of having information in a central location in order to make better decisions for the overall organization. In the last example, the lost desk, we again saw the advantage of having timely information, but there is something more subtle in that example.

"Did you notice that at least two people were entering the same data? There can be significant savings from having only one person enter the data. But the savings in the time it takes to enter something only once is just a part of the advantage. Perhaps an even bigger saving is in quality. How many of you really believe that the same information gets entered into the system each time someone else does it. Yeah, sure! And I'm Santa Claus. Just having one entry point for data that is then distributed is a very big advantage in terms of minimizing the chances of error."

Data entry issues

"OK, how many of you have address books? Wow, nearly everybody! How many of you have calendars that have your schedules? You know those little pocket things from your suppliers, or Palm Pilots, or something like that? Again, just about everybody. Now how many of you have your calendar up to date? Whoops, not so many hands in the air now. How about your address books, do you have the latest changes you know about? Now, even fewer hands are up. OK.

"So, how many of you have your secretaries maintain your calendar? OK, for those of you whose secretaries maintain the calendar, how many are up to date? OK, not very many hands are up? Why is that?"

Boy, I hope she doesn't ask me about my calendar or my address book. The last time I think I entered anything in the address book was in 1965.

"I'm really not going to embarrass anybody here. Let me guess that the reason that your calendars aren't up to date is a combination of some things you didn't tell your secretary about and some things you did say that didn't get entered. My guess is that the same thing is true of your address books. Some of you probably haven't put any changes in your address books for months. Instead, you have little bits of paper with new phone numbers sitting around someplace.

"Think of all the work required just to maintain individual calendars and address books. Everything that is scheduled needs to be individually entered by everyone involved. The same is true of address information. If we centralize this information, then only one person has to enter the new item in the schedule or change the address. At that point, everyone has immediate access to the current information. Now that's saving a lot of tedious work for people, not to mention the reduction in chances for error.

"What I am getting at here is obvious to you, I'm sure. Now R/3 won't do the data entry stuff for you and, if you don't enter it, it won't get distributed. Moreover, the data about the meeting had better be entered correctly or everyone is going to show up at the wrong place. There is an analogy about the discipline required for entering the data that I think would be clear to some of you.

"How many of you have material requirements planning systems? Not too many. Well, those of you that have MRP systems in place realize the importance of data accuracy and data entry discipline. As we learned in the implementation of MRP, you have to have the discipline to input the data every time material moves from one place to another place. If you don't, you won't know where materials are in the manufacturing facility. Inability to develop the discipline to do this consistently, accurately, and on a timely basis was often a major stumbling block to installing an MRP system. SAP R/3 requires the same kind of discipline, this time throughout the organization.

"For those of you who are in service businesses, how big a problem is it to account for your time? Yeah, I see your heads nodding. You see that is the same thing. If you don't enter the time in the system, then you can't bill the client."

Man, I think she's been in our shop. We are always forgetting to log time against projects for the design of new furniture or when we are getting ready for the big furniture market. We have guys who have more unaccounted-for time than accounted-for time. Yet everyone is working on something all the time. At least I think they are.

"I hope you have gotten the message here that there is an analogue between keeping your calendar and your address book up to date and the need for entering the information into the R/3 system if the system is to provide value for your company. I can't stress enough that this may mean that the roles of some of the people may have to change significantly."

We would sure have to do things differently to use this. Jerry isn't ready to feed this big system data. Once the data are captured, though, all kinds of things are done automatically. So the real problem is how you get this thing implemented? I remember the problems we had when we put in our material requirements planning system; many of those old timers just did not want to change and it took us forever to get the data right. How could we make the changes?

"I know what's on your minds. This can't be magic. You have all heard the horror stories about implementing ERP systems. We are working to improve that situation and, even though it may not be the most logical thing to bring up next, I'm going to discuss a way of getting the R/3 software up quickly. This is an innovative approach that capitalizes on our experience to get you using the system quickly, so that you're getting the payoff and are in a position to improve over time.

"Before I get started, though, I understand that the emergency donut delivery has arrived. Go get refueled and I'll conclude when you return."

13. SAP implementation—Accelerated R/3

Amanda started out the next session saying, "ASAP stands for Accelerated SAP and is SAP's approach to implementing the R/3 software. It is a way of helping you describe your company to the system. It systematically guides you through the tasks involved in getting R/3 up and running in your company.

"Keep in mind that ASAP is really not for everyone. It is generally for smaller companies or firms that are not interested in a complete reengineering of their processes. For those that can use it, though, it is a good way to get the software running very quickly.

"So what is ASAP? ASAP is a standard approach to implementing R/3. It carries your company through a sequence of steps built around several pre-structured activities that SAP has developed based on their experience in thousands of firms. They sequence these activities along what they call the 'Roadmap' (Figure 12), in five major phases. Each phase is completed in turn on the road to R/3 implementation. SAP calls these five major phases: Project Preparation, Business Blueprint, Realization, Final Preparation, and Go Live and Support."

Do I have to learn all these new terms? I have a life-size picture of Mr. McDougle listening to me say "Business Blueprint."

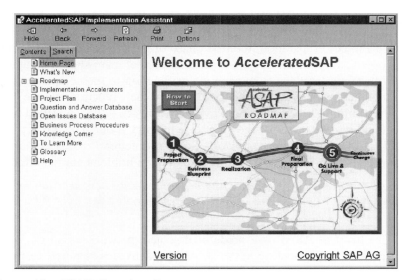

Figure 12: ASAP Opening Screen

"In more general terms, these are really quite intuitive steps. In Project Preparation, for example, you would be organizing the team, setting milestones, and so forth. The next phase, the Business Blueprint is where you describe to ASAP the way your specific company does business to help select the appropriate R/3 software options. As you have probably already guessed, Realization is where the software is configured and tested. In Final Preparation, you never would guess this: you train the users in their part of the system.

"You think you know what Go Live and Support means, but it is really only where you start to use the system. You know you will be able to enhance it over time. The idea is to get a basic set of processes running with R/3 and then improve on this basic implementation in the future.

"If this sounds like fairly standard project management—it is. The data are even in Microsoft Project format. To help the implementation team get organized, SAP provides six- and nine-month versions of the project. The six-month version is for smaller implementation projects and the nine-month version for the larger ones. There are ASAP programs for a single country and programs for multinational implementation projects."

Man, that was a good donut. Prof was right. I could gain weight. This ASAP might be a way for us to get up to speed quickly. I wonder what they did in Ohio. This is so much quicker than what I heard at the Rotary meeting. I better take notes on the details.

Project Preparation phase

"During Project Preparation, the first phase of the project, a major activity is the organization of the project team. The project team should be assembled with representatives from each major function in the company. These team members should be knowledgeable about their function and the company. In addition, they should be individuals who are fully committed to the project and will be there for the long term to carry it out. The project team should be given special space to work. Some people refer to this as the 'war room' which is an amusing way to think about an implementation effort!"

Hey! We have enough war as it is! I better not let the boss hear this or he'll use my office. I guess some of Prof's student interns won't work. I knew this wouldn't be cheap.

"The heart of ASAP is a predefined project network based on SAP's experience in implementing systems. All the activities required to install R/3 are included in the software along with suggested times for their completion. In the Project Preparation phase this standard project template is evaluated and modifications can be made based on the specific needs of the firm. We recommend, however, that you use the standard template. This is a way of getting the project going without stalling at the start over what changes to make.

"You probably know of firms that relied on consultants to install the system. Many of you have probably already been approached by your accounting firm or an independent consulting firm suggesting that they would be willing to help you implement SAP R/3. This is not all bad! True, you *can* use ASAP without help, but we suggest you get some outside consulting. There are three things to remember here. First, make sure your consultant knows about R/3. That is where you want the expertise. Second, you cannot delegate management decisions to the consultant. You know your company, the consultant knows R/3. Finally, we recommend that the consultant be on the project team."

> *Funny that she's pitching consultants. I wonder if Prof knows enough R/3 to do this for us. Then again, he already knows how screwed up we are and would probably refuse.*

"In our experience with six-month projects, the Project Preparation phase takes about 2.5 weeks out of the 25 weeks. That's about 10 percent of the project time."

Business Blueprint

"The second phase of the project is the Business Blueprint. Business blueprinting is the means by which the parts of the software appropriate to your company are configured. ASAP incorporates an innovative tool to help in this activity. SAP has developed a series of questions about the way you do business that the project team answers. Their answers guide the software in suggesting the processes that your company should use to conduct its business and configuring them to fit what you do. Examples would include taking orders from your customers, buying from your suppliers, or promoting an employee.

"You can see here an example for taking customer orders (Figure 13). Most questions require a simple yes/no, true/false, or select from the list kinds of answer. Some others may need details that require the project team to do some research and interviews to obtain the correct descriptive information. Once the questions are answered, ASAP generates a detailed description of how R/3 might be configured. Obviously, you have final control over which of R/3's processes your firm will use, but the ASAP suggestions are a very useful part of the business blueprinting activity.

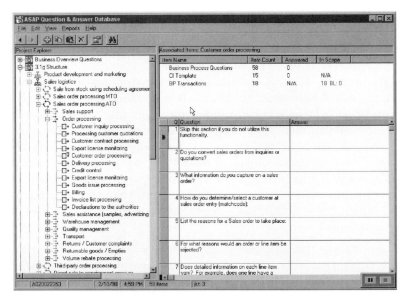

Figure 13: ASAP Question and Answer Database

"In fact, we think this is one of the most innovative applications of expert system technology we have seen to date. Using questions to investigate how you want your business to operate, ASAP suggests which processes to use."

This is cool! I bet Prof doesn't even know about this. I wonder if we can use this instead of Prof as a consultant. Hey, a break!

"Before the break we were talking about the processes that would be used in your installation. These processes are at the heart of the R/3 system. R/3 has, for example, a process for promoting a person, a process for running a mail campaign, a process for filling an order from the telephone, and many others. Remember, we said earlier that business blueprinting involves selecting exactly which processes will be used in your firm. ASAP helps you select from the hundreds of different processes contained in R/3.

"Another clever feature built into the ASAP software is a means for resolving issues. Whenever something that requires a decision surfaces during the project, the issue is documented within ASAP. Data associated with the issue, the parties involved, etc. are all documented. The system gives the parties involved 36 hours to make a decision. The idea is to keep the project on track, by requiring that the decision be made."

Does this mean I have to work on the weekends? I don't know if we have the discipline for this. Jerry can't even change his pants in 36 hours.

"The Business Blueprint activities represent about 5 weeks out of 25, or 20 percent of a six-month ASAP project."

Realization

"Phase three of the ASAP process is Realization. During this phase the actual R/3 configuration is completed, data from the legacy systems are converted, and the full system is tested. It is in this phase that the system is tested under full load conditions, similar to the way it will be used. It is best if people who will be actually using R/3 are also involved in this phase. Those that are, will become the trainers later in the ASAP project. This is an early opportunity to get them directly involved in the testing and implementation of the new system."

I wonder if we can train Jerry's clerk, let alone have her train others?

"The Realization activity takes approximately 45 percent of the time to complete an ASAP project; or more than 11 weeks out of 25."

Final Preparation

"Phase four, Final Preparation involves end user training. SAP offers courses appropriate for this level of training, but it is best if the users themselves, helped by the trainers, actually run these training programs. We can help, of course, both in training the trainers and end user training. The training should be completed as close to the actual 'go live' date as possible. In the Final Preparation phase, the users themselves should document the procedures for use, provide any special instructions that are needed to fit your organization, and organize a help desk.

"The Final Preparation takes approximately 25 percent of the ASAP project time, or more than 6 weeks out of a 25-week project".

Go Live and Support

"The final phase is Go Live and Support. This is where the starter's gun is fired. Going live with the system is just the beginning of an ongoing process of continuous training, learning, and improvement. This is where you learn the 'tricks' to make your use of the system more effective. It opens new ways of working inside the company and relating to customers and vendors. My objective, here, is to persuade you that Go Live doesn't mean you are done. You need to continue to train people and share knowledge to take full advantage of the system.

"The ASAP approach is designed to get you up and running on R/3 quickly. Many of the refinements are left for you to do later as you gain experience. For instance, you might use a single freight method at the start, adding others later or you might postpone any complex promotions until your people are comfortable with the system.

But SAP doesn't leave you on your own. For example, another innovative feature of the ASAP approach is an integrated quality assurance activity that is scheduled as part of the project. SAP wants their consultants to visit the project team periodically. This SAP expert comes to your company and interviews all of the key players on the project team."

If this guy keeps hanging around, it will be like a bad conscience if we are not on schedule. I guess that's his real job.

"The job of the SAP consultant is to provide a proactive functional and technical review. The visits are designed to point out potential problems before they occur. This expert ensures that the structured ASAP approach is being followed, that results are being documented, and that major issues are being resolved. This has been a successful feature of the ASAP approach. It is a way for your firm to get valuable time with an R/3 guru in a structured way."

I wonder how much that guy makes? I wonder if he would take my job and install this thing?

"I'm going to miss those of you who are leaving us. I hope you found what we have done so far useful. Of course, we'll talk about you as we get into the fun stuff later."

14. The R/3 views of the firm—Some detail

"That was fun last night. Thanks for the dinner. I had lots of perceptive questions about how to get R/3 implemented. Even after our discussion of ASAP, some of you are concerned about the horror stories you've heard and whether you need to fit your organization to R/3. Also, some of you feel that ASAP isn't for you. To help with these questions, I'll revise the schedule a little to get some more of the SAP view of the world into the day. I promise that we'll get to some demonstrations of the system, but the change may help to answer some of your questions.

"Okay, how does R/3 view the enterprise, the firm? How do all these things fit together from a company standpoint, not from a system standpoint? There are two things to say right up front. First, remember that the SAP R/3 programs are general so they can apply to all kinds of organizations. That means they are developed around generic processes that must be performed in any business. Second, even after configuring for your firm, remember that you may need to change some people's jobs to fit the new processes.

"One thing that may be difficult in learning about R/3 is understanding the jargon. R/3 uses the term 'organizational elements' to describe things in the company. Examples of organizational elements include the factories, the warehouses, the purchasing organizations, and the sales organizations. These elements enable the system to construct legal, organizational, operational, and other views of the enterprise.

"To draw on an analogy, think of these organization elements as 'codes,' the same codes we discussed before. In generating a report, you can sort on these codes. Accounting has codes for each cost center, for example. Marketing has codes for each product group, type of sale, distribution channel, region, and so on. That way they can cut their sales figures any way they want. Each group has their own reporting needs and the codes make the different views possible."

Yeah! Marketing cuts the figures every way but right!

"Let me describe an example of the use of views from the sales manager's perspective. As a manager in sales, I need to see how things are going by my different product lines. I would also want to see sales in different regions of the country. Since I need to pay my sales representatives, I need to track sales for each individual representative. To make this even more interesting, I have all kinds of different contracts with my customers. Some just place individual orders, others have blanket contracts. I need to know progress against a blanket contract and so on.

"Of course, I'm not the only one who needs various cuts through the data. My sales representatives need to know what is going on in manufacturing.

When, for example, will the order be completed, when will it be put on the truck, and how long will it take for the truck to get to the customer. They also may need to know when the marketing campaign is going to launch, how much can they promise to a customer, how much has a customer purchased this year, and so on.

"R/3 needs to be able to provide all these types of data instantly and uses the codes associated with the organizational elements as a means for doing so. Remember that the R/3 programs are built around the process flow diagrams included in the R/3 reference model. You know, like the diagram for booking a room? Well, we had to use codes for the organizer of the meeting, the attendee, and the room. That was so the system knew who was coming and where we were to have the meeting.

"The diagram you see now (Figure 14) is an overview of the way that SAP has structured some of the important organizational elements. They are collected in three areas. For example, some of the elements associated with the organizational view of the company are in Business Areas. They include companies, plants, storage, and purchasing. In Sales Areas we have elements like distribution channels, sales organizations, and divisions; like we just talked about. Control Areas contain elements that allow profit and/or cost to be viewed, for example, by divisions in the enterprise.

"The lingo here is important only to see the terminology that the SAP programmers used. The important thing is that R/3 has the capability of generating reports or views of the data to serve all the users of the system. In order to do this, the system needs codes for all the elements that might be needed for a particular cut of the data.

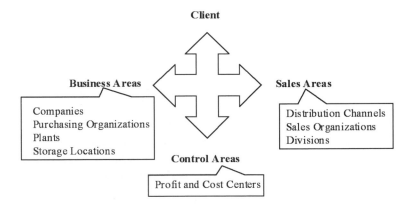

Figure 14: A Sample of the Organization Elements Used to Organize Information Within R/3

"Here we see client again. It is the highest level of integration in any implementation, most often the whole company. R/3 is designed so that multiple clients can be run within a single system. This might happen, for example, if you let each of your divisions have their own version of R/3. If you do this, though, no consolidated information can be obtained across the divisions by R/3. Each division or 'client' is independent. When a user logs on the system, the user logs on with a particular client and user code."

> *I wonder what this means for integrating with the Ohio plant. She seems to be saying we need to use a common set of codes in both locations to be able to summarize the data for Mr. McDougle. I guess this means that our raw material codes must be the same, as well as our accounting and customer codes. We would sure have to change a lot and we would even have to change codes on things that we buy from the same vendors as the Ohio people use.*

"Actually, we have just touched on a few of the major concepts to help you see how SAP organizes the program to enable you to get different views of your company. Now you have just enough terminology to make you dangerous or to use for dazzling people at cocktail parties."

15. A diversion—Dinner with Amanda

"Thanks Amanda," said Billy, "for coming to dinner with me. I appreciate your taking the time to join me, especially after having been out with the group last night. I'm really struggling with some of the terminology. I am the guy who will have to explain it when I get back to North Carolina, so I need to get it down."

"I know it is tough," replied Amanda, "so let me try to help you. Maybe it would be best if you told me what you think you understand and let me react to it."

"Before I start, you should probably know that the owner of our company is interested in implementing R/3 but is not computer literate at all. I'll need to explain it to him and he may ask me to actually implement the system if we go that way. You can see that I need to understand it very well."

Amanda said, "You know that I will be very helpful to you. I see the opportunity to sell another system and maybe I'll get to be the consultant on the job. I have always wanted to see western Carolina."

"You're certainly welcome any time," said Billy, "you don't need R/3 as an excuse. Let me start with my understanding. Maybe it is too simple, but I see R/3 as a box of Legos. You can make just about anything from them if you have the patience."

"That's interesting," replied Amanda. "I had not thought of it that way. Why don't you continue and we will see where the analogy might break down."

"Okay. I think of the box of Legos as being an R/3 system configured for a particular company. Anyway, with the box of Legos that I have I can build windmills, oil drills, Ferris wheels, and things like that. You even have directions to do things like that. I can't, however, build tanks, cars, or airplanes with that Lego set. I need another set to do those. The Legos are the individual processes, the things that you called 'best practices' that have been selected for the company. You can tell, I am a little confused."

"Well, that is an interesting analogy and the individual Legos do fit together like our processes. But it does not hold very well after that. The individual Legos are far more general than R/3's processes, especially after they have been configured to fit your company. You can, though, combine the processes to build a structure that works for your company. I find it interesting to think about the Lego kits as collections of those processes."

"The reason that I thought about Legos and Lego kits was it helped me understand configuration. I thought configuration was choosing which Lego set, or maybe it was choosing between a Lego set and Lincoln Logs. And then the size of the set or the specific Legos or Logs would be the second part of the configuration."

"I think the analogy has broken down," interrupted Amanda. "Let me try to use the SAP terminology and what you have seen in the seminar to make this a little clearer. SAP has developed hundreds of those processes that are documented in process flow diagrams. Each one does a certain task. We saw the one that reserved a room for a meeting and notified the participants. Your company might choose to use a different set of those processes than another company simply because you do different things or because you do things differently. For example, you might not want to use the room reservation capability. If you choose not to, though, there are some disadvantages. The programs that execute those process flow diagrams are all linked together so that . . ."

Billy interrupted saying, "Yes, I understand that, the integration. I'm still a bit hazy on configuration then. Is it more than choosing processes?"

"Yes. Remember the 'ors' in the process flow diagrams? Your firm might not pick the same ones as another firm. Also you need to specify who has the right to reserve rooms, order food, and so forth. Even in that little example, you can see there is more to be done than just use the process."

"That helps," said Billy. But I still don't understand how those processes relate to the business organization. You know, the functions like accounting, sales and marketing, manufacturing, and so on."

"Oh, I see. Remember I told you that there is a lot of confusion between the way SAP collects these process flow diagrams together and names them and the way you would like the collections named. All organizations seem to have different terms and conventions, all of which, by the way, can be accommodated in R/3, but our name choices may not match your names. That is the reason we have provided the flexibility to set up custom menus to fit your company. To use your Lego analogy, SAP may have Legos grouped into three 'functions' for a windmill: legs, braces, and propeller. You might have different Legos grouped by sides, crosspieces, and propeller."

Billy asked, "Is there no relationship then between what we call functions, or what we name accounting, manufacturing, marketing, and so forth, and the process flow diagrams?"

"Well, there is in the sense that the people who are doing order entry are most likely associated with sales or marketing. Similarly, the person who is scheduling production jobs is most likely to be housed in manufacturing. The process flow diagram for entering an order and for scheduling production jobs can be put in the box called manufacturing or the box called accounting, or whatever. It is more important to know that the collection of these process flow diagrams will do all of the jobs that are necessary for your business.

"I'm sorry I have got to leave now and go over the notes for the seminar tomorrow. But please feel free to ask any questions or contact me again if you are not clear."

16. At last—A customer order demo!

"It's time for some demos. I need to set you up for these, however. Remember that R/3 is a collection of individual computer programs. Among them are those that produce reports, send e-mail, and keep track of your calendar. The ones we are going to look at now provide screen forms for people to fill in to accomplish a task—like booking a luncheon meeting room. Here in the seminar, sometimes it will be difficult to remember how to get to a particular program. You might think there is no logic to where it is in the menus.

"On the other hand, think of the person who uses the system every day to do a particular job. That person will become very familiar with the programs that are associated with their job, just like you are now familiar with your e-mail and the other computer programs you use. I'll bet that the logic to them wasn't clear to start with either. Anyway, have patience with me and

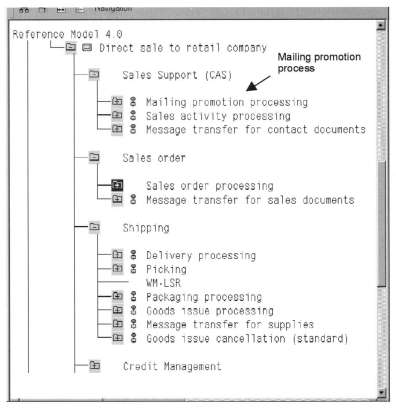

Figure 15: Order Handling Options

try to see how R/3 captures data in an orderly way and makes it available to all who need access to it."

I wonder why she is apologizing now. I liked the room-booking example, even though I didn't like having the nametags.

"In order to illustrate how R/3 can be used to help you manage a business, we are going to use a motorcycle manufacturing company. I have no clue why, but this company is commonly used in R/3 user training programs. We'll start with a typical customer order management process. I have brought up a screen showing the processes that support direct sales to retail companies (Figure 15). As you can see, there are many different processes available. Each process is documented with a process flow diagram like we saw earlier in the seminar.

"Activities in the customer order process may include the management of a mail promotion. R/3 has programs to maintain the mailing list. All customer interactions can be logged into the system using phone call record or mail response tracking. Also, order quotations can be integrated into the overall process and managed by the system. The slide (Figure 15) gives some feel for the kinds of processes that are included in R/3."

Whoops, that is a lot of detail! I wonder how much of that stuff Jerry does?

"At the motorcycle company, a typical sales cycle begins when a customer service representative receives an order from a retail dealer. Integrated into the R/3 system is the ability to receive the order via a wide variety of media other than voice or paper. These include fax, EDI, and Internet. Typical steps in processing an order would include order entry, creating the delivery transaction, invoicing the customer, processing the payment, and so forth. Here, way under the Logistics menu, is the form used to enter a cash sale order (Figure 16). It shows a completed form from the Cycle Concepts store that ordered 10 motor cycles, 15 headlamp kits, and 20 taillight kits.

"Of course, there are many other types of order forms available, including consignment orders, sales against a contract, rush orders, and returns. However the initial order is created, information is automatically carried from one transaction to another, requiring data entry only once.

"Also, the customer service rep has access to other programs that enable the rep to complete the job. During sales order taking, for example, the rep checks the customer credit limits, checks the availability of the items, and updates the cash forecast to reflect the sale, and the system automatically updates the data for the production of the items. That's probably a bigger job than any of the people currently involved in your order entry function has.

"To illustrate how the customer service representative checks availability of the item, we select one of the items on the order by clicking the box to

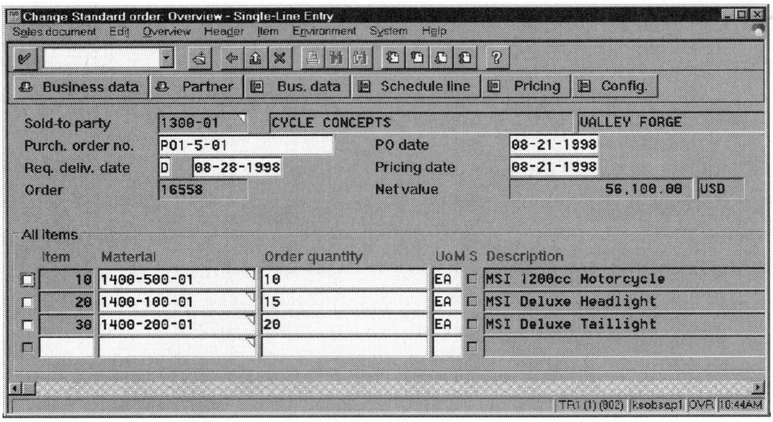

Figure 16: Cash Sales Order Entry Form

the left of the item. Then we run through the menu path: Item -> Schedule line -> Quantities/date -> Edit -> Shipping details. I know that going through the menus may seem like magic, but they quickly become familiar with a little use of the system. But there is also a short cut for those who use the system frequently for the same task. We could move immediately to the Shipping details display by using a unique code that R/3 has assigned to this screen (Figure 17)."

I'll take the shortcut every time. I'll bet all R/3 users have calluses on their mouse fingers.

"Keep in mind that there are many options for how a particular task might be handled. For example, the inventory sourcing process for an item can include options to obtain the item from stock on hand, or by a replenishment activity that triggers a production order or a purchase order. This process can even be configured to source material from an external supplier or from external warehouse sites. The first time an item is entered in the system, this sourcing information is included as well. There is great flexibility here.

"In our example case, the motorcycle is being shipped from our warehouse in New York. Notice the dates on the report (Figure 17). They provide an interesting insight into the R/3 integration. The 'material availability' date is the date when the item must be available in inventory for picking. This date is automatically calculated by working backward from the customer's requested delivery date, taking into account how much time is needed for delivery related activities such as picking, packing, loading, and transportation.

"The 'loading date' is when picking and packing must be completed so that the goods are ready to transport in order to reach the customer on time.

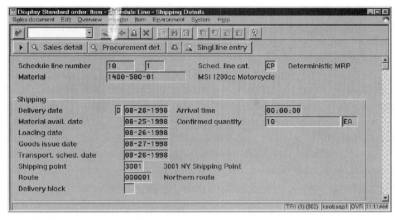

Figure 17: Shipping Details

Special packaging materials required for loading must also be available by this date. The 'transportation scheduling' date is when transportation must be arranged.

"Finally, the 'goods issue' day is when the goods must physically leave the shipping point. The system will automatically create a goods issued document to account for the outgoing inventory. The 'goods issue' date enables the accounting department to relate the movement of goods to the invoice.

"An obvious question is how did all of these dates get into the system. The time offset for the assembly operation is built into the material database. In the database, our 1200cc motorcycle is categorized as being manufactured on demand. The database includes a field for this type of item that indicates that manufacturing needs to be given a week to assemble them. For the 1200cc motorcycle, the system also knows how much notice to give the carrier and how long it takes the carrier to deliver motorcycles to our customer. The data about the carrier are included in the vendor database that is used by this program.

"Notice how all of the key elements of processing this order are scheduled using these dates. Activities required by production, the warehouse people, transportation, logistics, and accounting are all coordinated by the system."

This is certainly more comprehensive then the room reservation thing. The motorcycle guys look more like the Ohio plant than we do, though.

"The system automatically creates a packing slip and the picking list information for the warehouse management processes. When the item is picked, the system can print order-packing documents. Multiple orders for a customer can be automatically combined for shipment purposes. On confirmation that the goods have left the warehouse, the system updates inventory balances and makes appropriate general ledger entries. At each step in the process, transaction tracking is possible using the original customer order number created when the order was initially taken.

"The final step in customer order processing is billing and receipt of payment from the customer. Invoicing normally occurs after the product has been shipped to the customer and the data from the actual delivery documents is transferred to the invoice automatically. Options for invoicing by individual order, a group of orders, or on a regular billing calendar are available. Once the invoice has been released, financial accounting is notified. The receivable and revenue accounts are updated with a journal entry into the general ledger."

I suppose that our people do all this stuff by sending messages back and forth.

"The receipt of payment is handled by posting the amount against open items in accounts receivable. The customer payment processing includes receiving and recording the customer's payment, increasing the customer's available credit, reducing receivables, recording any cash discounts, and reconciling any differences in amount received compared to invoiced amounts.

"You can see the power of an integrated approach. Errors are minimized since the data for the order are entered once and are common in each step of the process. The precise status of the order from initial creation to final payment is available at any time to the users of the system."

Wow! This sure is a lot different from the way we handle selling our furniture. Also, somebody has to make those motorcycles and that requires a lot of coordination for ordering parts and fabricating all the pieces. They need material requirements planning. I'm going to ask her if R/3 has it?

"Thanks for the question, Billy; you woke some people up. Yes, R/3 has an extensive set of MRP programs. I'll show you some of their capabilities a little later in the demonstration. First, let me show you a few things about how R/3 supports purchasing."

17. Another demo—Procurement

"How many of you have worked in purchasing? Well, at least a few of you have. R/3 takes a very general approach to procurement so it might be different than what you are used to. Whether material is coming from a plant owned by the company or from an external source makes no difference to R/3. In addition, the system considers material that will be used in internal production processes and material that will be shipped to customers in the same manner. Even the bagels for our luncheon meeting in Germany are handled through the procurement programs.

"The procurement programs use data contained in the material master and vendor master records in the database. As we might expect in a totally integrated system, the material master records are the same whether they are used for finished goods or for raw materials. The codes are used for identification."

There are those codes again. I have a sinking feeling that something like "the wooden thing over there" won't work with R/3.

"Let's just walk through the overall procurement process. It is comprised of the following steps:

"There is a request for goods or services. This could be in the form of a purchase requisition created manually or automatically from the material requirements planning (MRP) programs.

"The source of supply is next determined. This could be an external vendor or an internal source such as a manufacturing plant or warehouse.

"The requisition is then linked to the vendor in the system.

"A purchase order that references the requisition is created.

"The system provides automated expediting and follow-up reminders to ensure the order is delivered on time.

"The goods are recorded as they are received into the warehouse using a purchase order goods receipt.

"The system compares the received order with the original purchase order and quantity received to validate the invoice.

"Payment is made, dependent on the payment terms and conditions defined for the vendor.

"The system can support different types of arrangements with external vendors. For example, if the item is purchased in large quantities on a regular basis from a single supplier, a long-term contract may be agreed upon. The purchase requisition can then release purchases against this contract. Alternatively, if you wish to spread purchasing across a number of suppliers, a quota agreement may be drawn up that splits the purchase orders into predefined ratios."

You know, this sounds like a very rational process. I'm not sure it could handle the change in hardware on that Atlanta desk, though.

"When the purchase requisition is released to the vendor, the data are copied into a purchase order with details from the vendor master record. Creating the actual purchase order can require special authorization if this type of control is needed.

"Here we have a screen (Figure 18) showing a purchase order form from R/3. This is an order for 100 of the Deluxe Headlight kits that are priced at $25 each and scheduled for August 26 delivery. Notice that the order dates and delivery dates are the same. This could be for a just-in-time order to a local wholesaler."

Or donuts to the seminar?

"The system can handle vendor contracts that include various quantity discounts, special scheduling agreements, and special quotas such as minimum or maximum order quantities. Service contracts are handled the same as contracts to purchase materials, thus providing a uniform screen look to the user.

"Different purchase order types, different general ledger account assignments, different cost centers, and different assets types can be assigned to the items purchased. It is even possible to spread the costs across several cost centers or projects when the order is created.

"Once a purchase order has been released, its status must be tracked by the system. R/3 has various types of reports that can be displayed to

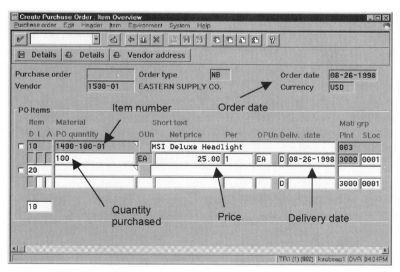

Figure 18: Purchase Order—Item Overview

show the status of purchased items. I want to show you a stock overview screen and some detail (Figure 19). The detail list showing the status of inventory at the New York site, was created by double clicking on the '3000 New York' line in the Stock Overview screen (Figure 19). The amount of material 1400-100-01 that is on-hand at warehouse location 0001 in New York is given here. Also, note the open order for 100 units from the purchase order that was created.

"Item data associated with the receipt are copied from the purchase order into the goods receipt document for use when the goods arrive. Goods receipt data are used to update purchase order history and vendor evaluation. Vendor performance history, including due date adherence and quality, can be viewed at any time.

"Full integration implies that general ledger records are automatically updated to reflect the increase in inventory. It is even possible to automatically generate an electronic mail message to inform the person that ordered the goods that they have been received. A complete purchase history is maintained for audit purposes."

It sounds so logical when she explains it. I wonder why all the war stories.

"Invoices are matched to the original order and payment is handled in accounts payable. Accounts payable pays all posted invoices that are due and not blocked for payment. Payment is based on the terms specified in the purchase order or in the vendor master. The payment program has been designed for international transactions and method of payment can vary depending on the country involved.

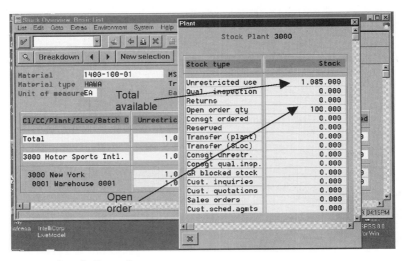

Figure 19: Stock Overview

"Standard management reports including order value by vendor, number of purchase orders by material type, and average value of purchase order by purchasing group are available. In addition, custom reports can be designed using a report formatter that is part of R/3. Information can also be quickly exported to a Microsoft Excel spreadsheet for more specialized analysis."

Wow! When I think of all the hands that touch our purchase process, it boggles the mind. All those folks' jobs would have to change.

"Take a break and we'll do some more when you get back."

18. For management—A financial application

Amanda started the next session with, "You are not hitting the donuts so hard today. What happened?

"Several of you suggested that the examples were too operations oriented, so here is a financial application. The programs are divided into five sets that provide different views of a company's current financial health and detailed operational performance. These are defined as follows:

"*Enterprise controlling*—an enterprise-wide view of financial reporting.

"*Treasury*—control of cash, banking, securities, and funds management.

"*Financial accounting*—core financial accounting integrated with subledgers. Financial accounting can be broken down into the following: general ledger accounting, accounts receivable, accounts payable, legal consolidations, special purpose ledger, and asset accounting.

"*Controlling*—management accounting for tracking overhead and profitability as well as production process control. Controlling can be broken down into overhead cost controlling, product cost controlling, sales and profitability analysis, and activity based costing.

"*Investment management*—capital management such as construction projects or capitalization of assets."

I think this is going to be over my head, at least over my overhead. I never believed you could control cost from the accounting sheets anyway. I always thought you had to change the way things were done in operations.

"R/3 organizes accounting information around external and internal users. External users require published information in conformance with legal requirements such as audits/annual reports, W-2s/1099 tax reporting, sales receipts, and other information. Internal users could be at any level in the company and require information on internal operations. This information would typically include performance data like cost and productivity numbers. Custom reports can be created and all data can be exported to Microsoft Excel spreadsheets for custom analysis.

"What you see here (Figure 20) is a report showing the contribution margin from the sales of different motorcycle models. This report has been custom designed and gives the percentages for the 1200 CC motorcycle compared to the other models.

"This report can be summarized graphically by clicking on a graphic icon on the top left of the report. I know these are difficult to see from where you are sitting. The 'navigation' area gives options for viewing the detail of the report. By clicking on 'Customer,' the sales by individual customers can be

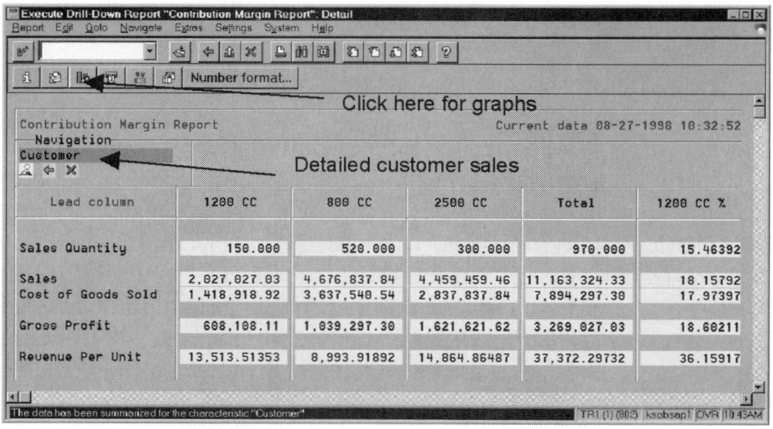

Figure 20: Contribution Margin Report—Summarized for All

seen. These graphic and optional levels of detail are standard features of all R/3 reports, even the customized ones."

We don't have anything like this capability. Do we need R/3 to get it though?

"Next we have a cost center report (Figure 21) for purchasing. There are two accounts related to this cost center. These are the salary account— 430000—and the depreciation account—481000. In our example, the planned, that is the budgeted, costs have not been entered, so the variance reporting is not complete; actually they are all unfavorable. On the other hand, with these unfavorable variances, they may look like budget reports.

"To create financial audit trails, every transaction processed by the system is represented by an electronic document. Documents are accessible in real time and are stored centrally for easy access. Data resulting from transactions posted to the system can be viewed at every level of detail from the original document to the summary report. For most reports, the system provides a drill-down capability, allowing you to go to lower levels of detail."

What is this? Oil drilling?

"R/3 is designed to automatically create the transactions needed to update the general ledger accounts. In many cases these transactions will update the subledger accounts that were created to track profit and/or cost. Of course, manual general ledger transactions can also be posted to the system. The subledger accounts are automatically updated in the general ledger through a reconciliation account that aggregates the information. For example, customer

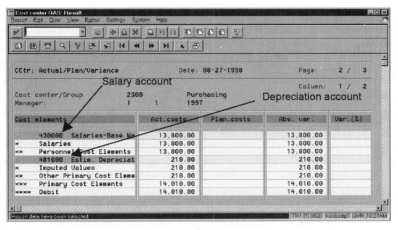

Figure 21: Cost Center Report for Purchasing

and vendor subledgers update the accounts receivable and accounts payable accounts respectively through reconciliation accounts."

I don't think I'll ever be reconciled to this stuff. I hope that there will be something that I can understand.

19. Just for Billy—A manufacturing example

"Well, Billy, we finally got here. Yes, R/3 does have material requirements planning—MRP for short. In fact you may remember that I told you some people think that R/3 is just an extra-strength version of MRP. As with most of the application programs, however, you will see that it is broader than you might be used to seeing with MRP. The programs support both manufacturing planning and execution. Manufacturing planning is the process of using forecasts and customer orders to create production and procurement schedules for finished products, component parts, and purchased materials. Manufacturing execution is the process of producing component parts, finished products, tracking all shop floor activities, and recording inventory movements.

"The manufacturing planning process can be broken down into three major steps. The first step is the determination of requirements. Sales forecasts are based on historical demand data and current order requirements. Historical data can be used in a variety of models, including moving averages and exponential smoothing. The forecasts from these are combined with actual demand data to create a composite forecast of demand for the company."

Wow! Here's something familiar for a change.

"The second step, master scheduling, is the process of determining how to meet this demand. Master scheduling, in many cases, may involve simply making the anticipated demand each period. If there is much uncertainty in the forecast, or significant seasonality in demand, a more complex plan can be developed. Such things as building safety stock to protect against uncertainty, or producing inventory in slack demand periods for peak periods, may be done.

"The actual master schedule is a manufacturing plan reflecting how demand will be met. The master schedule can include finished products, subassemblies, components or other items that require the use of capacity. Typically items included in the master schedule are those items that have a major influence on profits, have long lead times and/or consume critical resources. The programs can also use the master production schedule to project capacity requirements on key resources. The schedule can then be adjusted to compensate for anticipated problems.

"Our next screen (Figure 22) ties the forecasting and master scheduling parts of R/3 together. This screen depicts the 'Rough-Cut Plan.' In the first row are the anticipated sales for our 1200cc motorcycle either from the forecasting programs or manual entry. Next we enter the 100-unit target stock levels for the first four months of our planning period. The rough-cut plan is generated by determining the production required to meet these targets. We could have chosen to set 'target day's supply' and have the system

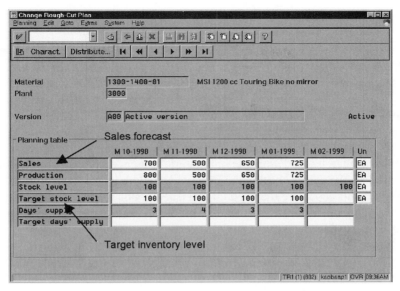

Figure 22: A Production Plan Design to Meet Target Stock

calculate a plan from this data. The system is very flexible in doing trial and error 'what if' analysis using this type of interactive screen. Once we are satisfied with the production plan from this screen we can enter it directly into the database and make it available to the master production schedule.

"The master production schedule is input into material requirements planning (MRP), the third step in the manufacturing planning process. The MRP program calculates detailed schedules for all the supporting assemblies, subassemblies, and component parts. Information on the parts necessary to produce an item is provided in a file called the bill of material."

So far, so good! I wonder if the bill of material can be changed during manufacturing like we do all the time. I think I'll ask her.

"No, Billy, you can't change the bill of material after you have started to produce the product. You can have a different bill of material for each product and even for each order so they can be very different. This is part of the flexibility of R/3.

"For the master schedule items, the MRP program creates planned orders that reflect the plan for meeting demand. These planned orders are then used to calculate the schedule for the component parts that are needed. This is a process known as 'exploding' requirements. These calculations consider available warehouse stock and any outstanding purchasing or production orders when determining how many additional products are needed."

Boy, those guys in the back are having more trouble with this than I did with the accounting demo.

"Remember that earlier I said both planning and execution are supported; well, execution starts when the planned orders are formally released into the production system. Routings describe the sequence of manufacturing operations required to produce a specific item. For each operation, the anticipated time and materials needed, together with equipment and tool requirements, are documented in the routing list.

"Materials are issued against the orders and their actual progress through the shop is then tracked while actual material usage, employee hours, etc. is captured by the system. When the order is completed a formal confirmation is created and goods are received into finished goods inventory. Finally, reconciling differences between actual and planned material and other resource usage and cost are recorded and the order is closed.

"Execution involves more than just managing the manufacturing of the item, as you can see. It also means capturing the details for tracking progress and cost accounting. If the item is produced in-house, costs are accumulated as the item consumes resources, primarily employee and machine time, as part of the manufacturing process. The cost, capacity, and scheduling of these resources are tracked by the system. In the case of outside purchases, the

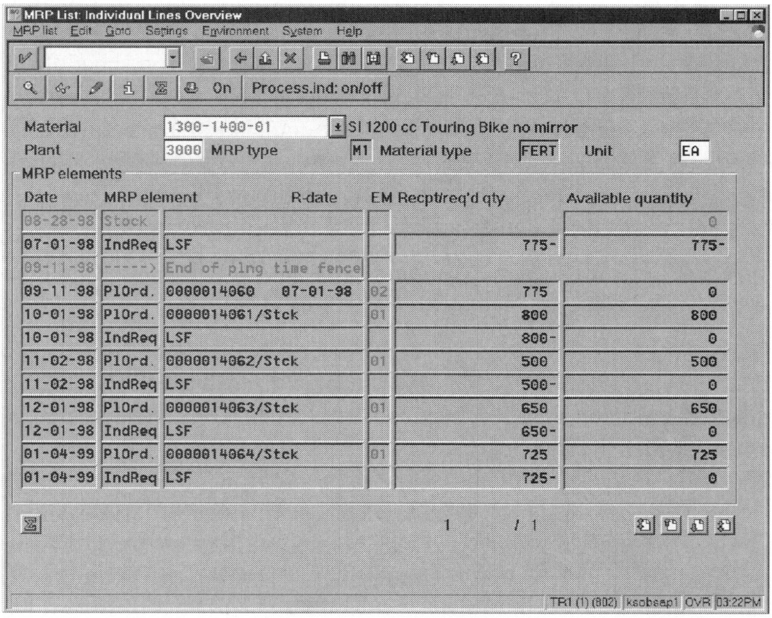

Figure 23: MRP List

planned orders are sent to purchasing and are released to vendors. Their progress at the vendor can be tracked as well."

> *I guess our old system is not as bad as I thought. If this is "best practice," we're pretty close. She makes the data entry sound automatic though. I know I've entered some of the data on the weekend after it happened rather than right at the time.*

"An extensive reporting system is provided by R/3. The next screen (Figure 23) is a report showing the results of an MRP run. It is for the SI 1200 cc Touring Bike. I wonder why there is no side mirror? Anyway, the 'IndReq' MRP elements represent the forecast sales, independent requirements for you purists, expected for the item. You can see the production plan from the planning report shown earlier (Figure 22) and carried into the master production schedule is 'exploded' here. The available quantities in this report don't show the safety stock requirements, the target stock levels, from before."

> *I wonder if that motorcycle comes with a sidecar option. I've always wanted one of those. I can see my wife and me now.*

"There are many additional reports available through the R/3 menus to support the planning and execution of manufacturing. The list shown on the slide (Figure 24) is a sampling. I'm not going to talk about these, but you production geeks can poke around in the menus during the break.

"Well, that gives you a quick view of a few of the capabilities of R3 and how some of the programs work. R/3 is really big and it takes literally weeks to learn about each of the application areas. We haven't really gone into the areas of human resource management, warehouse management, or project management, to mention a few."

- Master data—materials, bills of material, work centers, routings.
- Sales Order and Planning (SOP)—product group breakdown, product group usage, material usage, and planning situation.
- Demand management—total requirements, characteristics, and planning techniques.
- Master planning—planning result, planning situation, order report, and pegging.
- Production control—capacity planning, backorder processing, pegged requirements, pegged receipts, and stock/requirements list.
- Capacity planning—work center views for load, orders, pool, backlog, and overload.
- Kanban—plant overview, stock/requirements list, stock overview, and error display.
- Product costing—existing costs and standards.

Figure 24: Sample MRP Reports

20. Crunching the numbers—The hardware

"All right, this is going to be very different than the demos we have just seen. I'm going to talk about what underlies these programs. We'll look first at the hardware.

"SAP gave a lot of thought to organizing the computers to run the R/3 programs. As with the program itself, they made sure that there was substantial flexibility in how they did it. There is real power in their approach, because there is high degree of computing 'scalability.' Scalability refers to the ability to match the processing requirements to the needs of the organization over time. As more processing power is required, additional computers, storage or memory can be added to the system. As more storage is required, the database can also be expanded.

"Sure, it has always been possible to add more processing power to a computer system, but in the past that involved buying a new computer and scrapping the old. You no longer have to do this with our new way of sharing computers and the software running on the computers.

"To make scalability possible, the computers are organized into the three distinct tiers you see now (Figure 25). At the heart of the system is the database computer, called a server in this design. Since all the data used by the system are stored in a database, the performance of the database server is critical to the success of the system.

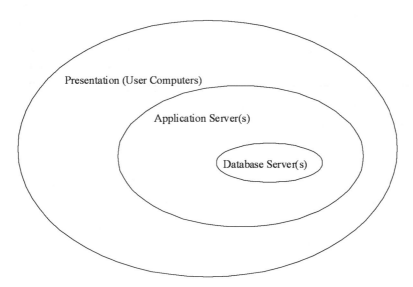

Presentation (User Computers)

Application Server(s)

Database Server(s)

Figure 25: Three-Tier Architecture

"The database server is a special computer designed to be very reliable. The disk drives, for example, are designed so that if one fails no data are lost and a new drive can be installed without shutting down the system. In addition, when more storage is needed it can be easily added by installing additional disk drives.

"These database servers can be purchased from many vendors. SAP provides the other programs, but the database program must also come from another vendor. There are a few suppliers of database programs that can work with R/3."

Hey! No sales pitch. This is something new.

"The next tier in the system is referred to as the application layer. These computers run the R/3 software. Although SAP supplies the software, hardware for running the programs must be supplied by other vendors. Once again, the application layer can be run on a single computer or on many, depending on need.

"The last tier is the presentation layer. This consists of the computers the users are actually using. You know the ones on their desks. The presentation computers can be regular personal computers, since the computers at the application and database tiers do most of the work. SAP supplies the software for the presentation computers. In fact, a lot of what you have been seeing is the output of the presentation programs.

"The term 'three-tier client-server system' is used to describe this approach to hardware support for the system. The client is the user of the system. Incidentally, this has nothing to do with the SAP use of the term client for the highest level of information integration in R/3. The servers are the 'application servers' in the middle layer. These computers are doing all the calculations required to provide the screens and reports needed by the client computers. The application servers also send the commands to the database servers to retrieve and store all the data used by the system."

"Many developments are on the horizon that will simplify the hardware issues. Soon it will be possible to access the system on the Web and the screens will have a Web look to them. I don't have any examples for you yet. But it should make life easier for future users."

If that doesn't happen soon, it sounds like we will have to buy new computers. I wonder if Mr. McDougle realizes this means that he may not be able to renew his club membership for next year? I should talk to the Ohio guys and see what they did.

21. Providing support—The software

"You have seen how complex the R/3 package is. There are some implications of this complexity, which lead to important management principles. You need to have knowledgeable people working on the implementation project in order to configure the system appropriately. When configuration is going on, you will decide exactly how R/3 is going to organize the database, which is difficult to change later. What's more, if you need to make changes to the system, you need to use the proprietary programming language, ABAP/4. Also, you can't just tack on a package you are currently using without some work. Finally, and most important, mistakes in the initial configuration may severely limit future options. This is not intended to discourage you, but to make clear that the considerable benefits of R/3 don't just happen automatically.

"I want to show you why R/3 is such a powerful system, so hang on. To grasp the real complexity of the collection of programs that comprise the R/3 system is difficult. However, I do want to attempt to give some feel for how the major groups of programs are organized and how this relates to data maintained by the system."

Oh, oh! She's gonna smoke me now! I wonder if this is the kind of thing that Prof is doing with his grant? I'm gonna get some more coffee.

"Here is a diagram that depicts the major components of the system (Figure 26). I'm going to give you a brief explanation of each of these boxes. Keep in mind that all of these things must be done no matter how the software and hardware is organized. In fact, you are all doing them now with paper slips, software, processes, and so forth. Overall, however, as you see how logically they are integrated, it's clear that R/3 is not all that different from what we might have seen before the three-tier client-server systems were developed. The big difference is that R/3 runs on a number of individual computers, and each user is even using an individual computer.

"On the slide (Figure 26) the Computer Center Management System is a group of programs that assist the system administrator in running R/3. One task this system performs is the assignment of the different application programs to the individual servers available for R/3. For example, the programs that support materials management and human resources can be run on the same computer or they can be run on separate computers.

"Since each server will be running multiple programs, the system administrator needs to assign programs to the available computers and to set priorities for running these programs. This allocation of resources and setting of priorities is often referred to as 'tuning' the system. Incidentally, when things go wrong, like when one of the servers gets overloaded, it's often because the system isn't tuned correctly."

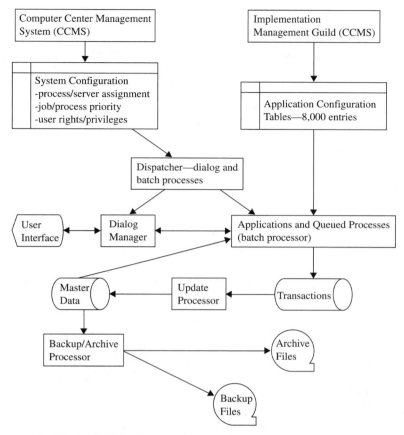

Figure 26: The R/3 Software Architecture

You know we don't have anyone in the company who can do this. I don't even know anybody who can do this. The computer guy doesn't have a clue about what we do in our jobs and I don't know if he knows a client from a server. I wonder who does this in Ohio.

"The system administrator also needs to authorize users for the system and assign each user specific privileges. This ensures users have proper authority to access certain applications. Many users, for example, would enjoy having the ability to change their salary anytime they wanted. I thought that might get your attention and that you'd be interested in how to change your salaries. Now you know. The programs that handle these authorizations are in the Computer Center Management System."

Interesting, using multiple servers for the different programs sure would increase our hardware costs. Well, maybe not. There are probably more trade-offs than just between one big computer and a number of smaller computers. I wonder if SAP gets a commission on all the computers sold to run R/3!

"In the upper right corner of our diagram (Figure 26) is the Implementation Management Guide. This is where the R/3 programs are configured prior to their use. Selecting options associated with each process largely does this configuration (Figure 27). A simple example would be the default currency used for the accounting reports. Another might be the definition of the group of users who can schedule rooms in a particular area.

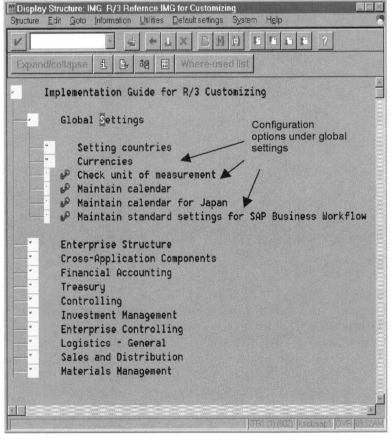

Figure 27: Implementation Management Guide (IMG)
Configuration Menu

"Configuring the system by specifying the 8,000 options in the configuration tables (Figure 26) allows R/3 to be tailored to the needs of an enterprise. Of course, the enterprise must often adapt to the processes supported by R/3. It is a two-way street. This task of system configuration requires considerable knowledge of the entire capability of the R/3 system and the way the firm does business."

I'm getting nervous again. Nobody is gonna figure out how to determine 8,000 options in one lifetime. There must be an easier way. I guess that is what ASAP helps do. And what is this stuff about adapting the organization? I think an example of when people would say you have to adapt your organization to the R/3 approach was in the nametag thing. I think I'll ask her about this.

"Billy, are you still worried about those name tags? Well, if you don't want name tags, don't select that option when you configure the system. But notice that the person who programmed that logic made it an option for those who want the name tags. If you really want something weird that isn't there, you can do it yourself.

"Also available through the Implementation Management Guide is the ABAP/4 programming language, a sample of which you can now see (Figure 28). This is the language, which some people claim is similar to the old programming language called COBOL, that was used to write the application programs included with the system. This is also the language that must

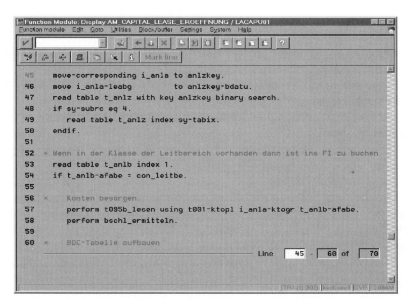

Figure 28: ABAP/4 Programming Language Example

be used to write custom programs that work within the R/3 system. Using ABAP/4 allows you to develop special applications that aren't covered within the standard R/3 programs. As you can see from our example, most of the programming has been done in German.

"There are many software programming companies around the world now specializing in ABAP/4 programming. But, SAP recommends that you not make major changes to the system since there is no guarantee that systems that have been modified, even with ABAP/4, will be compatible with future releases of R/3 software."

I'm just gonna call Mary Lou when I need changes.

"Using data supplied from the Computer Center Management System, the Dispatcher, shown in the middle of the slide (Figure 26), performs the actual assignment of applications to the server computers available to the system. The Dispatcher is programmed to balance the load on the system by moving applications between computers and adjusting program priorities according to the parameters supplied by the system administrator.

"The Dispatcher is managing two types of programs, the programs that support the users filling in screens and the programs that run the applications. The system administrator would normally give user screen programs the highest priority since this impacts their productivity. At night, priorities might be significantly different and long report programs might be run. The Dispatcher automates the process of making the R/3 system run efficiently."

But we don't have anyone around at night. I'm certainly not going to volunteer.

"The Dialog Manager in the middle of the slide (Figure 26) coordinates the communication between R/3 and the user. In a traditional real-time system, the user would have to wait at the screen for the database to update before being able to further interact with the system. R/3 separates the screen support from the actual updating to allow quicker response time. Oops, do you need a towel?"

What was that? Is somebody snoring? Jeez, somebody fell asleep and knocked their Coke off the table. What a mess! I hope there isn't a quiz on this stuff.

"To the right of the Dialog Manager (Figure 26) is the Applications and Queued Processes. These are the programs that perform the actual work within R/3. Remember that we talked about scalability earlier. This is an example of where the system can grow with your company

"Keep in mind that there may be either a single computer running these programs or many computers, and that single or multiple copies of the programs may be running. All this depends on the processing load placed on the R/3 system.

"The next program is the Update Processor. R/3 is structured so that the users, using application programs, create transactions whenever data need to be changed, added, or deleted in the database. These transactions are queued in a transaction file in the sequence received. The Update Processor prioritizes these transactions and updates the master database. Many problems associated with updating the database are solved with this simple mechanism for queuing and prioritizing data transactions.

"The final group of programs is the Backup and Archive Processor. These programs automate the process of creating backup copies of the database. This is one of the ways that we enhance system recovery in the unlikely event of a problem. In addition, old transaction data that represents the history of the firm are archived after the information is no longer needed by the system. The system has the ability to trace past transactions for correcting mistakes and for auditing purposes.

"I know you are ready for a break. Are there any quick questions?"

"What about the 8,000 options, isn't there an easier way to do this?"

"Yes, ASAP will help with that."

"My boss wants to only implement part of the system. Does that mean we still need to worry about all 8,000 configuration options?"

"When you implement only part of the system, you lose some integration opportunities but do simplify the configuration. The 8,000 options assume that you are implementing everything. Actually, no company would ever implement everything, so you don't need to deal with all 8,000. You only need to worry about those options that are important for the parts of the system you are using."

"Well just how much hardware is required to support a typical installation? Let's say we have 1,000 employees manufacturing a product that is distributed in the United States."

"This could be supported with a single database server and two to three application servers. Software costs would be on the order of $1 to $2 million. Consulting and training could easily run another $1 to $2 million. Typical yearly licensing fees would run about 15% of the initial software license cost or $150,000 to $300,000 for your 1,000-person firm. These are just rough ballpark figures. If some custom programming is needed, costs can easily be much higher.

"Let's take a break."

22. Course wrap-up—A sales pitch?

During the break Amanda came up to Billy and said, "Billy, you still look confused. Am I right?"

"Yes, and it is now getting to the point where I need to have things really clear if I am going to make sense when I get back to North Carolina. I am concerned about configuration. But, even more basically, I'm confused about the client code. It was not clear before and now I'm wondering if I could have a mixture of Lego sets and Lincoln Logs in the same client code," said Billy.

By this time there was a group standing around discussing various aspects of configuration and some of the other terminology. Billy was trying to explain the Legos and Lincoln Logs.

Amanda interrupted saying, "I think we have pushed that analogy about as far as it will go. It might be easier to think of this in the following way. The client code is the highest level of aggregation of information in the R/3 program. If it is helpful, you can think of this as being the Chairman of the Board position. Technically, SAP calls that an organizational element. The Chairman has all kinds of resources, locations, legal constraints, customers, and other things that are under his management. All of these are also organizational elements from an SAP standpoint. Remember that each organizational element has a code."

Billy replied, "Now I guess I didn't want us to get off on that issue. What I am really concerned about is configuration. Maybe it is related to the client code, but here's what I think I understand about configuration. I need to identify all of the plants, locations, legal relationships, people, products, customers, and so on with a code."

"Yes, that is right. In order for the Chairman to communicate with any of these things, these organizational elements, he will have to know their names or, in R/3 terms, to know their associated codes."

"Setting up all those codes could be a lot of work," mused Billy. "But that is only one part of the configuration process and I understand there is at least one more and that is choosing the processes that we want to use and specifying any alternative within them. Like the name tags or not."

"That's right," said Amanda. "There is one other aspect as well that may be a little more subtle. For each of the process flow diagrams that you choose, R/3 has to have the appropriate information to be able to execute the program. For example, if you want to be able to route your shipments by air or ground, the program must be configured to include both options."

"Man, we do that on the fly right now. I don't know that I could predetermine every alternative that we are going to need in the future."

"That's not necessary," said Amanda. "You can add some things to the database quite easily, like a new employee, a new customer, a new shipping route. These things can also be removed easily. It's more difficult to change things closer to the Chairman of the Board, things like creating a new plant or division, or acquiring a new company. Those things are harder to change at the moment. But you can be sure that SAP is working right now to make that easier in the future.

"We need to get back in there and wrap things up. The others are going to wonder what happened."

Back in the seminar room, Amanda said, "During the break, we had a lot of questions about configuration. At the risk of muddying up the water for some of you, I'm going to try another analogy, constructing a house. As you think about it, there are three 'levels' of activities that you must be concerned with. At one level there is the general specification of the house: number of bedrooms, basement or not, size, external orientation, internal layout, etc. In SAP terms, this is establishing the organizational elements for which we will need codes. The house, for example, might be given our client code. At another level, we look inside a room and make another set of decisions. Are there two ovens or one? What type of sink should be selected? Is there a deluxe refrigerator? This is like specifying the process flow diagrams that are to be used and which options will be selected for each.

"Finally, everything has to work together. There has to be both hot and cold water brought to the kitchen. The stove voltage must match the wall voltage. There must be extra outlets for other appliances that we don't know about yet, and so forth. That is like getting the data right in the database. It is a lot of work, but then it all has to get done for the system to work. Again, I need to point out that you are doing all of that now if you are providing a service or making a product. If you weren't, it couldn't be done. It is probably not very formal for some of you though."

Man, she's got that right.

"Please understand that you don't do this on a linear basis. The choices interact, just like they do for building a house. Remember when we looked at ASAP at the beginning of the seminar? The form that was filled out while we were doing the 'Business Blueprint' helps with some of this. Also, the screens that are used to enter data into the system require the data to be complete and correct. That is why it appeared so tedious to you.

"Well, we need to wrap up here. We have covered a lot of ground during the seminar. R/3 is designed to be a comprehensive solution to your business software needs. It covers everything including sales and distribution management, manufacturing and vendor coordination, complete human resource management, accounting, and treasury management. SAP is committed to provide our customers with the latest state-of-the-art business software.

"At this time I usually give the class a big R/3 sales pitch, but you have been so good, I'll just pass out these certificates. I hope to see you in the future and maybe I'll be lucky enough to be the consultant on your implementation team. Goodbye and good luck."

That was sure interesting, but I'm anxious to get home to North Carolina so I can get some good barbecue.

Back at the Plant III

23. The questions continue—SAP in Carolina?

"Sheesh," said Ruth as Billy walked in through the door of the Café, "What is wrong with you? Have you been used for a wrecking ball? It also looks like you're putting on a little weight."

"Ah, shut up!" retorted Billy. "When I got back from the seminar and climbed on the scales I decided I was going to have to lose weight or buy a new wardrobe. When I told my wife about it, she put me on a diet and made me start exercising. I got up early this morning and was doing a little jogging when Thompson's dog figured me to be an intruder. I quickly turned into a sprinter and came in early this morning to introduce a little normalcy to my life.

"Say, have you seen Prof? I want to talk to him about the seminar. I have more questions now than I did before I left."

"Well, I wondered how that went. We sort of missed you around here, but that didn't prevent us from talking about you. You know there are all kinds of rumors going around about Mr. McDougle and his brother's plant up in Ohio. People are worried that there might be some jobs lost if he buys that plant. Will some of you guys have to move up there? Do you know anything about it?"

Billy thought to himself that he didn't know of any changes other than what he had learned before he went to the seminar and so replied, "All I know is that Mr. McDougle's brother wants to retire, but other than that I don't know anything. In fact, you know I've been gone a week and I haven't had an opportunity to call back into the plant. Has Prof been coming in? I really have some things I want to talk to him about."

"Yeah, he's been around. Seems like he's been pretty busy with his project as well. Say, are you just going to stand around scaring the customers away or are you going to have something to eat?"

"Sorry. Yeah, I'll have coffee and a garlic bagel. I don't care how many people I scare off this morning, and it can't be worse than the way I feel or look now."

Billy reviewed in his mind some of the questions he still had from the SAP seminar. He really did hope there would be an opportunity to talk to Prof before he had to be in the office. Prof could at least help him think through some things before he had to meet with anybody at the plant. He knew he would be under pressure to answer a lot of questions about what he had learned.

As Ruth brought the bagel over and refilled his coffee cup, Billy saw Prof walk in and hailed him over to the booth. "Man, am I glad to see you," said Billy. "I have hundreds of questions left over from the seminar and I'm hoping to get my head around some of them before I have to face Mr. McDougle with the answers. To start with . . . ," he stopped suddenly as he was aware that Prof was staring at him.

Prof said, "Billy, you look like you slept with a blow dryer turned on high. Isn't that an added chin I see hanging down there under your ugly face? I thought you went to a seminar, not a sumo wrestler training camp."

"Do we have to talk about this? I have important questions. Yeah, I did gain a little weight and I'm trying to take it off. The jogging left me a little frazzled, that's all. Now, can we get to the questions?"

"I have a question too," replied Prof, "but it's about your sanity. What's up?"

Functional integration

"Well, thinking this through is a lot harder than I thought. In the seminar we seemed to go from big system integration ideas to unbelievable detail when we were working through some of the examples. In fact, some of the people just couldn't follow the detailed procedures necessary to perform even a simple task. Part of that was because it was so different, but part of it was because of the amount of data required to feed the system. All of those weird little codes and menu searches became overwhelming. The instructor said that some of those entries could be automated and that there were changes coming in the future, but I came away with an impression that the level of detail is incredible and the amount of training that would be necessary for our clerical staff would be staggering. In fact, I'm not sure some of them will be able to make the change.

"Not only are the details for handling the day to day transactions huge, but the installation of the system looks to me to be tough also. There were thousands of decisions that had to be made to install the system in any given location and it looked to me like many of those were not technical at all. I mean, they were things having to do with the way we do business as opposed to the way the computer operates."

"Now you're getting the hang of it," said Prof. "It is detailed and it is hard. The people in the organization must make the key decisions and that makes it tough. You're also right, there may be some people who won't be able to make the change. Twenty years ago we could have talked about taking away the typewriter and saying everyone had to use a word processor. Now it might be like taking the telephone away from everyone and telling them that they have to use some intergalactic e-mail system for communication. It would be tough for some people to learn all those new codes just to 'call' someone. What else did you learn?"

"Well, another thing," continued Billy, "is this bit about flexibility. There seems to be quite a bit of flexibility at configuration time in selecting the procedures you want to use, but it sure seemed to me like there wasn't much flexibility after that. I think what made it clear to me was the incredible amount of detail we had to supply just to do anything. In fact, the 'best practice' processes, as the instructor called them, are just general process flow diagrams for doing something. I don't see how they're called 'best practices' because they're so very general. In order to make them specific to your firm you need to configure all kinds of options and once they're set they're pretty well fixed. Suppose that we went through all of the configuration stuff. It's not clear to me that it would still fit our circumstances."

"You're asking the right questions, Billy. Particularly given the informality of your plant. You're raising an issue that makes me think about an idea that occurred to me in our work on our project at the university."

"Oops! I didn't even remember to ask you how that project was going," said Billy, "I'm sorry. How is it going?"

"Well, we're learning a lot but, like you, I still have a great number of questions. Let me tell you about this one theory that I've been working on. It seems that it goes back to our conversation a couple of weeks ago where we were looking at the difference between a common database and the ERP approach. Here, let me sketch out what I mean by this. See this thing here that kind of looks like a star?"

"Yeah."

"It's the common database sort of idea. See, the stuff goes in from the points of the stars to the center and from there people in the different functional areas

can take the information out as they want. This allows for a lot of individual customization in how information is used in each of the areas and provides great flexibility while preserving a common set of data."

"Hey, you guys!" interrupted Ruth as she poured more coffee. "Here's some more napkins, but maybe I should start covering the tables with paper like they do over at Fred's Barbecue. Also, you've been so intent I don't know if you realize what time it is."

"Yeah, you'll start charging us rent pretty soon," said Billy, "and I'll have to get a second mortgage on the house. We'll be out before too long. Thanks for the extra napkins."

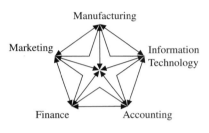

Prof continued, "Let me show you what ERP, say SAP, looks like. It's not a Chrysler emblem but an attempt to show you that there is a common database, but functions are linked by the system one to another and to the database. Well, you get the idea. Those links are specified by the ERP system and not by the people in the organization. That's why you need to worry so much about the data detail.

"Here's another thing I find interesting. Two of the leading suppliers of ERP systems, Baan and SAP, are both European companies. One is from the Netherlands and the other is from Germany. These countries, and organizations in those countries, have a long history of functional separation and hierarchical management. It's quite understandable that they would devise a system that was essentially based on centralization of information and decision making. Not only is the information centralized in a database to provide common information to the organization, but also to provide a central location for control. The specification of the linkages between functions also means that management understands not only what is done but how it is done. This is quite consistent with a hierarchical organization.

"On the other hand ERP providers like Oracle and PeopleSoft, which are based in the U.S. and, not surprisingly, out in California, have a different approach. Oracle, for example, supplies both database software and ERP application software. The common database is still an important aspect of their approach but their software is much more open to customization of the applications. That means, for instance, that R/3 could use Oracle as the database for their system. I don't know if country of origin is really the reason for it, but it just struck me that the more organic approaches seem to come from the U.S. and the more hierarchical approaches seem to come from Europe."

ERP implementation

"Something else that might be interesting to you is this little diagram I have been working on to show some options for implementing an ERP system. On one axis is the amount of flexibility in product offerings, reacting to customer changes, opening new facilities, etc. that your company needs to compete effectively. The other is the degree of centralized decision making that exists in the company. This is partly a cultural characteristic. For example, do you tell the foreman what to make next or can he or she decide? Anyway, here's what the diagram looks like.

High	Common Client Multiple Processes	Multiple Clients Multiple Processes
Flexibility Low	Common Client "Best Practices"	Multiple Clients Mostly "Best Practices"
	High	Low

Centralization

"Let me take you through the boxes and explain some of the options available. First the low flexibility, high centralization box. This is where I see that ERP vendors like SAP would like you to be. There is no need to open new plants, deviate from the 'best practice' processes, and so on. Remember, in SAP terms, that 'client' is the highest level for aggregation of system information. Firms in this box would only have one client and there would be common practices throughout. Data would be kept on one central server giving management the opportunity for centralized control. Of course, in your case, the folks in Ohio may not like North Carolina calling the shots or vice versa.

"To the right is the low flexibility, low centralization box. This is where there could be lots of 'little' ERP systems. For example, you could have one implementation of R/3 in Ohio and a second one in North Carolina. Each would be configured with the 'best practice' processes appropriate to them. Any centralized decision making would require some manual collection of information, but the people in each facility would probably be pretty happy with this, since they would have control over their own destiny.

"The high flexibility, high centralization box is where I would see a single client and multiple processes. Individual units of the company could use 'best of breed' processes. They would go out and find the best ways possible to support the jobs that need to be done. Of course gluing all of this together and maintaining it could be a nightmare, since applications could come from anywhere. To integrate this for the single client we would need to write or purchase computer programs to move key pieces of data between these 'best of breed' applications and the data base or do it the way you do now—little slips of paper. Orders that have been completed by manufacturing need to be reported to the accounting system, demand forecasts from marketing must be moved to the manufacturing planning system, and things like that.

"The last box is the high flexibility, low centralization box. It is here that I would think multiple clients and multiple processes would fit. The processes would be selected from 'best of breed' and individual clients could be established for different business units. Even within one of the business units, we could let all the functional units do whatever they think is best. The Manufacturing people would implement the software that they think is best. Accounting would get what they think is best, and so on. Here we get a great deal of flexibility, but the consolidation of information can come at a high cost.

"These boxes represent a combination of the amount of local autonomy a company needs to be able to respond to local conditions and the way it makes decisions. I'm looking for clever names for the boxes. I'm tempted to use political terms. So the lower left-hand corner would be Dictatorship, the lower right would be Feudalism, the upper left would be Socialism and, of course, the upper right would be Anarchy. You guys fall in the Anarchy box. With your need for high flexibility and low centralization culture, I sympathize with your concerns."

"Maybe that's why I'm worried about the support for our special applications," remarked Billy. "You know, we have a tremendous number of homemade programs that we've added to our MRP system in order to manage the customization and changes that our customers want in their products. I'm really concerned about SAP's willingness to support those applications, even if we can get them into the system. They were making noises at the seminar like we were on our own if we added applications, even if they were written in the ABAP/4 programming language of SAP. They warned us that when SAP supplied upgrades to the system they might not be compatible with our additions."

Prof broke in, "Here's maybe a way to think about the cost implications of trying to do something that doesn't fit the Anarchy box. First of all you simply can't move into the low flexibility row. Your market won't let you. You would be out of business. Said another way, the cost of reducing flexibility is infinite. You can move to the upper left, but there are costs of trying to centralize decision making as well.

"First there is the obvious cost of hardware, systems, and so forth of trying to centralize. That can be big, as you already know. Second, there is an organization cost to that change. It implies training costs, obviously, but some people simply may not go along with the loss of autonomy and will leave. And you know that it's always the best ones who have the options to do so. There will also be great stress as the rumors fly.

"The third type of cost involves configuration. You saw in the seminar how detailed it is for a single client, using common processes. Here you have 'best of breed' applications that need to be integrated into the system. Even subtler is the complexity of centralized management of all that you need to do locally to be responsive to the market. This fourth category of costs is often totally overlooked."

"Thanks, Prof, I think outlining costs that way will be helpful as I talk to Mr. McDougle. I do need to find a way to help him see my concerns."

"They are very real concerns, Billy. Incidentally, I've been working on a diagram that I'll try to remember to bring in tomorrow. The diagram shows information flows in ERP systems and I think I can pinpoint where your concerns are. In the meantime, I've got to get to the office . . ."

"But you're tenured!" interrupted Billy. "You don't need to show up at all do you? On the other hand, I've got to get over to the office or I won't find a paycheck."

"Yeah! Tenured! That means I can work any 16 hours in the day that I want to. See you tomorrow."

24. Back at plant—Things heat up

As Billy turned his car onto the highway for the short drive to the plant, he reviewed some of the things he had learned at the SAP seminar. It was clear that there was no way that McDougle Furniture could implement the system on their own. A lot of help would be needed to do the implementation right. There were other ERP vendors, but he hadn't learned much about them nor had Prof been particularly helpful on that score either. The thing that troubled him the most, however, was that R/3 appeared to lack the flexibility to easily accommodate some of the company's special needs.

Pulling into the parking lot, he was surprised at how many cars were there. Normally, Billy showed up early enough that there were only a few cars in the lot when it dawned on him that he was arriving much later than usual. As he went into the plant, he was greeted with a lot of razzing about his extra chin. It almost seemed as though Ruth had called ahead to set him up. There were a number of remarks also about his getting an extra week of vacation so soon after he had taken his regular vacation. Billy fended off all the teasing comments and asked one of the expeditors, Tom Maroney, whether there had been many problems.

"Well, we kept things rolling along pretty good until about Wednesday when the sales guys called us with a whole bunch of changes to that big order for the bank in Charlotte," said Tom.

"What kind of changes were they? Does it look like we're going to be late with the order? Is there anything that I need to do?" asked Billy.

Tom replied, "Not that I can think of at the moment. The biggest changes were in the display racks and bookcases for the reception area. They wanted more shelves and locking glass fronts on the cases. Oh, they also wanted a change in the finish. They want it darkened up, but that shouldn't cause any problems. The only other change was in some of the hardware and we're on that already. The shelving and locking doors meant that we needed to redo the bill of material and special order some additional stuff. It reminds me of all the problems we had with that big desk that went down to Atlanta a couple weeks back."

"Sounds like you guys are on top of it. Does it look like we're going to make the schedule?"

"It's going to be tight. We might have to slide a day or two, certainly not more than a week. I won't know until we've heard back from one of the suppliers today."

"Be sure to warn the guys over in sales. Remember how upset Jerry Mancora got when that Atlanta desk didn't get out of here on time. I don't think any of us want that again."

Tom replied, "You know, I'm becoming a fan of this just-in-time stuff. If we could get our products out the door in days instead of weeks, our customers wouldn't have time to change their minds."

"Yeah, but we wouldn't have any customers then. You know Jerry says how important it is to be able to accommodate their every whim. I agree, though, sometimes it feels like they are a bunch of spoiled brats and we're the ones that are spoiling them. You'll have to admit we're pretty good at it, though. How long did it take you to redo the bill of material and reschedule the stuff?"

"We were done by the morning of the day we got the changes bolted down. It wasn't a big deal from that standpoint."

"Great! Keep up the good work."

Billy went into his office to confront the pile of paper and e-mail messages he knew were awaiting him. As he began to go through them and make sure there was nothing that had a high priority, the phone rang. It was Mary Lou asking if he could come upstairs and see Mr. McDougle. "As soon as I finish answering this e-mail," said Billy, "It will be about 10 minutes. Is that okay? What's up?"

"I'm not sure, but he asked last week if you were going to be in the office on Friday. When I told him no, that you wouldn't get back from the seminar until that night, he just said okay. He seemed anxious to see you. Hey, if you learn anything about the rumors flying around, let me know. My family is all over me about whether I'll still have a job here or will we have to move to Ohio."

"I heard some of that over at Ruth's this morning. I don't think that is what he wants to see me about, but I'll let you know. See you in 10."

Later, when he walked into Mr. McDougle's office, Billy was greeted with, "Well, what did you learn?"

"Well, Mr. McDougle, I've been trying to think how to summarize that. I'm still not convinced that SAP is for us. At least not the whole package. I'm trying to talk with other people who know more about it before I make up my mind, but it's still up in the air as far as I'm concerned.

"Let me be a little more specific. The one fact that became very clear at the seminar was the tremendous amount of detailed management decision making that has to be done in order to use the system. It's clear that this is not a simple software fix for a firm. The amount of detailed decisions necessary to configure the system to match our business is really staggering."

"I understand we can get help with that," interrupted Mr. McDougle. "There are consultants around who have a lot of experience in implementing these systems. SAP's R/3 program—see I've learned something too—is apparently one of the most widely used, so that kind of expertise is available. Besides, we have the experience at the plant in Ohio. Those guys really want to help."

"I know there are consultants around," replied Billy, "and the SAP people provide some support as well. What was obvious to me, however, was that the kinds of decisions that need to be made are those having to do with the way the business is managed, not the way the software operates. As examples, the system needs to know whether or not we'll have finished goods inventories, whether we bill customers on completion or have progress payments, who has the authority to make changes in specifications, what people have the right to access what information, how we define particular common terms, and so forth.

"As you may know, I have been having coffee with a professor from the university who is doing a study of ERP systems. He's been very helpful in pointing out some of the things that have to be done in order to implement and use a system like R/3. He asked me to see how many different forecasts we had and I found we had three different forecasts for next month and I couldn't reconcile them. He also suggested that I take a look and see how many people are involved in booking a customer order and I gave up after a while because there were so many."

Again Mr. McDougle interrupted, "Couldn't we use your professor friend as a consultant? It seems to me that he has the right answers."

"That's an idea, but he doesn't have as many answers as he does questions. For example, he can't tell us which person should be responsible for defining and entering the single forecast that the system needs. That's something we would have to do. All those detailed questions I mentioned earlier are ones that we would have to answer from the perspective of the business. All the consultants can do is help us understand that the questions must be answered. Incidentally, there is some software called ASAP that helps in raising these questions and structures the implementation process. Even with this, though, it takes several months to install the system in fairly straightforward businesses."

"Several months! Wow! I think there's something you're not telling me," said Mr. McDougle. "Is there something else that's bothering you about the system?"

"Yes there is. I'm concerned about the flexibility of the R/3 approach to accommodate some of the special needs of our business. Just this morning, for example, when I came in I found that we had to reconfigure the bill of materials for one of the orders currently on the shop floor. We have our own software that does this for us and it's not clear that we can incorporate that software in the R/3 system. Even if we could, it wouldn't be supported as subsequent upgrades of R/3 came out. I'm concerned about that kind of flexibility to support the specific software enhancements that we've made here.

"But there's the more general question of flexibility as well. By this I mean that R/3 requires a substantial amount of discipline to follow the specified procedures that SAP calls 'best practices.' They are not best practices the way you and I would think of them, but they are fairly general procedures that can be tailored to perform specific functions or, in their terminology, support specific processes. For example, once the order entry process is configured, the procedure is quite rigid in terms of what data are put in, who does it, and when. This is the way that the system gets information that has precise definitions into a common database.

"What is troubling me is that the nature of the way we operate here doesn't mesh with that requirement. You know how informal we are in our internal relationships and even with our customers sometimes. This may be wrong in some sense, but it's the way we've done business for as long as I've been with the company and it's what our people, our customers, our suppliers, and others who know the firm expect from us. If we suddenly impose a great deal of formality on the place, I'm not sure what the results might be."

"Wow! I can see that I sent the right person." replied Mr. McDougle. "I knew you wouldn't be steamrolled by salespeople, nor would you be persuaded to simply accept all of their claims. I also figured you would be skeptical enough to raise the right kinds of questions, and it seems like you have. As they say in the melodramas, however, 'the plot has thickened.'"

"How's that?"

"Well, my brother has definitely decided to sell the plant and our most recent family summit meeting concluded with my agreeing to buy it on very favorable terms. So, I still have the issue of trying to integrate the two facilities and am still hopeful that R/3 might be able to do it for us. I think I want to hold an open mind on this and I'm going to ask you to do a little bit more research for me."

"Well, that explains a lot! There were rumors all over Ruth's Café this morning and even Mary Lou was asking me what was going on. Now I can see what the situation is. I think you need to get some information out to our people and to the community. There's a lot of worry about whether some of us will have to move to Ohio, whether they'll still be jobs here, and so on. If there's a great deal of uncertainty, it can be pretty hard on our efficiency. Besides, I can think of two or three people in the shop I would hate to lose if they felt their job might be in jeopardy. They've got friends at other plants that might be able to help place them. What are your plans on this and what can I say to the people who ask me?"

"Are you trying to get out of doing a little more research? Nah! I don't mean that, I know there are a lot of rumors going around. I know I'm going to have to make some formal statements, but I did want to talk with you a little bit before I did. In fact, I have the reporter from *The Citizen* coming over a little bit later this morning. He is going to write an article about what's going on and try to help me communicate with the community that there are no plans for any changes at all in the short run and maybe not even in the long run.

"If people ask you about it, you can certainly tell them that we're going to continue to operate the two plants independently for a while. There will be some travel back and forth between the two facilities as we learn from them and they learn from us, but I have no intentions of letting any people go or moving any people up to Ohio. My interest in ERP is to simply see if we could find a way of making the integration, particularly the accounting consolidation, of the two facilities easier.

"Let me tell you what I have in mind for you to do and you can help me in the community relations area as well. I'd like you to go up to the plant in Ohio and talk with their information systems guy about their R/3 installation. His name is Dan Bragg. He has been around Ohio for awhile and is quite a legend. I think they called him 'Dan-Dan the FORTRAN man' back in the old days.

"I'd like you to find out about how long it took them to put in the system, and what the difficulties were along the way. Decide whether or not you think they can be of any help to us if we decide to go that direction here. Just get any other information you can on how it's worked for them and what we might learn from it. I'd also like you to look over the plant and see what you think about it from your experience. I've been up there a few times and it looks like a pretty good operation to me, but it's different than what we do down here. I don't have your experience in manufacturing to understand what they're doing."

"When did you have in mind?" asked Billy. "You know I've just gotten back from the seminar and there's a pretty big stack of stuff on my desk. There have also been some changes out in the shop that maybe I ought to stay on top of, so I'd like to spend at least a few days here sorting out what's going on before I leave."

"Well, I think that's okay, but it looks to me like the plant runs better when you're gone anyway."

"What?"

"Just kidding! The staff you've built does a good job. They only come running to me once in a while when you're gone. I really do need some help getting my brain around this software. In fact, I've asked some friends of mine to give me a couple of contacts at other furniture plants in the area who've implemented R/3 and I've got a list for you. I haven't made contact with them yet but I've been assured they would be very happy to spend some time with you discussing their experiences.

"One of the companies thinks they are a close competitor of ours, so you might not be able to learn much about their manufacturing but they are open to visits to discuss their R/3 installation. They may be the best source of information for us here. I'd like you to visit them fairly soon. If you want, you could spend a couple of days here visiting local plants for half a day and working here for half a day but I would like you to be up in Ohio before the end of the week."

"I know, you just want to make sure the plant can continue to run when I'm gone. I suspect I'll come back and find my parking place taken, my desk moved, my office locked, and the softball trophy thrown in the trash barrel. I'll get on it right away. I want you to know, however, I still don't think I'm the guy for this job. I think you need somebody who knows a whole lot more about systems and computers and that kind of thing."

"No, I know I've got the right guy. Let me get you this list and we'll get you started."

Billy spent the rest of the day in the plant working on the paperwork on his desk and phoning to try and make appointments at a couple of the local furniture companies to learn about their installations. Everyone seemed to be real busy, and he never did get anything scheduled. He was interested in learning what some of the other furniture plants were doing with R/3. He decided to try again after he returned from Ohio.

25. Information integration—Off to Ohio

Prof arrived at Ruth's Café shortly after it opened. It was very early for him to be there and of course Ruth had to make a comment.

"Prof! What are you doing here so early? Oh, I see! Your suit looks like you've slept in it all night. I guess this is the way you guys over at the university get that rumpled look. It's really becoming!"

"Yeah, you don't realize what we have to go through to keep up our image. My wife thinks I'm absolutely crazy when I spend all night sleeping in a brand new suit just so I can get that 'Mr. Chips' effect. Do you really like it?" replied Prof.

"Would it make any difference if I didn't? What'll you have, the usual?"

"That will be fine. I was hoping I could catch Billy early. I found what it was that I was thinking about the other day and would really like to show it to him," said Prof.

"Yeah? I'd like to talk to him too. I'm really concerned about what's happening over at the plant. You know I've got family over there and they're worried about whether or not they're going to have a job next month."

"Well, I don't know anything about that," replied Prof. "But I'd be willing to bet the rumors are a whole lot worse than the reality. It always seems to be that way."

Prof sat down at the table and pulled a piece of paper out of his briefcase. He was looking at the lines and boxes when Billy walked in and Prof missed seeing him enter. The first time Prof was aware Billy was there was when Ruth yelled across the room, "Wow! Look at you. Are you getting married again? Don't sit over there with Prof, you two will clash!"

"Ignore her and come on over here," said Prof. "I want to show you the diagram I told you about the other day. I finally found it."

"Before you go over there and sit down, tell us what that suit is about. Prof just sleeps in his to get that rumpled effect for his classes, but that one you've got on looks brand new, Billy," said Ruth.

"Well, I've got to go to Ohio to visit the plant so I dug through my closet and found this suit in the back. I thought I'd wear it before the moths got to it."

"Oh! Talking about Ohio," said Ruth, "I've been meaning to ask you about what's happening over at the plant. You know my family is all worried about whether or not they're going to have jobs and they've been asking me to . . ."

"Hey! Not to worry! I talked to Mr. McDougle about that yesterday and he assured me that there won't be any changes in the operations at either plant and certainly there won't be any people from here moving up there. So you can tell them all to relax."

"What's going on?" asked Prof. "I always seem to be the last to know about these things."

"Mr. McDougle has decided to buy his brother's plant up in Ohio. You know, we talked about that awhile ago and at that time it sounded as though it was just a matter of trying to integrate the financial part of the business. Well, it turns out it's much more than that. Mr. McDougle wants to operate both plants and is now interested in seeing if we can install R/3 to cover both of them. That's why he's sending me up there."

"I guess that's why the rumors have been going around," said Prof. "Like I was telling Ruth earlier, it always seems like the rumors are worse than the reality. Ruth, I sure hope this works out okay for all your folks. I know Mr. McDougle has been a very honorable man and I'd stake my claim on his word. Billy, this means that this is just a lot more timely than I had thought."

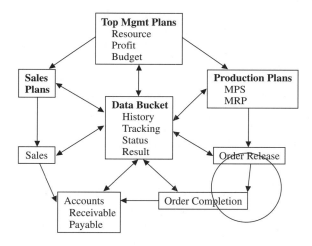

"What have you got?"

"Here's the diagram we were talking about the other day. This is a different way of looking at how ERP systems work, even those that are not focused on centralized management and control. See the data bucket there in the middle? That is where the common data are housed. That's why you'll sometimes hear the term 'data warehouse.' The overall chart will give you a pretty good idea of how information flows from the top management planning activities, through the functional area plans, to the execution and accounting activities. Of course there are lots more boxes and arrows going back and forth. I'd show you, but we have already used too many of Ruth's napkins."

Billy interrupted, "It looks comprehensive and I know it's complicated."

"It is comprehensive. That's the intention of these kinds of systems. The reason it looks complicated is that's the way business is. But what I wanted to show you is right down here on the lower right side where it's got MPS/MRP and Order Release and Order Completion. That's the part of the system where your manufacturing needs vary the most from R/3."

"What do you mean?" asked Billy.

"You've told me a lot about how frequently you change orders and even designs once they start through manufacturing."

"Yeah! That just happened to us recently. We had an order going through the shop and the customer wanted some stuff added to it and some hardware changed. It meant that we had to completely redo the bill of materials and order some new stuff. But my guys are good at that. They got it taken care of pretty quickly."

"That's what I mean. You can see that what you need to have is something between Release and Completion that allows you to modify the orders as they're going through the shop. And you need to keep track of changes, due dates, and capacity, as it's happening. I think you've told me you've got a homegrown system that does that pretty well, but whether it will integrate with some of these ERP systems or not is an open question. It's almost sure that the application won't be supported if there are changes to the software later on."

"Well that's just exactly what I was beginning to wonder and was one of the issues I raised with Mr. McDougle. You know, he's asked me to go up to Ohio. He also wants me to visit some other plants in the area that have implemented R/3, but I just don't see how I am going to have time for that.

"I think he's really serious about this. It looks to me like his feeling is that we can put in a single system that does everything for both plants. I guess he feels this will save some money and will make it easier for him to manage and consolidate the results from both plants."

"Did he tell you what to look for? What's the exact purpose of your going up there? Do you know?" asked Prof.

"I think there are really two agendas," replied Billy. "I do think he wants me to look over the plant and assess it from a manufacturing point of view. Despite his experience, he feels he would like another pair of eyes just sort of looking the place over. But the other thing is that he wants me to see how the R/3 system is working up there and whether or not I think we can use it down here. I'm not sure how I'm going to go about assessing that, but I am interested in seeing what kind of shop they're running. I might learn some tricks for this place."

"Well, you probably already know this, but let me give you a few things to look for and maybe some things to be aware of."

"Ruth! Can you bring us over some more coffee, Prof's about to start a lecture."

"Yeah! You better take notes; this is going to be on the final," remarked Prof. "Let me just mention a few things about the shop itself and that's where I'd suggest you really start. I'm sure you already know you want to get some feel for their volumes, inventory turns, number of suppliers, number of customers. Do they make to order or make to stock? How specialized is their equipment and how skilled is the labor? In addition, how do they schedule and run the shop? Finally, what kinds of shop floor control systems are necessary to keep it running? I'm guessing that Mr. McDougle is probably also interested in having you assess how well this is all being done."

"I think you're right," said Billy. "He really does want some kind of an evaluation."

"You know the manufacturing drill," continued Prof. "All I'm really suggesting here is that you simply look at the plant to figure out what things are different from your plant, and why. That's pretty straightforward. What may not be as clear, especially as you think about the possibility of involving SAP, is the need to look at some of the other areas. Remember you found that there were multiple forecasts and a whole bunch of people involved with order entry at your place. You might check some of the details of how they work with their customers and how the accounting works. For example, how is customer billing done? Are there progress payments? Do they age accounts receivable and does the process vary by vendor? What do the accounts payable look like? Who configures orders? How are the forecasts prepared? You know, just look at some of those other areas also."

"You know, I think you're right. I need to make a few notes on the other areas. I'm less knowledgeable about those, but I don't want to forget to look at them."

"Well, let me give you the best advice I know," said Prof. "Beware of the computer guy. I'm guessing he'll stick to you like a wet T-shirt. He'll be all over you thinking of R/3 as *the* solution. He'll think of it in terms of an Information Technology or IT solution, not a management solution. Make sure you get to talk to some of the other people up there, especially those who are using the system now."

"Thanks. I know Mr. McDougle wants me to spend some time with the IT people but I'll heed your advice. You know, for a guy in a rumpled suit you're okay."

"Same to you fella! Let me know how it comes out, and don't sleep in that suit."

A Different Business IV

26. High-volume efficiency—The Ohio plant

As Billy got out of the taxi at the entrance to the Ohio plant he noted that it was not as big as he expected and there were a large number of trucks at both ends of the facility. He also felt a bit eerie entering a building called McDougle Furniture that didn't look at all like the facility back home. He entered the reception area and gave his name to the receptionist saying he had an appointment to speak with Mr. McDougle but was a little early. The receptionist asked him to have a seat and said somebody would be there shortly.

As Billy sat down he couldn't help but notice how spartan the reception area was. There was a framed copy of the mission statement that was prominently displayed next to the receptionist's desk, a catalog with some of the company's products, a plaque indicating the company was ISO 9000 certified, and a couple of softball trophies in a display case.

Very soon a young man entered the reception area and introduced himself as Mr. McDougle's secretary. He led Billy back into the offices. There was no mistaking Mr. McDougle. He looked very much like his brother and immediately showed some of the same warmth and friendliness. Once in the office, Mr. McDougle asked Billy if he'd like a cup of coffee. He turned to a pump pot thermos bottle and drew a cup. He handed it to Billy and drew one for himself as Billy thought to himself what a great idea to have the coffee right in the office.

"I'm delighted to have you here," said Mr. McDougle. "It makes it seem like we're getting closure on this transfer of ownership. You know, of course, that I have mixed emotions about this but my wife is absolutely right. I've been promising her some traveling time and we've simply not been able to get it in. It's also great to have the business stay in the family.

"Now, I understand a major part of your purpose in being here is to look at our SAP system. We're really happy with it and probably couldn't even continue to do business if we didn't have it. I think the best procedure, if you agree, would be to have our information technology person, Dan Bragg, walk you through the system. Mr. Bragg has been involved in the SAP project since we started it and knows all the details from top to bottom."

"Well, that's fine but I've got a couple of other things that I'd like to see as well," Billy interrupted. "Eventually I do want to look at your SAP system, but first I'd really like to get a feel for the factory, the products, the production processes, and something about how you do business. That way I'll have a better understanding of how R/3 helps you do it. In fact, I'd really like to start with a look around the factory. I feel a lot more comfortable there than I do around the computers and I can get a much better feel for the business. If that wouldn't interrupt your operation too much, it would be very helpful to me."

"Fine! I can understand exactly why you want to do that. I'll have Larry Underhill take you through the factory. He's our manufacturing guru and you guys can babble away in shoptalk all you want to.

"At some point, though, you should talk to Dan Bragg. He really can explain the SAP system in its entirety and I think that would be something you would like to learn about as well. I know it's something my brother's very interested in and I think we can help you get the system running down there. With our experience and the fact that we're in the same business, we should be able to save you guys a lot of the agony that we went through here.

"I'll turn you loose with Larry and plan on having lunch with you and Mr. Bragg. Is there anybody else you can think of that you might want to have some time with while you're here?"

"Yes. I would like to talk to someone from accounting and maybe a couple of the order entry clerks and inventory planners to get a feel for what they do."

"Well, we can have you meet with some of the staff after lunch, but I don't think they'd be able to answer the kinds of questions you would probably want to ask. I will see if we can get our chief accountant to join us. If not, I'll make sure you can meet with her after lunch."

Mr. McDougle turned to his phone and called Larry into the office and made the introductions. Billy liked Larry immediately and felt he would get honest answers to any questions he might ask. As they left Mr. McDougle's office, Larry suggested that they go into his office for an overview of the plant layout and process before going out into the factory. Billy agreed and found himself seated behind another cup of coffee looking at a plant layout.

"The material flow is really very simple," explained Larry. "It comes in one end, flows through the process, and out the other end. Well, at least that's the theory. Actually, we do pretty well most of the time in moving the product through the plant on a pretty linear basis. You probably saw all the trucks outside. We try to operate here on a just-in-time basis. Trucks are unloading raw material almost all day long at one end of the plant and trucks are taking away completed orders at the other end of the plant. I have a dream of some day unloading a truck on the receiving end, and then having the driver drive around to the shipping end to load the same truck with the finished product. We're really not there yet though."

"Wow! If we thought about that at our shop," said Billy, "we'd have time to wreck the truck on the way around the building, rebuild it, bring it back, and still wait for the product to come out the shipping end. How long does it take for an order to go through the shop?"

"It depends. I'm sure you knew that would be my answer. Most of the orders go through in a few hours. Even if there's a problem, it's rarely more than two days before we're on the outbound truck."

"Surely that doesn't include all of the order cycle time, does it?" asked Billy.

"No. If we talk about the total order cycle being from the time we get a confirmed order to when it's on the truck, it's a matter of a few days but rarely more than a week," responded Larry. "But, let me continue.

"The trucks bring in raw material several times a day, as I said, and we have long-term relationships with just a few suppliers. It's pretty simple. We mostly use plywood, composition board, some solid wood, hardware, and a little bit of finishing material. Almost all material comes in pre-finished and cut to standard lengths and widths. We can quickly pull the material that we need to assemble products. We do a tiny bit of cutting to length, some machining activities, a small amount of edge trim work, but very little finishing. Then we package the product and send it off to our customers."

"What kind of machining do you do?" asked Billy.

"Well, as I said, we do some trimming of standard length boards that will become shelves or braces or things like that. Most of the machining, though, is drilling and routing for the installation of the fasteners and to provide holes for mounting doors, shelf pegs, and that sort of thing. In fact, that's one of the first parts of the operation out there."

"How many vendors do you have?"

"Oh, about 30 for most of our business. We get a real break on the price with the volumes we provide for these guys."

"What kind of volumes are we talking about?"

"We have a standard desk model that is real popular around here. I'd say that we ship between 450–500 of those units a day. The same is true of one of our shelving units. The number may vary a bit depending on the orders we're filling on a particular day. We probably fill some five to ten orders a day."

"Wow! We don't do that kind of volume in a year in our shop. In fact, I'd be hard pressed to think what a 'standard' desk might be at our place. Everything we do is different. I can't even think of a standard board or finish," said Billy.

Larry continued, "We couldn't do this kind of volume if we didn't let our suppliers do most of the cutting, finishing, and provide us standard sizes that are common to a lot of our products. About the only thing we do in finishing is the edging. Here we put a strip of wood tape on the edge of a freshly cut board. Occasionally, we need to touch up the finish or the surface of something that's been damaged in transit or marked up somehow. But it's pretty rare. Our biggest headache here is packaging."

"Packaging? What do you mean? We just wrap our stuff in moving blankets and send them on their way," said Billy.

"No, everything that goes out of here is wrapped in cardboard, strapped, and boxed for shipment. We have to match the right cardboard pieces and boxes with the products or we can't fit them together. The volume of cardboard here is huge. We package the fasteners and screws in plastic bags and put them in each box, but that's much less of a problem."

"It sounds to me like you're really mostly assembling and packaging. Do I have the picture right?" asked Billy.

"Yes. As you can see from the plant layout, raw material comes in and there's only a small amount of raw material storage. That's where we sort the material as it comes in and get it ready to go into the routing and cutting operations. The packaging material comes in and moves directly into a packaging inventory. We have roller conveyors in the shop so we can move this material through quickly. The next areas are finishing, which I already said was pretty small and strapping, where we strap together the shelves, sides and tops, for example. The pieces eventually go into a cardboard box that will be sent to the customer.

"Another activity is pulling together the hardware and fasteners. We put these in a plastic bag with an assembly instruction sheet. It doesn't take a lot of space but, again, we have to get it synchronized with the right batch of wood parts coming down the line.

"The final step is the final packaging where we insert the plastic bag, staple and seal the outer layer, and move the product over into a very small finished goods area. We don't hold much finished goods inventory here. It's mostly a staging area for shipping out but we'll occasionally hold some of our more popular items for a short period of time."

"How much inventory are we talking about?" asked Billy.

"Oh, just a couple of days worth. We get nervous when there is very much. There is just no place to put it. I don't really think about it very much, as long as the suppliers do their job and the customers keep providing us with their estimates of what they need in the future. We can pretty well match things up. The customers usually give us forecasts several months into the future for the product lines and some estimates of how they think they'll break down by model. We get pretty good information from our major customers. We are even tied into their systems in some cases. We are committed to replenish their inventory within a few days after they've finalized an order.

"We're only talking about 300 products in roughly 10 or 12 families here. The sales guys and the customers know pretty well how the finish options and accessories work out, so it's not a real big deal."

Billy queried, "How stable are the product lines? That's a big number of products to me, but my guess from your standpoint with the volumes you've got it isn't huge. Do they change very much?"

"No, they're pretty stable. We probably change the product line 15 to 20 percent a year, something like that. The sales guys always want to do more, of course, and we always want them to do less, but it's pretty stable. We work with our customers on what they want. They do most of the design work. The customers don't want a huge number of stock keeping units in their inventory so we're able to control that pretty well. The amount of part commonality is very high, also. We work hard with the customer's designers and our suppliers to make as much product as we can from as few raw material part numbers as possible. That also really helps us on the supply side in concentrating our efforts. Should we go look at the shop?"

"Yeah, I'd really like to do that. First, though, how many customers are we talking about here?" asked Billy.

"Well, we've got just a few big ones that account for most of our volume. This would be your Wal-Marts, Kmarts, Office Depot, and so on. There are a few other smaller customers and we still do business with some local retailers here in Ohio that are leftover from the past, but they really are a small part of the volume. Since most of our products are for general and home offices, they tend to be things like computer desks, bookshelves, storage cabinets, desks, and other things oriented to the office. That actually helps us in keeping the number of parts pretty small since they can be assembled in a variety of different ways. Let's go take a look at the plant."

As Larry led Billy through the shop from raw material to finished goods there were several things that came to Billy's attention. There really wasn't much inventory to be seen and everything in the shop seemed to be in motion on conveyers or being worked on at a machine or being packaged into the final carton. Roller conveyors were throughout the shop, moving the product from one area to another and finally to the shipping dock. In the machining area, the number of computer controlled machine tools struck Billy. He asked Larry about this.

"We went to computer controlled machines sometime back to increase our flexibility," replied Larry. "We've been able to program the few machining operations that we have and with our standard parts, we can very quickly move from one configuration to another. This has helped us do mixed batches of product for our customers. For example, we may have an order for 40 desks of a particular kind in two different colors, a dozen computer tables, 20 book-shelves in different sizes, and so on. We can almost justify doing those on a one by one basis now. These machines can change over very quickly. There are not many people in here because it doesn't take very many people to run the machines. Most of the programming work takes place back in the office.

"We also make use of some simple fixtures in the machining area and in final assembly to help speed things up. These fixtures help us position and stack pieces quickly. The standard sizes have really made things fairly straight forward."

Billy noticed that there weren't many workers around. He did notice, there was one person who wore a uniform that made it look like he worked for a different company. He was in the area where the fasteners and the hardware were being put into plastic bags. He asked Larry about that.

"That's one of our vendors bringing us some inventory," said Larry. "For a lot of our hardware we have asked local companies to keep us supplied. They know about how much our volumes are going to be, we provide them information on what we're doing, and they keep our inventory bins topped up. It's worked out really super for us. We've not had a shortage with any of the hardware or fasteners since we started doing this. We just don't even worry about it any more."

"Boy, we couldn't do that at our place, we don't even know until the last minute what kind of hardware is going to be put on some of our stuff. I don't see a lot of people in the shop. Do you have trouble getting workers?" asked Billy.

"No, we just run ads when we want people. We have pretty high turnover in the shop. I think some of the companies in the area know that after someone's worked with us for a while they're pretty disciplined and careful in their work habits and pretty reliable on the job, so they hire them away. It helps keep our wage rates low though."

"Isn't there any training, or learning period? How do you get the people up to speed on the jobs?" asked Billy.

"It's not really a problem. It takes just a few days for the people in the shop to learn the jobs. We do everything we can to keep things pretty simple. You will see also that each unit that's going through the shop has a clear set of instructions with pictures that go with it. So it's pretty foolproof. We do have a final inspection like everybody does, but it's really mostly just to make sure all the parts are there. It's pretty hard to screw up, though. The carton looks too long or won't close if there is something wrong. Sometimes we have a problem with hardware, but that's where we put our good people.

"We do work with the people to make sure they understand the importance of careful handling and that sort of thing. We don't want dented shelves or frayed edges or anything like that going out and it's really not been a problem."

"I don't see any finished product around here anywhere. Don't you assemble the products at all to make sure they go together or do any testing of that kind?" asked Billy.

"No. We're really pretty cavalier about that. When you go into one of the stores where our furniture is sold you'll often see some of the pieces assembled and sitting around as sample units. The people in the stores do that and if there's a problem they'll report back to us. Also, there is a customer response card in the instruction booklet. If there is something hard to do we'll hear from them and check to see if adjustments need to be made. But once it's designed, the machine tool programming and fixtures are set, and a few test units are assembled, we don't worry about that at all."

Finally they reached the finished goods area and there were cartons of product around but there wasn't much space for finished goods. Quite a bit was on roller conveyors lined up at the loading dock. The trucks were being loaded from these conveyors. Billy could begin to see how it might indeed be possible to pull some material off of an inbound truck, run it through the machine shop, strap some things together, wrap some cardboard around it, and put it on the same truck before it left the lot. The differences between what these guys were doing here and what he was doing back in North Carolina were just overwhelming to him. He did want to find out what Larry's reaction was to R/3 before he went to lunch and so he raised the subject.

"Larry, you know that one of the things I'm here to learn is how you guys like your R/3 software and whether or not that's what we ought to be thinking about using down in North Carolina. I did see the computer in your office but I don't see a lot of them out here on the floor. I'm really wondering, is it something that is run out of the other offices or what?"

Larry responded, "It's made our life tremendously easier. In fact, I don't really do very much with the system at all except to occasionally go in and see what's being planned for some of our big customers. I do that just to make sure our suppliers are aware of what's going on and that we're not messing up too badly in matching the supply to what the customers want. Besides, you're right, it is mostly run out of the office area. There is a little data entry here, but even that is mostly automated with bar codes and readers.

"Now, we do have to use the system a lot when we change the product line or make model changes and that sort of thing. We work very hard to make sure we've got the right information in the bills of materials, the pricing files, and that sort of thing. If that kind of information gets screwed up, we really have a mess on our hands. So there's a lot of work getting the new design in, but once it's there the computer just does its thing.

"Remember the paper that was traveling with the units as they were going down the conveyors out there in the shop? Those are generated by the system. There's an application that pulls off some information and writes that little report and pulls down the picture that rides with the unit until it goes out into the truck. And in fact, you've just given me a great idea. We could leave that picture right in the carton and the customer could use that to verify that everything was there."

"Was it a difficult task to put the system in?"

"Well, you need to talk to the computer guys about that. I understand they got a lot of help from some of our customers and suppliers, but the manufacturing types weren't involved very heavily in the effort. One of our accountants was pretty deeply involved, though. Of course, we went to meetings and did some training. We knew that life was going to be different, but we were already making so many changes in order to accommodate the requirements of our customers that SAP wasn't a big deal for us. We thought that SAP might make us more efficient and we'd have to lay off some people, but that didn't happen. We were growing at the time, so there was plenty of work for everyone and that has continued. Some people changed jobs, though, and others had theirs changed by SAP.

"Hey, it's just about time that I get you back to Mr. McDougle's office or you're going to miss lunch. I think he's got one of the best local restaurants lined up for you."

27. An R/3 success—A pleasant lunch

As Billy returned to Mr. McDougle's office, he was greeted with, "Hey, there you are. I was just about to send out the Saint Bernard dogs. I knew once you production guys got together you'd be yacking up a storm." Mr. McDougle continued, "Let's go. The others will meet us at the restaurant and I can tell you a bit about them on our way over."

Billy turned to Larry Underhill and thanked him for the factory tour. "I learned a lot out there, Larry, and appreciate all the time you took with me. I'm still really struck by the differences in what you do compared to what we do and I'm sure I haven't absorbed it all. Can I reserve the right to come back and talk to you again or give you a phone call?" asked Billy.

"You sure can. I really enjoyed talking with you and hope we have an opportunity to swap war stories again sometime," replied Larry. "Enjoy your lunch."

As they got into the car and started out towards the restaurant, Mr. McDougle explained to Billy that they were going to one of the local restaurants that featured Amish cooking. "I sure hope you're hungry! These people really know how to feed a person. It's just simple home cooking, but it's marvelous," said Mr. McDougle.

"I'm looking forward to it. The walk around the plant really did whet my appetite," replied Billy. "Who's going to join us at lunch?"

"I've got several people coming to meet you. I was able to get the chief accountant to join us. Her name is Pat McDougal, and before you ask it, she's no relation. She's a graduate of the local Business College who's done a wonderful job for us. She can probably answer some questions about the accounting system that I wouldn't even be smart enough to ask. She also was a big help in getting our system up and running.

"I also have Jerry Edwards, one of our sales reps. I thought you might want to talk to him about how they get information from the customer and their view of how the system has helped them work with the customers. He's really very knowledgeable and worked for a couple of big retail organizations in the past. His experience has really been helpful to us."

"Thanks! Great! I presume Mr. Bragg, the IT guy is going to be there as well," said Billy.

"Yes. He will be there and has told me he's reserved the rest of the afternoon to talk with you if you want to spend the time. Ah, here we are."

As they pulled up to a plain looking building, Billy noticed that the foyer was crowded with people. Mr. McDougle said, "Don't be worried. I've got a reservation. It always looks like this at noon and it's even worse at dinnertime. The place is popular."

After the introductions were made, everyone was seated and the orders were placed, Billy turned to Pat McDougal and asked, "So, Pat, how's life after R/3?"

"Good question! Sometimes during the implementation I wondered if there would ever be any life afterward. I spent weeks getting all those account codes set up for our suppliers and customers. I even went to SAP school to learn about the accounting and MRP programs."

"Well, I can share some of your misery, having just finished a SAP seminar myself. I won't ask you for all the gory details in front of everybody, but I sure didn't understand everything our instructor presented us," said Billy.

"Me too. I've learned a lot since then, though. In fact, even though the system has done a lot of things for us and makes our life easier in a lot of ways we're all still learning to use it and there are probably many things we aren't doing as well as we could," said Pat.

"Well," asked Billy, "what about the traditional activities like billing and accounts payable? You know, things like that."

"Our billing and accounts payable have changed tremendously over the last few years, but it's more because of the way our business has changed than it is because of R/3. With most of our major suppliers we have virtually no paperwork and no accounts payable. We have so little inventory here that we use back flushing to determine what to pay. As soon as we finish something, we use the bill of materials to calculate the material that must have gone into that item. We accumulate that information each day, use it to reduce our raw material inventory and to pay our suppliers. We have very little paperwork associated with those transactions. We do an electronic transfer to their accounts on a frequency that depends on the contract with a specific company.

"The only real exception to that is for the suppliers of our hardware. I don't know if you saw them out in the factory, but they replenish the inventory themselves and bill us periodically. We use a summary of the bill of materials for the items produced in that period to estimate what the bill should be and, normally, pay it without question.

"We had a summer intern from the university here a couple of years ago. She did a project for us that produced a program for making estimates of the amount of hardware used for various sales volumes and mixes. We use that estimation procedure occasionally just to make sure our hardware bills are reasonable."

"Well, that's an awful lot different than the way we do it in North Carolina. I'm not as familiar with the accounting as you are, but I know our accountants spend time every now and then determining what our accounts payable age is and worrying about the reconciliation of the invoices with the changes in raw material and prices. What about the sales side? Have there been many changes there?" asked Billy.

"Yes, there have. We have something like the same process operating on the sales side, but we're the supplier and we get payment from our customers. Actually, there seems to be a lot more electronic connection on that side. I'm not sure how it all works. You can ask Mr. Bragg about that. As I understand it, we ship product to our customers, they read the bar codes on the product that comes in, and then transfer funds to our account covering the amount of product they've received. Like in our payment for raw materials, the frequency of this depends on the specific customer and terms of the contract. We haven't had to do a lot of reconciliation. There are occasional returns that we need to make up."

"Let me embarrass you a little and ask a bit about life after R/3, again. The system is quite comprehensive, but may also be pretty inflexible. Did you have problems getting people to use it?" asked Billy.

"Yes. I ran a lot of training sessions. It took some of our clerks a long time to appreciate the demands of the system. If you don't enter something into every field the system asks for, it won't let you move ahead. With the old system, only key information had to be entered. The system assumed a lot. After all, our customer base is fairly small and we knew them pretty well. We've pretty much gotten used to the discipline required and, as I said before, are learning how to use the system to do more things than we originally anticipated. We are also learning how to have the system enter some of the information for us."

"I'm curious, did you integrate the hardware cost estimation program with R/3," asked Billy.

"No. It runs on a spreadsheet that we have on one of the PCs in the office. We pull the volumes and product mix off the R/3 database and use it in the program."

Billy turned to the sales representative, Jerry Edwards, and asked him about the use of R/3 information on the sales side. Jerry replied, "Most of the information we use is electronically transferred from our customers by their buyers. The buyers are pretty knowledgeable and they have projected buying plans that they provide to us. The plans form the basis for our master production scheduling here.

"I'm sure you're familiar with MRP. That's what we use to explode the requirements for production back through the shop. We negotiate with our customers over the amount of commitment and risk that we each share. There's confirmed order information that gets converted into a fixed shipping schedule for each customer. This information is anywhere from one to three weeks into the future, depending on the customer. Beyond that, the information that the buyers provide us is planning information. We have agreements that indicate we'll be paid for any raw material commitments we make to cover these plans. Information further out is simply to provide us their best guesses on what the future looks like.

"I'm sure you saw some of the finished goods inventory we maintain. There's not very much of it and it's mostly our high-volume items. So we need the planning information from our customers in order to make production schedules that will match our shipping requirements.

"All of the basic information is communicated to us electronically through our Electronic Data Interchange connections. I understand it took quite a bit of time and several technical changes to link us to our customers this way, but it really has helped. We put in some data traps, filters that look at the orders and plans as they come from our customers and determine whether or not they're reasonable. The summer intern that Pat talked about was involved in that project for us as well, and it's been very helpful. We can almost always spot a new buyer when they start work. The data traps keep signaling that the plans are higher or lower than expected or have the wrong product mix. It is integrated into the system. We couldn't wait to do it in the office. Things just happen too quickly around here."

"That's interesting. Again, it's very different from what we do. I guess from what you say, you're not concerned about progress payments or a lot of customer involvement in product design. How does the design process work? Do you guys do it all?" asked Billy.

"No. We work very closely with our customers on changing the products. You probably already heard from Larry that he fights us constantly to keep the number of products down and when we look at design changes with our customers we argue that it's in their best interest to spread things out when they introduce new products. So far we've been pretty lucky in doing that. We only change the designs a couple times during the year and we've tried to make the time periods different with different customers, but that's not worked out the way we'd like. The customers like to use new designs to pick up sales in traditionally light seasons, so a lot of changes tend to be done at the same time."

Mr. Bragg interrupted, "I've really been interested in this conversation because I don't often get to hear these points of view. Most of the time I just sit in my office and take abuse from these guys. The system's slow, the reps need more information, why can't I do X, you know, the usual things programmers have to put up with. I agree with what Pat and Jerry have said. We're all learning how to use the system better and, even though I had experience before with R/3, I'm learning more about it everyday myself."

Mr. McDougle interrupted, saying, "Hey, they're going to sweep us out of here if we don't leave. Let me suggest that we go back to the plant. Billy can spend some time with Dan discussing the information technology parts of this. Dan's going to be key to any collaboration that we have with you guys anyway, so time spent with him will be very valuable. In fact, you can ride back with him so you can get an early start on your conversation."

Once in the car, Mr. Bragg started the conversation by saying, "I'm looking forward to working with you on this project. Mr. McDougle has told me a lot about his brother and your plant. It looks to me like we've got an awful lot in common and I think I can save you guys a whole bunch of work. You've already heard from Pat and Jerry how much they like the system and my personal opinion is that we couldn't do business without it."

Billy laughed.

"What's that for," asked Mr. Bragg, "Did I say something wrong?"

"No," said Billy. "I just wondered if it was a requirement that you be named Jerry in order to be a sales representative. Our sales guy is named Jerry Mancora and it just struck me that they have the same first name."

"We actually have two Jerrys in sales. In fact they are both Jerry Edwards. It really causes confusion sometimes."

"How does R/3 keep them straight?" asked Billy.

"Well, it uses the match codes. Everything in R/3 is coded and the two Jerrys have different codes. Great, we're here. Let's park and I'll take you to my office."

Once settled in Mr. Bragg's office, with the obligatory cup of coffee, Billy asked, "How long did it take you to get R/3 up and running? I've heard a lot of war stories about implementation and even about some firms that have been working at it for years without having gotten it finished. What was it like for you?"

"It really wasn't bad. It was a matter of a few months. Most of the companies that have problems getting R/3 implemented are much bigger. The firms I know around here that have implemented R/3 are fairly small and have done so in a matter of a few months. You know, of course, that there's a special software package called ASAP that can help with the configuration of the system."

"Yes," said Billy. "I heard about that in the SAP seminar that I went to. Did you use that?"

"No. We had a lot of help from our customers. In fact, they really insisted that we implement ERP of some kind and they steered us toward R/3. The real reason they wanted us to get the system running was to help support their Electronic Data Interchange systems. They look forward to using the Internet for future communication. We agree that it will probably be much less expensive than the EDI links. We're a long way from that now, but when the time comes we'll be ready."

"Did your customers actually do the configuration for you? I thought that was the most difficult thing to do and was what described your operation. I wouldn't think your customers could do that for you."

"No, but they did supply some consulting help. SAP had some people helping as well. I have also had some experience with R/3 in the firm I worked for previously, and that gave us a leg up. I don't think I mentioned it, but our suppliers were involved as well. Some of our wood suppliers, the plywood company for example, had R/3 already installed and knew the ropes. We actually had quite a bit of help.

"I have to admit that Pat did a great job as well. She just learned all about the system. Since she knows so much about how this business operates, she knew the answers to most of the key questions. Also, she is a great teacher and the clerks caught on quickly."

"Let's see, if you had suppliers, customers, you, Pat, and some SAP people working on it, that's already quite a crowd. Did you have other people involved in the implementation?"

"Yes. We involved key people from each of the areas of the plant. For example, Larry was involved in the manufacturing part of our activities."

Billy interrupted, "Did you give any thought to any of the other ERP systems? There are several of them on the market and there are differences among them. I'm afraid I don't know much about those differences, but would be interested in your opinion."

"No, we didn't consider other systems. Not very seriously anyway," replied Mr. Bragg. "You see with the experience that I had, the help of customers and vendors, and the popularity of R/3 in the furniture industry, we didn't really spend a lot of time evaluating other choices. There may be something better out there, but we didn't think it was worth a lot of effort on our part to try to find it—if it existed. It was more important that we get up and running. We needed to start providing value to our customers and good information to our suppliers quickly.

"And we can really see the results. We've become a lot leaner in our operations and our overhead has gone down as well. That's happened even though the sales, production volumes, and transaction volumes have all gone up. I'd say that's a pretty good indication of success."

"Yeah, it's hard to argue with success," replied Billy. "I really do appreciate your offer of help, as well. If we start down this path, it's pretty clear we're going to need all the help we can get. I know Mr. McDougle, that is, our Mr. McDougle, not your Mr. McDougle, is very interested in having a common system. So he's very supportive."

Next, Billy and Mr. Bragg were involved in a technical discussion over whether or not the computer system in Billy's North Carolina plant would be sufficient or whether they'd have to invest a lot of money in additional capacity. It looked like there would be some investment required, but the basic equipment was there. Billy was sure that the computer cost would not be the big item, anyway, and decided that he would need to follow up on the details of that to be sure. He was convinced the hardware wasn't really where the benefits or the problems would arise.

As he got ready to leave, Billy again thanked Mr. Bragg for his offer of help. In turn Mr. Bragg assured him of his full support. "You know Billy, installing R/3 in North Carolina should be a real piece of cake. I bet we can even get a great deal from SAP on the software license. It seems to me that our operations are so similar and Mr. McDougle, yours not mine, really wants R/3 installed, so I think you should rely on us. I don't see why we can't simply bring down our configuration and use that as a guideline for your operation. Now, there may be some places where we'll need to make some minor changes, but it looks to me like it shouldn't be any problem at all.

"I'd love to see us set a record for implementation. In fact, I don't see any reason we can't get the system up and operating in your shop and have the integration complete in time for the transition. That would enable Mr. McDougle to start his travels this summer without having to worry about the business. I know that's just a few months off, but it's really doable."

"Well, I really appreciate your enthusiasm and offer of support, but I'm still a bit of a skeptic. I guess that's why I was asked to be involved with this. It does sound pretty easy, but as a manufacturing guy, I've always found that the easier it sounds the more traps there are on the voyage. Anyway, I'm sure we'll be back up to talk to you and I'm also sure we're going to have you down to spend some time with us. Thanks again for your help."

As Billy started back to North Carolina, he realized he needed to talk to a neutral person and looked forward to having a bagel with Prof the next day.

28. Back in Carolina—Ruth's vacation

As Billy entered Ruth's Café, he heard Ruth's familiar voice ringing out across the room, "Hey, Buckeye! Good to see you back. I don't know if you've seen the paper or not but there's an interview with Mr. McDougle in there. It seems like he's saying the same things that you had said the other day. It looks like there isn't going to be any transfer of people or lost jobs or anything like that. Do you still agree with him? Or did they offer you a job up there in Ohio?"

"Nah, they didn't offer me any job, Ruth. I don't think they liked my suit. Actually, that's such a different operation up there that I don't see how any of our people could be of much help. I'll have a garlic bagel this morning. Maybe it will keep Mr. McDougle from talking to me," replied Billy.

As Billy slid into the booth, he saw Prof enter the Café and signaled him to join him. As Prof approached, he said, "Hey, welcome back. Ruth, I'll have the regular. Well, Billy, what did you learn?"

"Man, that's a very different operation than ours. They make more stuff in a day than we make in a year. Well, not quite, but the volumes are just amazing. They sell to places like Staples, Office Depot, Kmart, Wal-Mart, you know, those sorts of places. So they have a limited number of customers. Heck, we don't even know who our next customer is going to be. Their designs are fixed until they come out with new products, which is only once in a while."

Prof interrupted, "I'm delighted to hear you talking this way. It sounds like you spent some time talking to the plant people and the sales people."

Billy went on to tell Prof about Ohio's electronic money transactions with customers and suppliers, how the factory was setup, the differences with the North Carolina operation and other details of the Ohio plant. He described the different people he met, commenting especially on Mr. Bragg and the role that the accountant played in the implementation.

Prof responded, "You sure talked to a lot of people and it sounds like you asked the right kinds of questions. Tell me more about the computer guy."

"Well, you were right with your advice. Actually, I asked to start the whole visit with manufacturing and then had lunch with sales, accounting, and him. Later, I spent some time with him in his office. He thinks we just ought to carry the whole system over here and install it. He's willing to help and everything."

"What do you think?" asked Prof.

"I don't think so. It is such a different facility. There is just no way we could use their configuration in our plant. At least not in manufacturing. The differences are just too great.

"It might be possible to use some of the other parts of R/3 here, but even there I think we'd need to do some configuration that would be different. If we have to use R/3, my inclination at the moment is to use just the accounting programs. This would be a lot easier than changing our MRP system. If we did accounting and finance, that should make Mr. McDougle happy. The accountant, Pat McDougal sure seemed to know her stuff. If Mr. McDougle could get her to come down here, she could be a great help on the accounting programs."

Prof added, "That sounds like a pretty good idea to me. Having part of the system implemented might satisfy Mr. McDougle's interest in consolidating the numbers and having some expert help in that area would make life easier. His interest in R/3, obviously, is because of the other plant, but I would think his biggest concern would be in the financial reports provided by the accounting programs. From what you've told me, it's very clear that you can't use the Ohio plant configuration directly."

Billy responded, "That's about where my head is at the moment. There is some benefit, I suppose, in being able to consolidate the financial statements of the two operations and that seems to be what Mr. McDougle wants. If we could just keep our current manufacturing program and develop a way to transfer the data that the R/3 accounting programs needed, I'd be happy. We process so few orders that it might just be easier to enter the R/3 data manually.

"Well, that's what I think I'll suggest to Mr. McDougle and we'll see how far we get. I don't know of any other real heavy pressures on us to do anything else."

"Hey, you guys, I'm going to take a vacation," said Ruth.

"What?" said Prof and Billy almost together. "What are we going to do for breakfast?"

"Well, you'll survive. You realize how many years it's been since I've actually gone and done something like this? I'm not leaving right away though. I'm giving you a little bit of warning, but I'm really looking forward to getting away from all the rumors about your plant. I'm going to see some of my relatives in Florida. Who knows, I might even take in DisneyWorld," continued Ruth.

"Well, you deserve it," said Billy. "But I'm gonna miss you."

"Same here," said Prof. "Boy, I better lay in a supply of bagels."

29. Decision at the top—A mandate for the plant

As Billy pulled into the parking lot he was surprised at the absence of cars, especially since he was running a little late. In particular, he was struck by the fact that Jerry Mancora's car was not in its usual parking space. Jerry had recently been coming to the office early to get his paper work done, so he could spend the morning on the phone selling furniture. As Billy entered the building, he decided to go directly into the factory rather than to his office. He wanted to make sure his impressions of the differences between the Ohio plant and this one were as great as he had thought.

He'd only been on the floor for a couple of minutes when Tom Maroney, the expeditor, came up to him and said, "Hey! I've got good news."

"What's up?" asked Billy.

"You remember I told you we might have a problem with that set of furniture we have been building for the Charlotte bank lobby? Well, the customer agreed to pick up air shipment costs for the special hardware and the vendor said no problem, so we're back on schedule."

"You guys always seem to be able to work miracles," said Billy, "But I think you're spoiling our customers. You did say the customer was going to pick up the cost of air shipments, right?"

"Yeah. They agreed to do it when Jerry explained to them that delivery of the hardware would probably be late if we did not ship by air. We're still going to have to track it, though. It's tight."

"Well, keep on it," said Billy. "Just let me know if it looks like there's another problem. We certainly don't want any unpleasant surprises at the last minute."

As Billy continued his rounds through the plant, he couldn't help but wonder whether or not the R/3 program that was up in Ohio would be able to handle the air shipment transaction. He was sure that they had never shipped any order by air. He wasn't even sure how it would be handled here, but wasn't worried about it at all. When he returned to his office he read on an e-mail message from Jerry Mancora saying Jerry was going to be visiting Veneble, a local company that had installed an SAP system fairly recently. Jerry indicated that he didn't want to be surprised later on, nor did he want the only perspective on the system to be the manufacturing perspective. "I wonder what that's about?" mused Billy.

A short time later, not surprisingly, Mary Lou called Billy and asked him to meet with Mr. McDougle as soon as possible. Billy said he would be up within the next five minutes and asked what was up.

"Well, you know, it's his interest in what you learned up at the Ohio plant. I know he's been talking to people here about what needs to be done in order to integrate the two operations."

"I hope I don't disappoint him too much. It's not clear to me that we're going to be able to do as much integration as Mr. McDougle would like," responded Billy. "I'll be right up."

As Billy entered the office, he was greeted with "Hey, Billy, what did you learn?" Mr. McDougle continued, "I'm really anxious to get your perspective on the plant up there. From what my brother tells me, and what I've seen before, it really almost runs itself."

"Well, not quite. It is a lot different operation from what we have here and that's probably what struck me the most," said Billy.

As Billy relayed to Mr. McDougle the differences between the two plants, Mr. McDougle seemed politely interested but somewhat distracted. Finally, Mr. McDougle interrupted, "Yeah, I know there are big differences between our two operations, but what about R/3? What did you learn about that?"

"They seem to think they couldn't run their operation without it," Billy replied. "They're so intimately connected to their suppliers and their customers that they really didn't have much choice in what they installed. It was very obvious to me that their use of EDI for sharing information and processing transactions is what drove a lot of the decision. They chose R/3 because some customers and suppliers used it and they could get help from them in the configuration and implementation of the system."

"If they're so happy with it, we should be able to use it here. Don't you agree?" asked Mr. McDougle.

"I've given this as much thought as I could with the limited exposure I've had," replied Billy. "I'm really concerned the system is not flexible enough for us to use in our manufacturing operations. Those guys up there have so few changes and such high volumes, it's unreal. Here we change constantly, and that's not easy to do with R/3. Up there the customers and suppliers really pushed them. They really didn't have any choice.

"Here's what I think we should do—at least to start. I know you're anxious to begin to pull the businesses together so you can consolidate the financial statements and better understand the operations at both places. To do that, I suggest we implement the R/3 accounting programs and not try to do any of the others for the moment. This will force us to clean up our data, have good definitions of the information that goes in the database, and it will put us in the position to have timely financial information for everybody. I think that for the time being, at least, we should keep our current MRP system. We can feed the accounting programs our sales and production information separately.

"I think we get a majority of the benefit for our business here from having the consolidated accounting reports. What is absolutely clear to me is we can't configure the system like the Ohio plant has theirs configured. I know that Dan Bragg really wants us to simply put his system in down here, but it won't work," continued Billy. "That's my opinion anyway. I don't see how we could possibly make R/3 fit the rest of our situation, even though we can integrate the accounting programs."

"Well, I'm sorry to hear that," said Mr. McDougle. "I had hoped we would be able to save some money and time by just bringing their expertise down here. Let me do some more checking around on my own. In the meantime, I'd appreciate it if you would continue learning what you can about the application of R/3 to our kind of business.

"You can go out and visit some other plants if you want to or spend some time with that friend of yours from over at the university. Let's keep in touch on it and I'll let you know if there's anything more specific I'd like you to do. Thanks for your help."

As Billy left Mr. McDougle's office he had a feeling that Mr. McDougle wasn't persuaded. He wasn't sure what more he could do to bolster his argument but decided he would call a couple of his buddies in the local furniture industry and see what more he could learn.

Over the next few days Billy continued to work around the factory and did call several furniture manufacturers in the local area. He found that most of the ones that had implemented R/3 were firms that designed their own product line for the furniture shows and then simply built the furniture as the customers' orders came in. R/3 seemed to be working well for all of them. The major difficulty they had was in configuring the combinations for fabric colors and wood finishes. These companies had operations that were a little more complex than the Ohio plant, but they were all making standard products with just a few options.

Billy stopped in at Ruth's Café every morning, but he was never able to see Prof. Ruth said something about Prof being out of town on some project.

In the office, he caught up with Jerry Mancora and asked him about what he had learned in his visit to the local furniture company that was running R/3. Jerry explained, "They're really happy with their new system. They have information on where orders are in the plant, when customers can expect delivery, when orders have left the plant, all that good stuff we seem to have trouble getting here."

"You did visit Veneble Furniture, didn't you?" asked Billy. Jerry nodded in the affirmative. "Well, I know that company and they make standard products. They're a lot different than we are. Did you ask how long it took them to implement the system and what kind of training they did? Did they lose any people? Did you talk to any of the manufacturing or financial people?"

"Hold on. No, I visited mostly with the sales people and a couple of the general managers. They seem so happy I didn't think it would be worthwhile to talk to anybody else," replied Jerry. "I get the impression you're not too happy with our using R/3 here. Have you talked with some of the other companies around here?" asked Jerry.

"Yes, I have," replied Billy. "You're right, many of them are quite happy with R/3. I'm simply not sure it's the system for us."

Later that same day Billy was surprised to get a call from a consulting company in Chapel Hill, North Carolina. The consultant told Billy that Prof had told them about Billy's interest in R/3 and his skepticism of the appropriateness for his company. The consultant went on to explain that their company did a number of installations of R/3 and most of their customers were quite satisfied with the results.

There were some customers, however, that the firm would not recommend for R/3 installation. These were companies that had very little experience with formal information systems, didn't appear to have the discipline nor training capability to develop people to use R/3, had changing information system requirements, and/or were dependent on a great deal of flexibility for success. Of course, at the end of the conversation, the consultant offered the help of their firm in evaluating the appropriateness of R/3 for McDougle Furniture and helping with the implementation if it was deemed worthwhile.

Later that week, Mary Lou called and asked Billy to come up to Mr. McDougle's office. She said she didn't know what it was about, but assumed it was about the computer because Mr. McDougle had been on the phone with Mr. Bragg in Ohio for quite some time. Billy muttered under his breath, "Oh great!" He told her it would be just a few minutes. He wanted to grab his notes from the meeting in Ohio before he came up.

As he entered Mr. McDougle's office, Billy was ushered to a chair and Mr. McDougle started in immediately. "Billy, I don't think we can wait much longer on a decision on R/3. I would like to have the decision made and have us down that road pretty well by the time the paperwork for the transfer of ownership of the Ohio plant needs to be finished up. In fact, anything we can do to help integrate with the Ohio operation before then would be worthwhile. I have spent a little bit of time these last few days talking with other furniture company owners in this area and with a couple of people down in the trade association office. I have also talked some more with the people up in Ohio. I've gotten some good and some conflicting information. I would like you to go over your recommendation with me one more time."

Billy went through his arguments for implementing just the accounting programs of R/3. He reviewed his concerns about the lack of flexibility and the need to incorporate their current manufacturing programs in order to meet the manufacturing needs. He repeated his observation that the local companies he talked with all made catalog furniture with fixed designs and, therefore, had quite different operations.

Mr. McDougle listened carefully and then said, "I remember that when I asked you to begin to look at this I said I thought you could keep us from making a mistake. I know you've tried to do this and have some very legitimate concerns, but I'm coming out on the other side of the fence. I've talked to some of the same companies that you have and they do express a lot of satisfaction with R/3. The concerns I've heard have come from companies that underestimated the time and cost for implementation. But they didn't have the resources that we have access to.

"The knowledgeable people I've talked to down in the trade association office say that they think R/3 will become a standard for our industry. I really would not want to be behind the eight ball if that does happen. And even if it doesn't, it still seems like it's a pretty good system.

"You know that Dan Bragg has offered to bring down all of his expertise and even share his configuration information. He is convinced that this will speed up the implementation process enormously and save us a lot of consulting fees. In fact, he thinks we can set some kind of SAP implementation record. He's had experience with this in a couple of different companies and we could use his knowledge. He tells me that he thinks we could be operational in less than three months if we allow him to do a lot of the configuration. I'll admit I find that offer very tempting."

"But their configuration simply won't fit our business!" said Billy. "They have stuff going through there so fast that they make more in a day than we make in months around here. Maybe more than we make in a year. They also had a lot of help from their customers and from their suppliers. We don't even know who our next customer is going to be. I'm really skeptical that it will work for everything and urge you to consider implementing just the accounting programs. It is also important that we get Pat McDougal down here to help get the accounting programs configured right and to train the people."

"I knew you'd feel that way. That's why I wanted to talk to you. I really think we should go with the full implementation. Look, if it doesn't work, we can always go back to what we had before and will at least have the parts of R/3 that we want," said Mr. McDougle. "You've not succeeded in convincing me otherwise, so I'm going to go ahead. Dan Bragg said he'd be available over the next two to three months to help and that it was a good time for them. They finished their fall and Christmas rush so he's got time available. Remember, our fallback position is to go back to what we have now."

"Only if we're still in business!" said Billy.

30. It happens—Starting the R/3 journey

For the next several days Billy didn't hear anything more about R/3. In fact, he didn't have an opportunity to see Prof either. He spent his days working around the plant, meeting with his staff, and attending to some of the problems that arose on a day to day basis.

At one point, Tom Maroney stopped by and asked Billy if some overtime could be authorized. The reason, according to Tom, was to make sure the furniture that was destined for the Charlotte bank lobby would be finished on time. "After all, the customer did agree to use airfreight in order for us to get the hardware here on time. I would really hate for us to be late with this shipment," said Mr. Maroney.

"Why do you think we need it?" asked Billy. "Are we behind on the project?"

"Well, you remember that batch of wood we've been seasoning? When we got into it to put some of the finishing trim on the furniture, we ran into some poor quality. We can still use the wood, but it will have to be for inside braces and that sort of thing. It isn't good enough for finishing trim. So we've had to do a lot more sorting and some special cutting in order to get the pieces up to snuff. We might be able to make it without overtime, but if you authorize three to four hours we've got a fallback in case we run into another problem."

"Yeah. Go ahead. It seems to me that the customer has really worked with us on this one, and I agree, we don't want to be late," replied Billy.

The next morning, Mary Lou called and asked Billy to join with some of the other managers for a meeting with Mr. McDougle in the afternoon. The meeting was to discuss the implementation of R/3 and somebody from the Ohio plant was going to be down to join the meeting. Billy realized this was likely to be Dan Bragg and the train was about to leave the station. He told Mary Lou he'd be up and asked her if there was anything special he should bring. She informed him there was nothing special and then asked, "What's going on here? I'm not sure I understand this R/3 thing. I thought you were the one who was supposed to be learning about this? Does this have anything to do with the fact that Mr. McDougle is taking over the plant in Ohio?"

"Well, Mr. McDougle wants a common system between the two plants. Since they already have R/3 running in Ohio, Mr. McDougle thinks it would be a good idea for us to have it here too. The computer guy from Ohio has had experience with this and is the one who's been responsible for putting it in up there. I guess that's the reason he's down here."

"Does that mean I'm going to have to learn a new system?" asked Mary Lou.

"I'm not sure," replied Billy. "I don't know exactly how it will be set up for our operation. It probably won't affect you very much, since I presume you'll still be using your word processor. We will probably use the R/3 e-mail system though, so you will have to learn how to use that. It probably will affect the accounting types more than anybody and maybe the people in the factory and sales operations. I just don't know yet. Maybe I'll learn more at the meeting this afternoon."

"Well, I hope you'll tell me if there's something that I should know. It's bad enough worrying about our jobs with the plant acquisition and now we've got this system to worry about. I'll see you this afternoon."

Billy looked around the room as people were getting ready for the meeting to begin. He had his cup of coffee as did other people, but there was not much of the usual friendly kidding going on. Dan Bragg was there as well as Jerry Mancora and some other managers from accounting, sales, and purchasing. Jerry was seated right next to Mr. Bragg and they were talking quietly. On the other side of the room, the purchasing guy was saying something to the accountant and so Billy sat down with his notebook and cup of coffee toward the end of the table.

When Mr. McDougle entered the room he sat at the head of the table next to Mr. Bragg and Jerry and explained to everybody that this was the initial meeting of the R/3 implementation committee. A couple of people next to the accountant buzzed with surprise and one said, "Wow!" Mr. McDougle then formally introduced Dan Bragg as the information technology manager from Ohio and said Mr. Bragg would be heading up the effort and the company was fortunate to have a person with his experience and background to work with. He then turned the floor over to Mr. Bragg.

"Good afternoon," said Mr. Bragg. "I'm really looking forward to this. I know some of you probably have heard the war stories about R/3 and some of you may not even know exactly what it is. Let me assure you that the war stories come from organizations that don't have experience with the system and don't know how to configure it to match their operations. As you know, we have a furniture operation up in Ohio, and I've had experience with R/3, so none of that will be a problem for us. With regard to those of you who don't know anything about the system, we will address that in the course of the implementation.

"The real advantage we have here is that we can save both time and money in implementation. We'll save time because we've already installed the system in Ohio and a lot of the technical detail has already been taken care of. We'll save money because we won't need to hire outside consultants to help us make technical decisions and we already know the furniture industry. Also, we have very little additional hardware that we need to purchase. In fact, I think we could be a showcase installation and that would bring a lot of visibility to the company. If we put this on an aggressive timetable, we could even set a record."

Billy interrupted saying, "Mr. Bragg, you know I've studied your operation and talked with some of your people and I've told Mr. McDougle as well that I'm really concerned about our simply plugging in your software package. Our operation is so different that I really don't think it will fit."

Jerry Mancora replied, "Billy, I know you have this concern but you and I have both talked with furniture companies in the area and Mr. McDougle has talked with people in the trade association and I don't think we have a choice. R/3 is becoming the standard for the industry and the firms I've talked with were all very happy with it."

Mr. McDougle interrupted and said, "Billy, that's why I have you on the implementation team. You are skeptical about the right things and ask the right questions. I want you to prevent us from making any mistakes. I want you to work with Mr. Bragg in making sure everything works well. We want to continue to provide the level of service and quality to our customers that they've learned to expect from us. I want to move quickly to integrate with the Ohio operation and I'm authorizing us to move forward in giving full support to Mr. Bragg and this activity. I certainly hope you'll support the effort."

"Thanks Mr. McDougle. I appreciate your vote of confidence," said Mr. Bragg. "I'm going to hand out some material on the basic structure of the system. I think we need to get right down to the meat of this thing. I'm going to try to meet with each of you individually and see what questions you have and then we'll convene again in a day or two. For us to achieve the schedule I've set, we'll need to meet nearly every day and most of those sessions will be working sessions. Again, I'm looking forward to working with you."

The next morning as Billy pulled into Ruth's parking lot, he saw a big sign in the window that said, "Starting next week Ruth's will be closed for several weeks." The sign went on to say that Ruth was taking an extended vacation. As he entered the Café, the regulars were all there, including Prof, but they were huddled around Ruth. "Get over here Billy!" said Prof. "Put some money in the pot, we're buying Ruth a bikini for her vacation."

As Billy dipped into his billfold to pull out a donation he looked in the pot and said, "That's not enough money to buy a bikini for Ruth. Remember you don't get much for your money when you buy those things." Then Billy ducked as Ruth took a playful swipe at him.

Billy motioned for Prof to come sit and asked Ruth for coffee and bagels. As they sat, Prof said, "Boy, I'm going to miss Ruth. She's really taking a long vacation. But she deserves it. The timing is pretty good for me though, I'm going to be away interviewing some companies for my research project."

"Well, I've got a lot going on over at the plant too," said Billy. "We're implementing R/3 and I'm on the implementation committee." He went on to describe to Prof the meeting and the decisions that had been made and voiced his skepticism again about the program.

"Billy, I'll be straight with you," said Prof. "The decision's been made. You may have doubts, but your job now, as a manager, is to get behind this thing and make it happen. At times all of us are put in positions where we have to do things we don't agree with entirely. Hopefully, this will be good for the organization. It seems to me that now is the time you need to use all your talent to make the system the best possible under the circumstances."

Billy was surprised at the strength of Prof's comment, but finally replied, "Prof, I know in my heart of hearts you're right. It doesn't do me any good to complain about what's going on, it just makes it harder for the other people. It's tough for me but I appreciate your splashing some cold water on my face."

After wishing Ruth a happy vacation and saying once again how much he'd miss her, Billy went over to the plant.

There was a memo on his desk from Mr. Bragg setting up a meeting for the next day and containing some initial thoughts on the implementation steps. The first of these was the establishment of a date when the North Carolina plant would switch over to R/3. Billy was surprised when he saw it. The date indicated a much shorter time period than any of the other implementations he had heard about.

As he looked down through the program that was outlined, he saw that it was very heavily concentrated in the area of software configuration, hardware acquisition, and software testing. There was very little training and nothing about bringing more people on board to maintain the system after it was implemented. Furthermore, he saw that Pat, the accountant from Ohio, was not on the distribution list. Apparently, she was not part of the implementation team. Billy made a mental note that he would have to address these issues in the meeting the next day.

Just as he got up to go out on the factory floor, his phone rang. He picked it up and was surprised to find that someone from the consulting company in Chapel Hill was on the other end. They wanted Billy to come down for an interview and to talk with some of the senior partners in the firm. They knew quite a bit about Billy's work at McDougle's. They had even learned of his taking the SAP course and of his visit to Ohio. Billy was impressed with the information network that the consulting company had. Billy said he'd need to think about it, but would call them back tomorrow.

The next day at the meeting of the implementation committee, Billy did express his concerns. It was clear from the reaction of Mr. Bragg and Jerry Mancora that they felt that more training was not necessary and any questions that people had they could get answered simply by calling up to Ohio. They also didn't see the need for having anyone to maintain the system after it was implemented since it would be connected to the one in Ohio and would be managed from there. The other people on the committee were very non-committal but seemed to be going along with what Mr. Bragg said.

Billy asked Mr. Bragg about Pat's involvement in the project. He was told that Pat had just submitted her notice and would be leaving the company soon. She was going to have a baby and felt the stress at work was just too much. After the baby was born, she might be available for some part-time consulting.

After the meeting, Billy walked through the plant talking to people. He also talked to some people in accounting and sales, to Mary Lou, and to a few others. He asked each what they knew about the R/3 system and the implementation plans. He was devastated to learn that the rumor mill had been working frantically. Clearly, no one had any real facts about what was going on and the guesses were all over the map. The conversations helped him think through his position and, with clear thoughts about the situation, he knew what he had to do.

When he got back to his office he drafted a careful memo describing an alternative implementation plan that included a lot more public discussion of what was going on, a lot more training, and the use of a consultant. He felt that this might help configure the system to meet the McDougle Furniture Company's needs. He was determined to give his ideas one last chance with the implementation committee.

He then called the consulting firm back and said he would come down for an interview. They wanted to meet him for dinner and a meeting with the partners that night. Things were moving a lot faster than he thought possible. A quick call to his wife and her words rang in his ears: "Go for it!"

That night, after a pleasant dinner and with surprising speed, a partner with the consulting company discussed what they wanted to do in the furniture industry, assessed Billy's qualifications, and made him an offer. After he got home that night, Billy discussed the position with his wife. He wanted to make sure that he was not just overreacting to the situation at the plant. But it did look like an opportunity he could not pass up.

Billy went into the office the next morning and asked to meet with Mr. Bragg before the next implementation committee meeting. At the meeting he explained that he had been talking to people from various parts of the plant and was concerned that they didn't know what was going on. He said, "Look, there is already uncertainty over the purchase of the Ohio plant and the rumors about R/3 are rampant. These people are concerned that they will be replaced by a computer, or, at best, have to learn whole new jobs. I think that there needs to be much more communication with these people or they will leave."

"Well, maybe you're right. When I know enough about what the system will look like, I'll call a meeting and do a demonstration," replied Mr. Bragg.

"I don't think you understand, they need to be involved," said Billy. "Here is a way that I think we can do it. I'd like you to look this implementation plan over and consider it for the meeting this afternoon. I'll present it if you would like."

Mr. Bragg looked at it and said, "Whoops! This doesn't meet our timetable. Do you really think we need so much time and so many people to do this? Well, I'll consider it and you can present it at the meeting."

At the meeting, after some preliminary remarks, Mr. Bragg announced that Billy wanted to discuss an implementation schedule that would take a lot longer than the one already in place. Mr. McDougle, looked at Billy and asked what this was all about. Billy explained about his discussions with people in the plant and how he felt they should be involved. He told the group that he had worked up an alternative plan that did take longer but got more input. Mr. McDougle wanted to know if the new plan would finish the project by the time that he took over the Ohio plant. Billy said, "No." At that point Mr. McDougle said he didn't think he could support it and asked if anyone else had any questions about it. When nobody responded, he turned to Mr. Bragg and said, "Well then, let's get back to work."

After the meeting was over, Billy returned to his office and drafted a letter of resignation. That evening, he discussed it again with his wife. They agreed that he should pursue the consulting opportunity.

The next morning Billy attached his memo on the revised implementation plan to his resignation letter. He personally delivered it to Mr. McDougle and explained that the consulting job was a great opportunity for him and that he just wasn't sure he would be very effective on the implementation team. He said one more time that he felt more strongly about the concern among the people than about the configuration issue and urged Mr. McDougle to consider changing the implementation plans along the lines outlined in the memo.

"Well, I'm not surprised you're leaving but I am disappointed," said Mr. McDougle. "I know it's been frustrating for you. I really appreciate what you've done around here. I certainly respect your decision but wish I could count on you to help us keep the factory humming in the future. Maybe you took too seriously my comment about the factory running better when you are not here, but you know I didn't mean it. If you do decide to go through with this, you have my full support and I wish you every success. If you want to come back and make an honest living again, give me a call."

31. The aftermath—Ruth's Café reopens

Prof entered the Café earlier than usual, anxious to see Ruth and learn about her vacation. As he entered, he ran to Ruth, giving her a big hug and said, "Wow! What a tan! You look beautiful!"

"Well, you do too, Prof. I really enjoyed my vacation but I'm glad to be back. I'm anxious to tell you guys about it," replied Ruth.

The door opened and Billy walked in. He spotted Ruth and also greeted her with a big hug. Prof greeted Billy with, "Billy, is that another new suit?"

"Yeah. Like it? It's my consulting suit," replied Billy. "But I want to learn about your vacation, Ruth."

At that moment the door opened and a couple other customers came in and Ruth found herself occupied with them. Prof motioned to Billy to sit down and said, "It's been a long time. I've heard rumors that you'd gone to Chapel Hill. Is that true?"

"Well, not quite. I've taken a job with a consulting company in Chapel Hill, but I'm staying up here. I'm helping them with their furniture industry practice and I'm still getting broken in. But here's the ironic twist. Mr. McDougle called these guys at somebody's suggestion," Billy eyed Prof very accusingly, "and asked them to help straighten out the mess that had been made of the R/3 implementation in the company. So, I'm up here now, charging consulting rates, trying to help them out."

"Well, I might have heard something about problems over at the plant, but you don't really think I'd tell Mr. McDougle to call up your company, do you? But I can't tell you how good it is to see you again," said Prof. "What happened at the plant?"

"Well, probably the worst thing is what happened to the people. They are very demoralized and some pretty good people have left, others are looking around for jobs. They don't understand the new system and can't get it to do what they need to have done. So they are trying to manually do what our old system did for us and are generally frustrated. People are still the key to running a business even if you are using R/3. I have even heard, for example, that things aren't running so smoothly in the Ohio plant since Pat—that's the accountant—left to have her baby.

"The manufacturing guys at the plant here are going crazy. They can't turn on a dime like they did before, so costs are going up as they add inventory and try to build patches in the operation to gain flexibility. Here's one example of the changes they're facing. They tell me that, just like they do in Ohio, they now have to get approval to buy some of the supplies that they used to just go get.

"Customer service has gone down. A customer called yesterday, and wondered about an expected delivery. But there was no information in the system about the order. Apparently, they had to make a change in the bill of materials. In order to do that they created a fake customer order for a new product. It sounds like the fake order was not properly entered in the system by the sales department, so manufacturing never even heard about it. They went ahead and made the wrong item. So things really got screwed up."

"So what do you think happened?" asked Prof.

"You mean about the plant?"

"No. In implementation."

"Let me see if I can summarize," said Billy, "I think there are three broad areas where things came unzipped. At the very first it was the way we got started on the project and the objectives that were established. Second, was the lack of involvement and use of the people who really knew how the place ran. Finally, I think that too many corners were cut on the configuration of R/3."

Prof said, "I'm taking notes. Elaborate."

"Remember how we got started. Mr. McDougle and I learned about SAP about the same time. We had different sources and interests, however. I think he was very honest when he told me to learn about the R/3 system and said I'd be unbiased. As things evolved, though, he became more interested in seeing if it would serve his needs to integrate with Ohio and I was concerned about whether it would work for this plant. Right there we have different goals.

"When he discovered the expert, Mr. Bragg, in Ohio and learned that other furniture companies were using R/3, I began to look a little foolish in his eyes. By the time that Jerry Mancora found out that some other marketing people in the industry were raving about R/3, I think that the decision to go ahead had been made. It's silly, I know, but I think the idea of being able to set some kind of record for implementation became a goal as well. It fit with Mr. McDougle's timetable for taking over the Ohio plant and Jerry probably saw great publicity through SAP."

"How about the people, Billy?" asked Prof.

"Yuk! Let's start with me. You gave me sound management advice when you said there are times when you just have to buckle down and make someone else's plan work. I did start to do that, but when Mr. McDougle said that he couldn't support me, I realized I was on the outside of the politics. I still don't know if I was running away from that when I resigned or if I was running toward the new job. Anyway, that's history and you can't look back.

"It was a lot worse with the other people. When I found out how little they knew about what was to happen, I knew that the plant was in trouble. The people on the implementation team weren't even informed. They didn't know beans, and here they were with an expert and 'the boss.' They couldn't support me or argue with Mr. Bragg. They simply weren't equipped to do so."

"How about the Ohio guy, Mr. Bragg?"

"Look, it would be real easy to blame him, but he was really somewhat innocent despite his experience. He saw an opportunity to set this record and really gain some fame among his computer friends. I don't think he knew the amount of work that Pat McDougal did at the Ohio plant, so he couldn't know what would be required here. I'm disappointed that he didn't listen, but you can't lay all the blame for this at his feet."

"And what about the configuration? You said you thought there were problems with that as well," Prof asked.

"I know a lot less about that than some of these other things because I wasn't there when they did it. From what people tell me, though, it is clear that many things don't fit the plant. Here is what I think happened. Mr. Bragg thought that they could simply install the configuration from Ohio and then put in what 'few' changes would be necessary for North Carolina. Some of the obvious changes were probably made, but the subtle omissions are now haunting them. Things like the need for approval for purchases and the lack of ability to change the bill of material when the product is on the floor.

"Remember there was the pressure to get the system working by the time Mr. McDougle took over the Ohio plant. Configuration is simply not an area where you can take shortcuts."

"Hey, I don't know when I have been quiet for so long," said Prof. "This is helpful to me, though, since I am still involved in those studies of ERP. So, what lessons have you learned about ERP in general and R/3 in particular?"

"I certainly understand that I am not an R/3 expert. My job is on the management side of things, so you are not going to get a lot of technical stuff from me. I look at ERP systems simply as integrated software that can help a firm integrate the organization's information. They provide comprehensive, orderly ways of entering plans and events in the database. From there, they provide information for making decisions but they don't make decisions. They are certainly not silver bullet solutions to a company's problems.

"What's more, a firm can't derive a competitive advantage from one. Maybe a firm can get some operational efficiencies and maybe someday it will be necessary to have one. But they are generic, like accounting systems. Do you know of any company that has gained competitive advantage from their accounting system?

"Here's a little prediction for you. In the future, there will be schools producing something like certified ERP professionals. Also we will find the programs in ERP becoming more standardized, just as accounting systems have done over the years. Sometime later, managers will find their homogenous ERP systems not producing all the information they need to run their companies. Then, just like happened with accounting systems, managers will augment their systems to get what they need."

"Whoa!" Prof interrupted. "You're really sounding like a consultant now. I'm not paying you by they word. What else have you learned?"

"Well, at least I feel better now! You already know that ERP can work for any firm anywhere. In fact, at some level all firms must integrate their information to get the job done, even if they do so manually. So the issue is simply a matter of cost versus value. Of course it is not easy to measure the costs or the value. I think your four-box matrix with Dictators, Anarchy, and so on is a helpful way of thinking about this. It points out, at least, where the cost will be high. Management will have to determine the value."

"Thanks, I'm still working on that idea," said Prof.

"You know there may be a couple more dimensions to that matrix," said Billy.

"At least," replied Prof.

Billy continued, "There are several circumstances where I now think the decision to invest in an ERP system is a no brainer, it should just be done. These are firms for which the change costs are small. For them, I think it is appropriate to just to go ahead and get started with ERP. An example might be some new company that doesn't have a lot of special processes already developed. There may be a size factor as well. For instance, small companies that don't have dedicated information systems people. Of course the firms in the low flexibility, high centralization part of your matrix would be candidates as well.

"These firms also have the benefit of something like ASAP to help them configure the system. Some of them don't even have a very good understanding of the way they do business, so going through an exercise like ASAP forces them to document it. If it's possible, it's even a good idea for such companies to start with a bare bones implementation and improve it as they go. But whatever they use, it's important to configure the system to match the way the company does business. The furniture plant here discovered that."

Prof asked, "But wasn't there a problem in trying to tie the North Carolina and Ohio plants together?"

"Yes. It's interesting to speculate on whether the two plants should be run under the same R/3 client code. Technically it is feasible. Certainly, when you think about it from an Accounting or Human Resources standpoint, there are probably no problems. Bills are paid and checks are taken to the bank. People need to be paid. There are many similarities between the two locations.

"But high-volume, standard product and low-volume custom production are just very different. For example, there is no need to track orders in Ohio. They are just made too quickly. In North Carolina, tracking orders is critical since it takes so long for them to be completed. Also, in North Carolina it is important to keep track of how much time workers are spending and how much each component costs. This information is important to track profitability for each order.

"Of course, there may be some advantages to running under the same client code. For instance, some material requirements might be consolidated for bigger discounts. But even that is questionable since wood, the most used raw material at both plants, is very different in terms of the type and quality between them. Even though the manufacturing planning and control processes for both plants could be run under the same system, who needs all that extra complexity?"

"How would you summarize what you've learned?"

"Oh, that's really easy. There are three simple rules for installing an ERP system. The first is talk. The second is communicate and the third is discuss. There are technical problems, true, but people solve them and people solve the systems problems. The people need to know what is going on. As people understand how they relate to one another and how to use the system to help them do it, the benefits increase. The wisdom is in the people. The system can help them apply it."

"Wow! Do you want to come and give a guest lecture?" asked Prof. "Those are good insights and are consistent with what I am learning."

"You can't afford me now. You should have asked me when I was at the plant," replied Billy.

"Well, I tried," said Prof. "Anyway, what more do you know about the local problem? Is McDougle's business going to survive?"

"I don't know. It's just a terrible thing to see so many people with such good intentions so traumatized. Apparently, they ran the computer guy out of town on a rail. Although he still is trying to manage the system from Ohio, I haven't heard anything more than I told you about what is going on up there. The amount of extra work the people are doing down here just trying to keep the shop running is really staggering. I guess it is a basic demonstration of the goodwill of people. I hope we'll be able to help them out because I'm really fond of the place and I would like to see Mr. McDougle succeed. Only time will tell."